Ao Haru Ride

The scent of air after rain...
In the light around us, I felt your heartbeat.

11

IO SAKISAKA

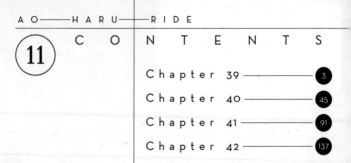

C O N T E N T S

S T O R Y T H U S F A R

Futaba Yoshioka was quiet and awkward around boys in junior high, but she's taken on a tomboy persona in high school. It's there that she once again meets her first love, Tanaka (now Kou Mabuchi), and falls for him again.

Futaba starts dating Toma. As their class heads to Nagasaki—a place that holds painful memories for Kou—Futaba is worried about Kou but tries to keep a friendly distance from him to put Toma at ease. For Kou, sunsets make him remember his mother's death, but now he is able to replace that memory with a new one—laughing together with friends. Futaba is happy to see Kou overcome his painful past and start to move forward.

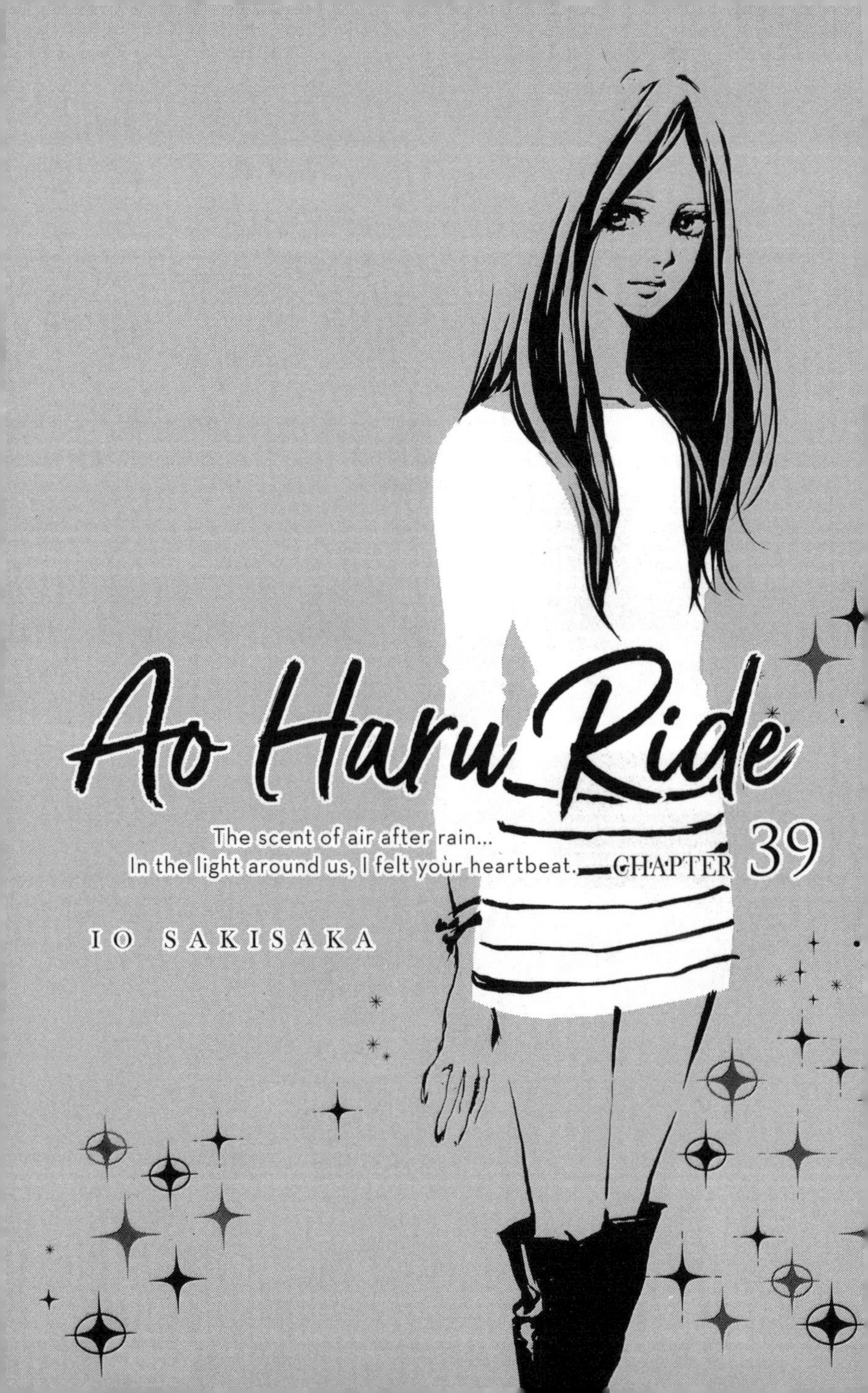
Ao Haru Ride
The scent of air after rain...
In the light around us, I felt your heartbeat.
CHAPTER 39
IO SAKISAKA

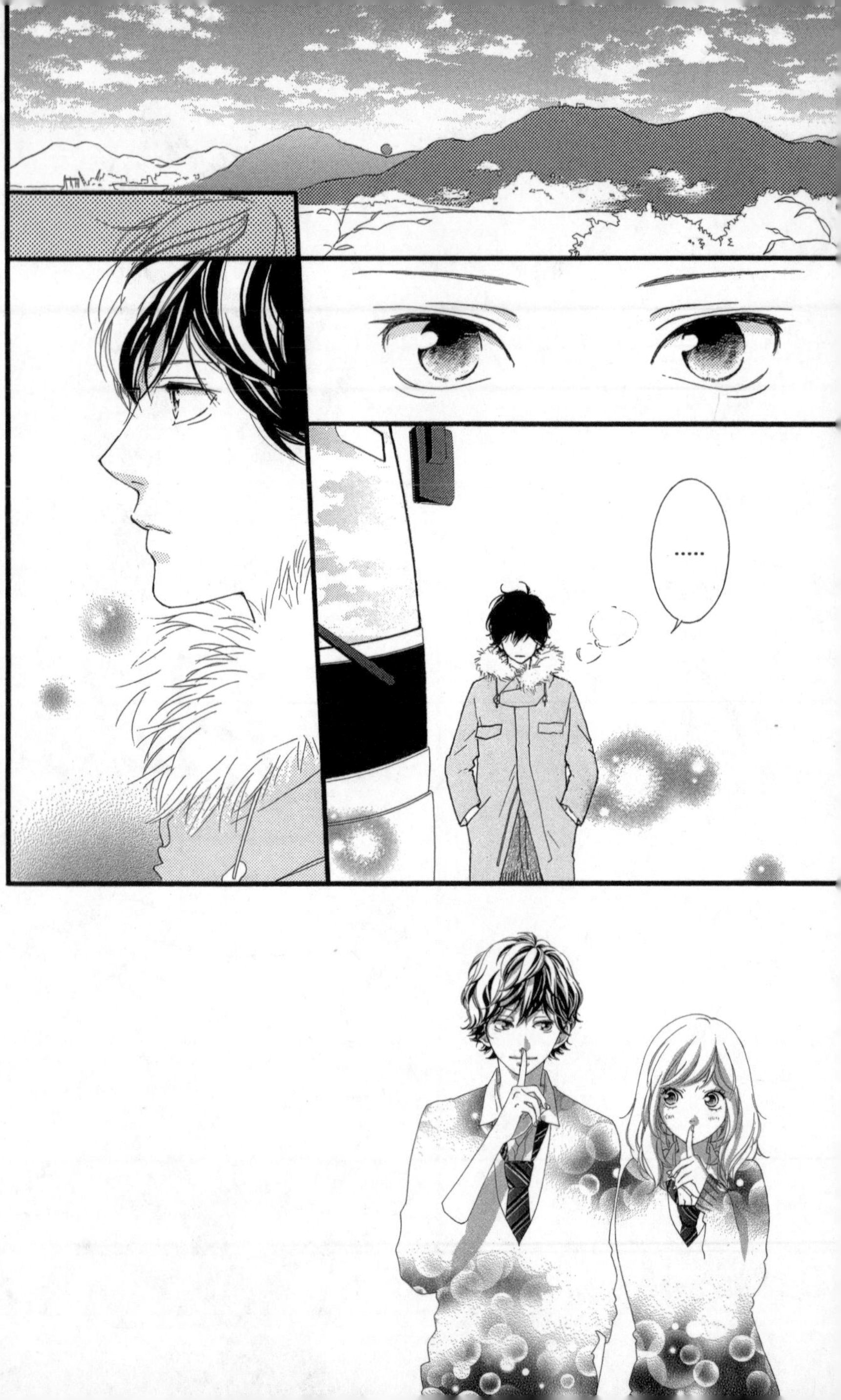
......

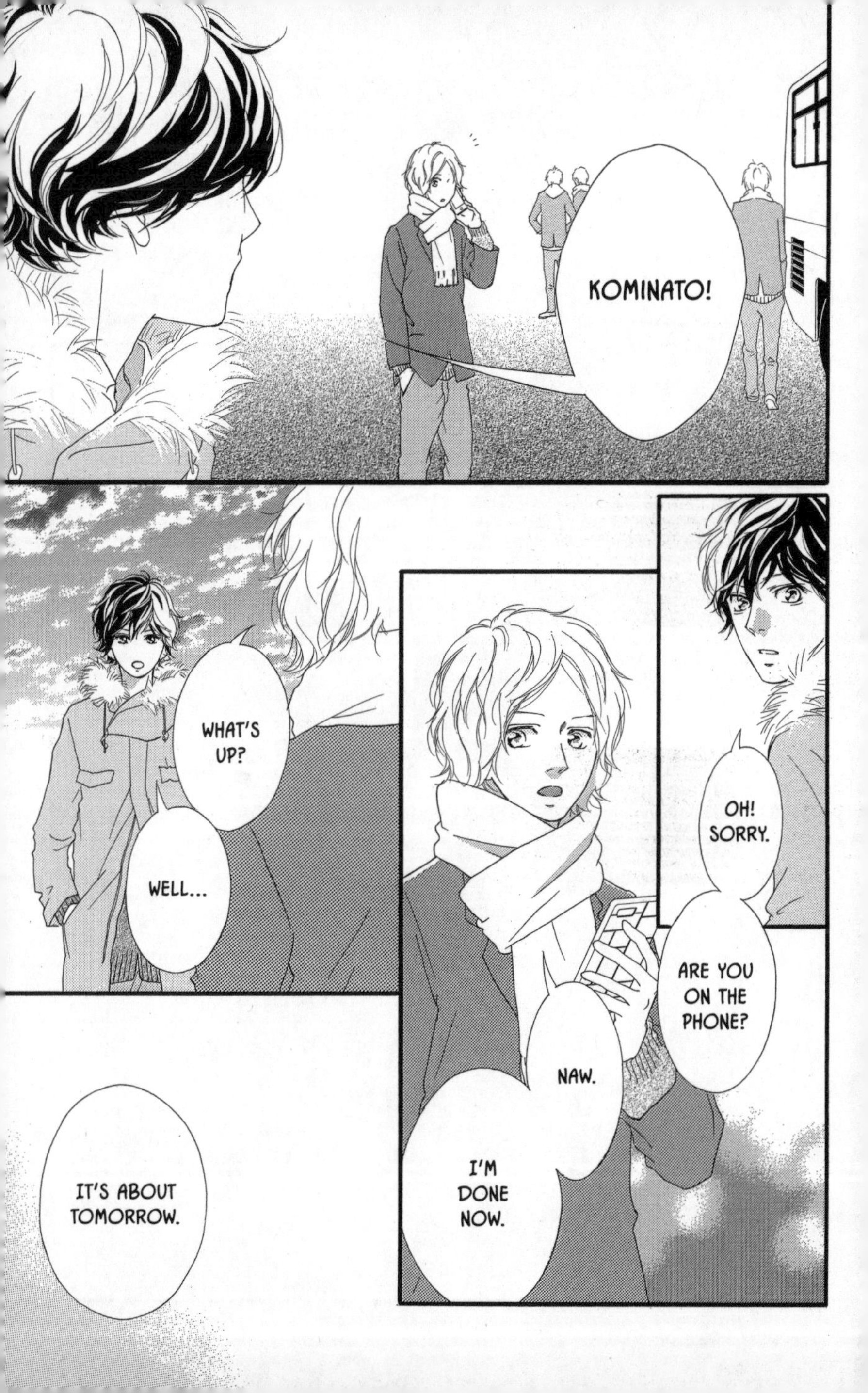
KOMINATO!
OH! SORRY.
ARE YOU ON THE PHONE?
NAW.
I'M DONE NOW.
WHAT'S UP?
WELL...
IT'S ABOUT TOMORROW.

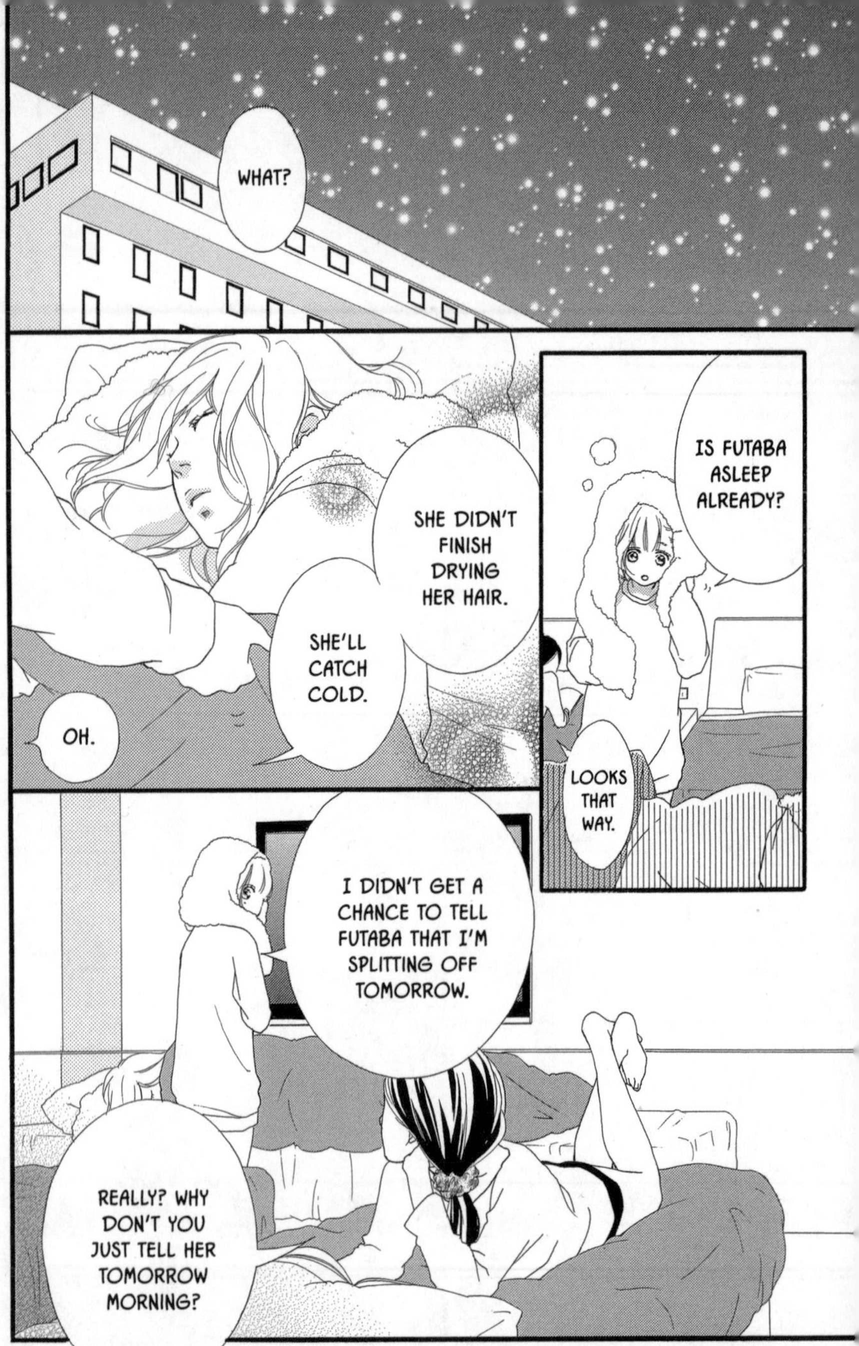
WHAT?
IS FUTABA ASLEEP ALREADY?
LOOKS THAT WAY.
SHE DIDN'T FINISH DRYING HER HAIR.
SHE'LL CATCH COLD.
OH.
I DIDN'T GET A CHANCE TO TELL FUTABA THAT I'M SPLITTING OFF TOMORROW.
REALLY? WHY DON'T YOU JUST TELL HER TOMORROW MORNING?

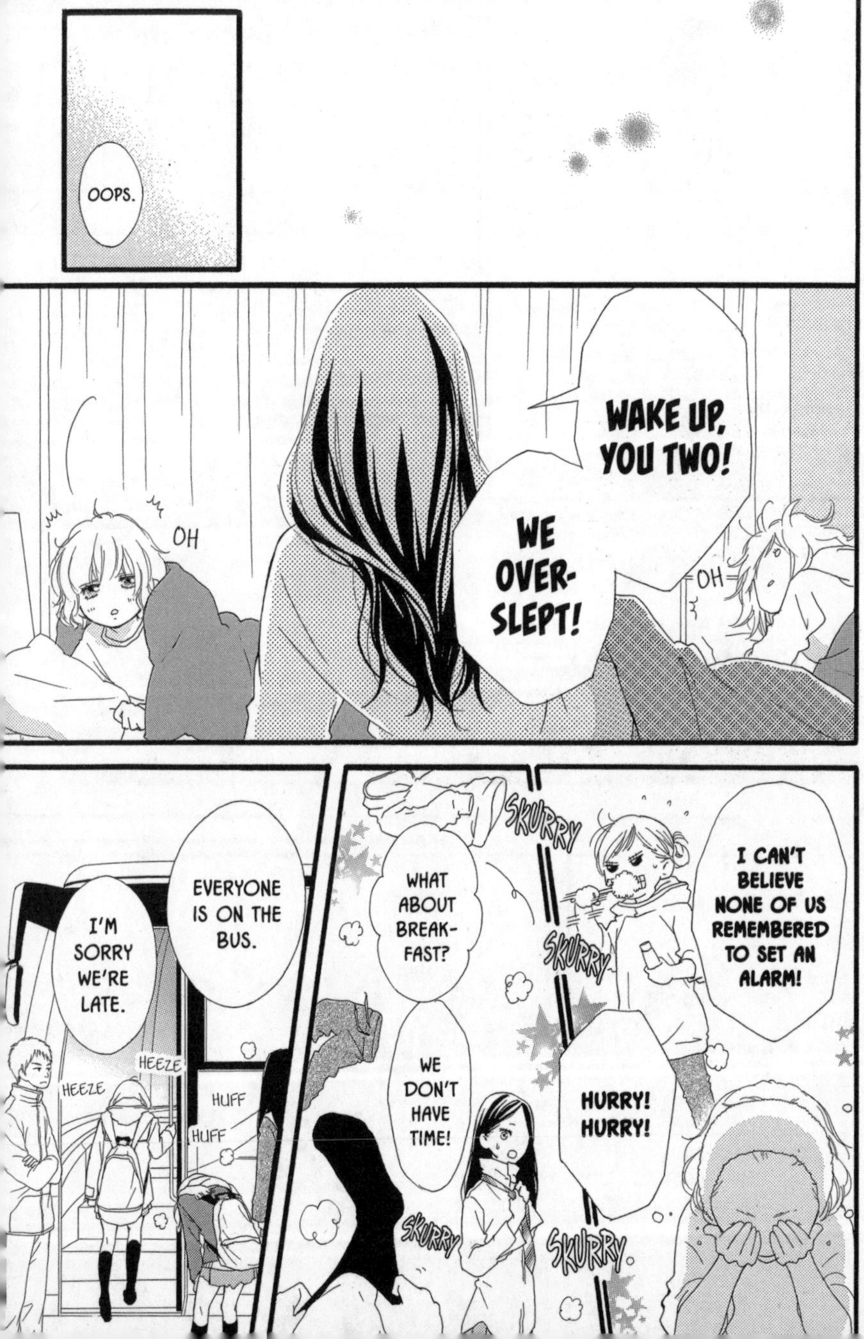
OOPS.
WAKE UP, YOU TWO!
WE OVER-SLEPT!
OH
OH
I CAN'T BELIEVE NONE OF US REMEMBERED TO SET AN ALARM!
SKURRY
SKURRY
WHAT ABOUT BREAK-FAST?
HURRY! HURRY!
WE DON'T HAVE TIME!
SKURRY
SKURRY
EVERYONE IS ON THE BUS.
I'M SORRY WE'RE LATE.
HEEZE
HEEZE
HUFF
HUFF

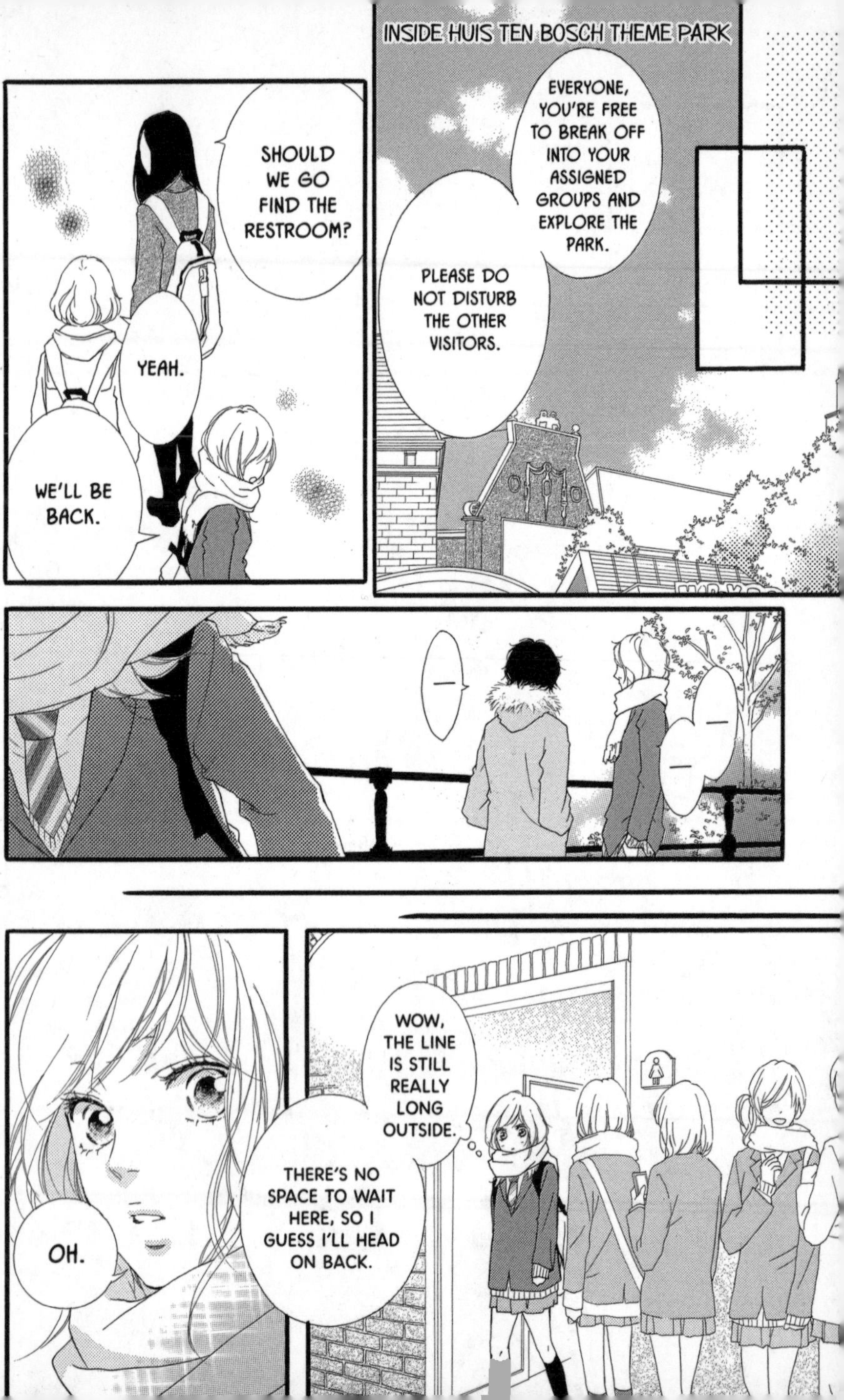
INSIDE HUIS TEN BOSCH THEME PARK
EVERYONE, YOU'RE FREE TO BREAK OFF INTO YOUR ASSIGNED GROUPS AND EXPLORE THE PARK.
PLEASE DO NOT DISTURB THE OTHER VISITORS.
SHOULD WE GO FIND THE RESTROOM?
YEAH.
WE'LL BE BACK.
—
—
—
WOW, THE LINE IS STILL REALLY LONG OUTSIDE.
THERE'S NO SPACE TO WAIT HERE, SO I GUESS I'LL HEAD ON BACK.
OH.

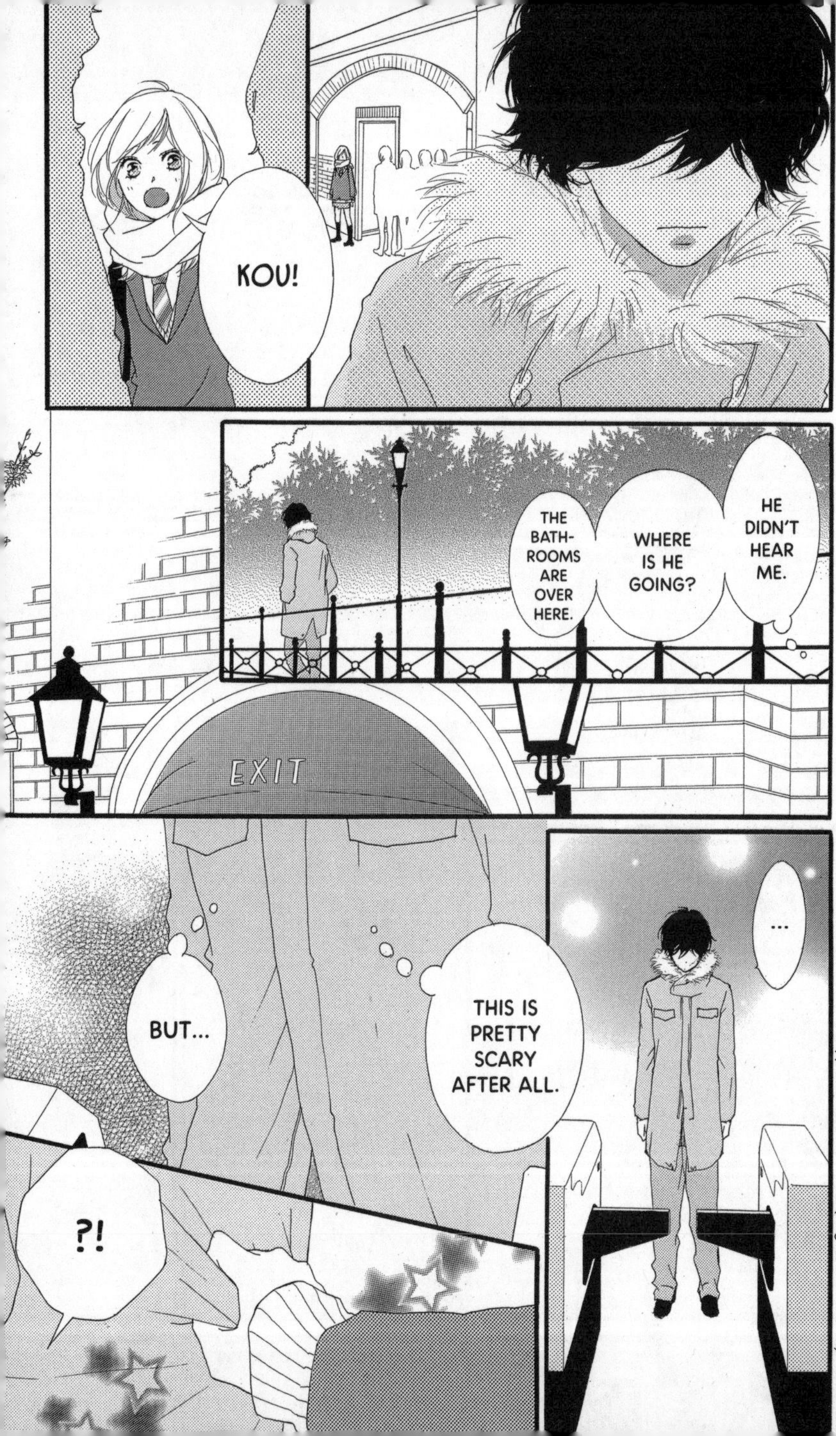
KOU!
HE DIDN'T HEAR ME.
WHERE IS HE GOING?
THE BATH-ROOMS ARE OVER HERE.
EXIT
...
THIS IS PRETTY SCARY AFTER ALL.
BUT...
?!

Produced with the support of Huis Ten Bosch (Nagasaki Prefecture)

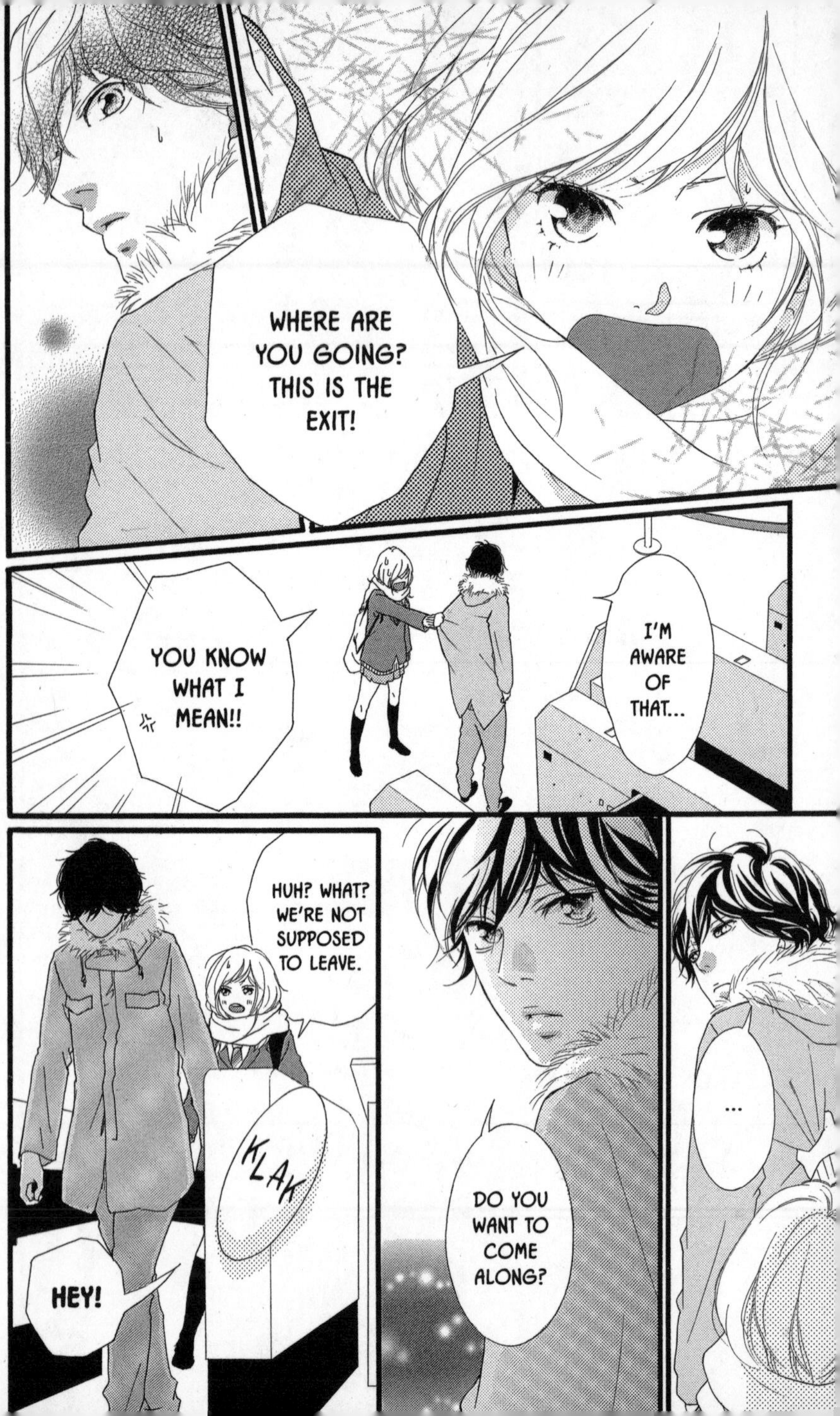
WHERE ARE YOU GOING? THIS IS THE EXIT!
I'M AWARE OF THAT...
YOU KNOW WHAT I MEAN!!
...
DO YOU WANT TO COME ALONG?
HUH? WHAT? WE'RE NOT SUPPOSED TO LEAVE.
KLAK
HEY!

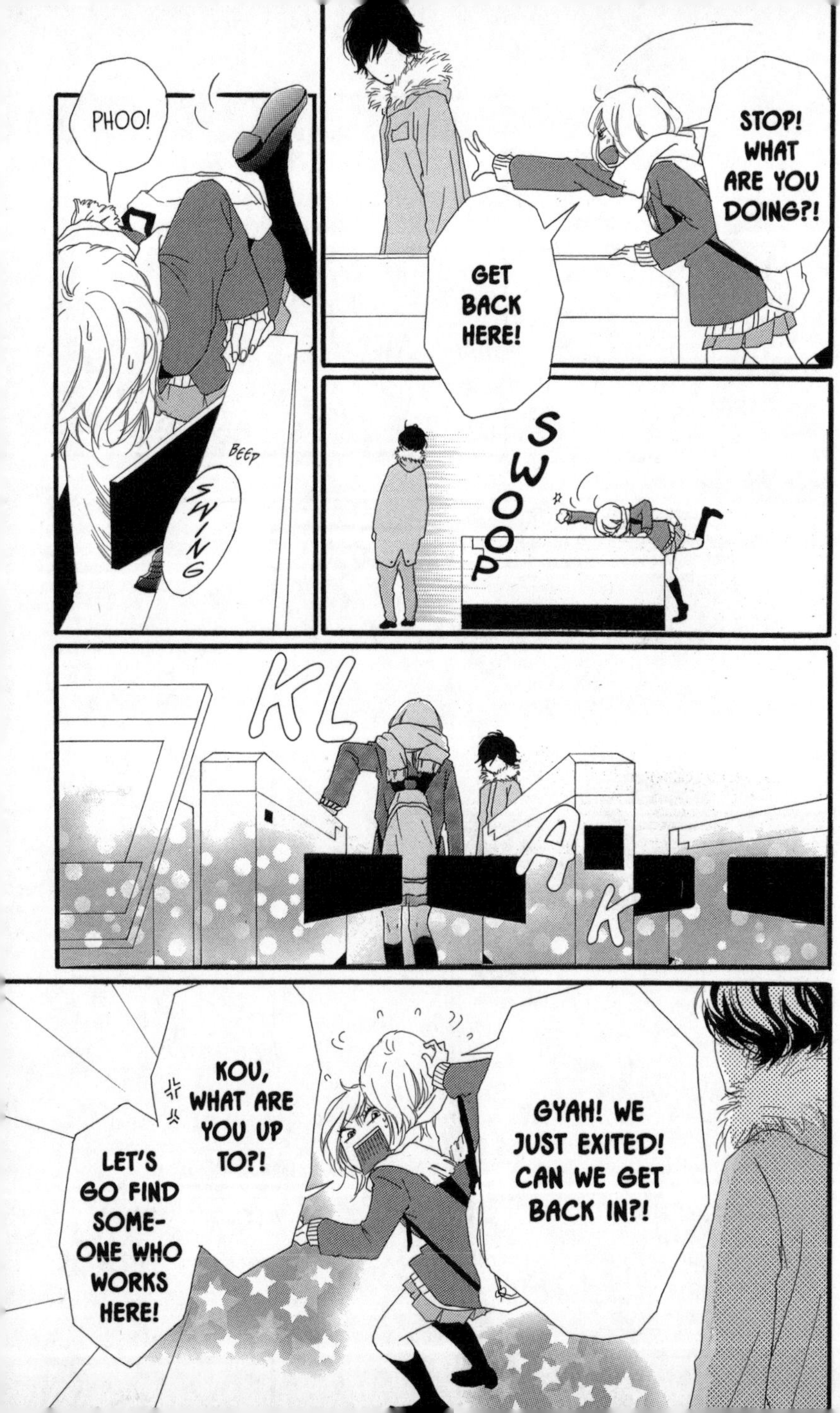
STOP! WHAT ARE YOU DOING?!
GET BACK HERE!
SWOOP
PHOO!
BEEP
SWING
KLAK
GYAH! WE JUST EXITED! CAN WE GET BACK IN?!
KOU, WHAT ARE YOU UP TO?!
LET'S GO FIND SOME-ONE WHO WORKS HERE!

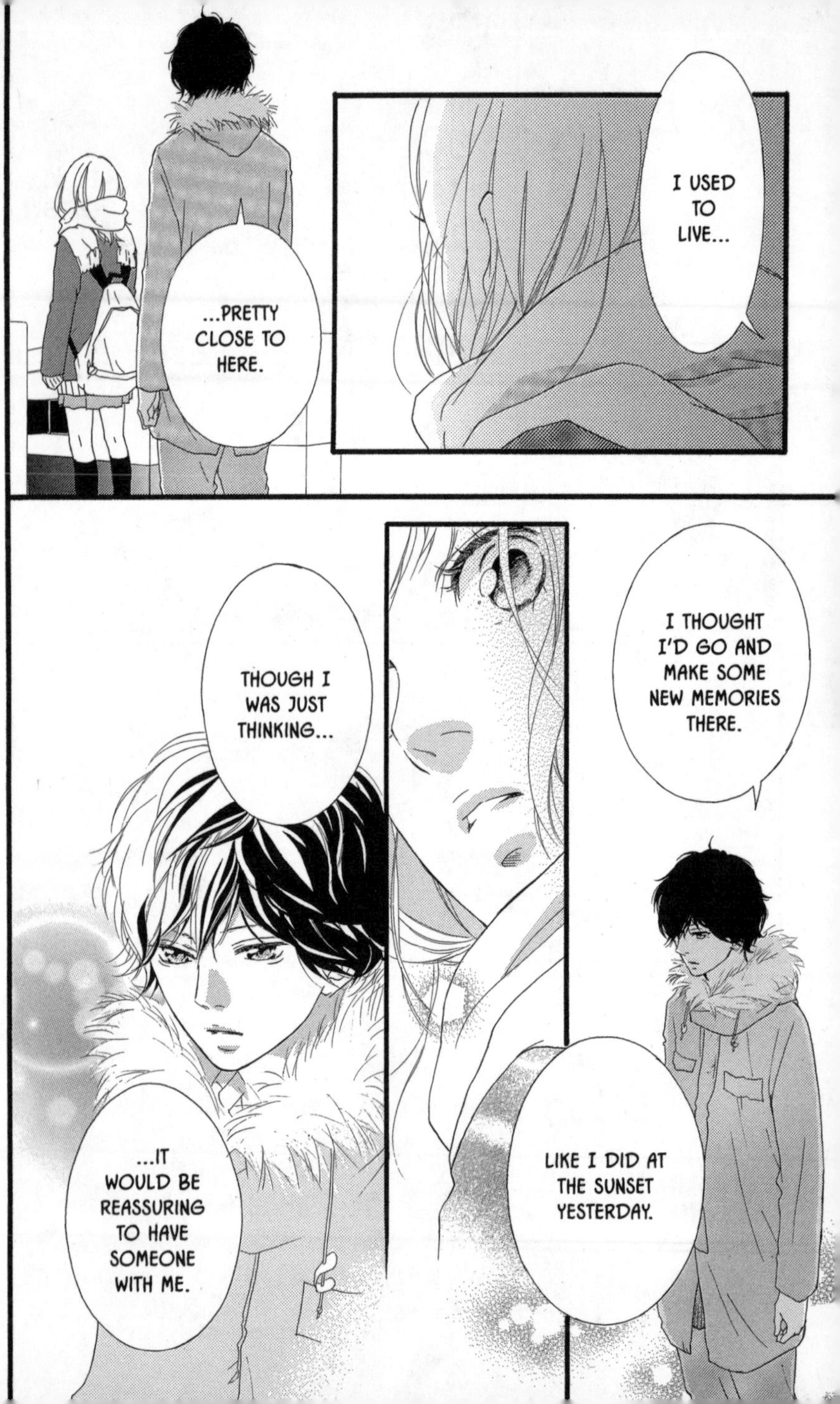
I USED TO LIVE...
...PRETTY CLOSE TO HERE.
I THOUGHT I'D GO AND MAKE SOME NEW MEMORIES THERE.
LIKE I DID AT THE SUNSET YESTERDAY.
THOUGH I WAS JUST THINKING...
...IT WOULD BE REASSURING TO HAVE SOMEONE WITH ME.

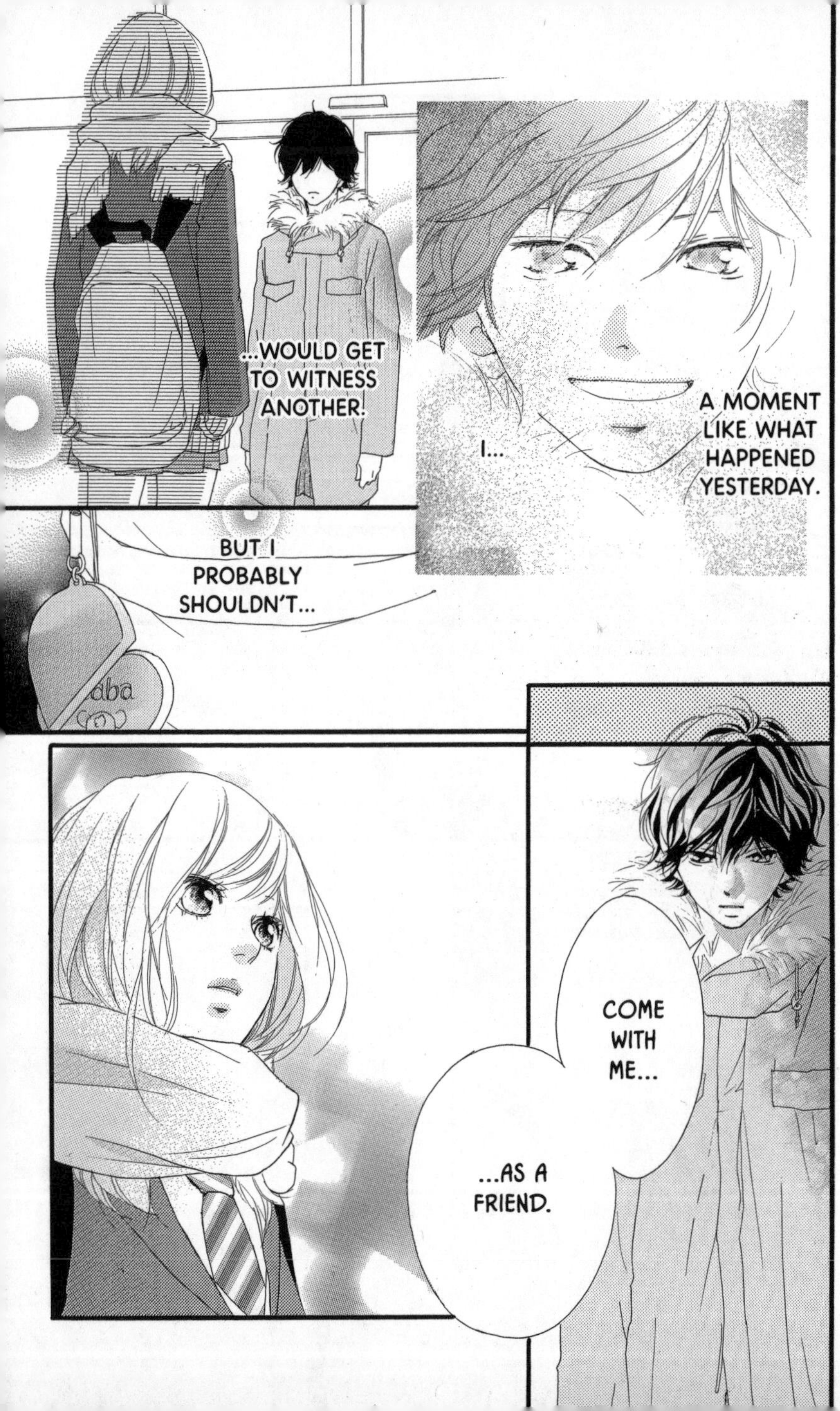
A MOMENT LIKE WHAT HAPPENED YESTERDAY.
I...
...WOULD GET TO WITNESS ANOTHER.
BUT I PROBABLY SHOULDN'T...
COME WITH ME...
...AS A FRIEND.

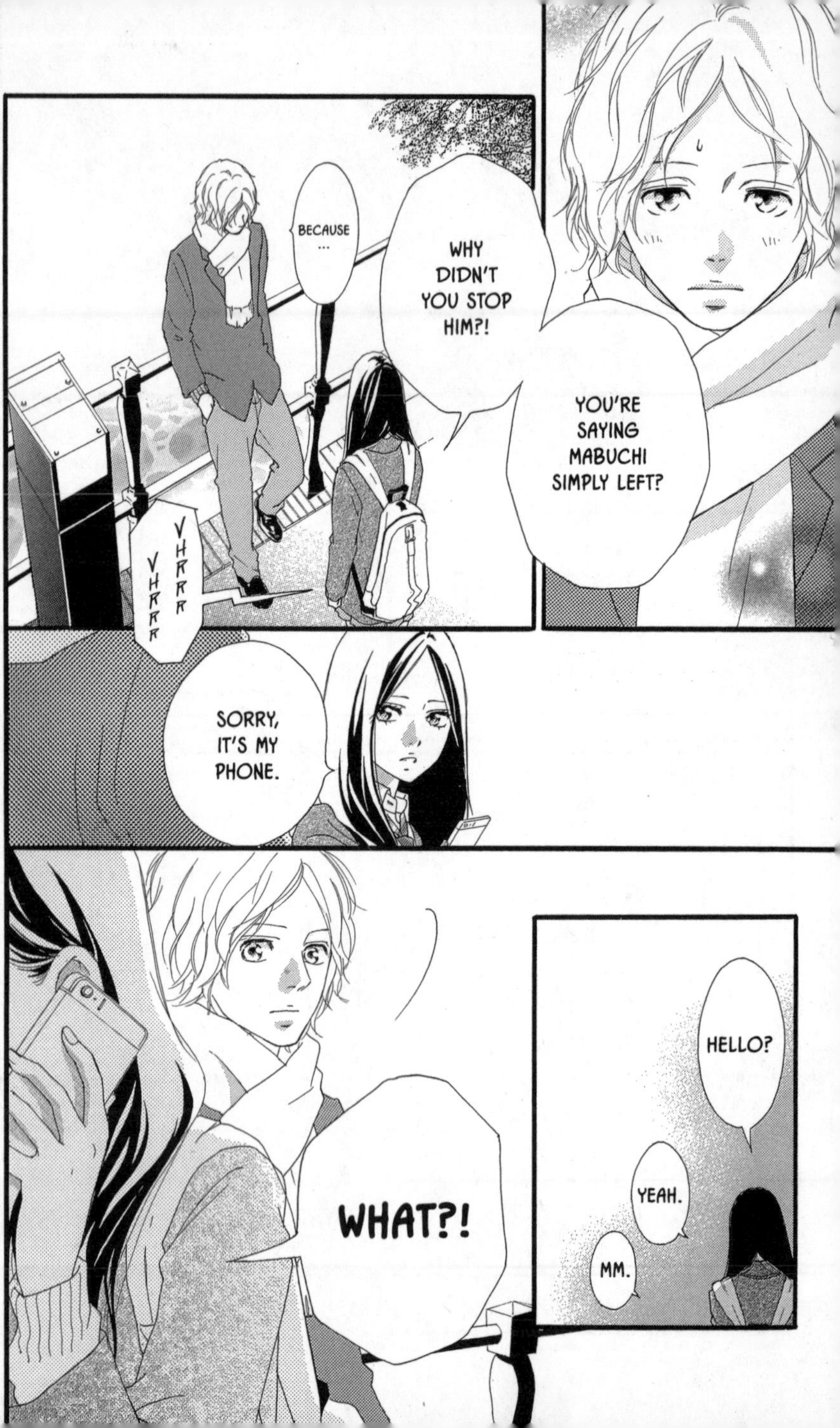
YOU'RE SAYING MABUCHI SIMPLY LEFT?
WHY DIDN'T YOU STOP HIM?!
BECAUSE ...
VHRRR VHRRR
SORRY, IT'S MY PHONE.
HELLO?
YEAH.
MM.
WHAT?!

The other day, for the first time in about five years, I had a hamburger from a fast food restaurant. Sadly, it wasn't that I was avoiding them, but I had just stopped going out. After such a long time, the one I ate was indeed delicious! Anyhow, I've been eating hamburgers upside down for ages.

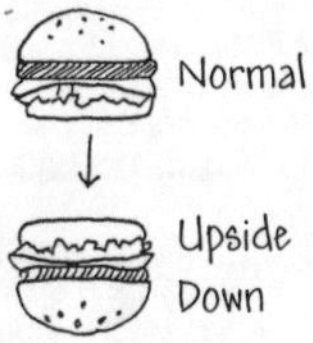
Normal
Upside Down

Why? Even I don't know. For some reason I hold them that way. Perhaps I think it's more comfortable or that it makes them easier to eat? Although... I think that can't possibly be the case. It really is a mystery to me. And when I ate that hamburger for the first time in years, sure enough, I flipped it over without even thinking. Next time, if I don't forget, I'd like to dig further into why I eat it that way.

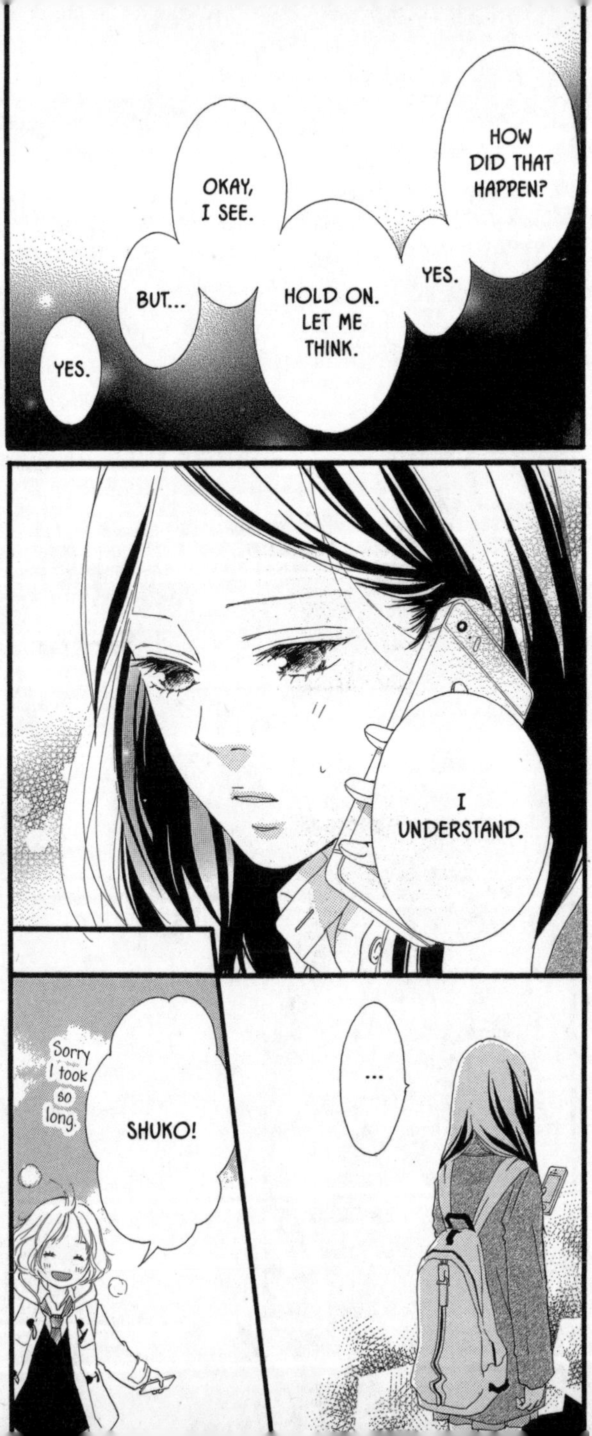
HOW DID THAT HAPPEN?
YES.
OKAY, I SEE.
HOLD ON. LET ME THINK.
BUT...
YES.
I UNDERSTAND.
...
SHUKO!
Sorry I took so long.

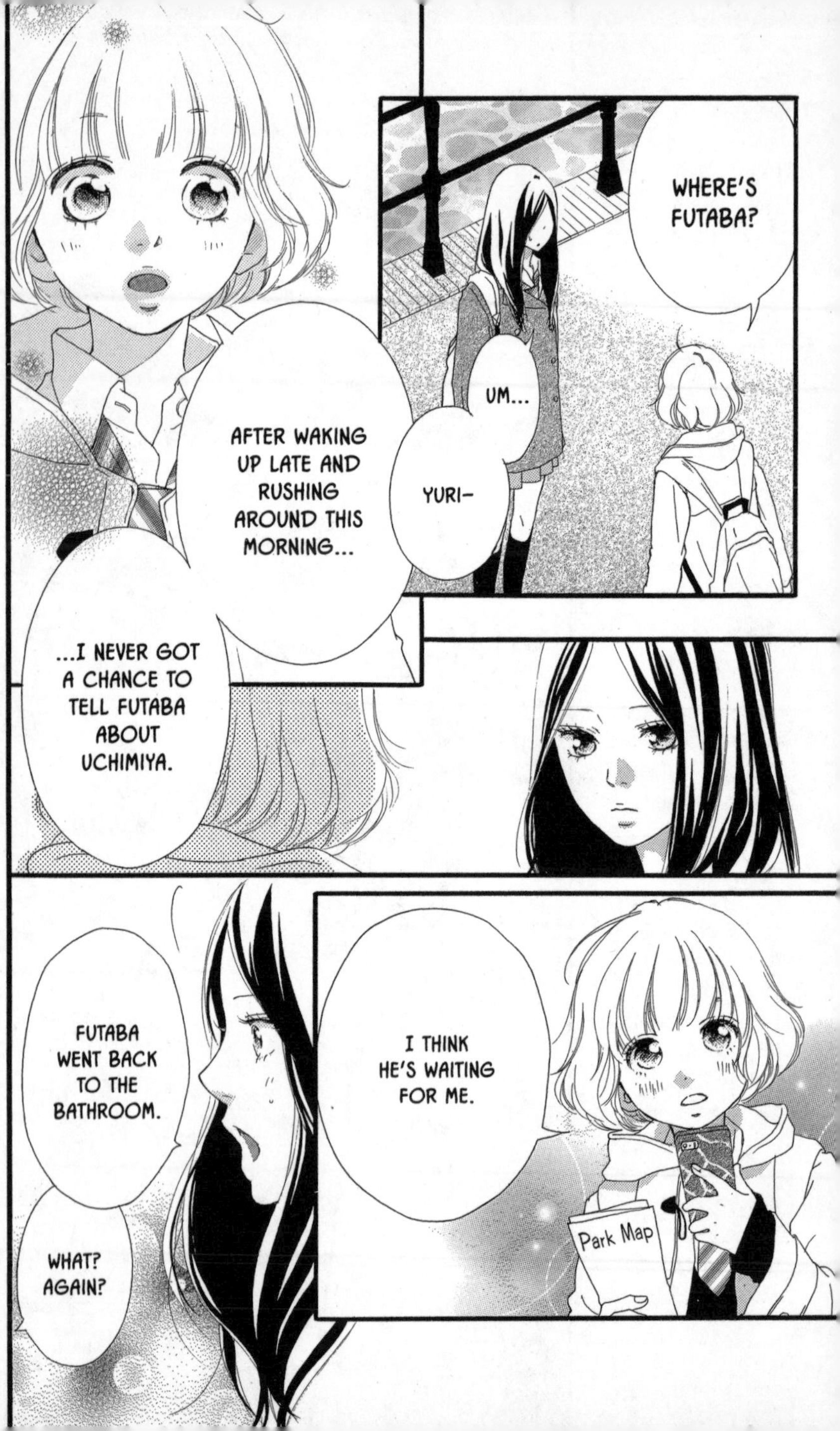
WHERE'S FUTABA?
UM...
YURI-
AFTER WAKING UP LATE AND RUSHING AROUND THIS MORNING...
...I NEVER GOT A CHANCE TO TELL FUTABA ABOUT UCHIMIYA.
I THINK HE'S WAITING FOR ME.
Park Map
FUTABA WENT BACK TO THE BATHROOM.
WHAT? AGAIN?

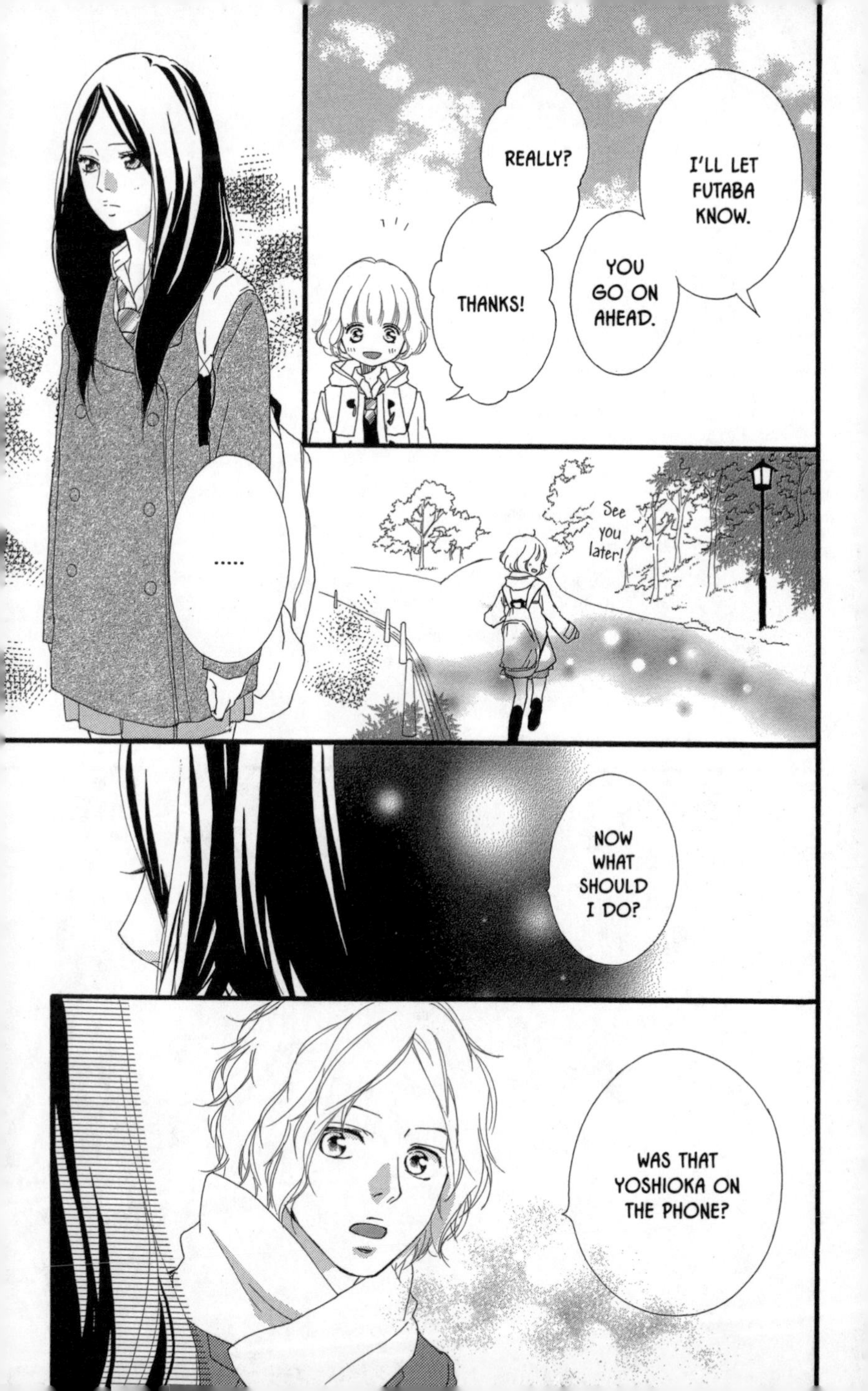
I'LL LET FUTABA KNOW.
YOU GO ON AHEAD.
REALLY?
THANKS!
See you later!
.....
NOW WHAT SHOULD I DO?
WAS THAT YOSHIOKA ON THE PHONE?

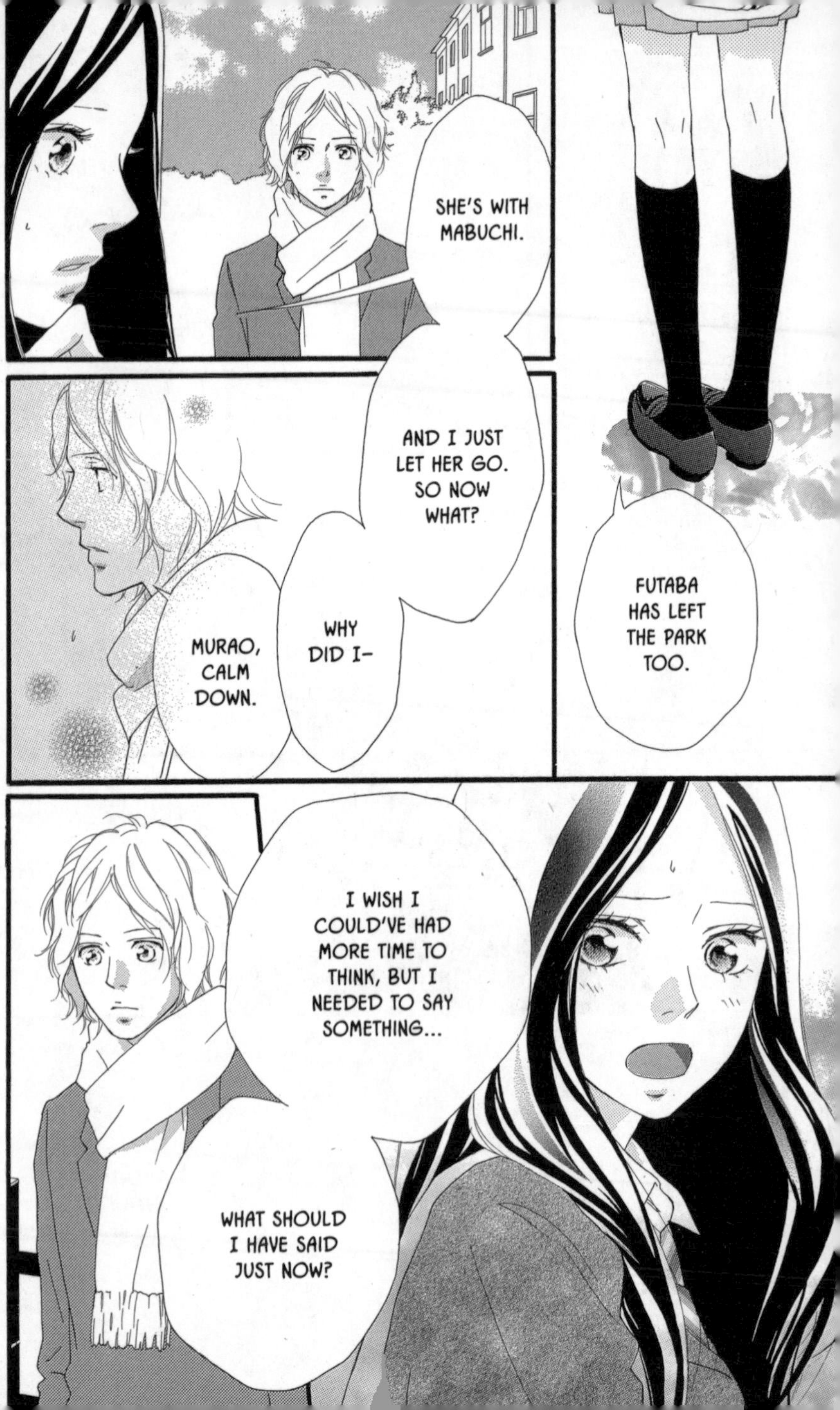
FUTABA HAS LEFT THE PARK TOO.
SHE'S WITH MABUCHI.
AND I JUST LET HER GO. SO NOW WHAT?
WHY DID I–
MURAO, CALM DOWN.
I WISH I COULD'VE HAD MORE TIME TO THINK, BUT I NEEDED TO SAY SOMETHING...
WHAT SHOULD I HAVE SAID JUST NOW?

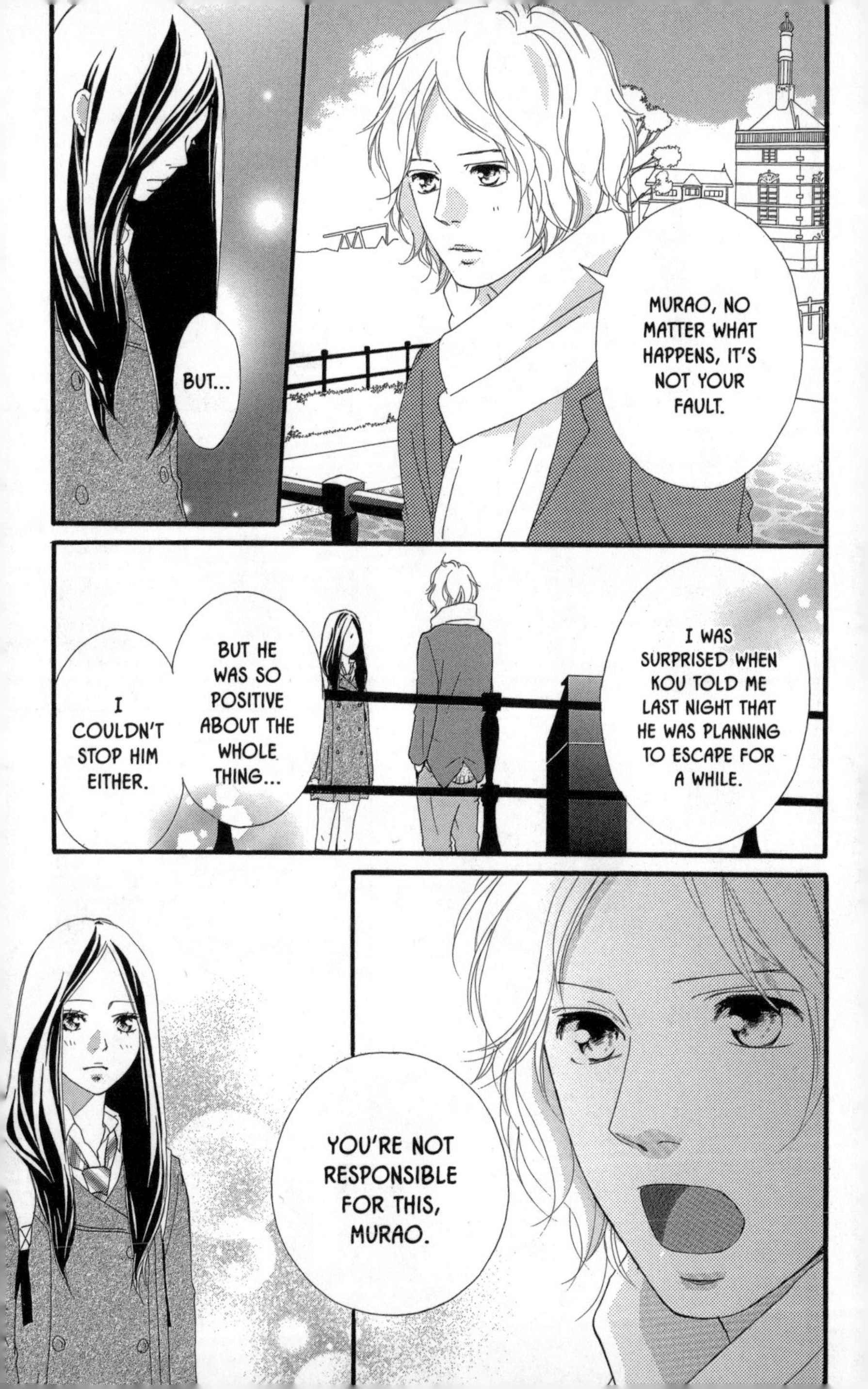
MURAO, NO MATTER WHAT HAPPENS, IT'S NOT YOUR FAULT.
BUT...
I WAS SURPRISED WHEN KOU TOLD ME LAST NIGHT THAT HE WAS PLANNING TO ESCAPE FOR A WHILE.
BUT HE WAS SO POSITIVE ABOUT THE WHOLE THING...
I COULDN'T STOP HIM EITHER.
YOU'RE NOT RESPONSIBLE FOR THIS, MURAO.

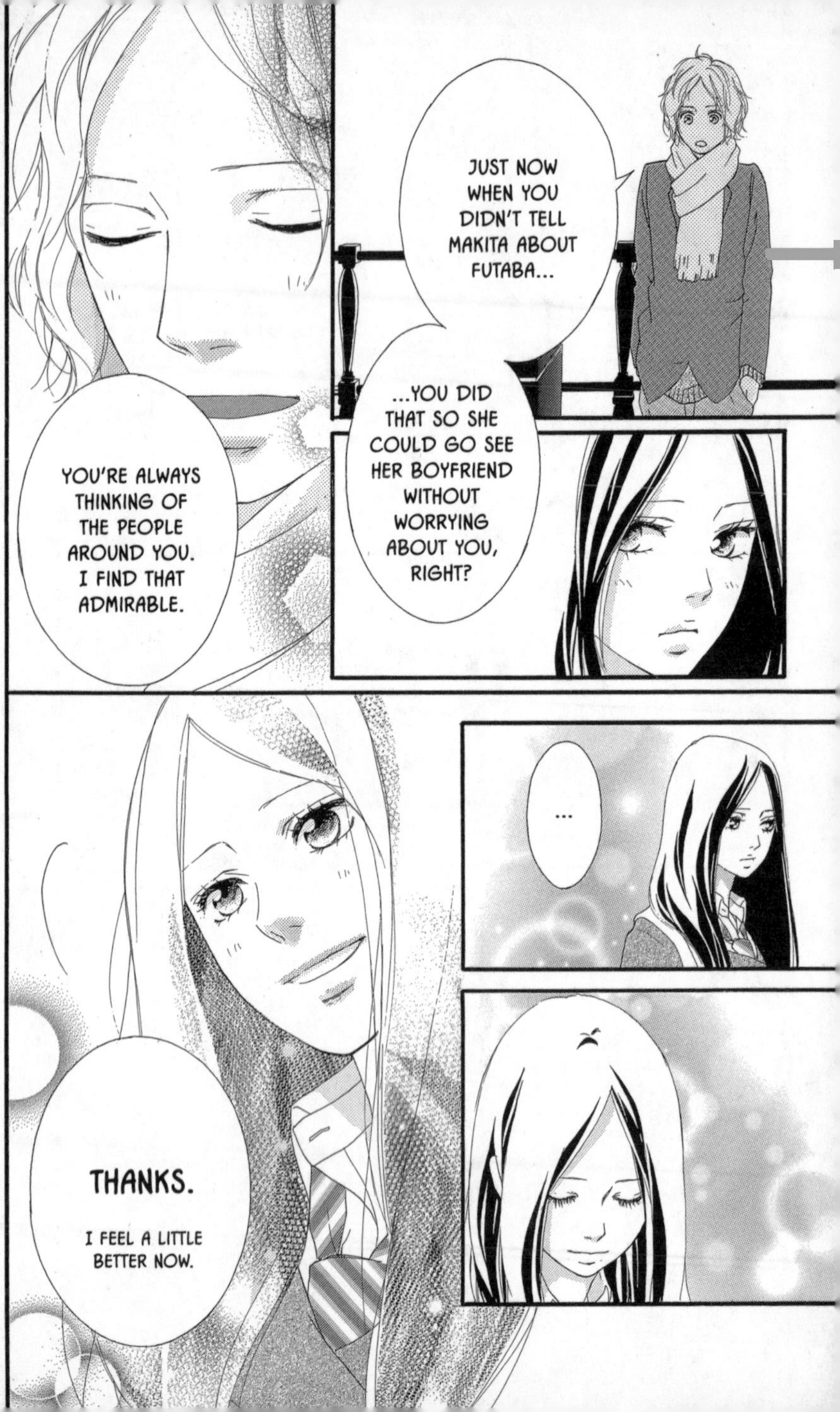
JUST NOW WHEN YOU DIDN'T TELL MAKITA ABOUT FUTABA...
...YOU DID THAT SO SHE COULD GO SEE HER BOYFRIEND WITHOUT WORRYING ABOUT YOU, RIGHT?
YOU'RE ALWAYS THINKING OF THE PEOPLE AROUND YOU. I FIND THAT ADMIRABLE.
...
THANKS.
I FEEL A LITTLE BETTER NOW.

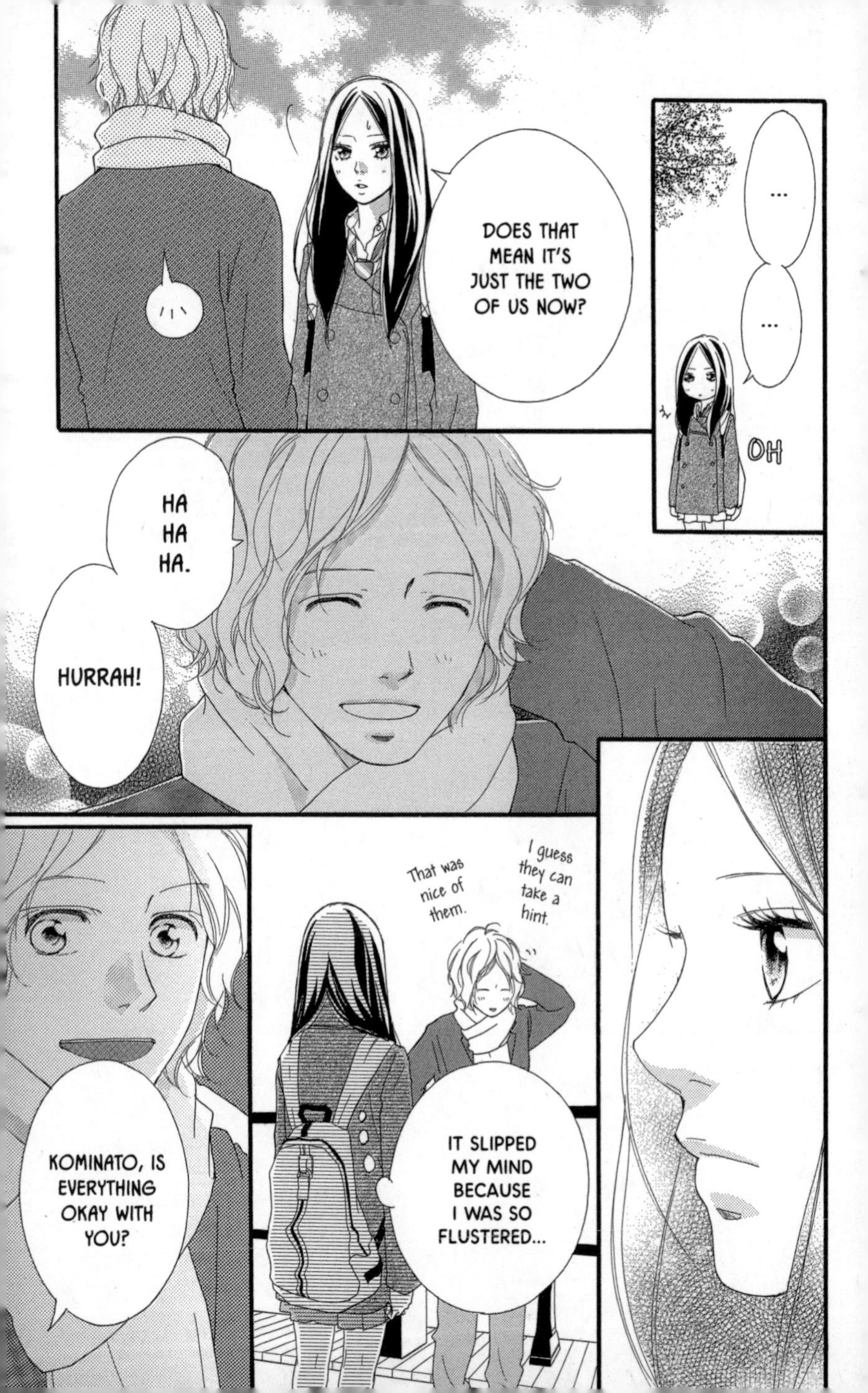
DOES THAT MEAN IT'S JUST THE TWO OF US NOW?
...
...
OH
HA HA HA.
HURRAH!
I guess they can take a hint.
That was nice of them.
IT SLIPPED MY MIND BECAUSE I WAS SO FLUSTERED...
KOMINATO, IS EVERYTHING OKAY WITH YOU?

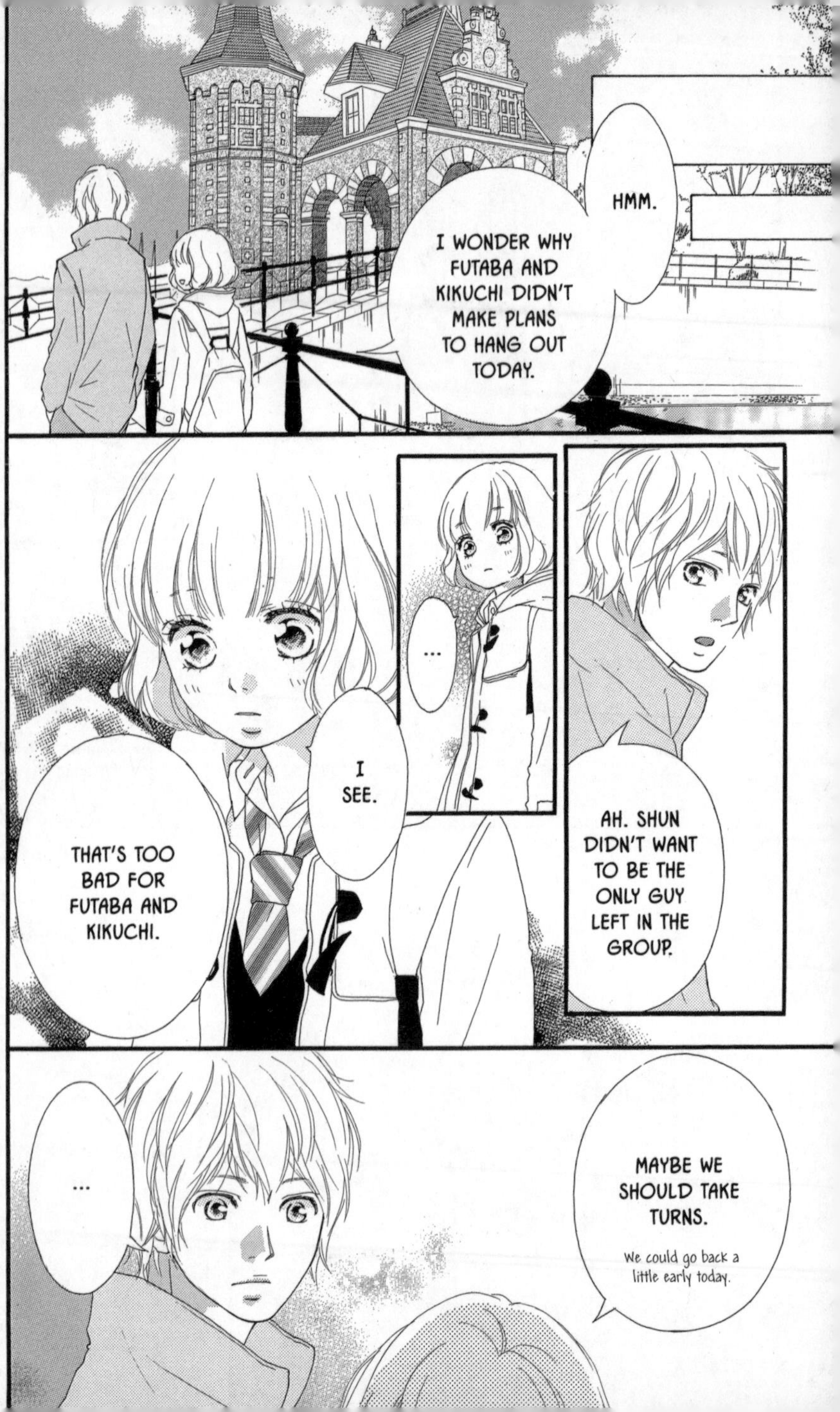
HMM.
I WONDER WHY FUTABA AND KIKUCHI DIDN'T MAKE PLANS TO HANG OUT TODAY.
AH. SHUN DIDN'T WANT TO BE THE ONLY GUY LEFT IN THE GROUP.
...
I SEE.
THAT'S TOO BAD FOR FUTABA AND KIKUCHI.
MAYBE WE SHOULD TAKE TURNS.
We could go back a little early today.
...

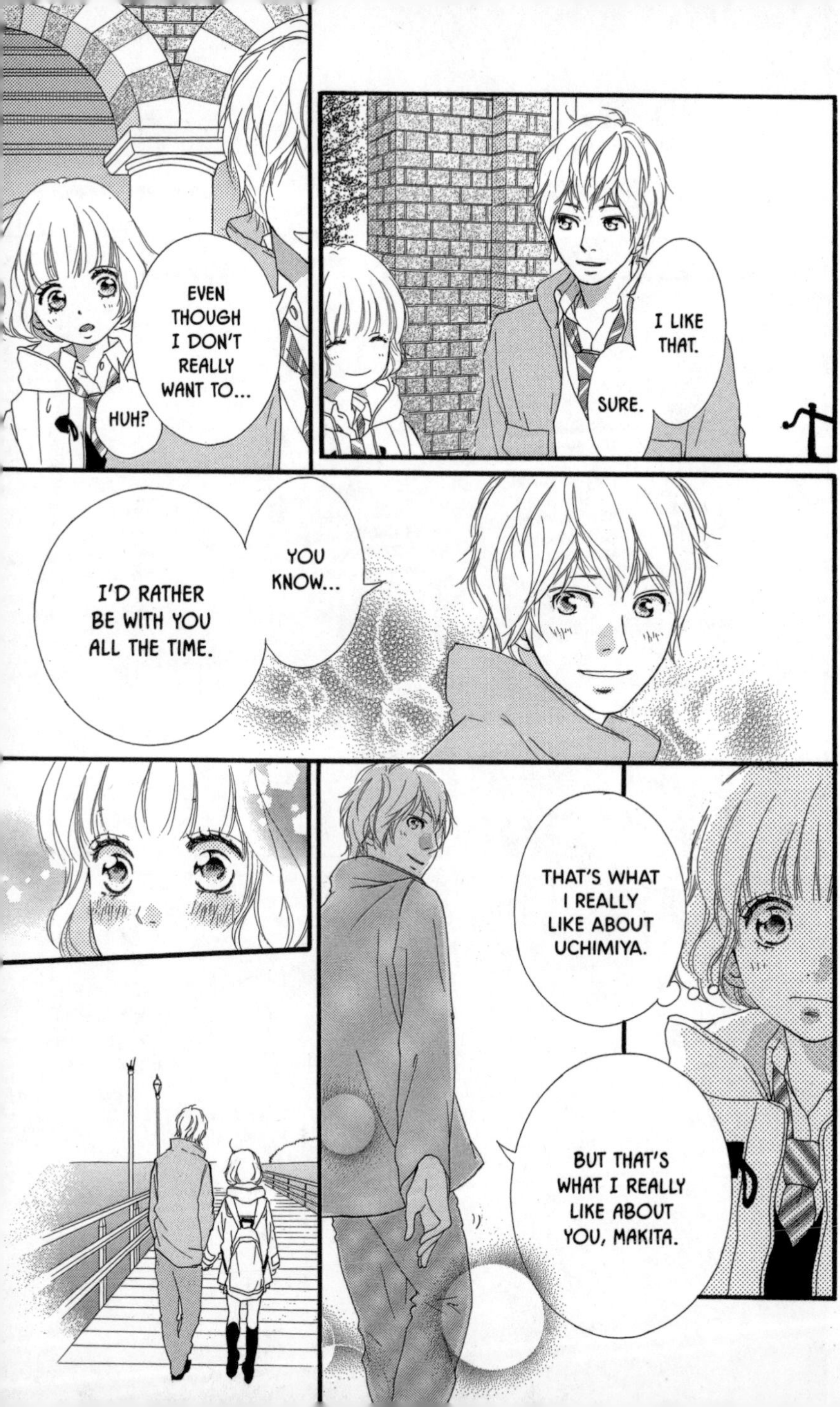
I LIKE THAT.
SURE.
EVEN THOUGH I DON'T REALLY WANT TO...
HUH?
YOU KNOW...
I'D RATHER BE WITH YOU ALL THE TIME.
THAT'S WHAT I REALLY LIKE ABOUT UCHIMIYA.
BUT THAT'S WHAT I REALLY LIKE ABOUT YOU, MAKITA.

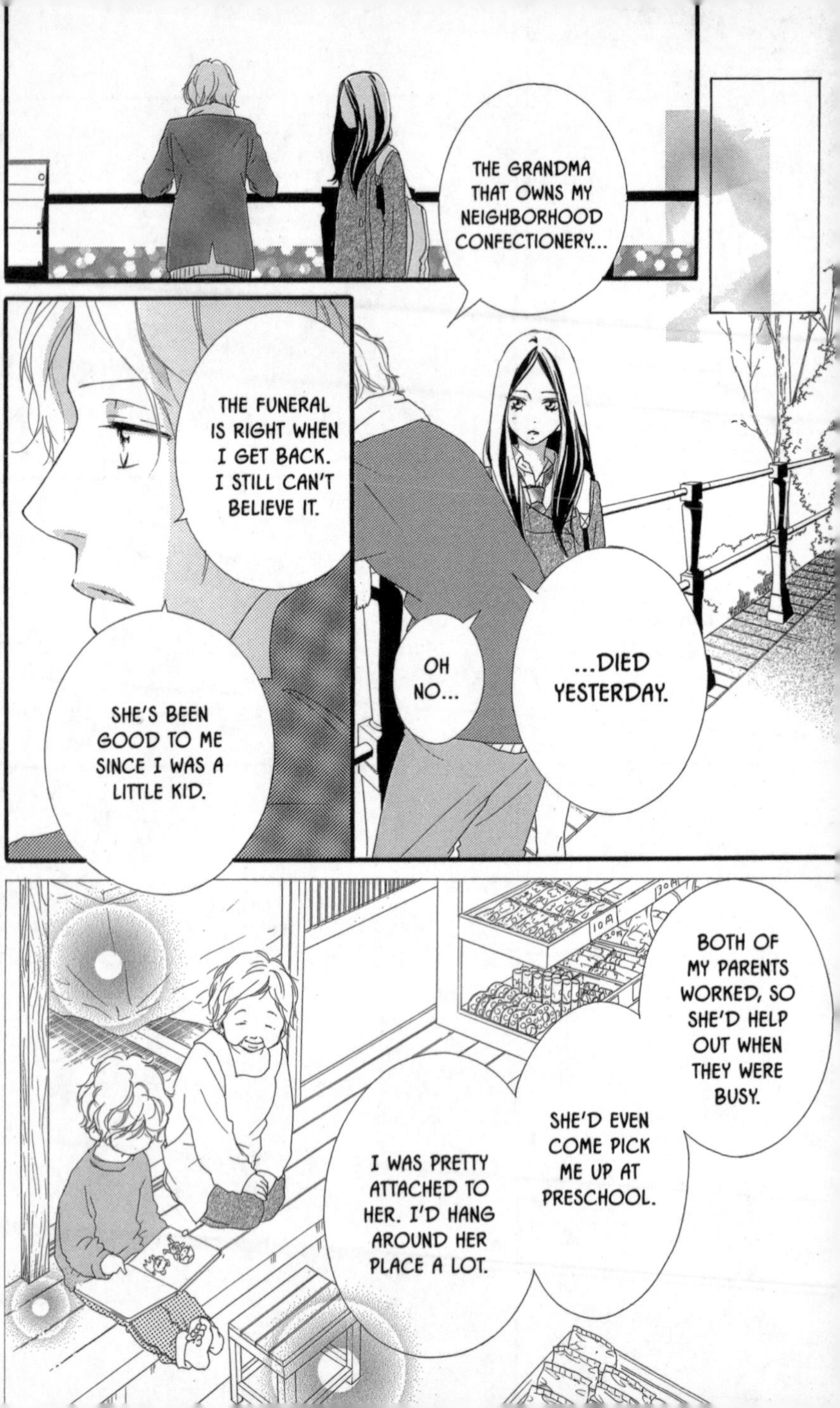
THE GRANDMA THAT OWNS MY NEIGHBORHOOD CONFECTIONERY...
...DIED YESTERDAY.
OH NO...
THE FUNERAL IS RIGHT WHEN I GET BACK. I STILL CAN'T BELIEVE IT.
SHE'S BEEN GOOD TO ME SINCE I WAS A LITTLE KID.
BOTH OF MY PARENTS WORKED, SO SHE'D HELP OUT WHEN THEY WERE BUSY.
SHE'D EVEN COME PICK ME UP AT PRESCHOOL.
I WAS PRETTY ATTACHED TO HER. I'D HANG AROUND HER PLACE A LOT.

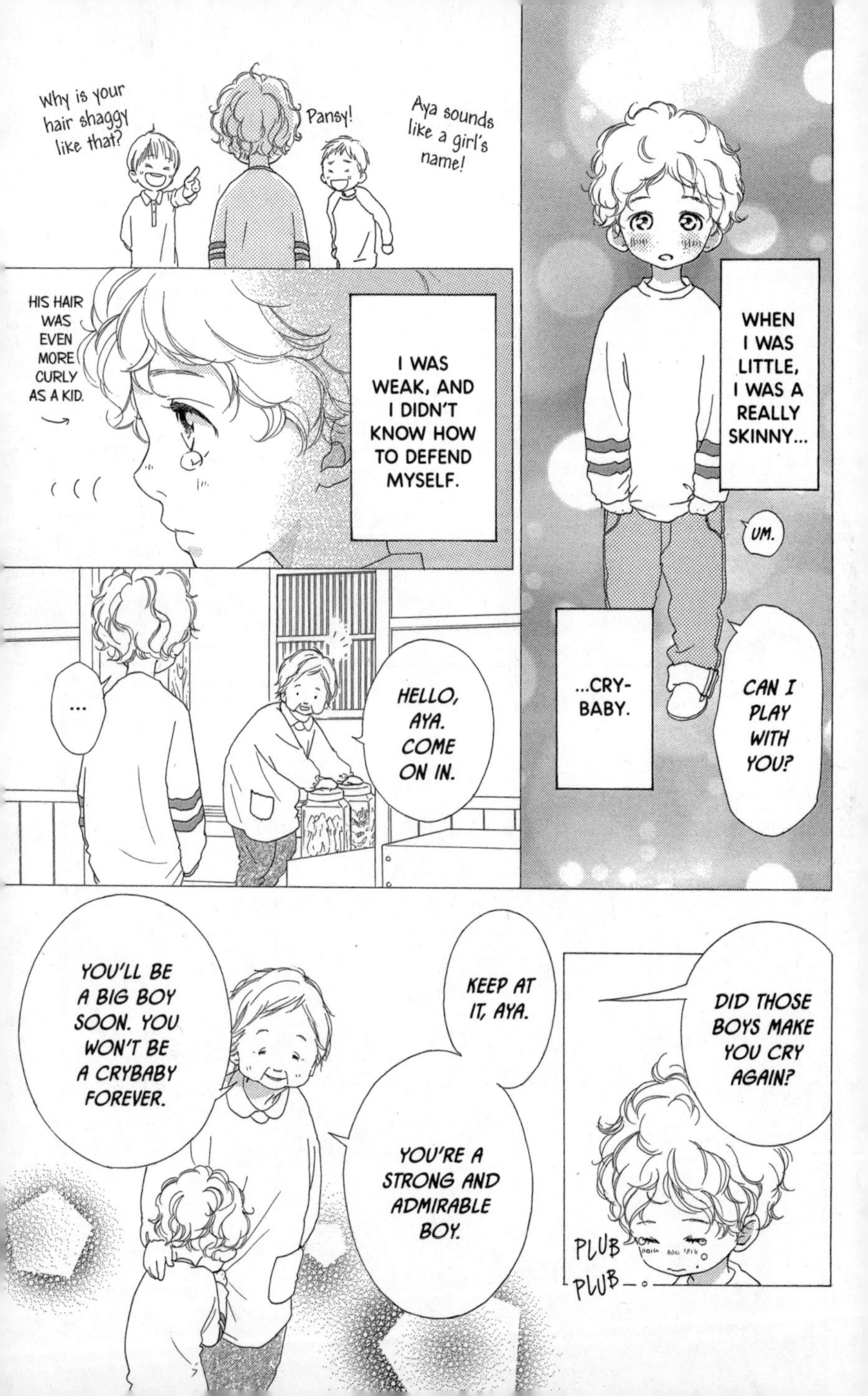
WHEN I WAS LITTLE, I WAS A REALLY SKINNY...
...CRY-BABY.
UM.
CAN I PLAY WITH YOU?
Aya sounds like a girl's name!
Pansy!
Why is your hair shaggy like that?
I WAS WEAK, AND I DIDN'T KNOW HOW TO DEFEND MYSELF.
HIS HAIR WAS EVEN MORE CURLY AS A KID.
HELLO, AYA. COME ON IN.
...
DID THOSE BOYS MAKE YOU CRY AGAIN?
PLUB
PLUB
KEEP AT IT, AYA.
YOU'RE A STRONG AND ADMIRABLE BOY.
YOU'LL BE A BIG BOY SOON. YOU WON'T BE A CRYBABY FOREVER.

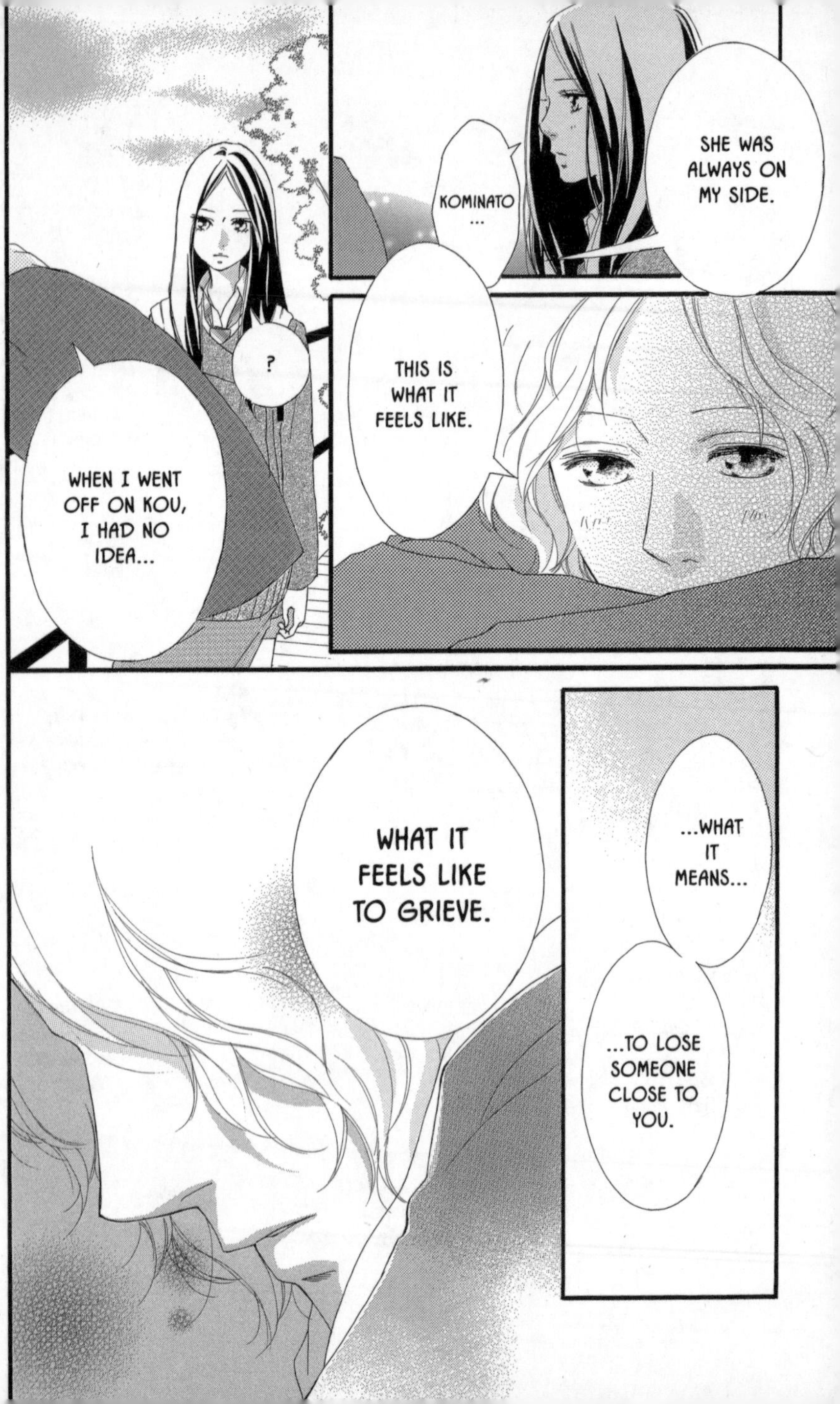
SHE WAS ALWAYS ON MY SIDE.
KOMINATO ...
THIS IS WHAT IT FEELS LIKE.
?
WHEN I WENT OFF ON KOU, I HAD NO IDEA...
WHAT IT FEELS LIKE TO GRIEVE.
...WHAT IT MEANS...
...TO LOSE SOMEONE CLOSE TO YOU.

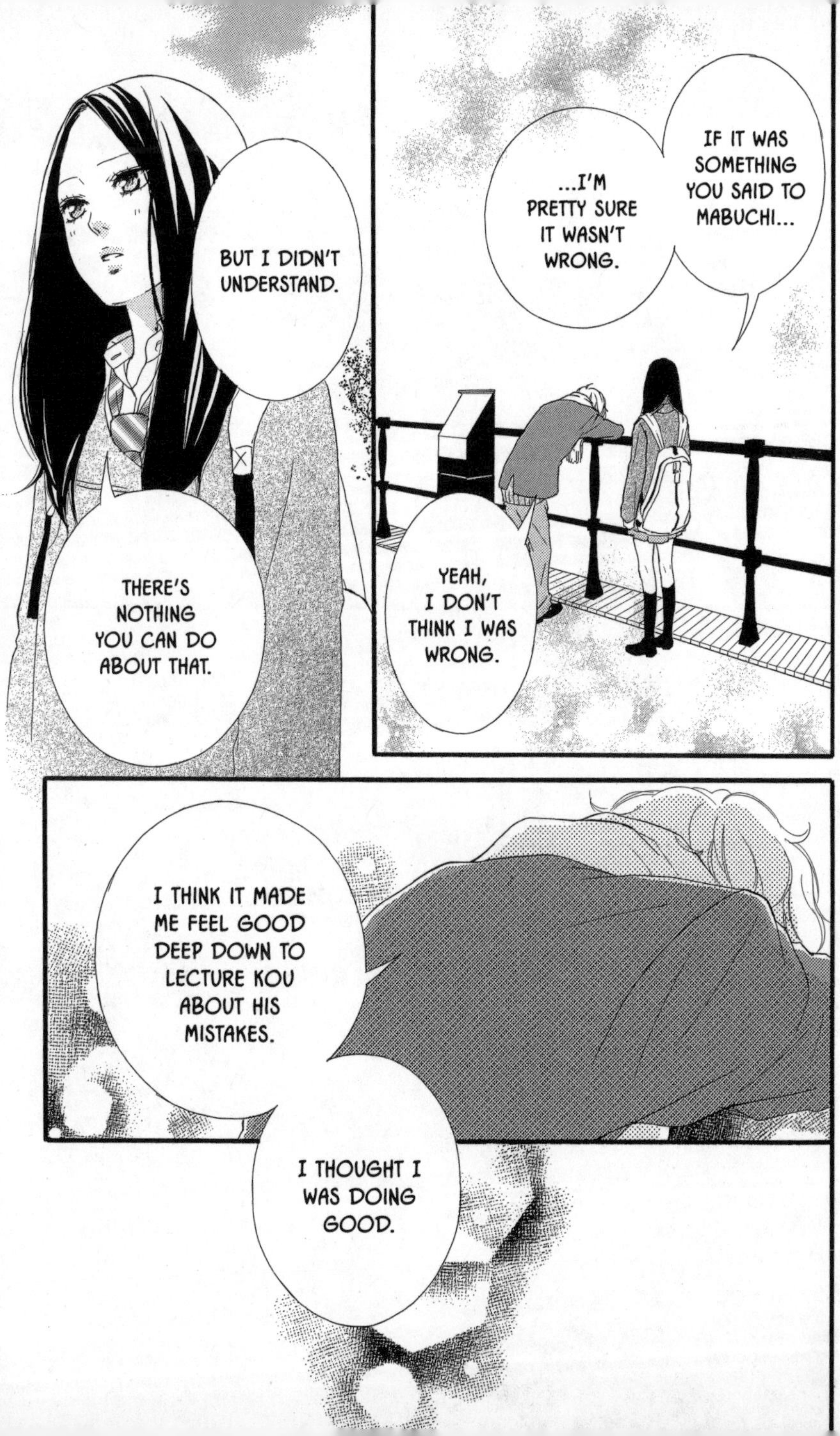
IF IT WAS SOMETHING YOU SAID TO MABUCHI...
...I'M PRETTY SURE IT WASN'T WRONG.
YEAH, I DON'T THINK I WAS WRONG.
BUT I DIDN'T UNDERSTAND.
THERE'S NOTHING YOU CAN DO ABOUT THAT.
I THINK IT MADE ME FEEL GOOD DEEP DOWN TO LECTURE KOU ABOUT HIS MISTAKES.
I THOUGHT I WAS DOING GOOD.

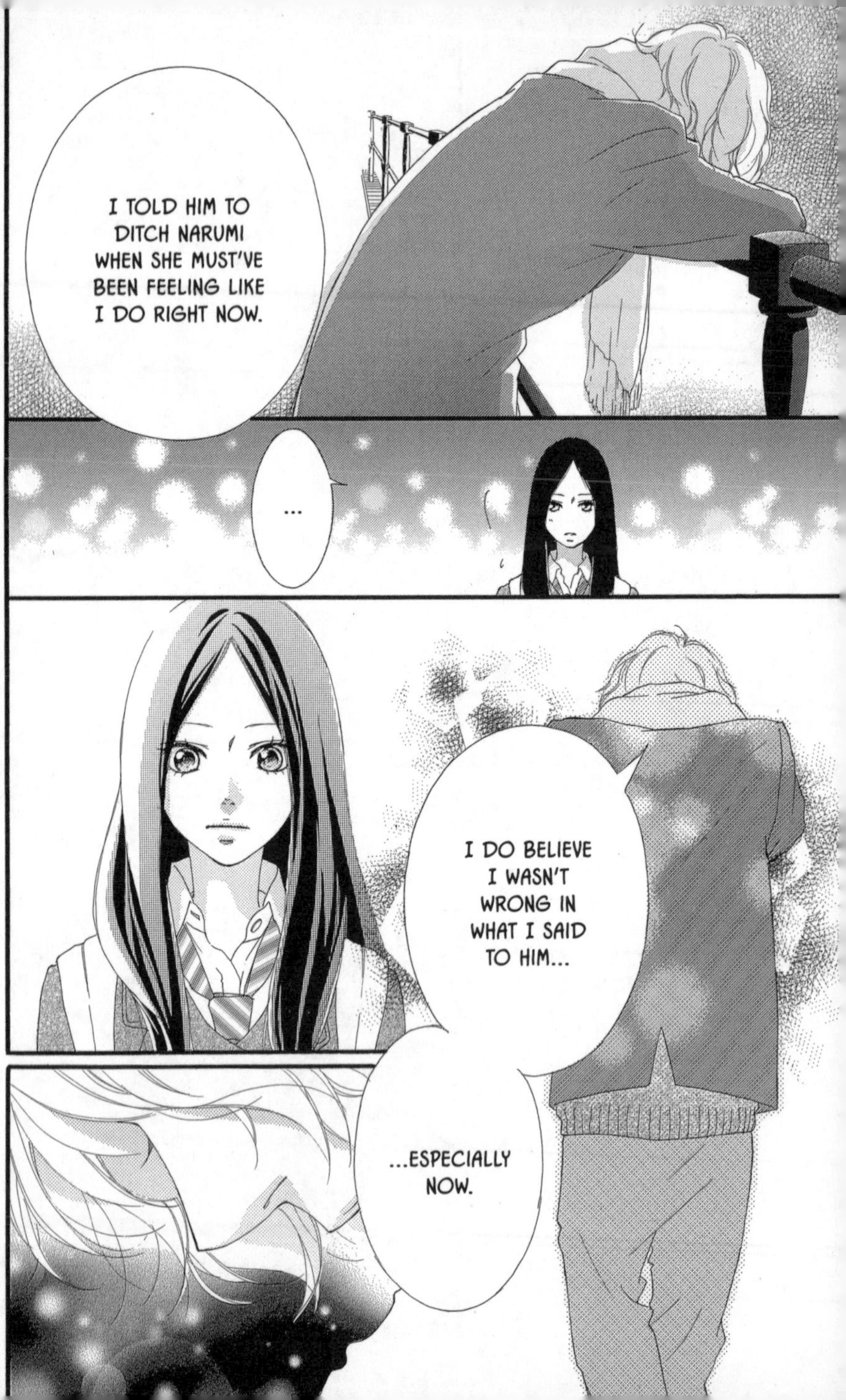
I TOLD HIM TO DITCH NARUMI WHEN SHE MUST'VE BEEN FEELING LIKE I DO RIGHT NOW.
...
I DO BELIEVE I WASN'T WRONG IN WHAT I SAID TO HIM...
...ESPECIALLY NOW.

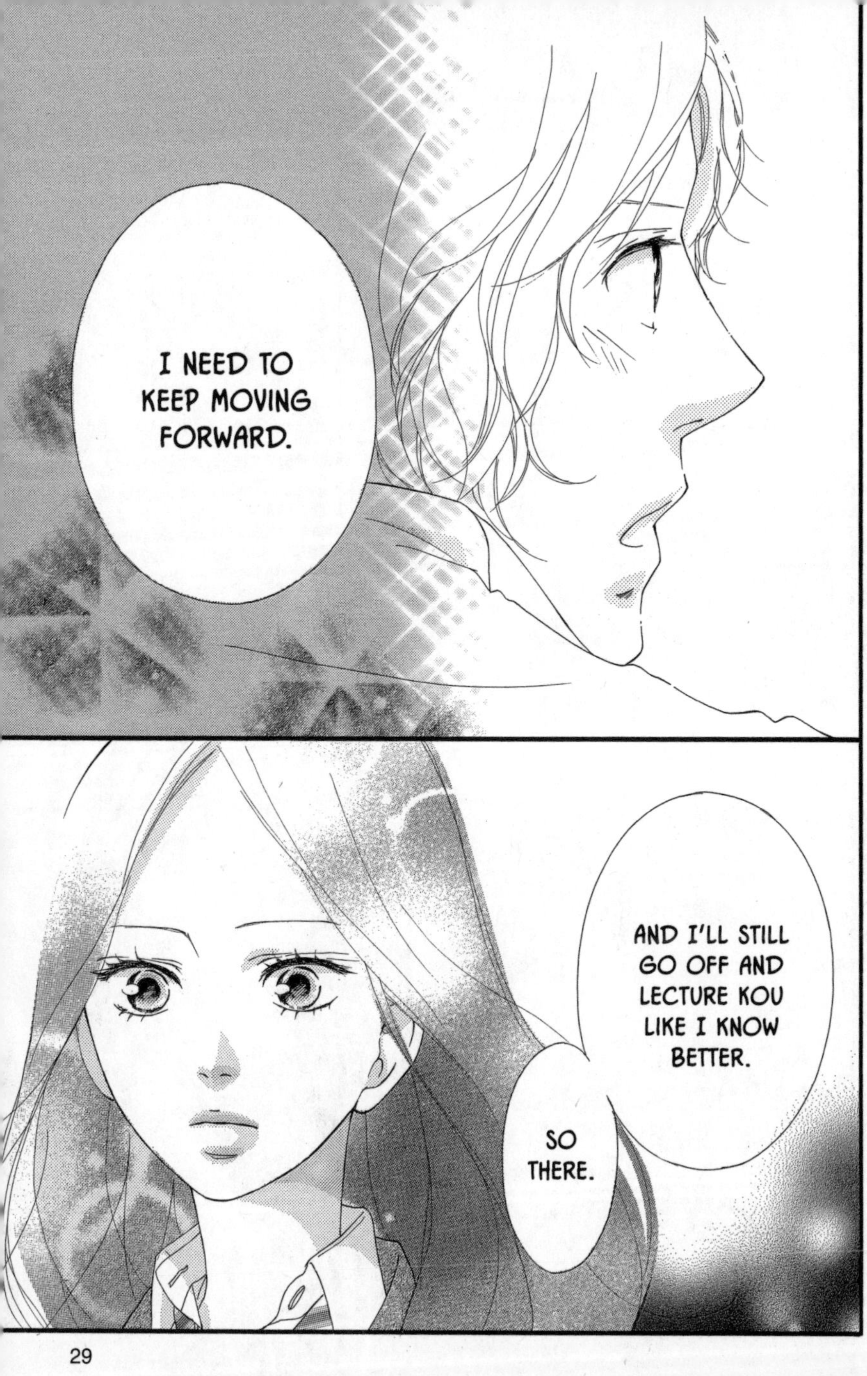
I NEED TO KEEP MOVING FORWARD.
AND I'LL STILL GO OFF AND LECTURE KOU LIKE I KNOW BETTER.
SO THERE.

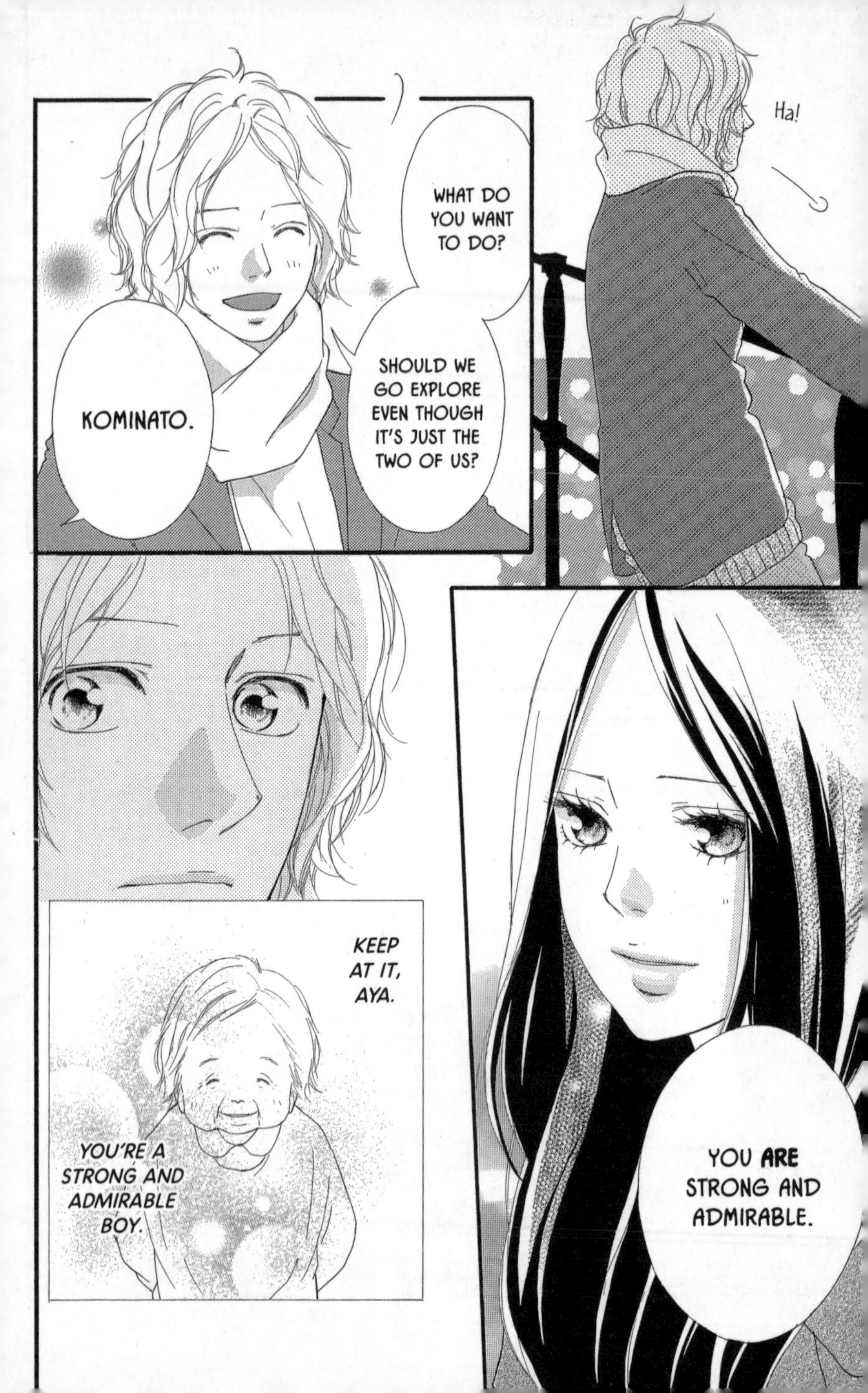
Ha!
WHAT DO YOU WANT TO DO?
SHOULD WE GO EXPLORE EVEN THOUGH IT'S JUST THE TWO OF US?
KOMINATO.
YOU **ARE** STRONG AND ADMIRABLE.
KEEP AT IT, AYA.
YOU'RE A STRONG AND ADMIRABLE BOY.

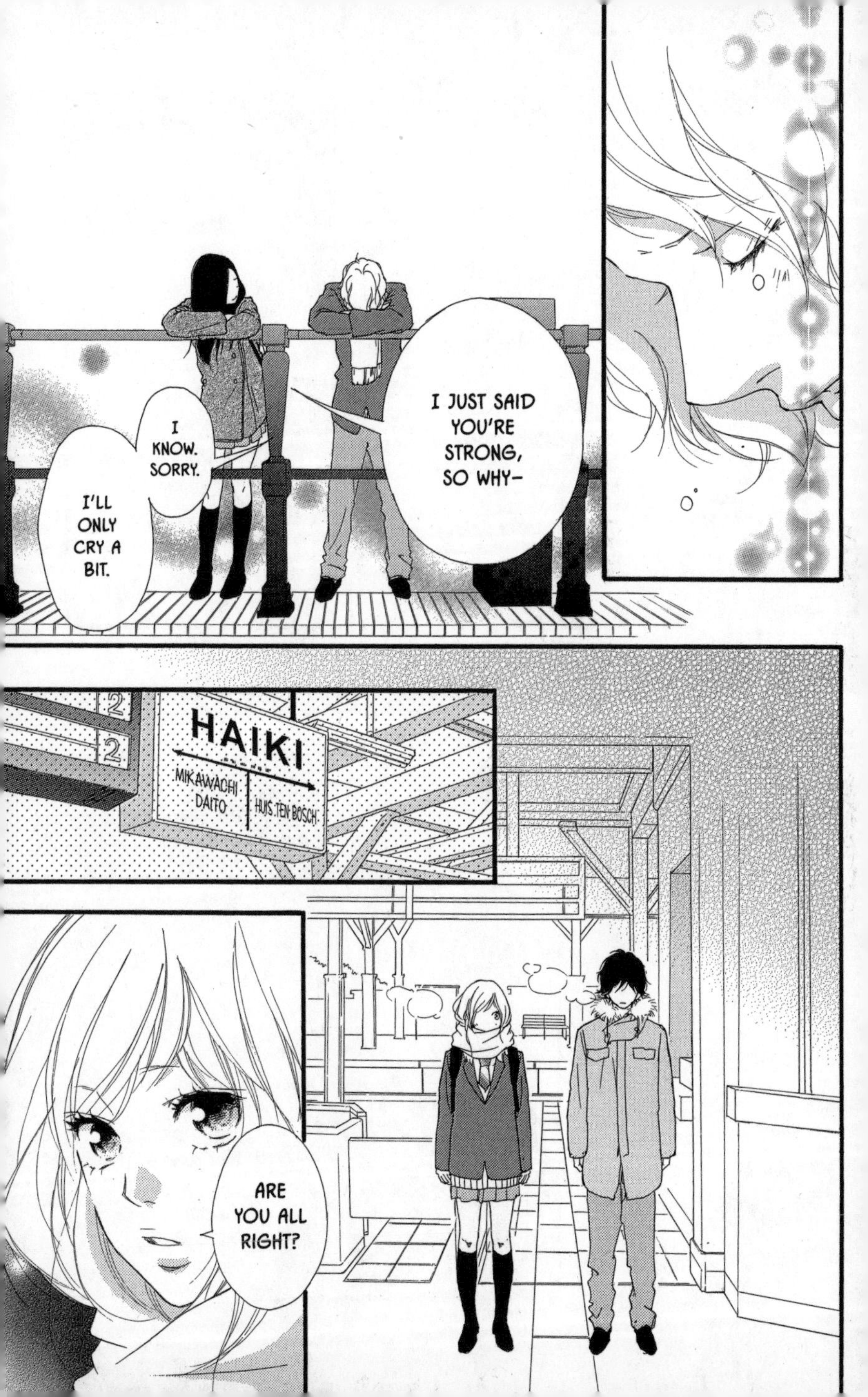
I JUST SAID YOU'RE STRONG, SO WHY–
I KNOW. SORRY.
I'LL ONLY CRY A BIT.
HAIKI
MIKAWACHI DAITO
HUIS TEN BOSCH
ARE YOU ALL RIGHT?

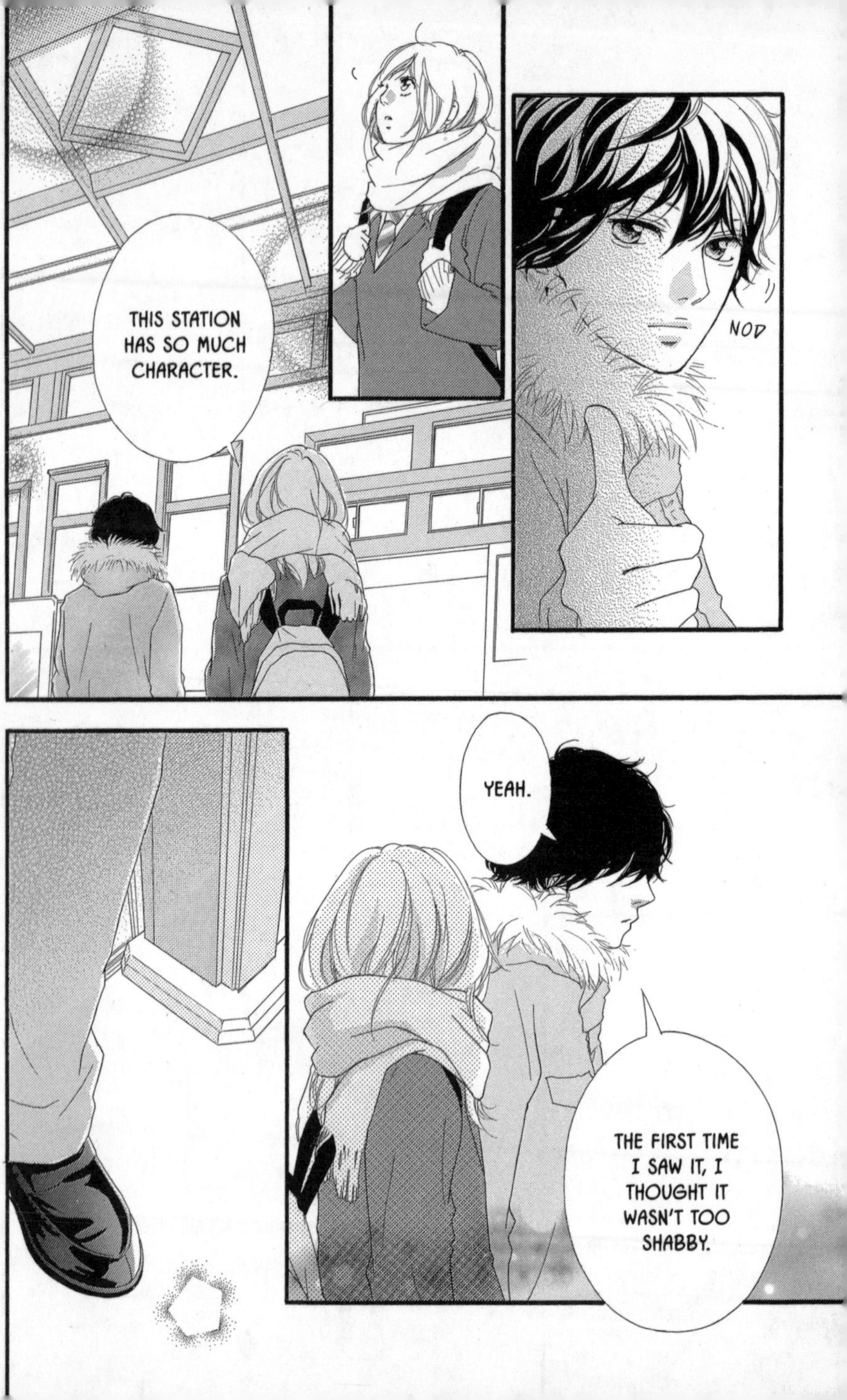
NOD
THIS STATION HAS SO MUCH CHARACTER.
YEAH.
THE FIRST TIME I SAW IT, I THOUGHT IT WASN'T TOO SHABBY.

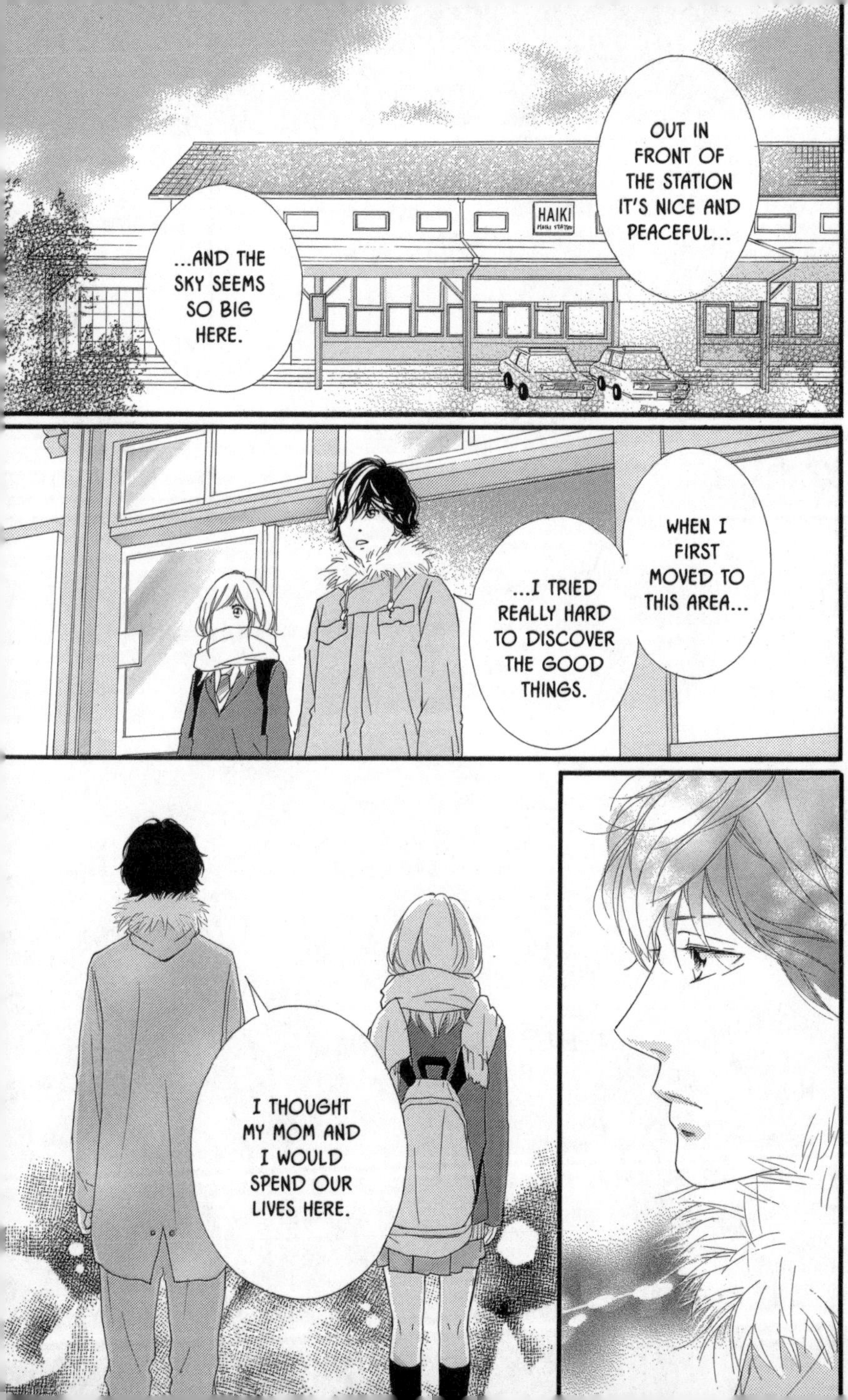
OUT IN FRONT OF THE STATION IT'S NICE AND PEACEFUL...
HAIKI
...AND THE SKY SEEMS SO BIG HERE.
WHEN I FIRST MOVED TO THIS AREA...
...I TRIED REALLY HARD TO DISCOVER THE GOOD THINGS.
I THOUGHT MY MOM AND I WOULD SPEND OUR LIVES HERE.

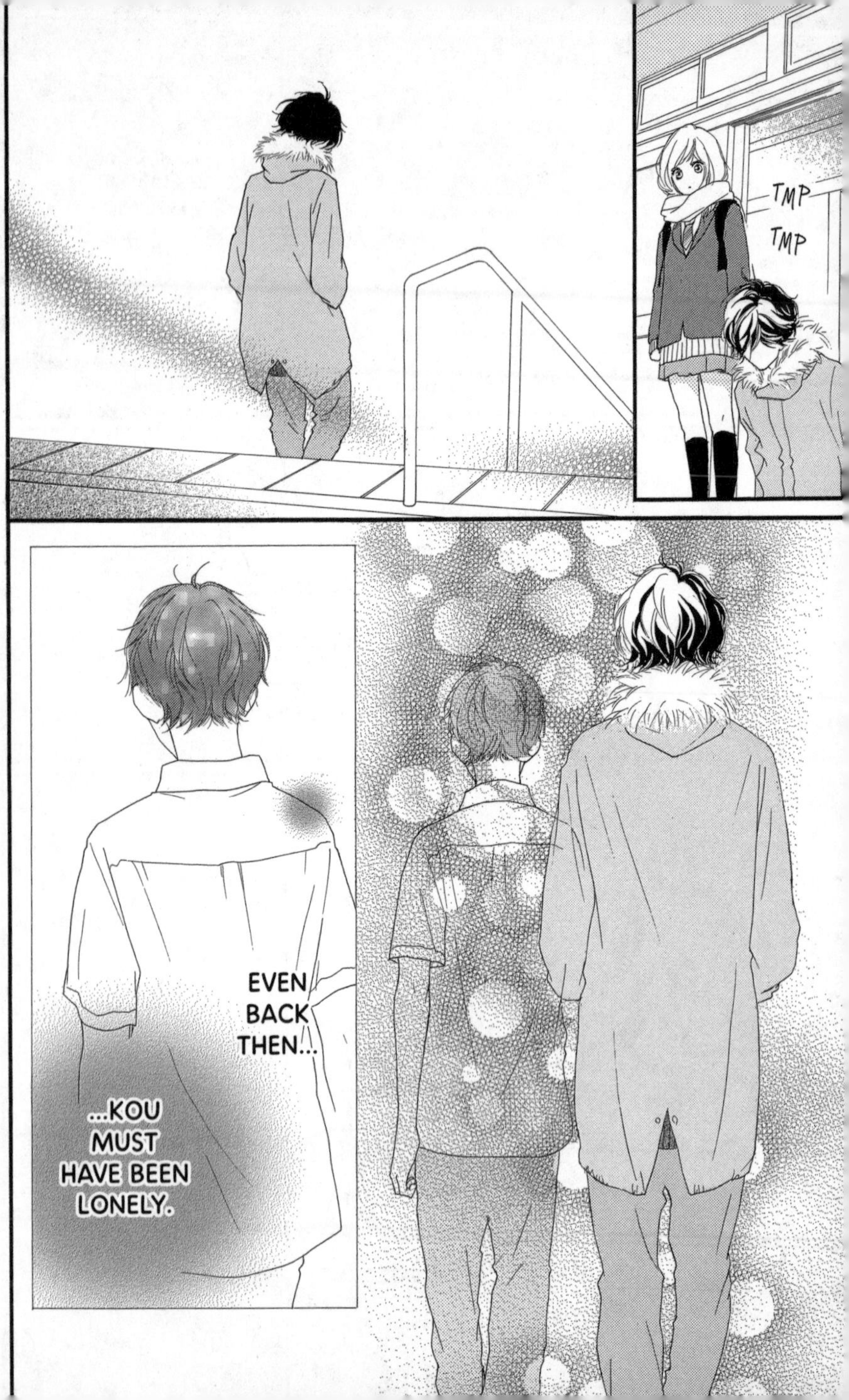
TMP
TMP
EVEN BACK THEN...
...KOU MUST HAVE BEEN LONELY.

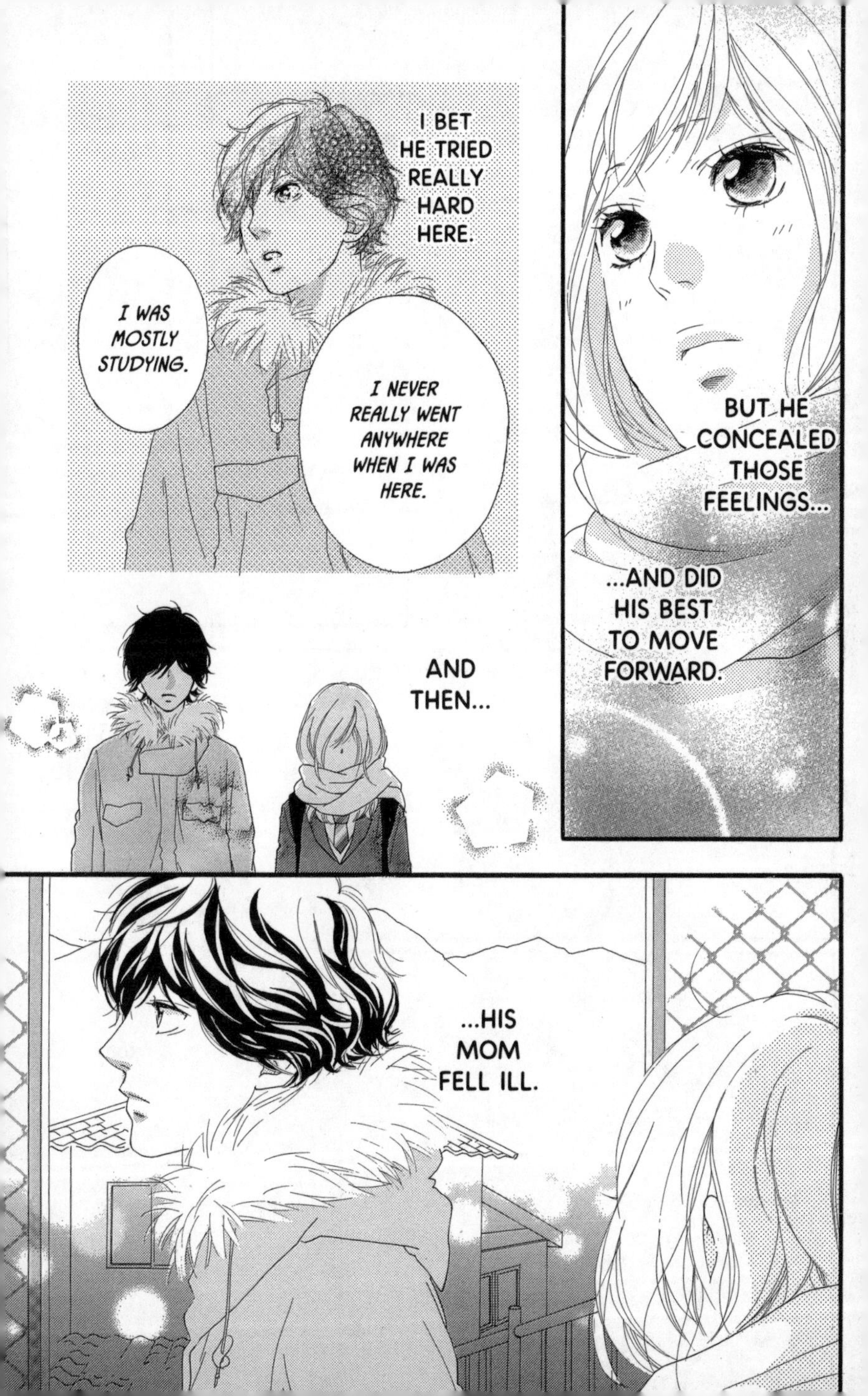
BUT HE CONCEALED THOSE FEELINGS...
...AND DID HIS BEST TO MOVE FORWARD.
I BET HE TRIED REALLY HARD HERE.
I NEVER REALLY WENT ANYWHERE WHEN I WAS HERE.
I WAS MOSTLY STUDYING.
AND THEN...
...HIS MOM FELL ILL.

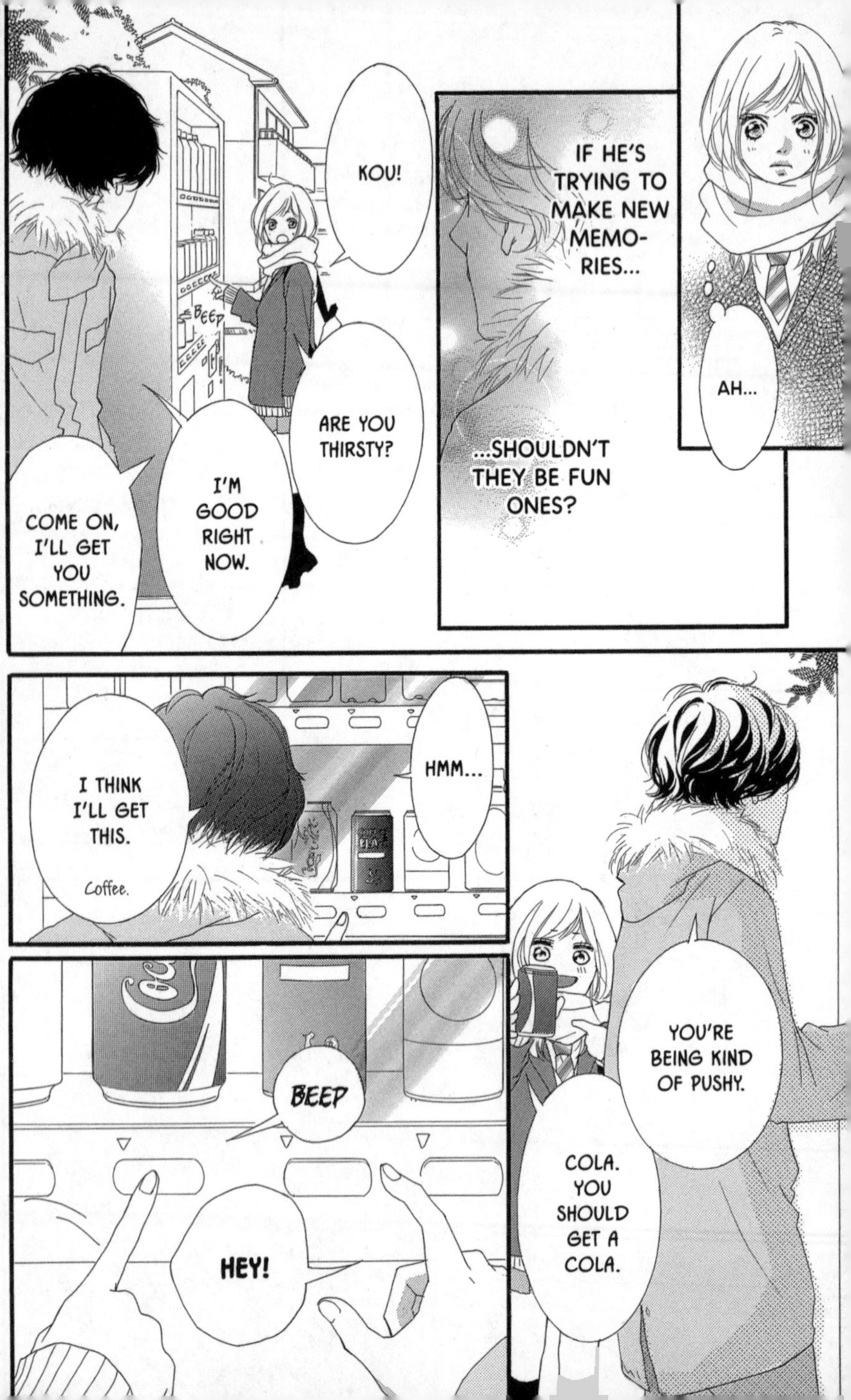
AH...
IF HE'S TRYING TO MAKE NEW MEMORIES...
...SHOULDN'T THEY BE FUN ONES?
KOU!
BEEP
ARE YOU THIRSTY?
I'M GOOD RIGHT NOW.
COME ON, I'LL GET YOU SOMETHING.
YOU'RE BEING KIND OF PUSHY.
COLA. YOU SHOULD GET A COLA.
HMM...
I THINK I'LL GET THIS.
Coffee.
BEEP
HEY!

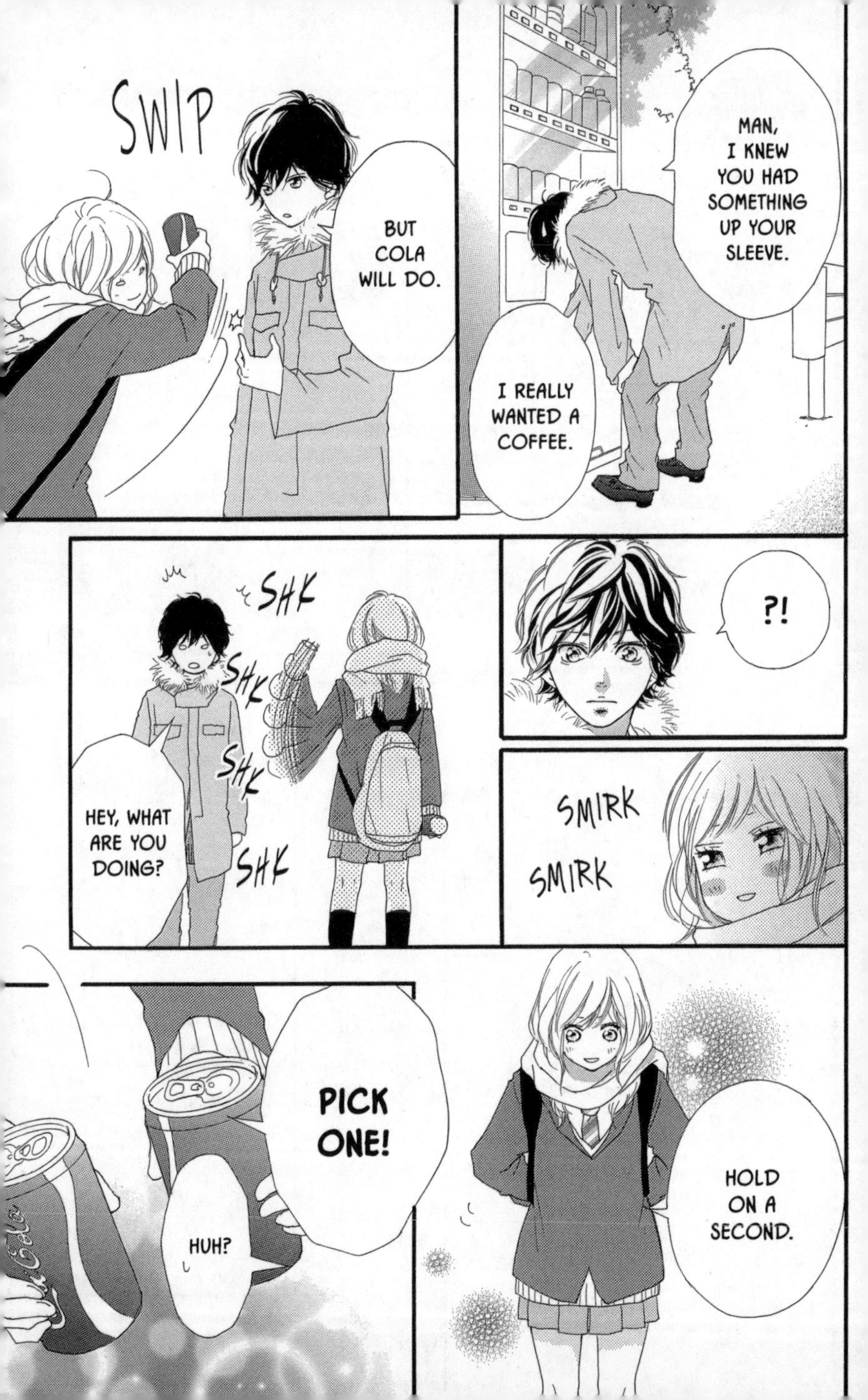
MAN, I KNEW YOU HAD SOMETHING UP YOUR SLEEVE.
I REALLY WANTED A COFFEE.
SWIP
BUT COLA WILL DO.
?!
SMIRK
SMIRK
SHK
SHK
SHK
SHK
HEY, WHAT ARE YOU DOING?
HOLD ON A SECOND.
PICK ONE!
HUH?

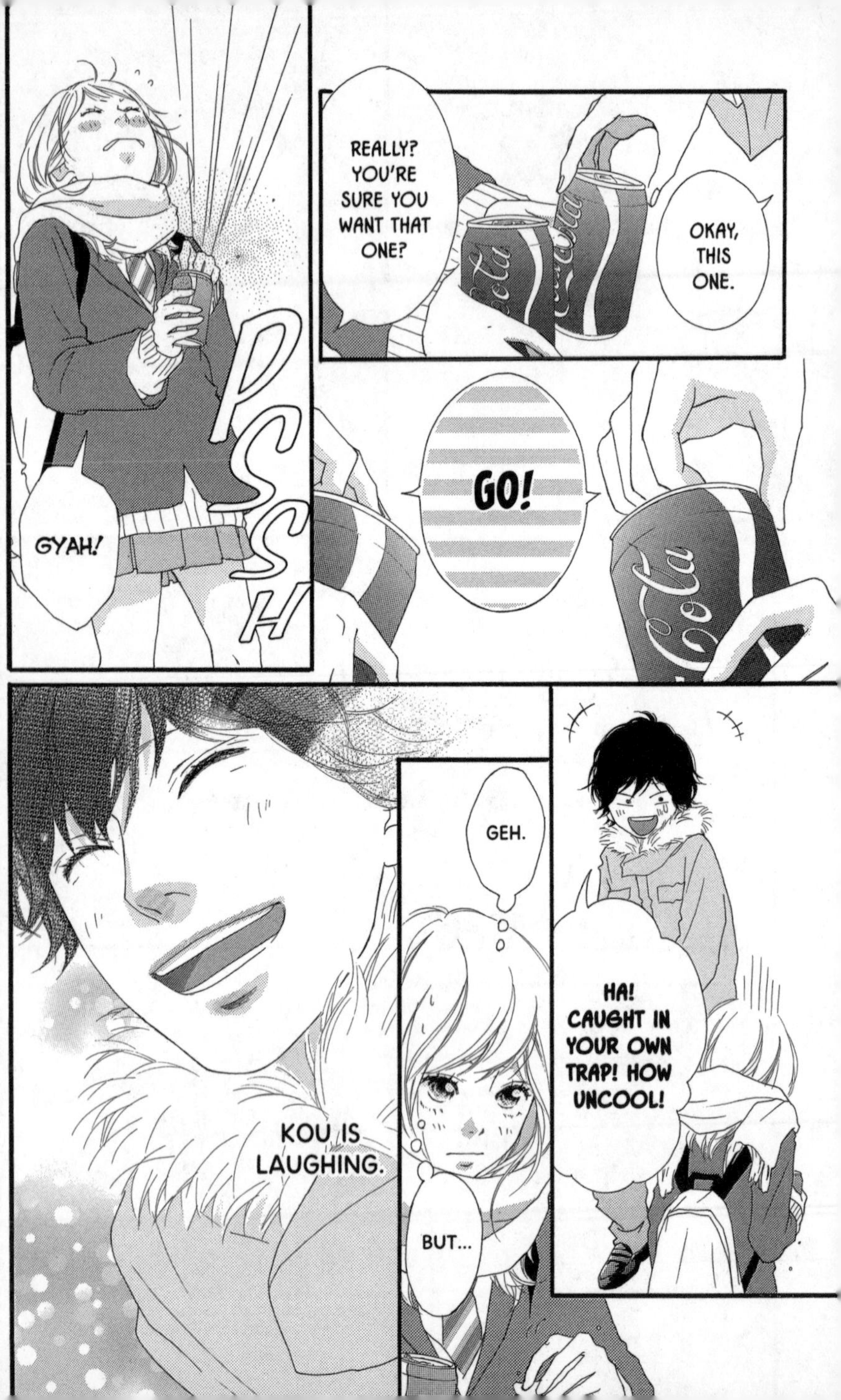
OKAY, THIS ONE.
REALLY? YOU'RE SURE YOU WANT THAT ONE?
GO!
GYAH!
PSSH
HA! CAUGHT IN YOUR OWN TRAP! HOW UNCOOL!
GEH.
BUT...
KOU IS LAUGHING.

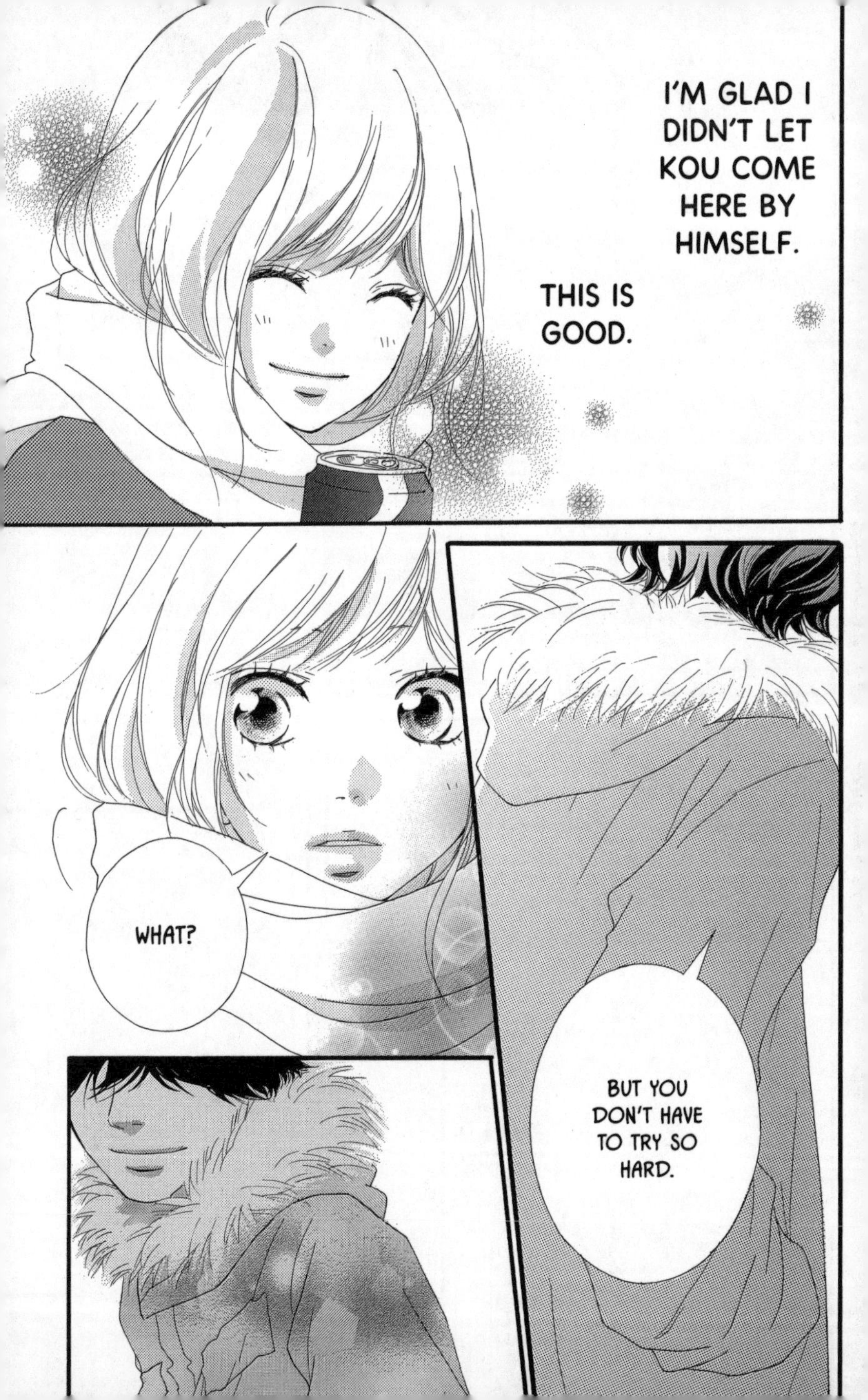
I'M GLAD I DIDN'T LET KOU COME HERE BY HIMSELF.
THIS IS GOOD.
BUT YOU DON'T HAVE TO TRY SO HARD.
WHAT?

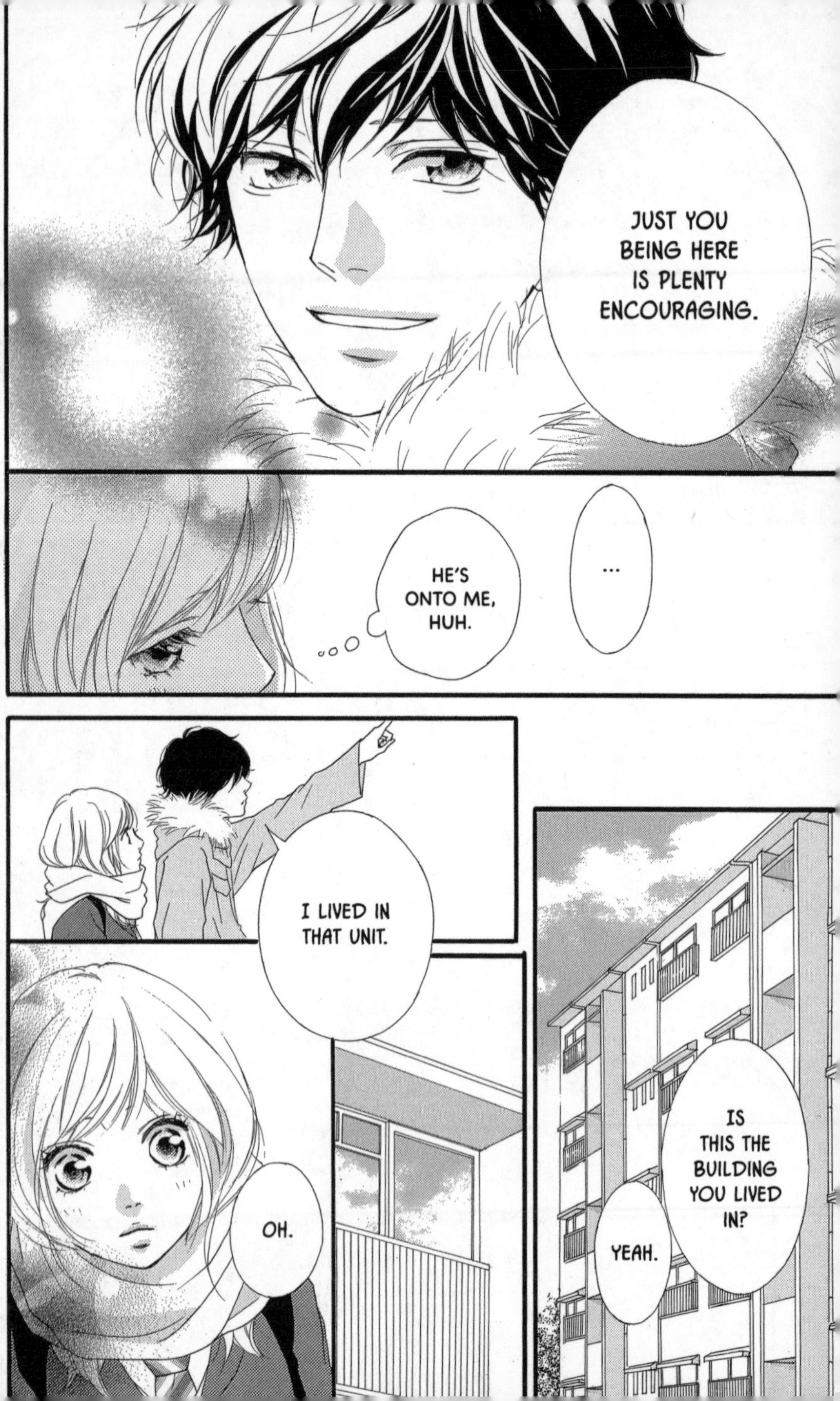
JUST YOU BEING HERE IS PLENTY ENCOURAGING.
...
HE'S ONTO ME, HUH.
IS THIS THE BUILDING YOU LIVED IN?
YEAH.
I LIVED IN THAT UNIT.
OH.

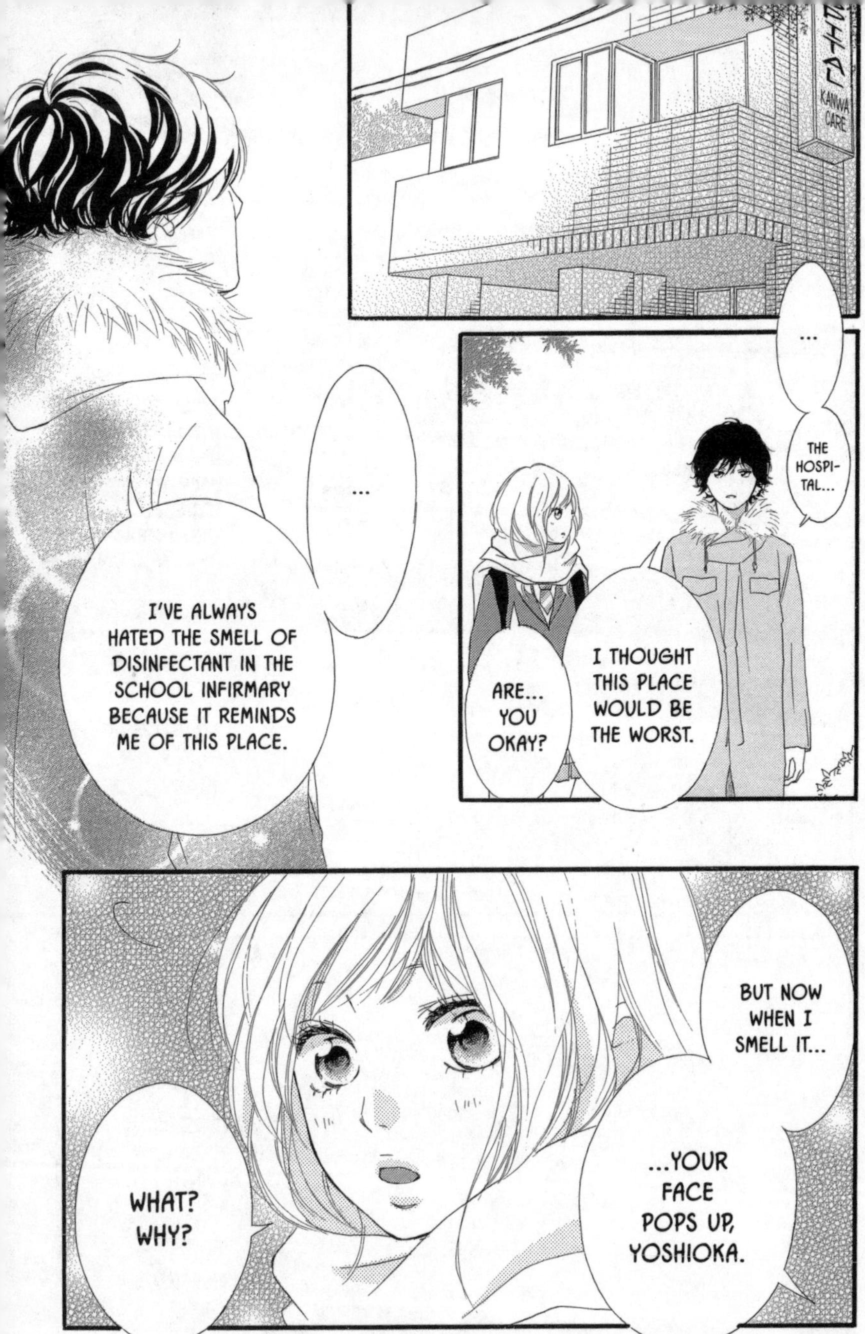
KANWA
CARE
...
THE HOSPITAL...
I THOUGHT THIS PLACE WOULD BE THE WORST.
ARE... YOU OKAY?
...
I'VE ALWAYS HATED THE SMELL OF DISINFECTANT IN THE SCHOOL INFIRMARY BECAUSE IT REMINDS ME OF THIS PLACE.
BUT NOW WHEN I SMELL IT...
...YOUR FACE POPS UP, YOSHIOKA.
WHAT? WHY?

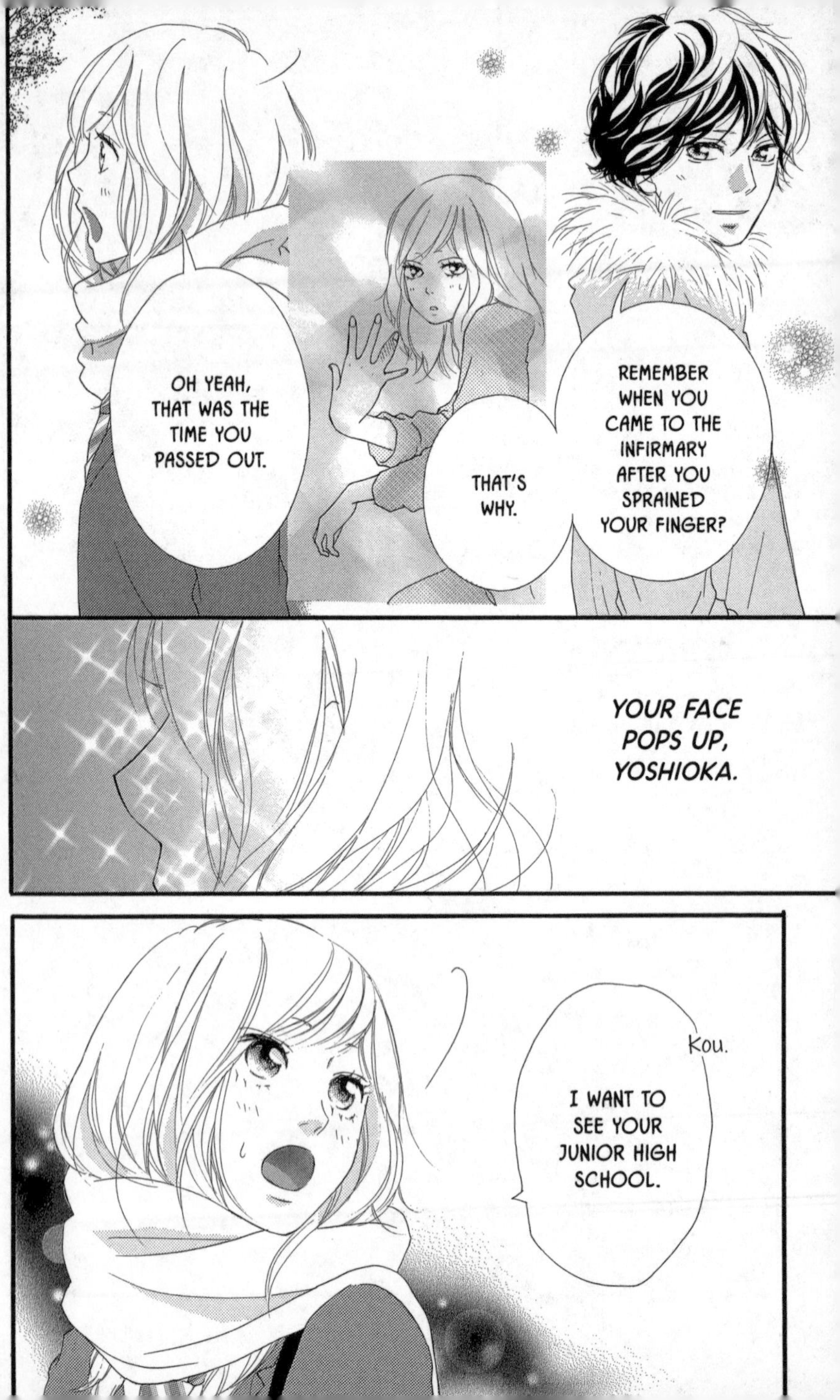
REMEMBER WHEN YOU CAME TO THE INFIRMARY AFTER YOU SPRAINED YOUR FINGER?
THAT'S WHY.
OH YEAH, THAT WAS THE TIME YOU PASSED OUT.
YOUR FACE POPS UP, YOSHIOKA.
Kou.
I WANT TO SEE YOUR JUNIOR HIGH SCHOOL.

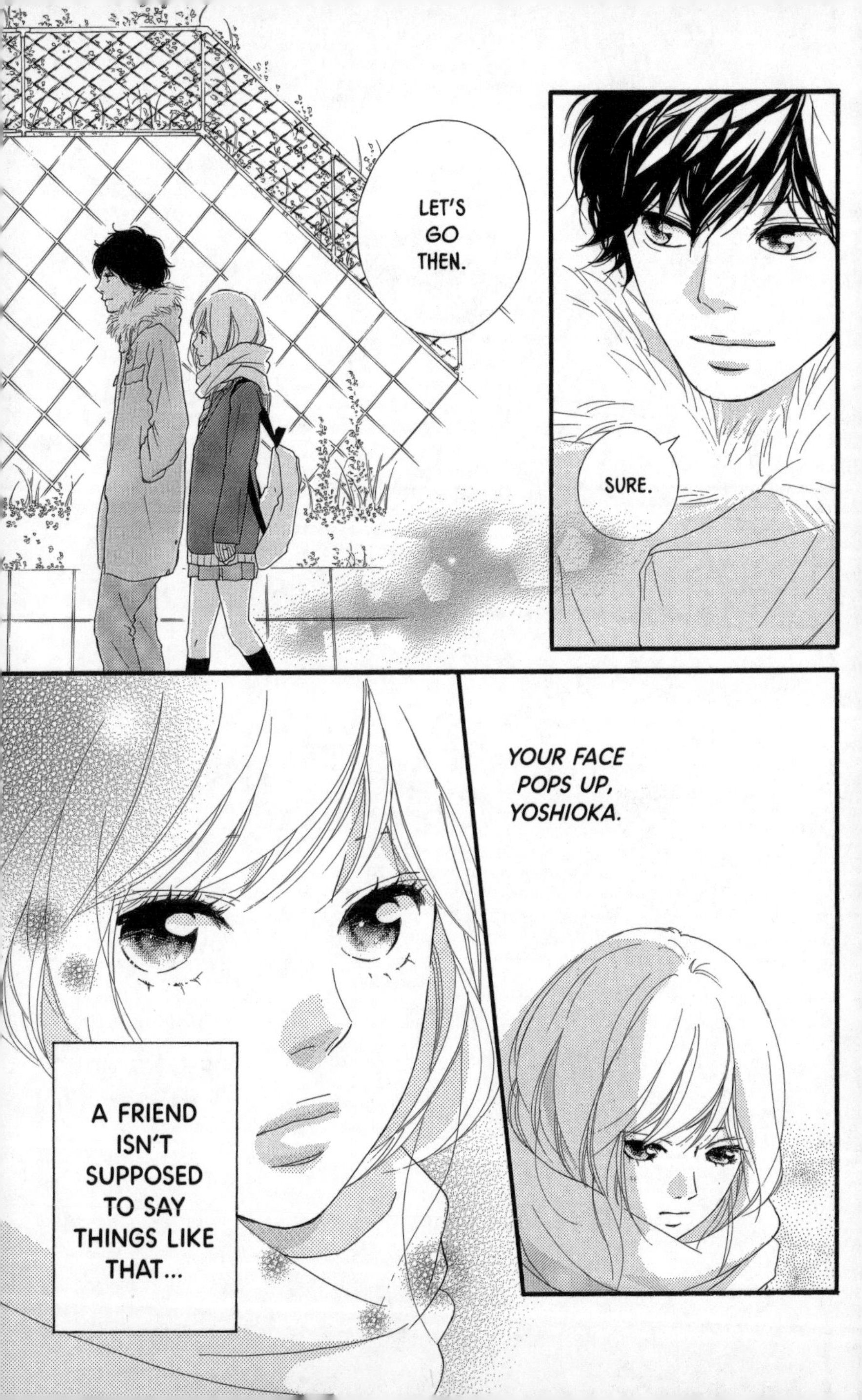
SURE.
LET'S GO THEN.
YOUR FACE POPS UP, YOSHIOKA.
A FRIEND ISN'T SUPPOSED TO SAY THINGS LIKE THAT...

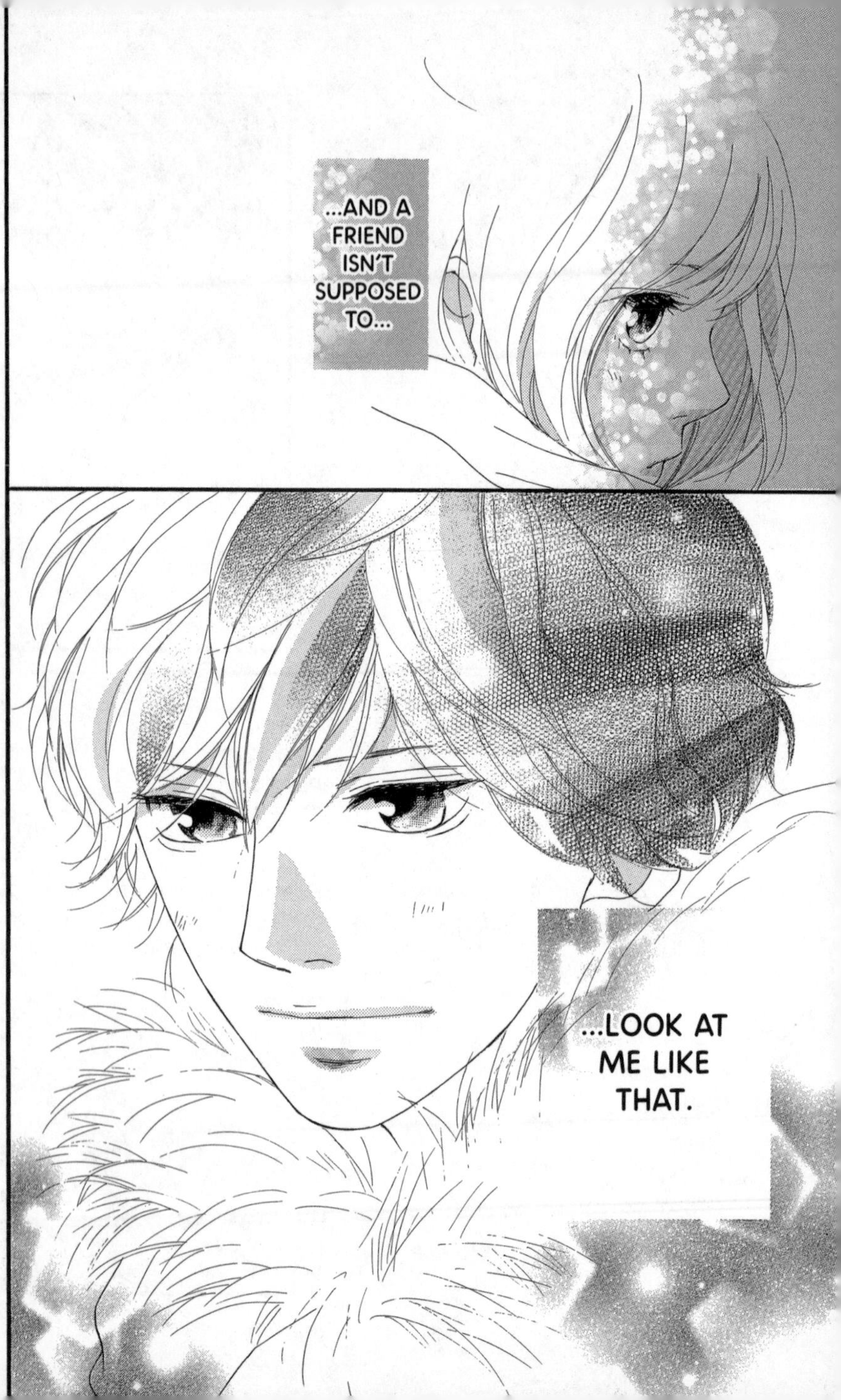
...AND A FRIEND ISN'T SUPPOSED TO...
...LOOK AT ME LIKE THAT.

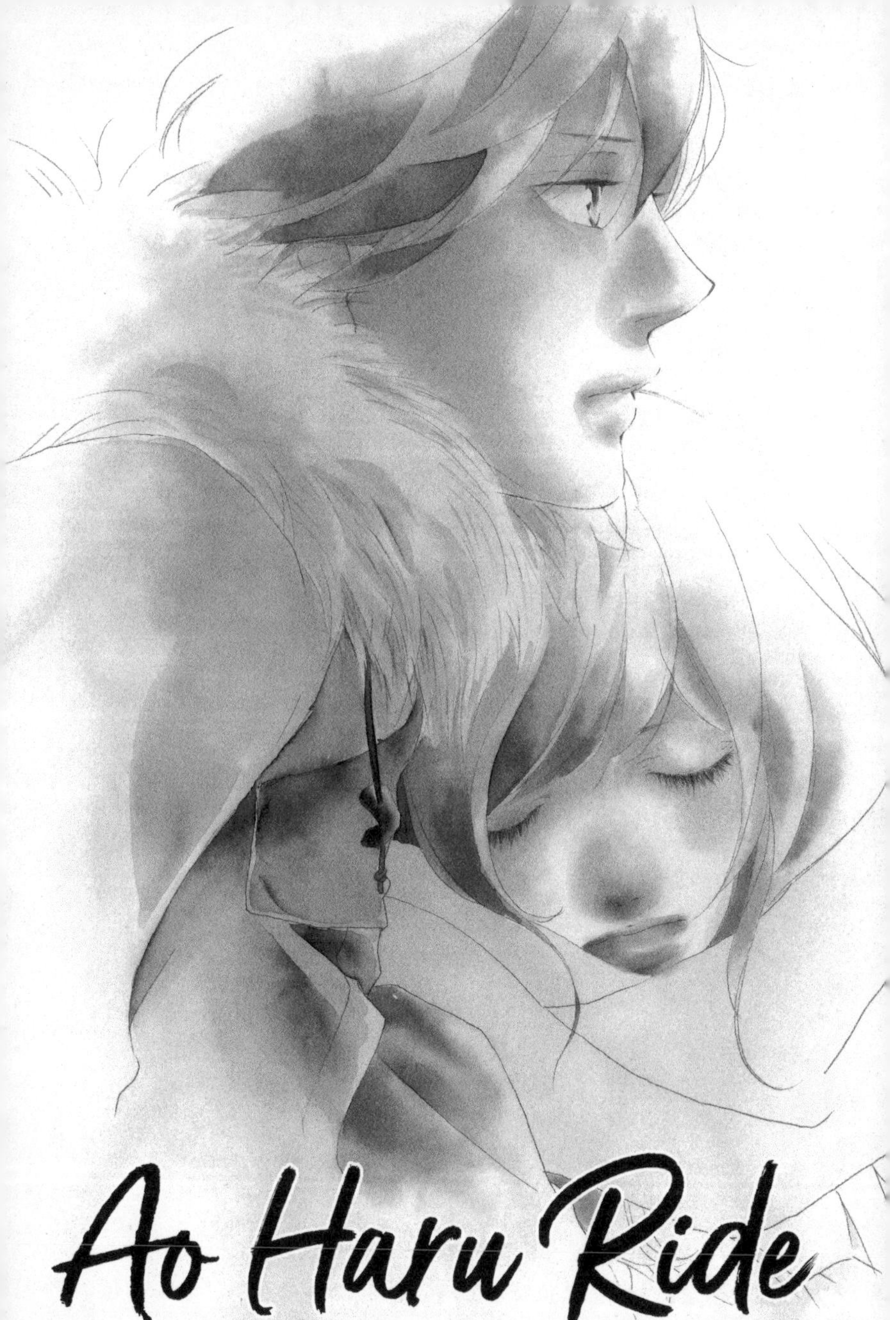

Ao Haru Ride

The scent of air after rain...
In the light around us, I felt your heartbeat.

CHAPTER 40

GREETINGS

Hi! I'm Io Sakisaka. Thank you for picking up a copy of *Ao Haru Ride* volume 11.

This volume feels like I am venturing into unknown territory. When I started this series, I saw my characters exactly as I planned them. But as the story unfolded, I started to learn more about them and understand each one more deeply. Of course this is a good thing, but it also means that the plot I originally started with doesn't always end up as planned. A storyline I had originally thought was good may end up useless and kicked to the curb. I may say to myself, "Actually, he would never do something like that." Because I know my characters so well now, I have to be honest with them by laughing it off and making the change... Actually, that was a total lie. In reality, I'll click my tongue with intense disappointment and I'll cry, cry, cry as I throw out that storyline.

Though these kids don't really follow my direction, I hope you keep reading to see what they do and enjoy volume 11 through to the end.

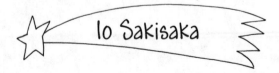
Io Sakisaka

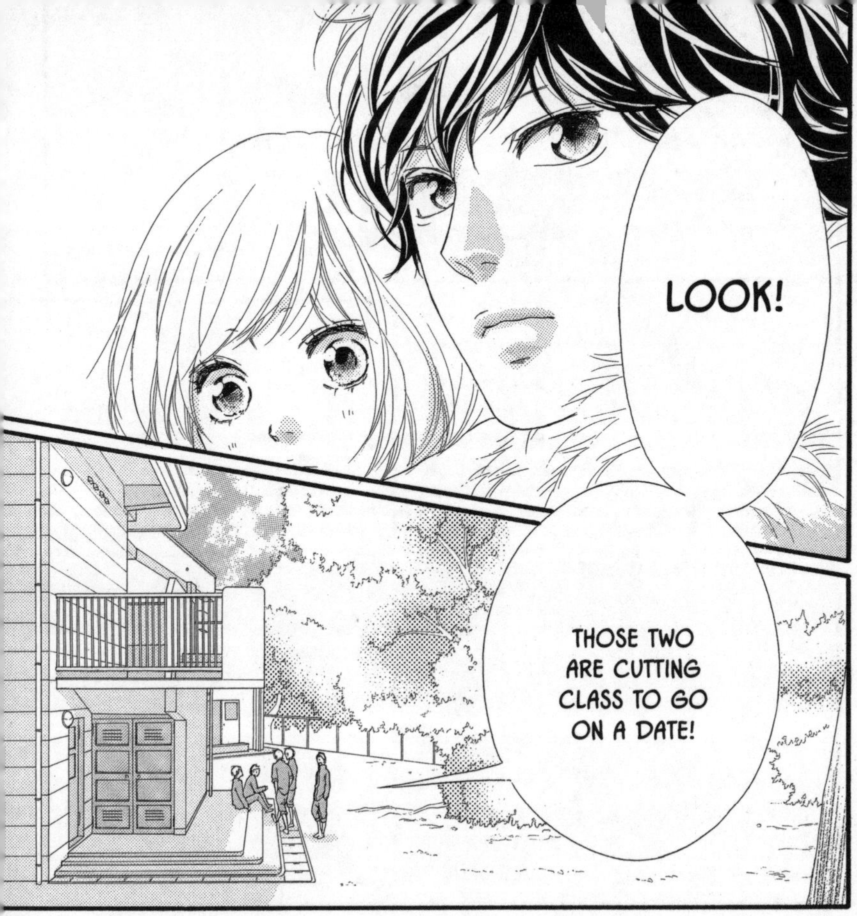
LOOK!
THOSE TWO ARE CUTTING CLASS TO GO ON A DATE!

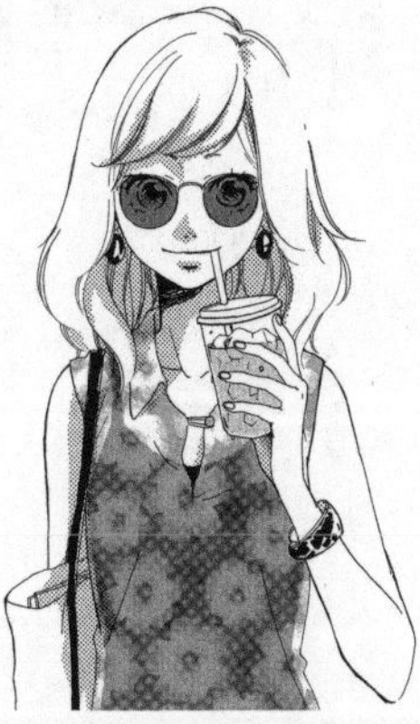

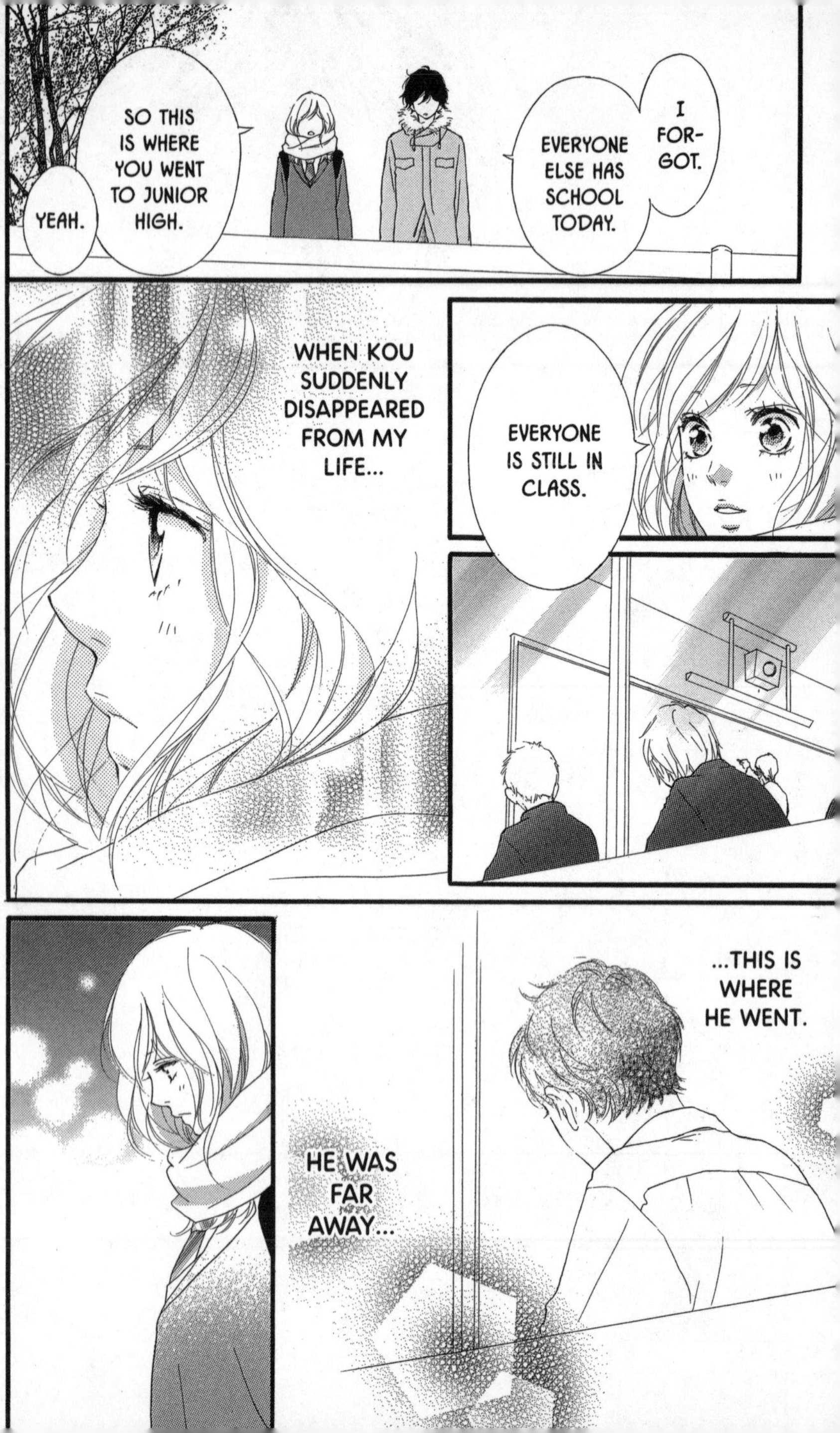
I FOR-GOT.
EVERYONE ELSE HAS SCHOOL TODAY.
SO THIS IS WHERE YOU WENT TO JUNIOR HIGH.
YEAH.
EVERYONE IS STILL IN CLASS.
WHEN KOU SUDDENLY DISAPPEARED FROM MY LIFE...
...THIS IS WHERE HE WENT.
HE WAS FAR AWAY...

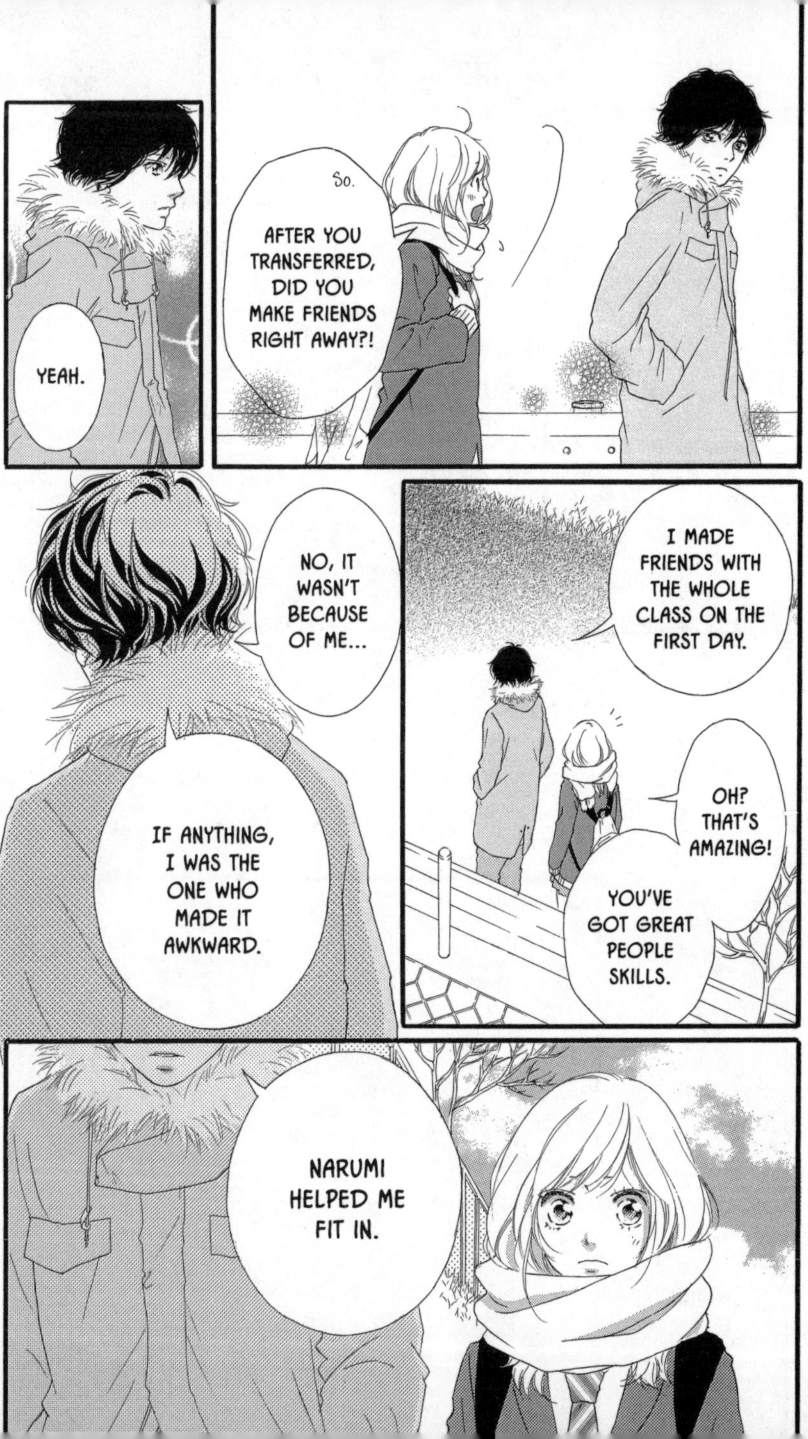
So.
AFTER YOU TRANSFERRED, DID YOU MAKE FRIENDS RIGHT AWAY?!
YEAH.
I MADE FRIENDS WITH THE WHOLE CLASS ON THE FIRST DAY.
OH? THAT'S AMAZING!
YOU'VE GOT GREAT PEOPLE SKILLS.
NO, IT WASN'T BECAUSE OF ME...
IF ANYTHING, I WAS THE ONE WHO MADE IT AWKWARD.
NARUMI HELPED ME FIT IN.

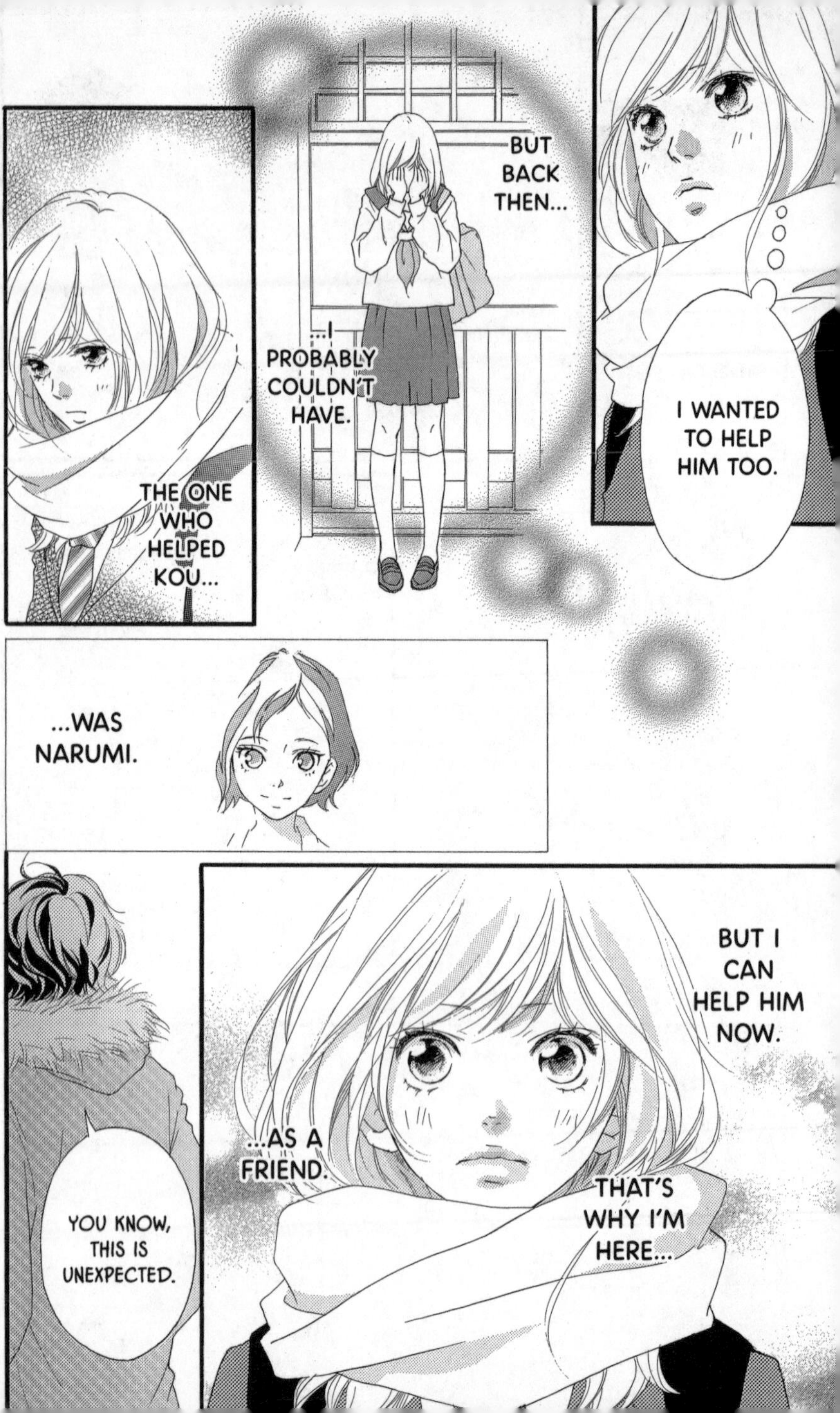
I WANTED TO HELP HIM TOO.
BUT BACK THEN...
...I PROBABLY COULDN'T HAVE.
THE ONE WHO HELPED KOU...
...WAS NARUMI.
BUT I CAN HELP HIM NOW.
...AS A FRIEND.
THAT'S WHY I'M HERE...
YOU KNOW, THIS IS UNEXPECTED.

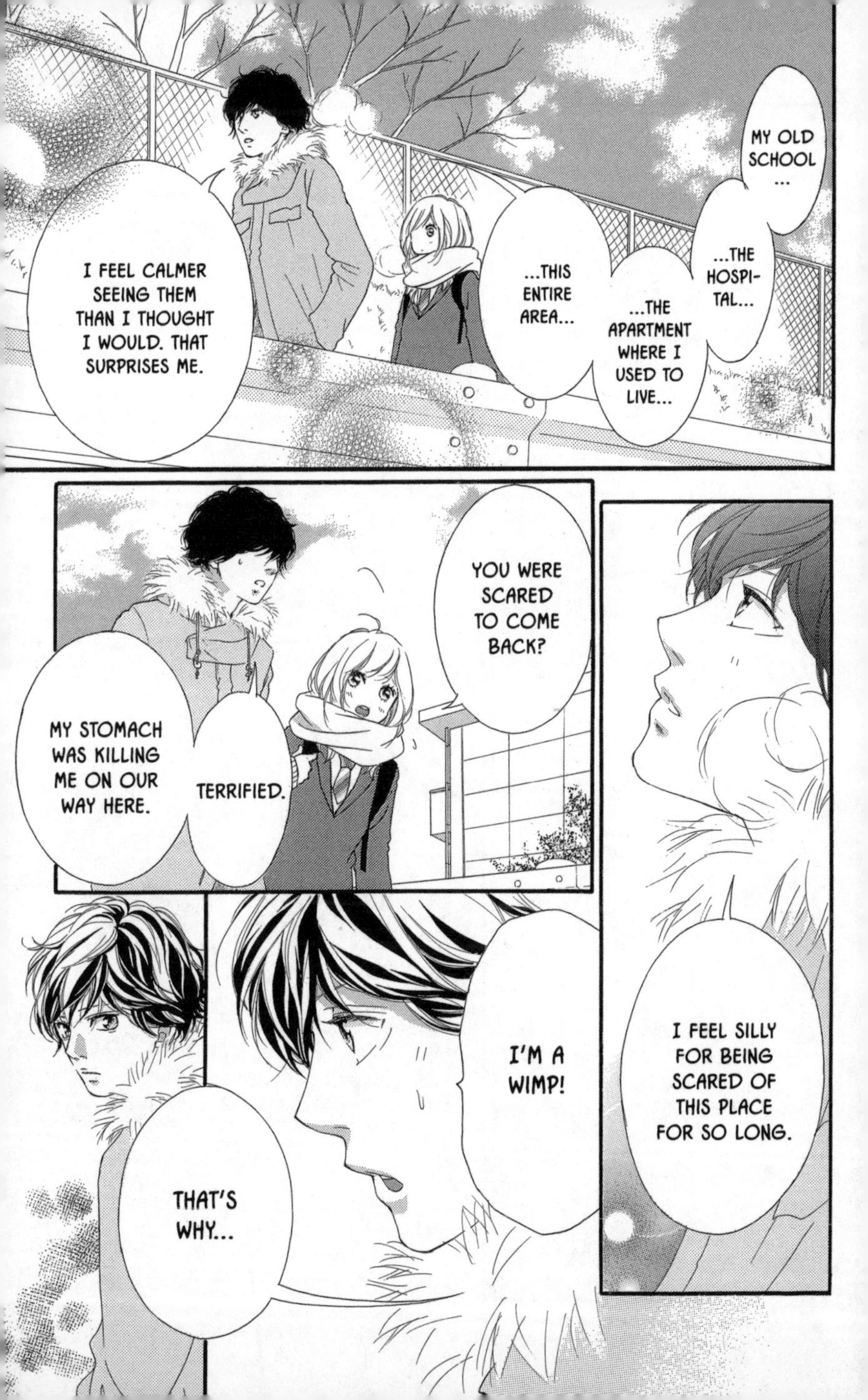
MY OLD SCHOOL ...
...THE HOSPITAL...
...THE APARTMENT WHERE I USED TO LIVE...
...THIS ENTIRE AREA...
I FEEL CALMER SEEING THEM THAN I THOUGHT I WOULD. THAT SURPRISES ME.
I FEEL SILLY FOR BEING SCARED OF THIS PLACE FOR SO LONG.
YOU WERE SCARED TO COME BACK?
TERRIFIED.
MY STOMACH WAS KILLING ME ON OUR WAY HERE.
I'M A WIMP!
THAT'S WHY...

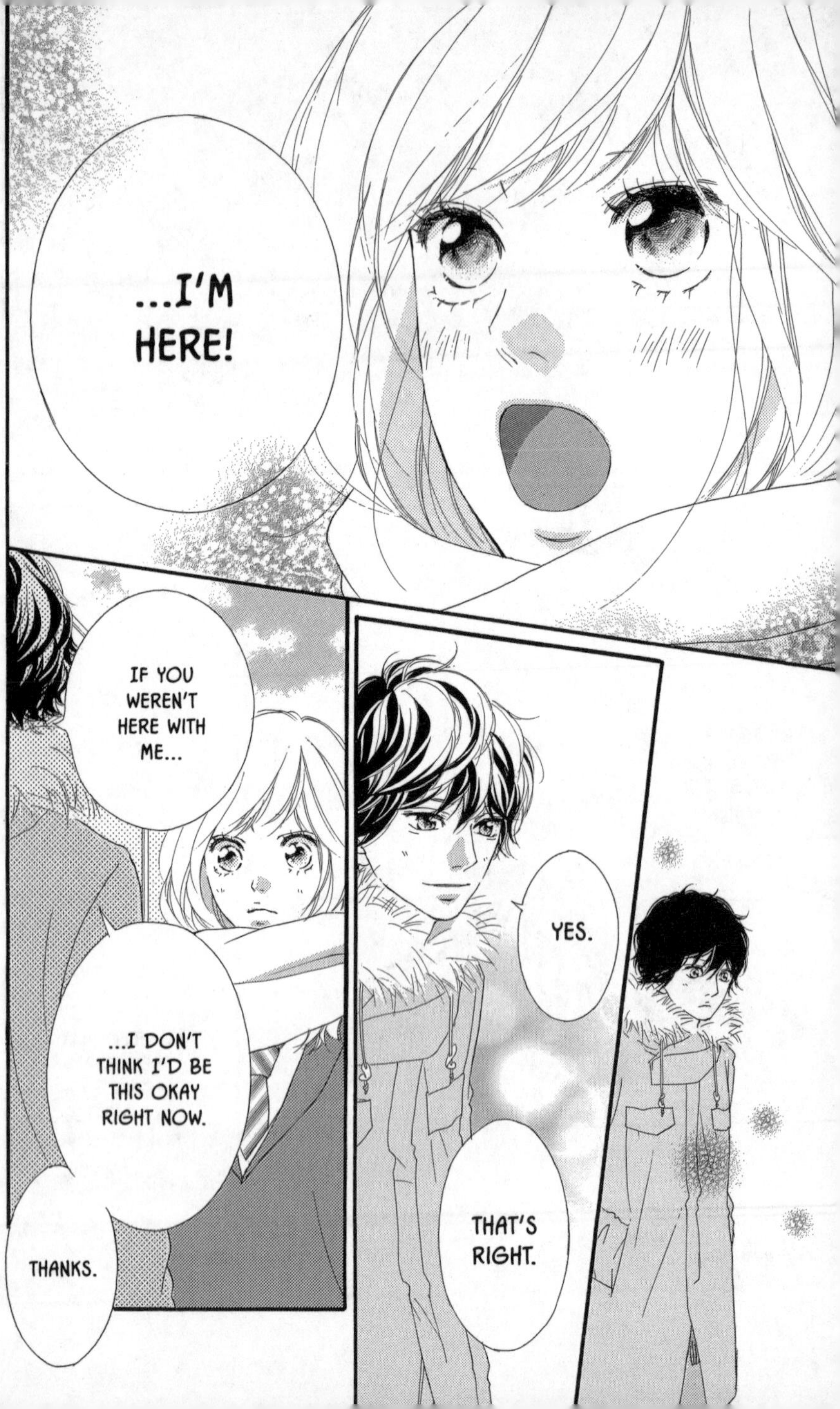
...I'M HERE!
YES.
THAT'S RIGHT.
IF YOU WEREN'T HERE WITH ME...
...I DON'T THINK I'D BE THIS OKAY RIGHT NOW.
THANKS.

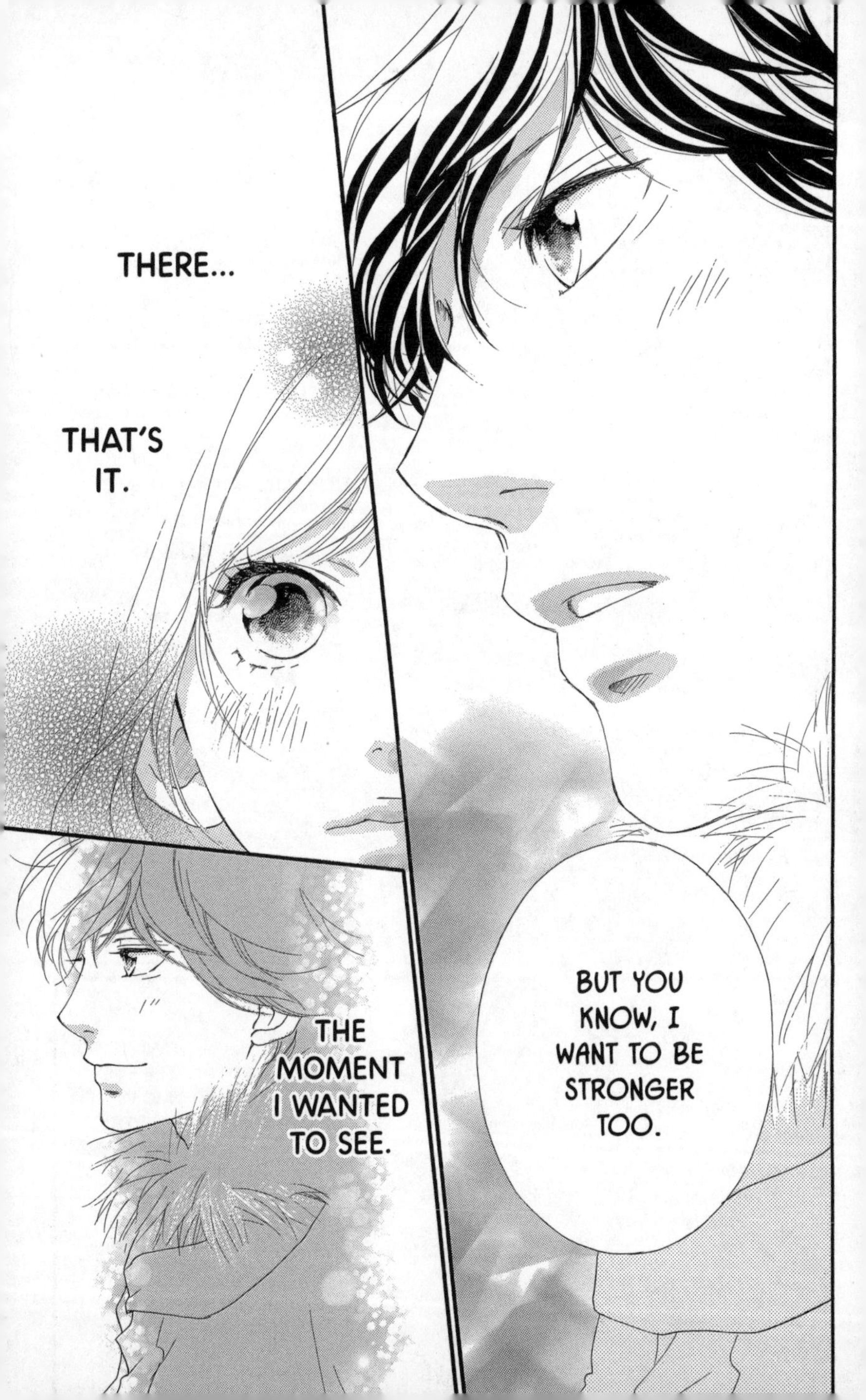
BUT YOU KNOW, I WANT TO BE STRONGER TOO.
THERE...
THAT'S IT.
THE MOMENT I WANTED TO SEE.

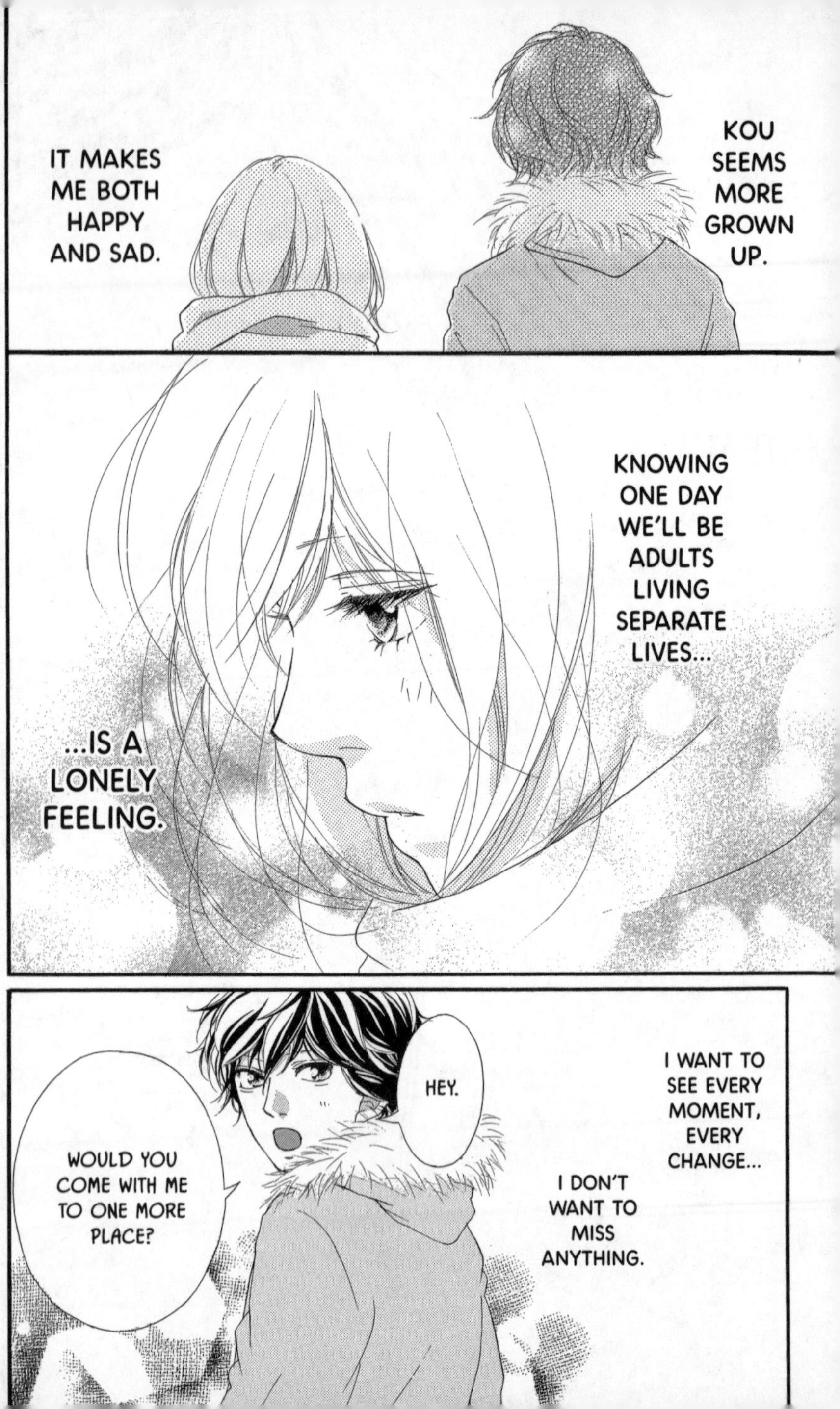
KOU SEEMS MORE GROWN UP.
IT MAKES ME BOTH HAPPY AND SAD.
KNOWING ONE DAY WE'LL BE ADULTS LIVING SEPARATE LIVES...
...IS A LONELY FEELING.
I WANT TO SEE EVERY MOMENT, EVERY CHANGE...
I DON'T WANT TO MISS ANYTHING.
HEY.
WOULD YOU COME WITH ME TO ONE MORE PLACE?

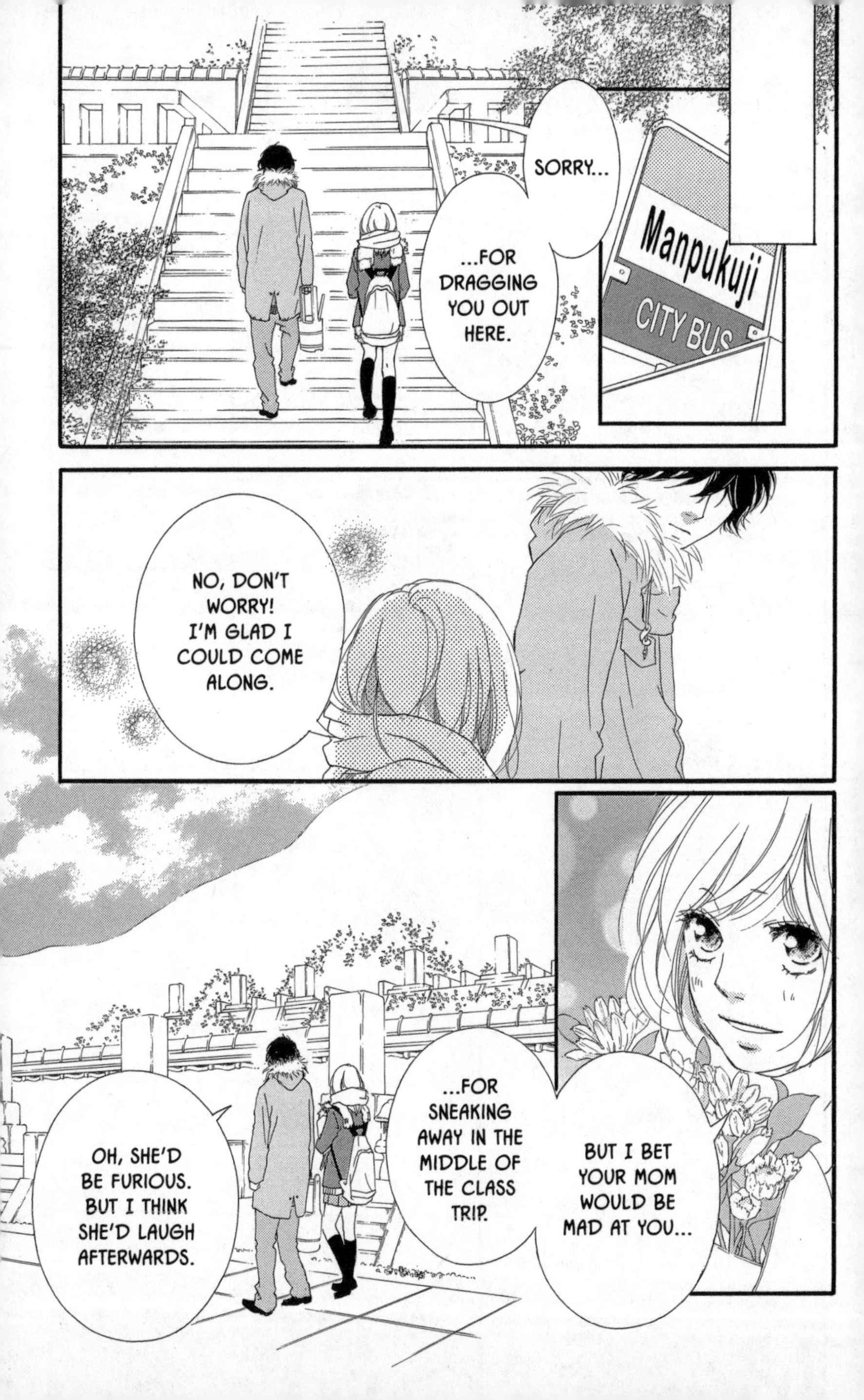
Manpukuji
CITY BUS
SORRY...
...FOR DRAGGING YOU OUT HERE.
NO, DON'T WORRY! I'M GLAD I COULD COME ALONG.
BUT I BET YOUR MOM WOULD BE MAD AT YOU...
...FOR SNEAKING AWAY IN THE MIDDLE OF THE CLASS TRIP.
OH, SHE'D BE FURIOUS. BUT I THINK SHE'D LAUGH AFTERWARDS.

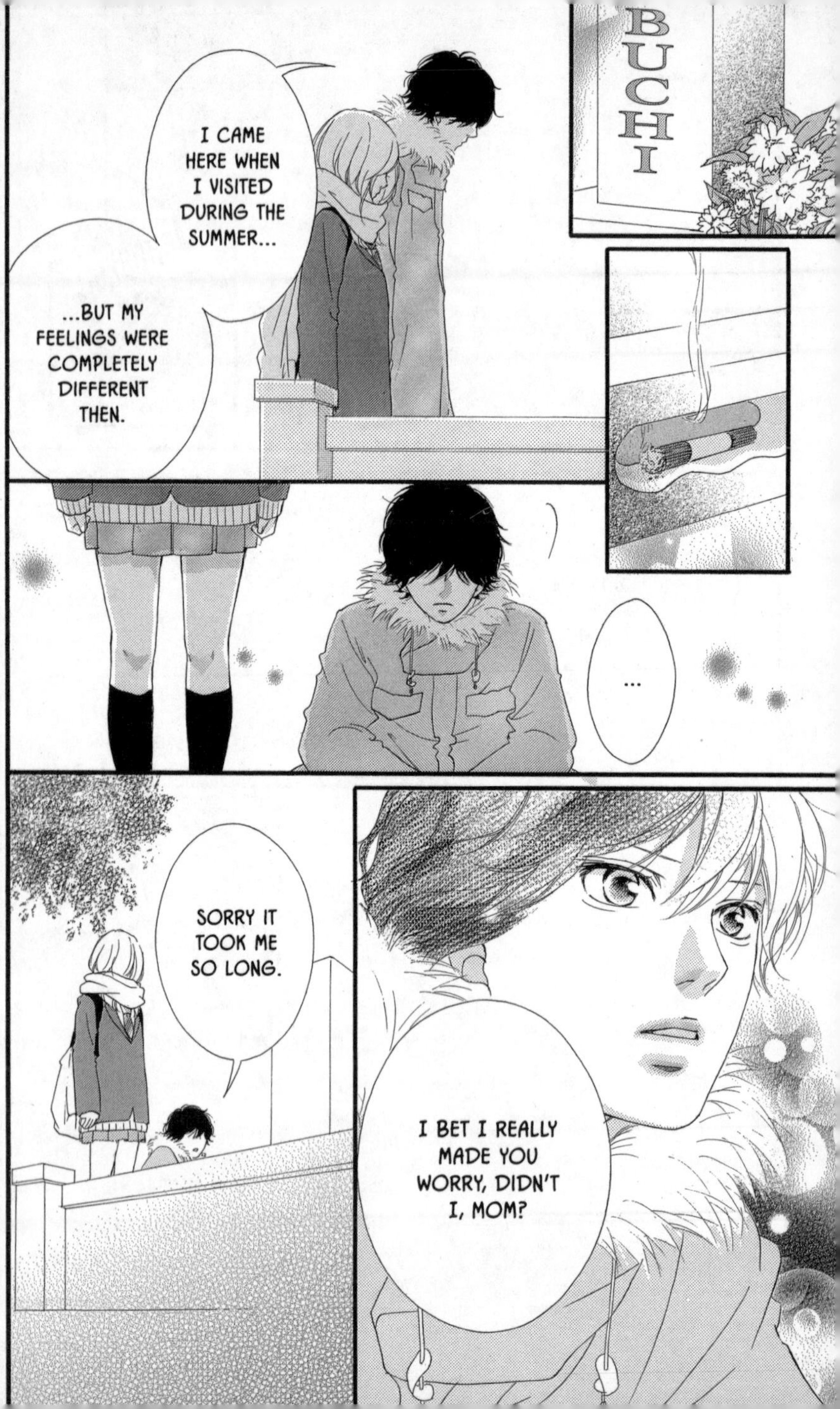
BUCHI
I CAME HERE WHEN I VISITED DURING THE SUMMER...
...BUT MY FEELINGS WERE COMPLETELY DIFFERENT THEN.
...
I BET I REALLY MADE YOU WORRY, DIDN'T I, MOM?
SORRY IT TOOK ME SO LONG.

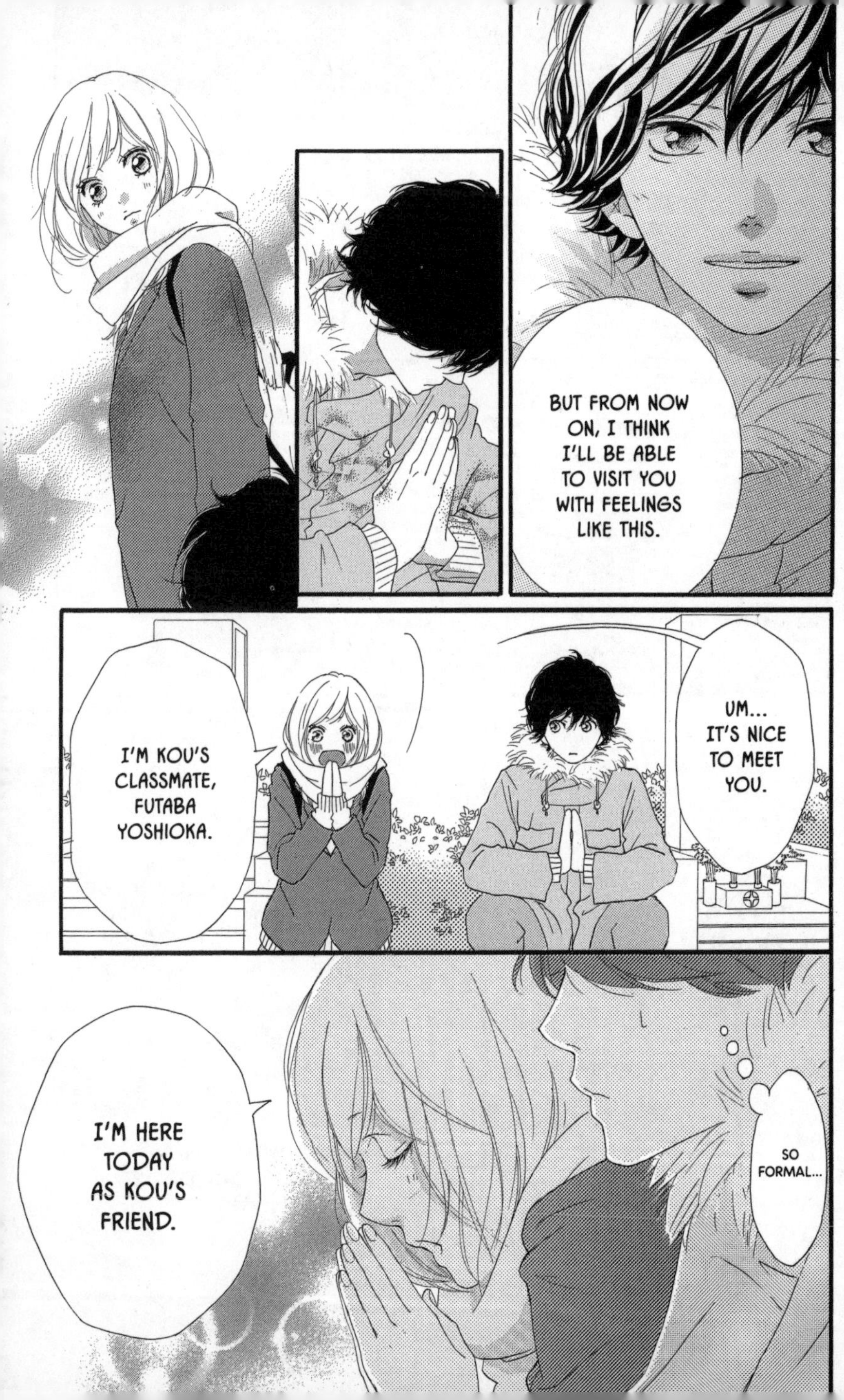
BUT FROM NOW ON, I THINK I'LL BE ABLE TO VISIT YOU WITH FEELINGS LIKE THIS.
UM... IT'S NICE TO MEET YOU.
I'M KOU'S CLASSMATE, FUTABA YOSHIOKA.
SO FORMAL...
I'M HERE TODAY AS KOU'S FRIEND.

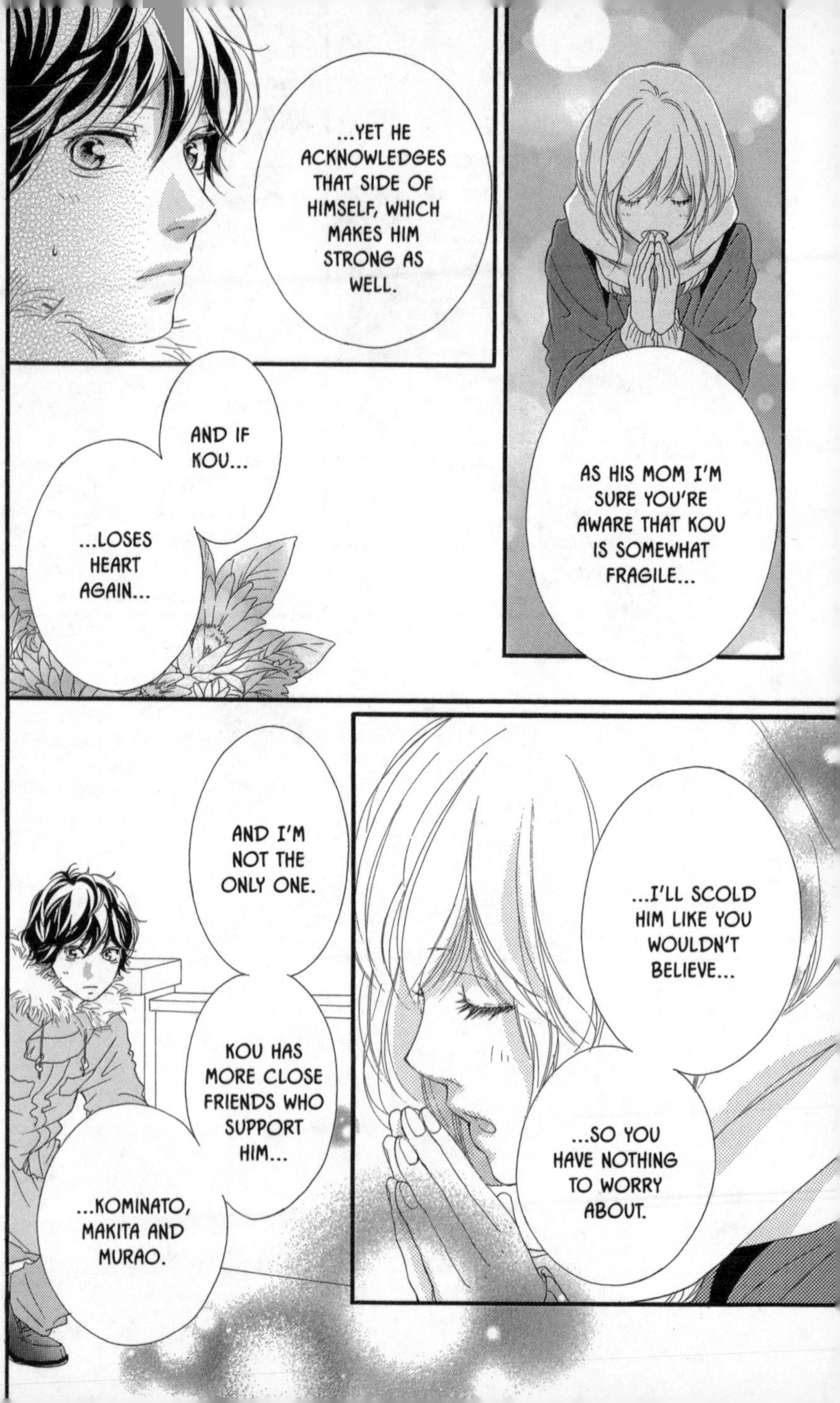
AS HIS MOM I'M SURE YOU'RE AWARE THAT KOU IS SOMEWHAT FRAGILE...
...YET HE ACKNOWLEDGES THAT SIDE OF HIMSELF, WHICH MAKES HIM STRONG AS WELL.
AND IF KOU...
...LOSES HEART AGAIN...
...I'LL SCOLD HIM LIKE YOU WOULDN'T BELIEVE...
...SO YOU HAVE NOTHING TO WORRY ABOUT.
AND I'M NOT THE ONLY ONE.
KOU HAS MORE CLOSE FRIENDS WHO SUPPORT HIM...
...KOMINATO, MAKITA AND MURAO.

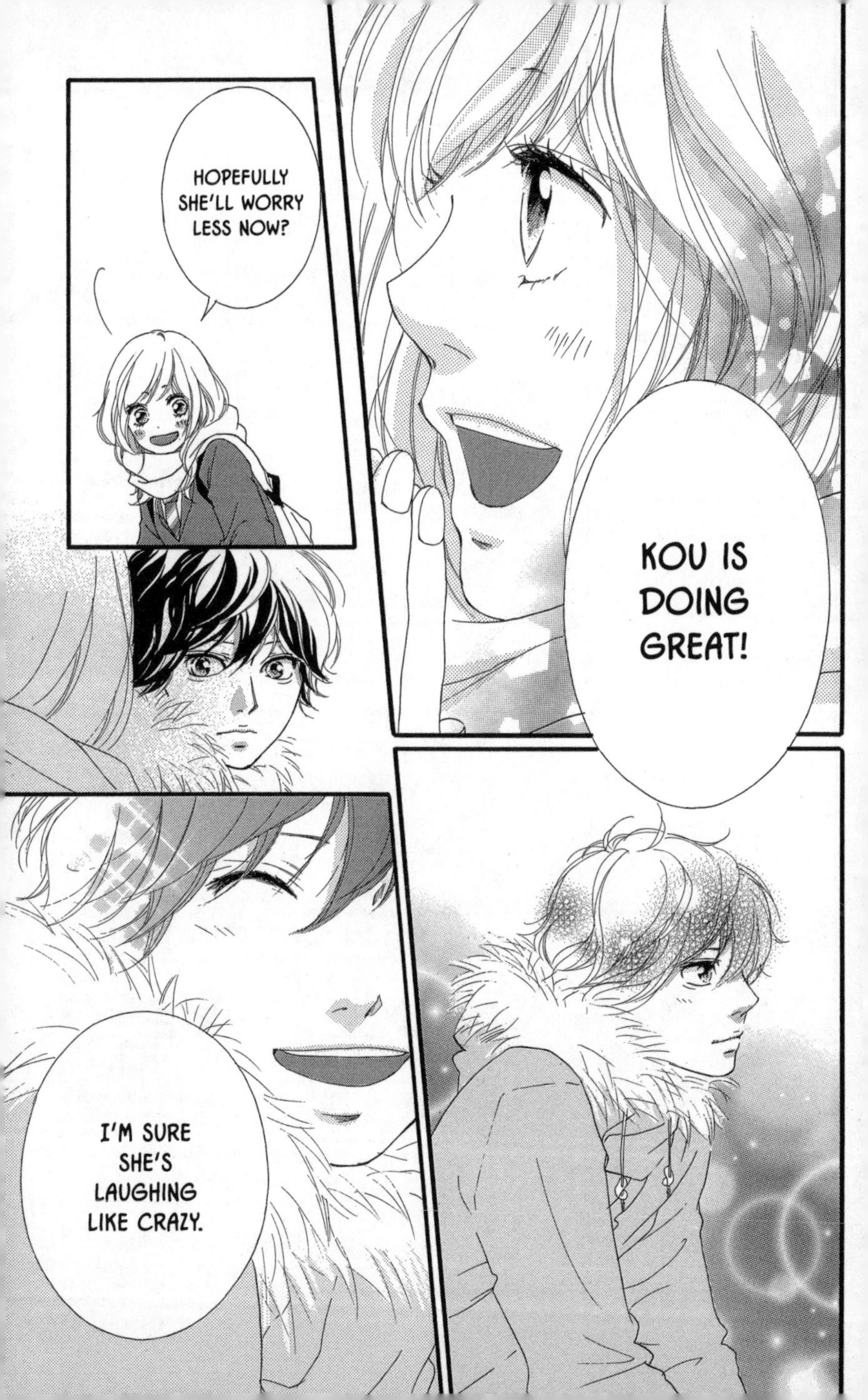
KOU IS DOING GREAT!
HOPEFULLY SHE'LL WORRY LESS NOW?
I'M SURE SHE'S LAUGHING LIKE CRAZY.

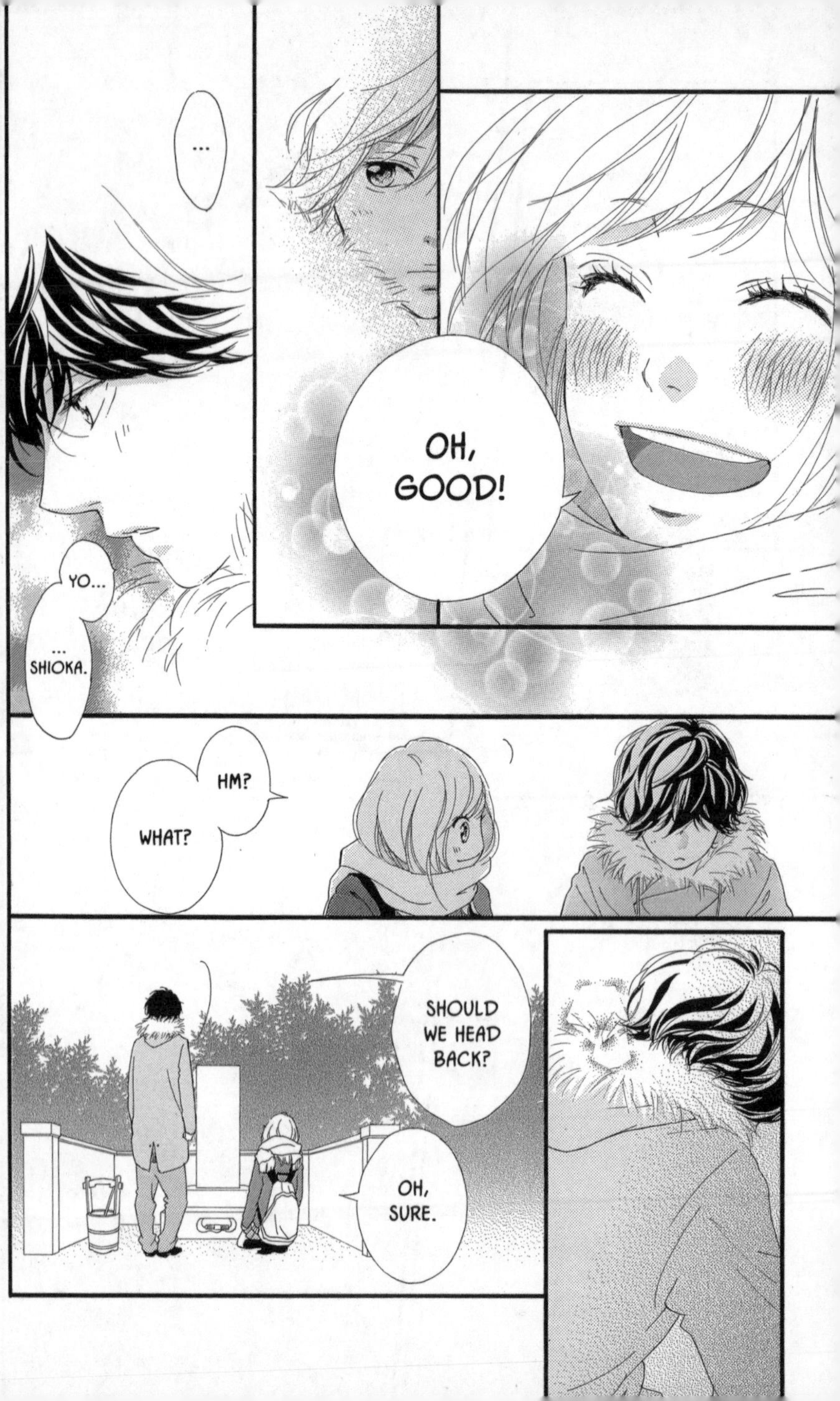
OH, GOOD!
...
YO...
...SHIOKA.
HM? WHAT?
SHOULD WE HEAD BACK?
OH, SURE.

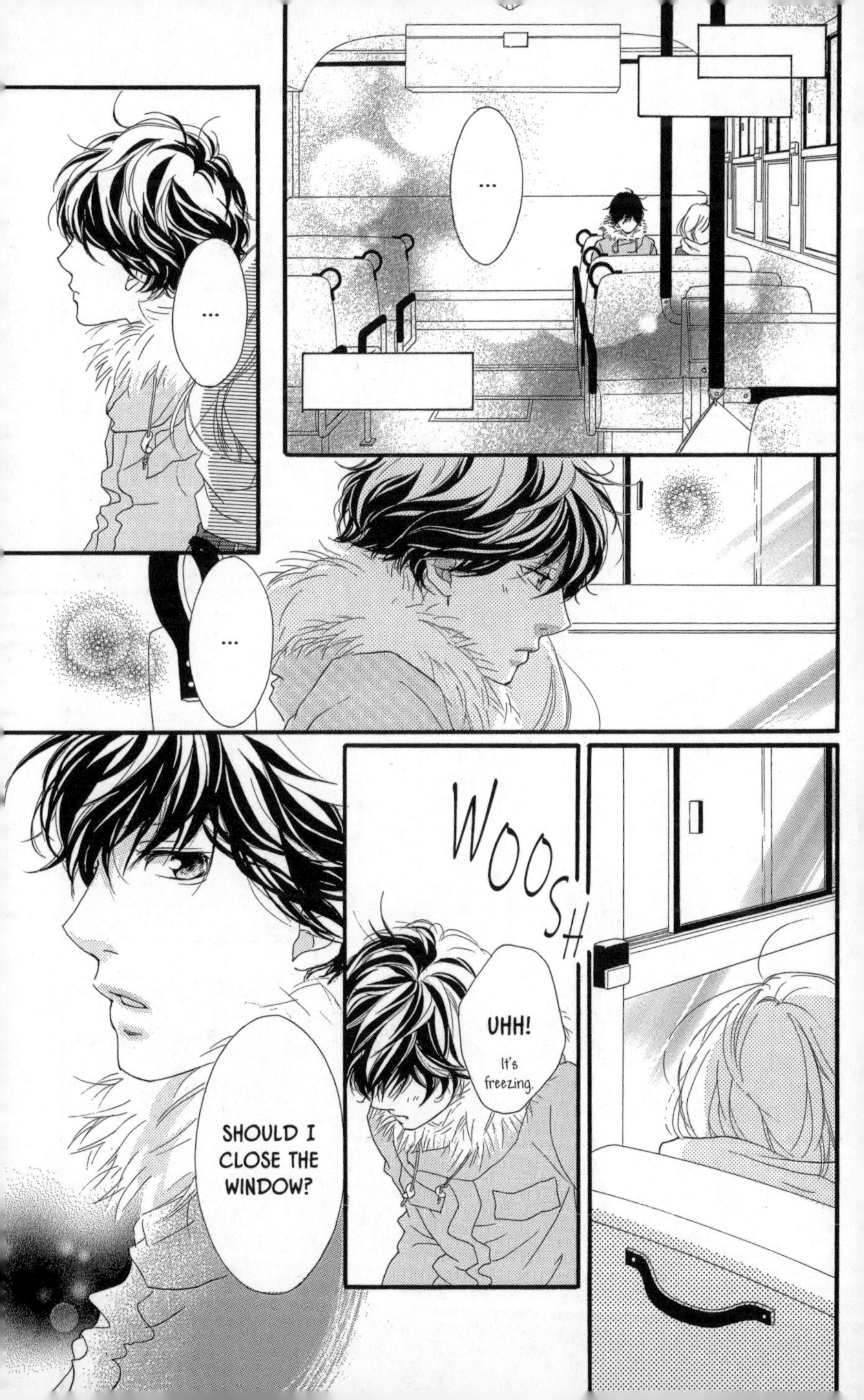
...
...
...
WOOSH
UHH!
It's freezing.
SHOULD I CLOSE THE WINDOW?

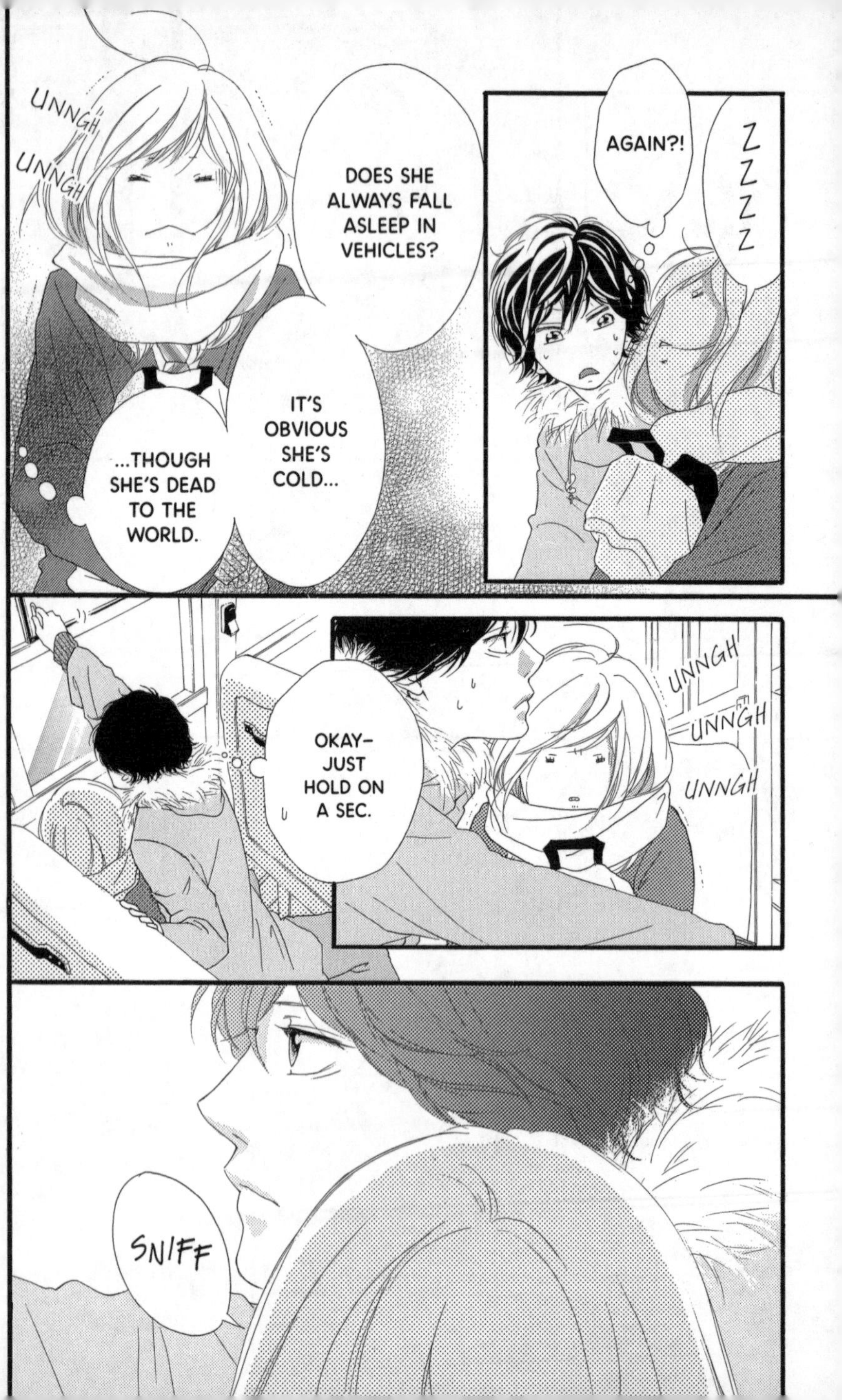
Z Z Z Z
AGAIN?!
UNNGH
UNNGH
DOES SHE ALWAYS FALL ASLEEP IN VEHICLES?
IT'S OBVIOUS SHE'S COLD...
...THOUGH SHE'S DEAD TO THE WORLD.
UNNGH
UNNGH
UNNGH
OKAY–JUST HOLD ON A SEC.
SNIFF

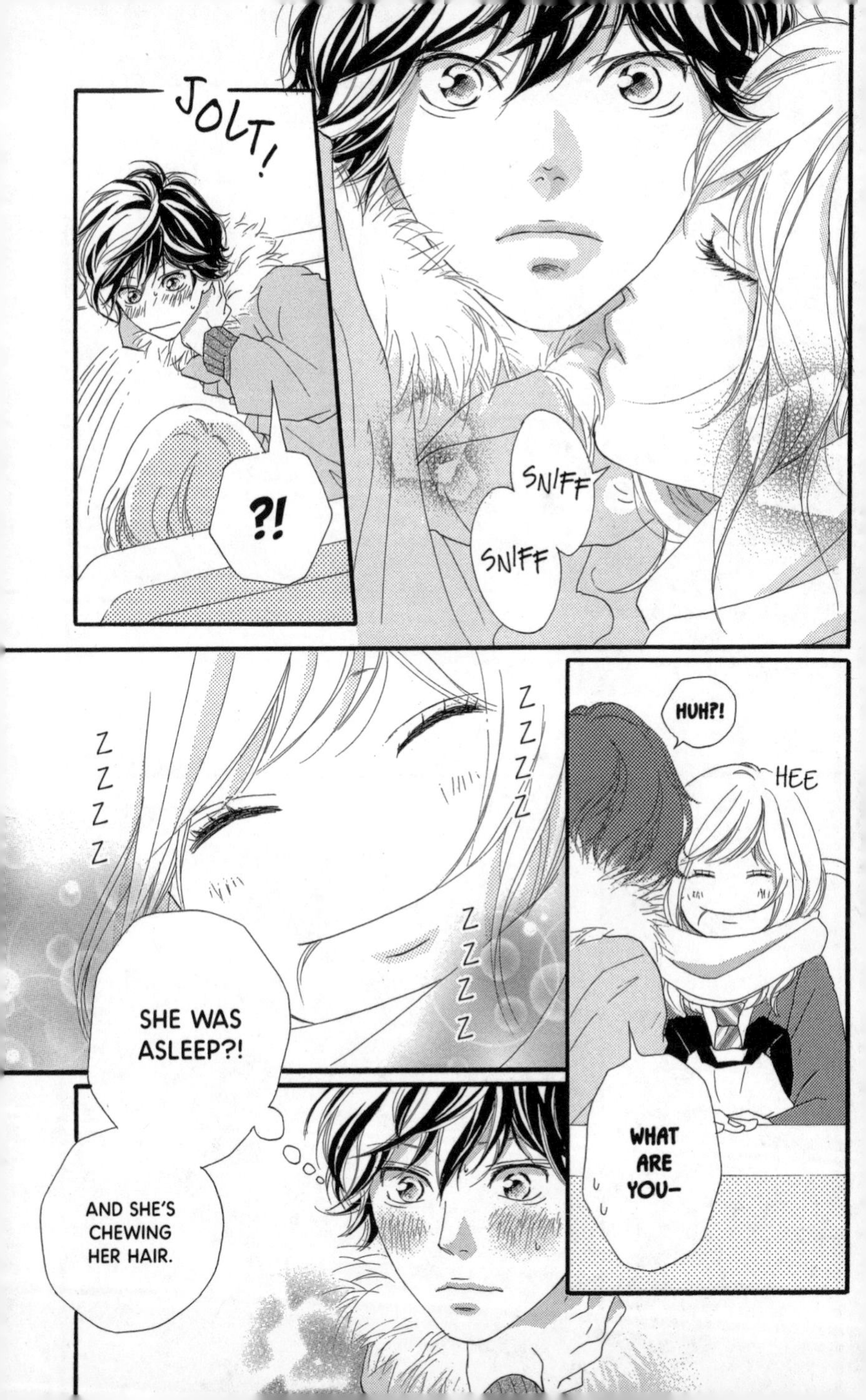
SNIFF
SNIFF
JOLT!
?!
HUH?!
HEE
WHAT ARE YOU—
ZZZZ
ZZZZ
ZZZZ
SHE WAS ASLEEP?!
AND SHE'S CHEWING HER HAIR.

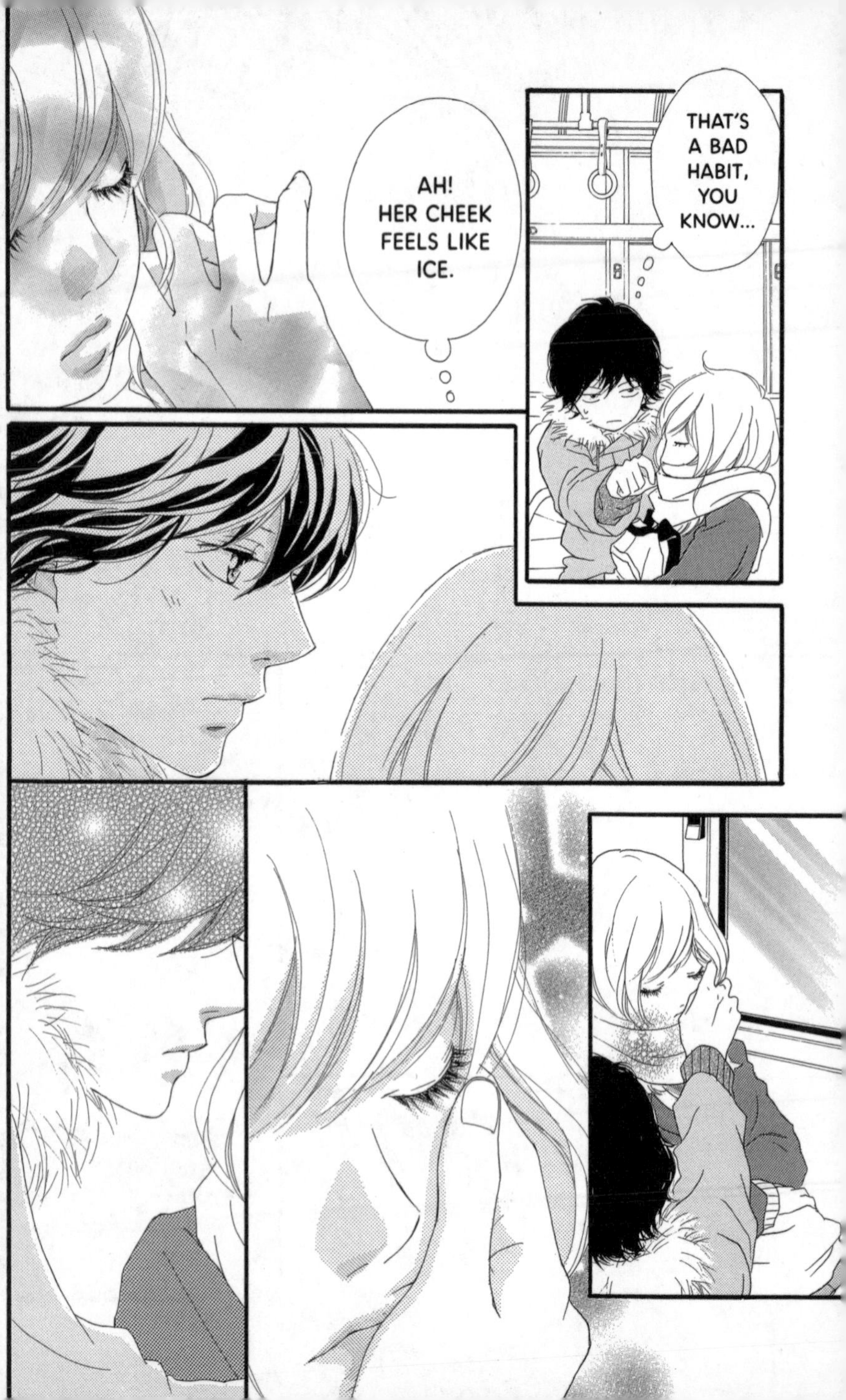
THAT'S A BAD HABIT, YOU KNOW...
AH! HER CHEEK FEELS LIKE ICE.

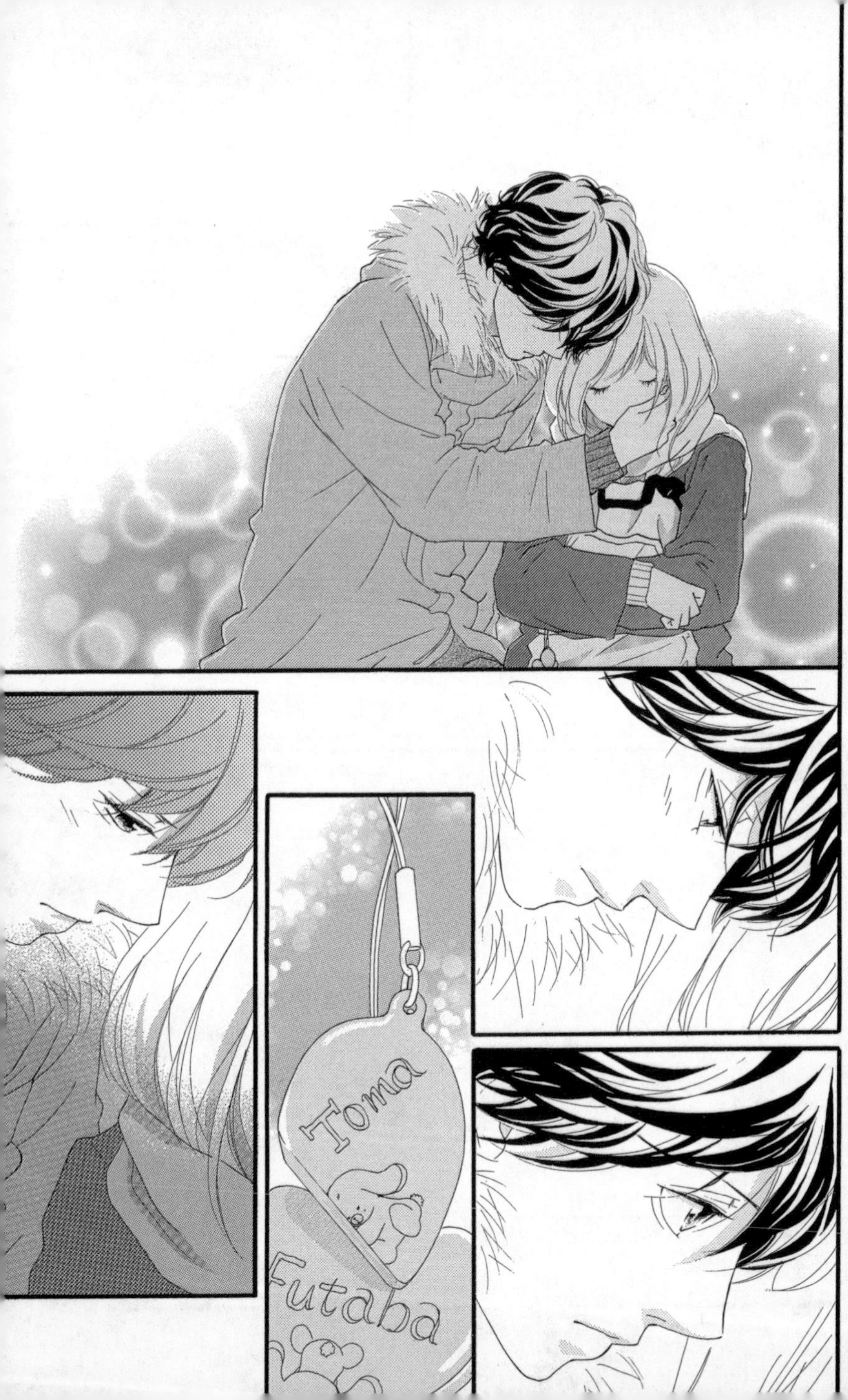
Toma
Futaba

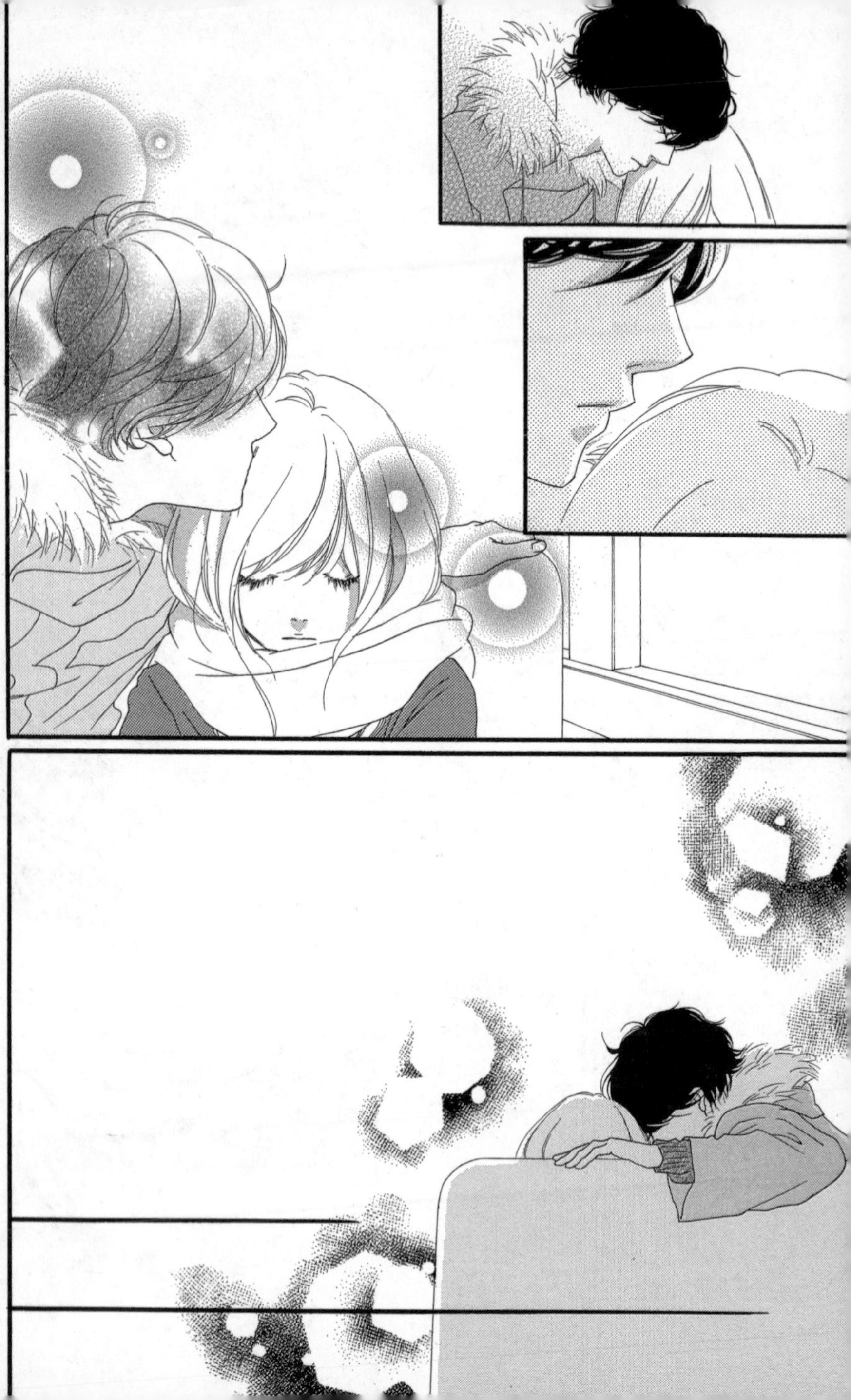

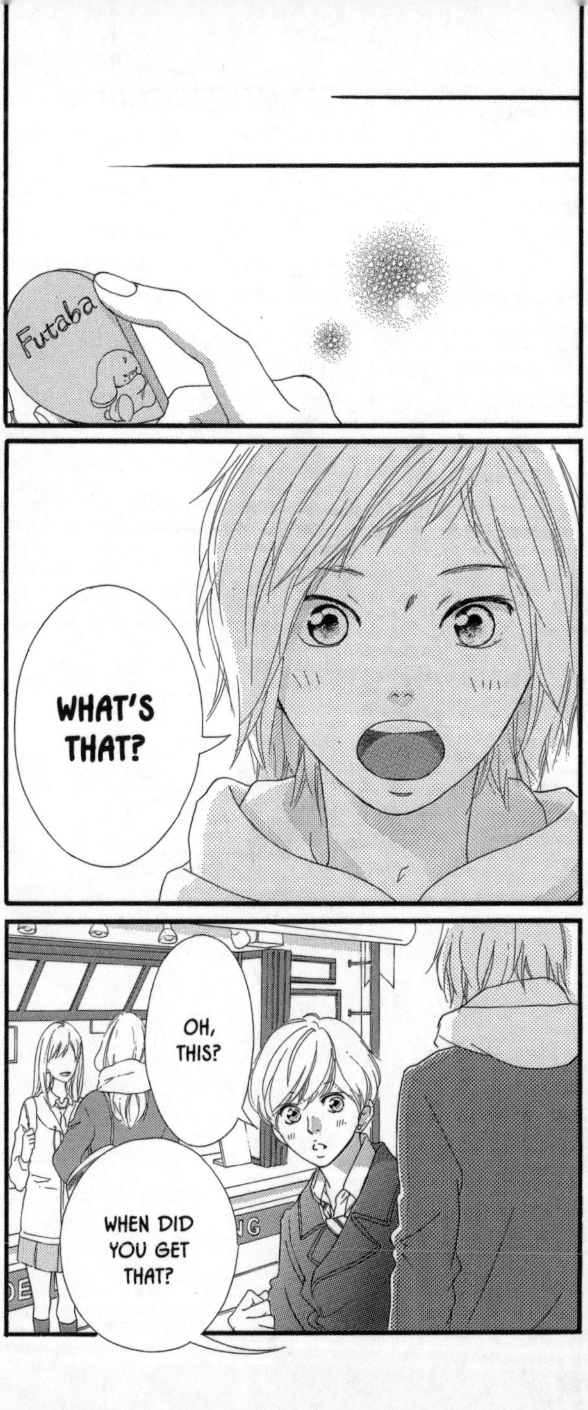
Futaba
WHAT'S THAT?
OH, THIS?
WHEN DID YOU GET THAT?

Mr. Toshiya Momozono appeared in volume 3 and volume 7—you may remember him as "Peach." (I made up his given name just now.) I knew another teacher who was called "Peach," but his real name and his appearance were completely different. I had so little interest in that teacher that I don't even know where his nickname came from. If you were to ask me if I'm worried he'll find out I created a character using his nickname, I'd tell you I'm not. When Mr. Momozono gets mad, his eyes turn into isosceles triangles.

Since there's some space left, here's a mini bio for him:

- Toshiya Momozono
- Birthday: 3/9
- Blood type: AB
- Height/weight: 5'6"/196 lb.
- Subject: History
- Favorite food: Crab cream croquettes
- Least favorite food: Pears
- Favorite music: THE OFFSPRING

I'm out of space, so I'll stop here.

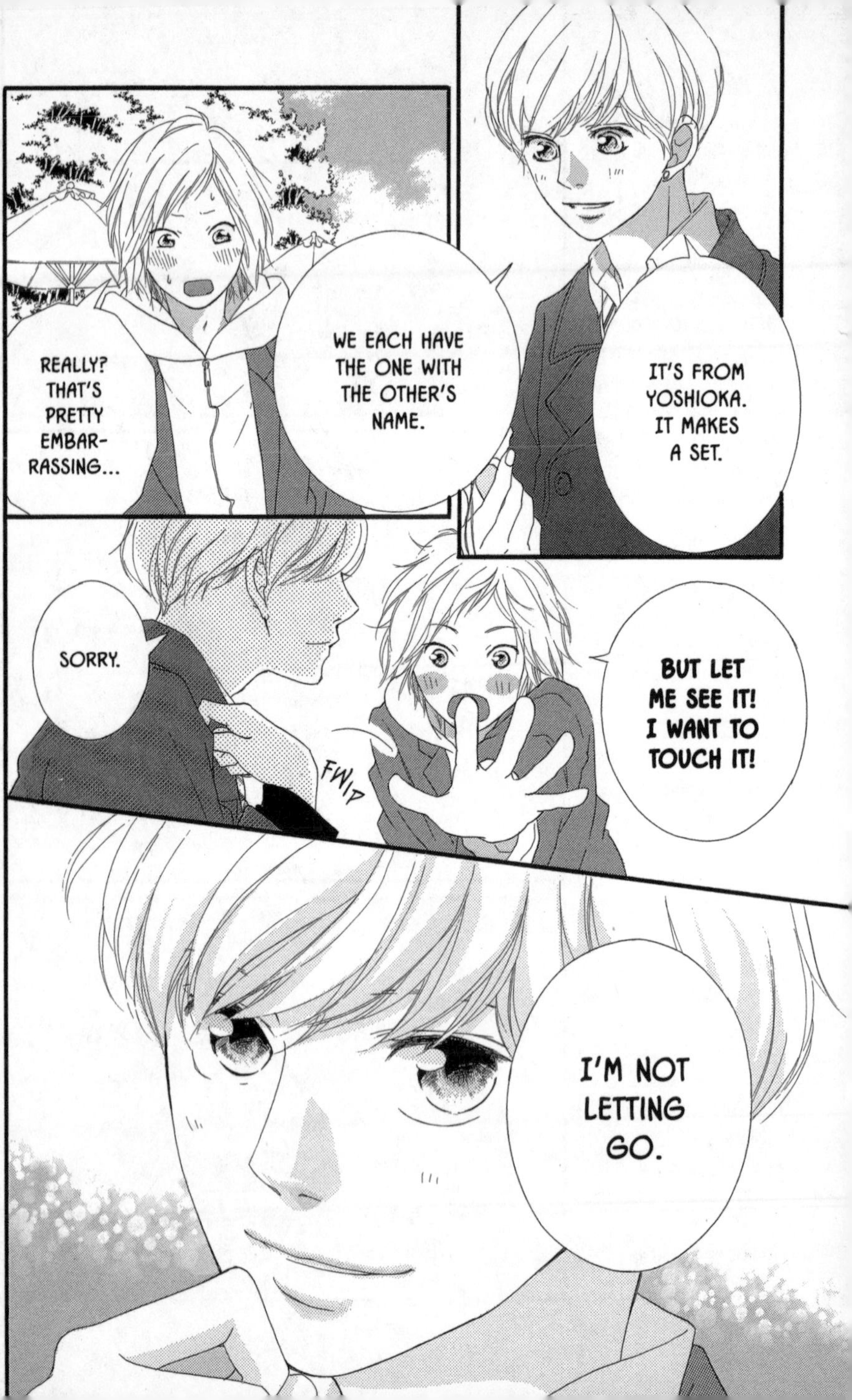
IT'S FROM YOSHIOKA. IT MAKES A SET.
WE EACH HAVE THE ONE WITH THE OTHER'S NAME.
REALLY? THAT'S PRETTY EMBAR-RASSING...
BUT LET ME SEE IT! I WANT TO TOUCH IT!
FWIP
SORRY.
I'M NOT LETTING GO.

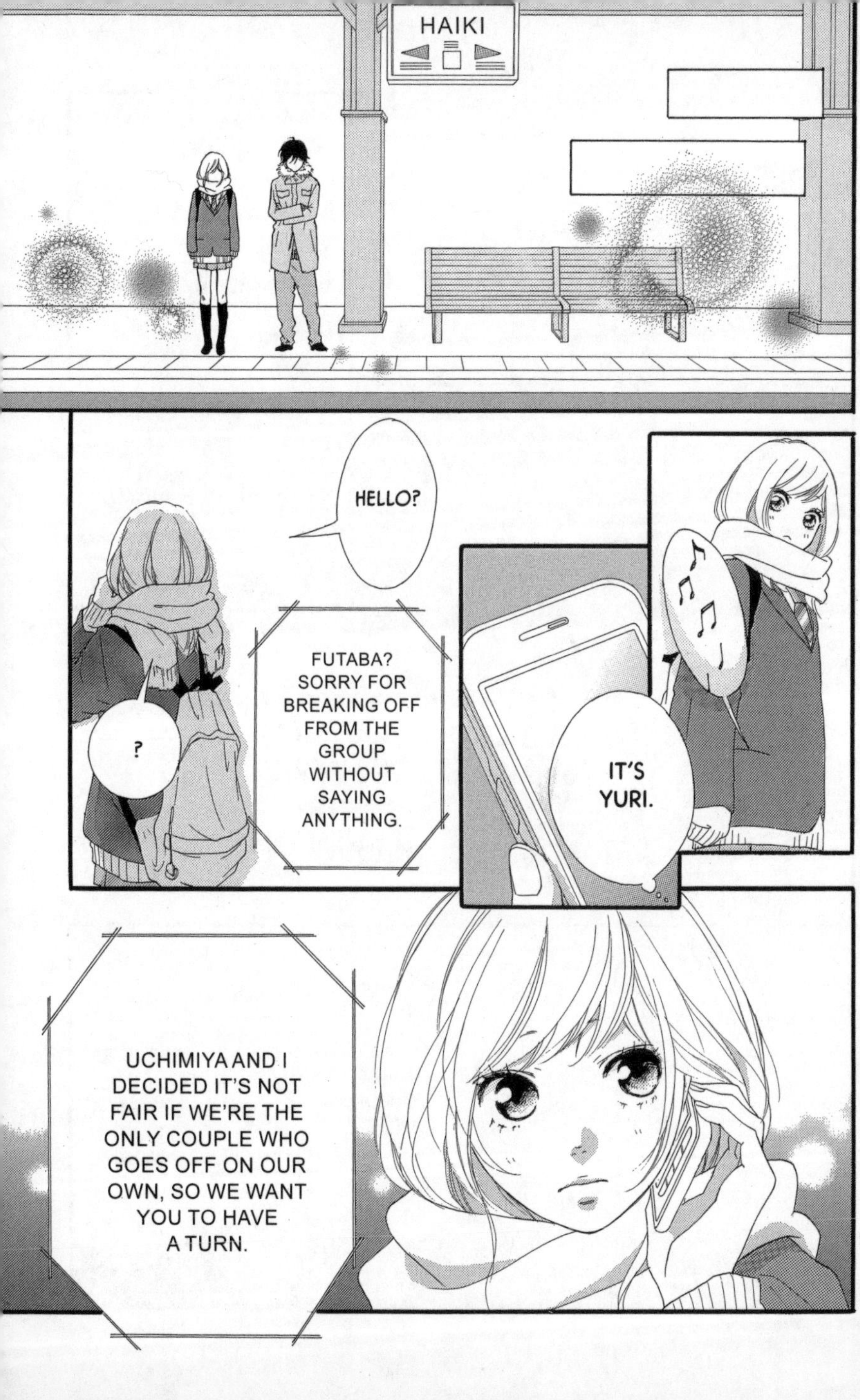
HAIKI
♪ ♪ ♪
IT'S YURI.
HELLO?
FUTABA? SORRY FOR BREAKING OFF FROM THE GROUP WITHOUT SAYING ANYTHING.
?
UCHIMIYA AND I DECIDED IT'S NOT FAIR IF WE'RE THE ONLY COUPLE WHO GOES OFF ON OUR OWN, SO WE WANT YOU TO HAVE A TURN.

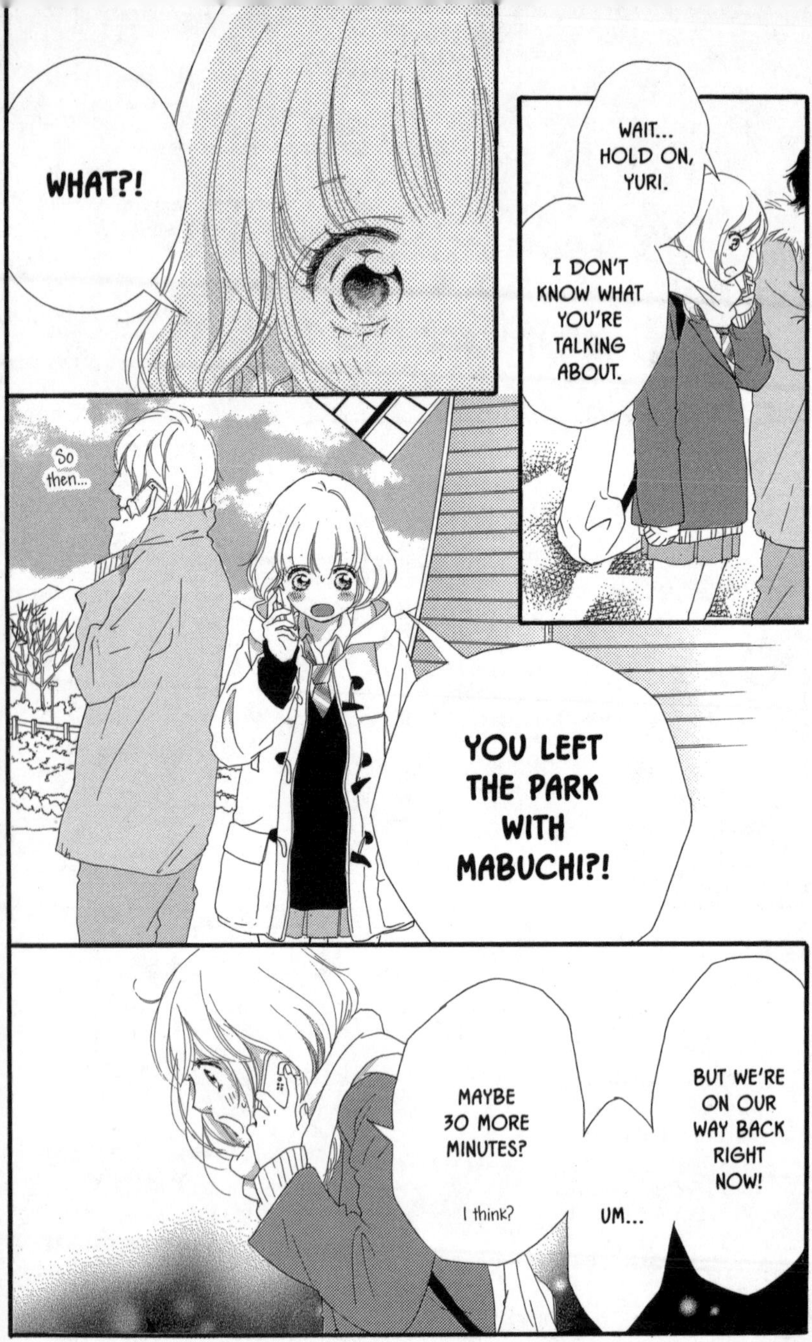
WAIT... HOLD ON, YURI.
I DON'T KNOW WHAT YOU'RE TALKING ABOUT.
WHAT?!
So then...
YOU LEFT THE PARK WITH MABUCHI?!
BUT WE'RE ON OUR WAY BACK RIGHT NOW!
UM...
MAYBE 30 MORE MINUTES?
I think?

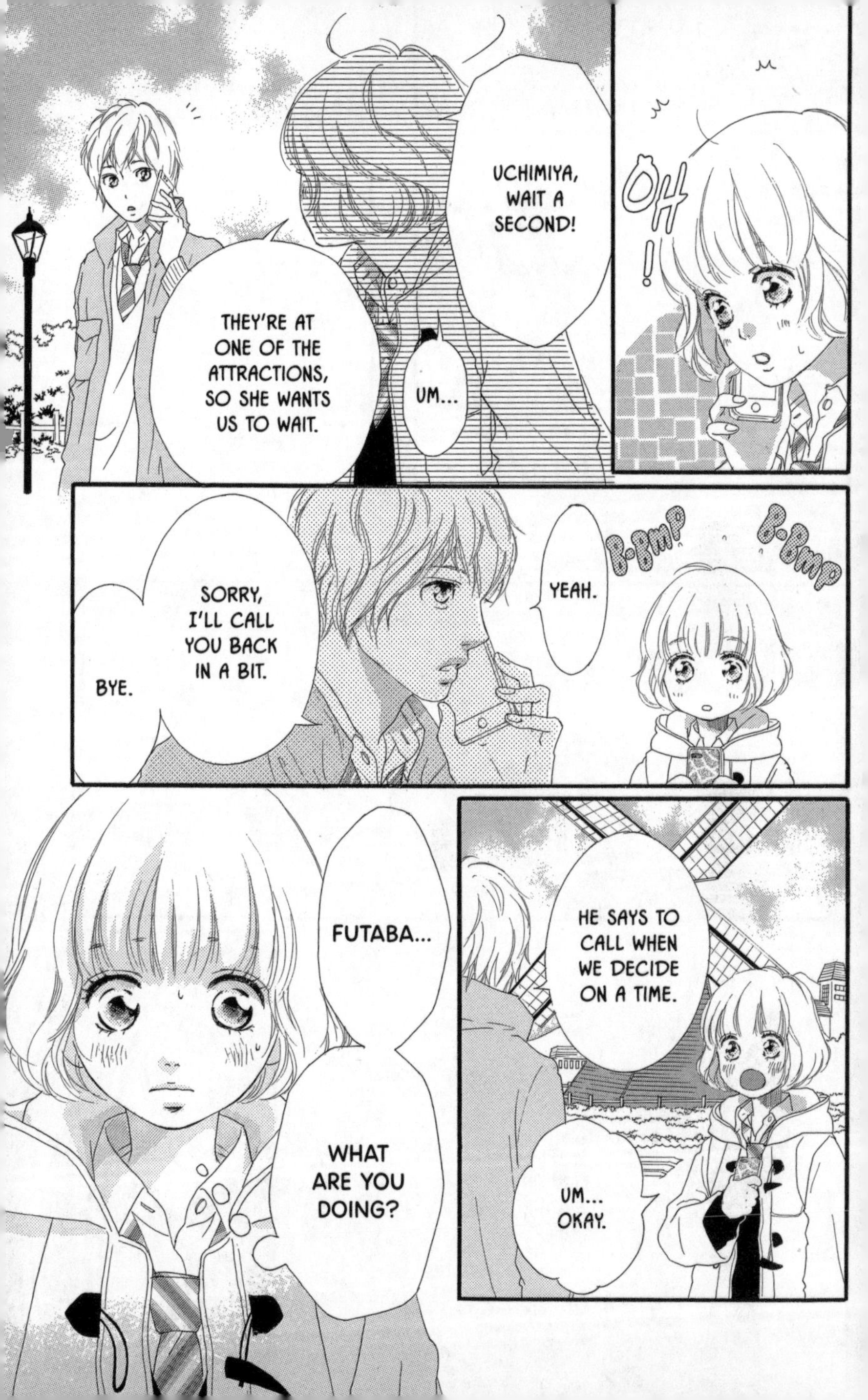
OH!
UCHIMIYA, WAIT A SECOND!
UM...
THEY'RE AT ONE OF THE ATTRACTIONS, SO SHE WANTS US TO WAIT.
B-BMP
B-BMP
YEAH.
SORRY, I'LL CALL YOU BACK IN A BIT.
BYE.
HE SAYS TO CALL WHEN WE DECIDE ON A TIME.
UM... OKAY.
FUTABA...
WHAT ARE YOU DOING?

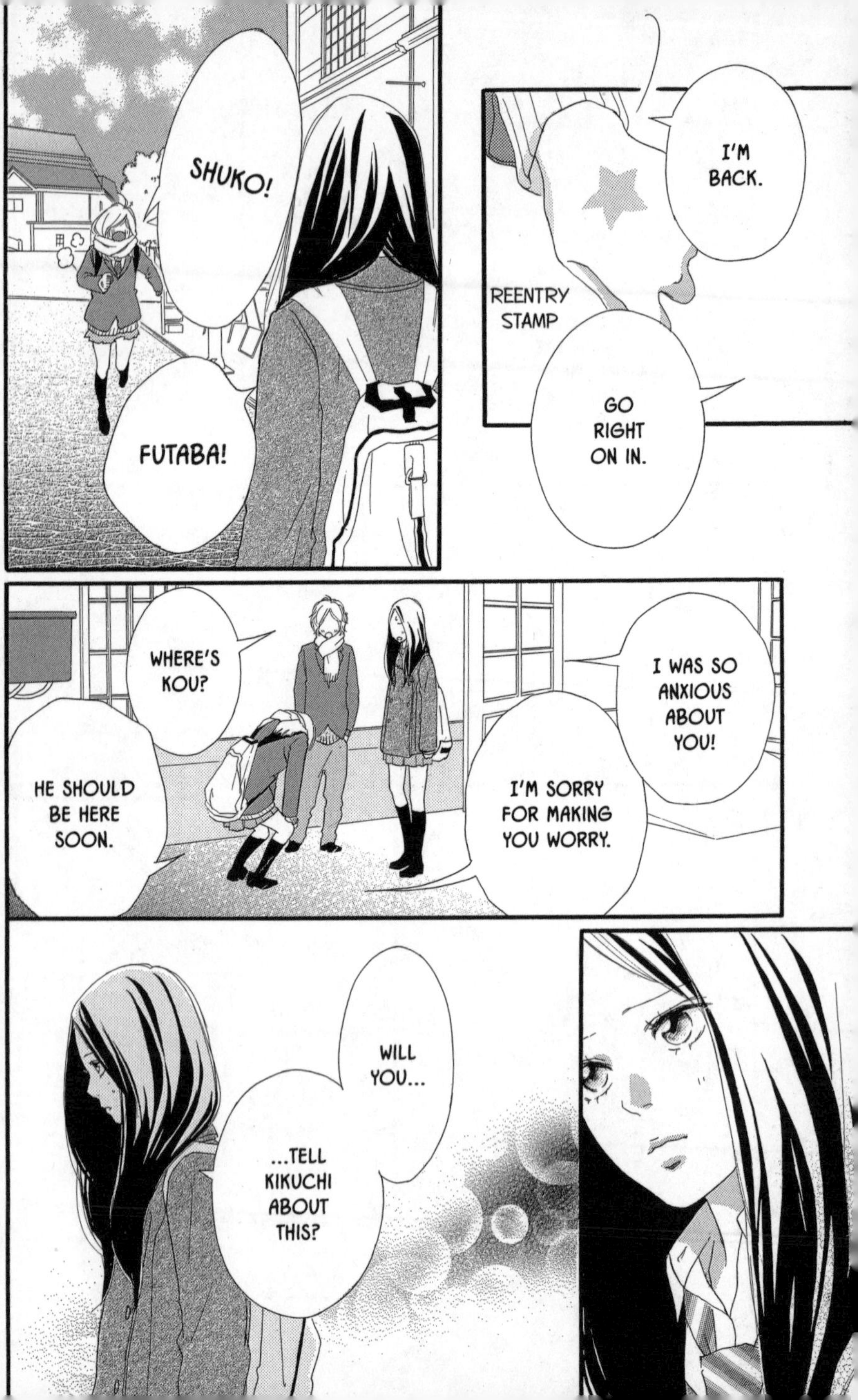
I'M BACK.
REENTRY STAMP
GO RIGHT ON IN.
SHUKO!
FUTABA!
I WAS SO ANXIOUS ABOUT YOU!
I'M SORRY FOR MAKING YOU WORRY.
WHERE'S KOU?
HE SHOULD BE HERE SOON.
WILL YOU...
...TELL KIKUCHI ABOUT THIS?

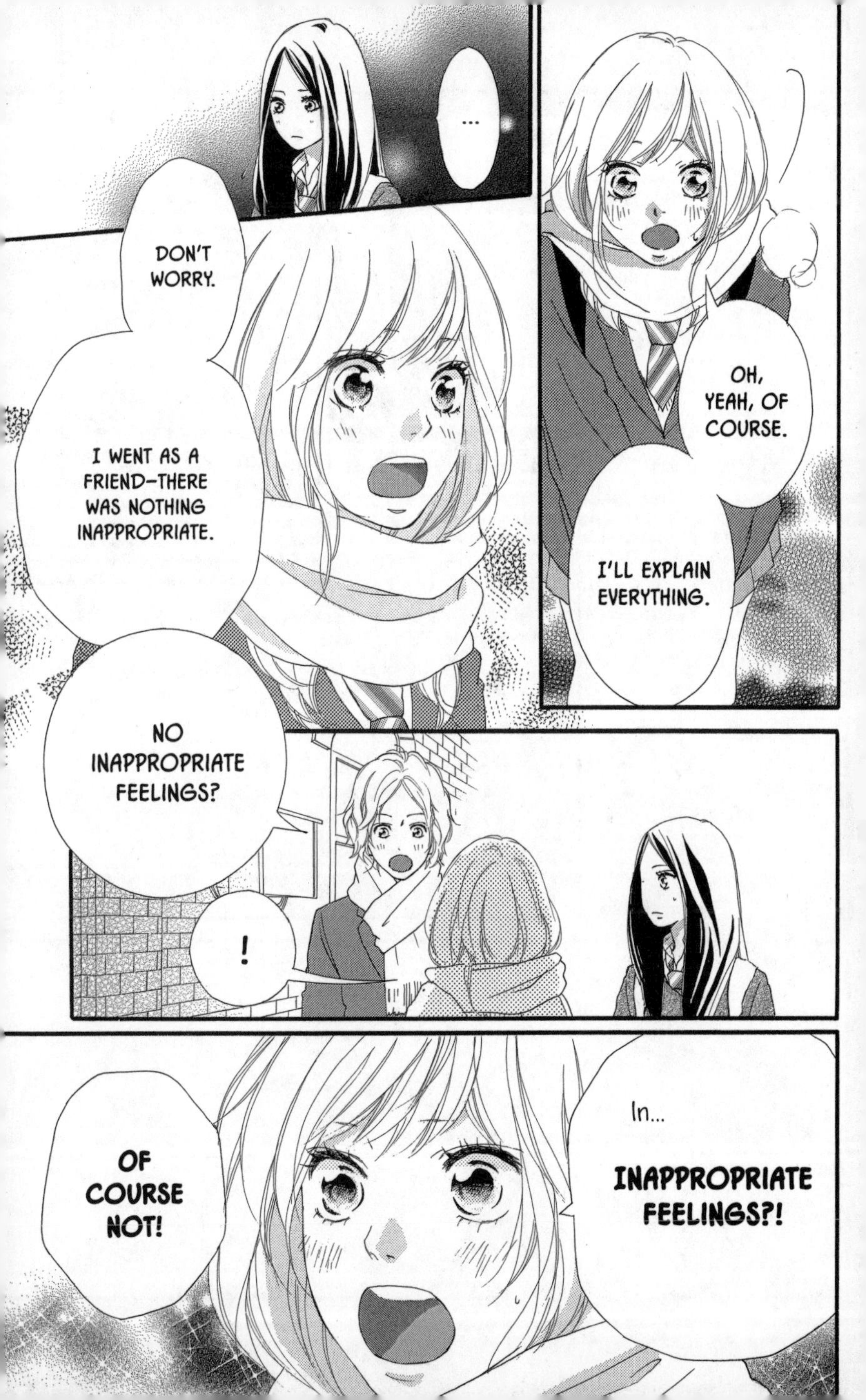
OH, YEAH, OF COURSE.
I'LL EXPLAIN EVERYTHING.
...
DON'T WORRY.
I WENT AS A FRIEND—THERE WAS NOTHING INAPPROPRIATE.
NO INAPPROPRIATE FEELINGS?
!
In...
INAPPROPRIATE FEELINGS?!
OF COURSE NOT!

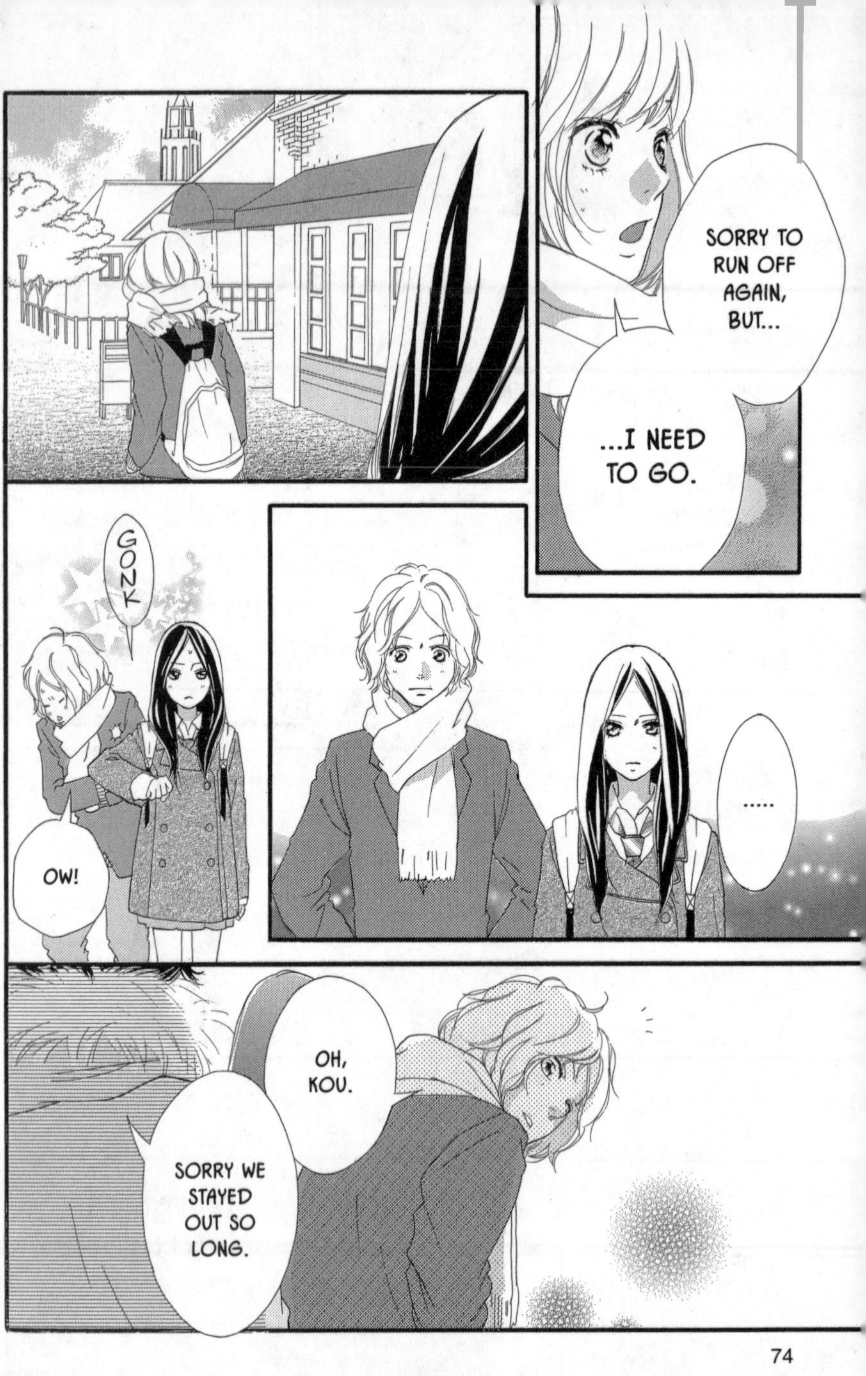
SORRY TO RUN OFF AGAIN, BUT...
...I NEED TO GO.
.....
GONK
OW!
OH, KOU.
SORRY WE STAYED OUT SO LONG.

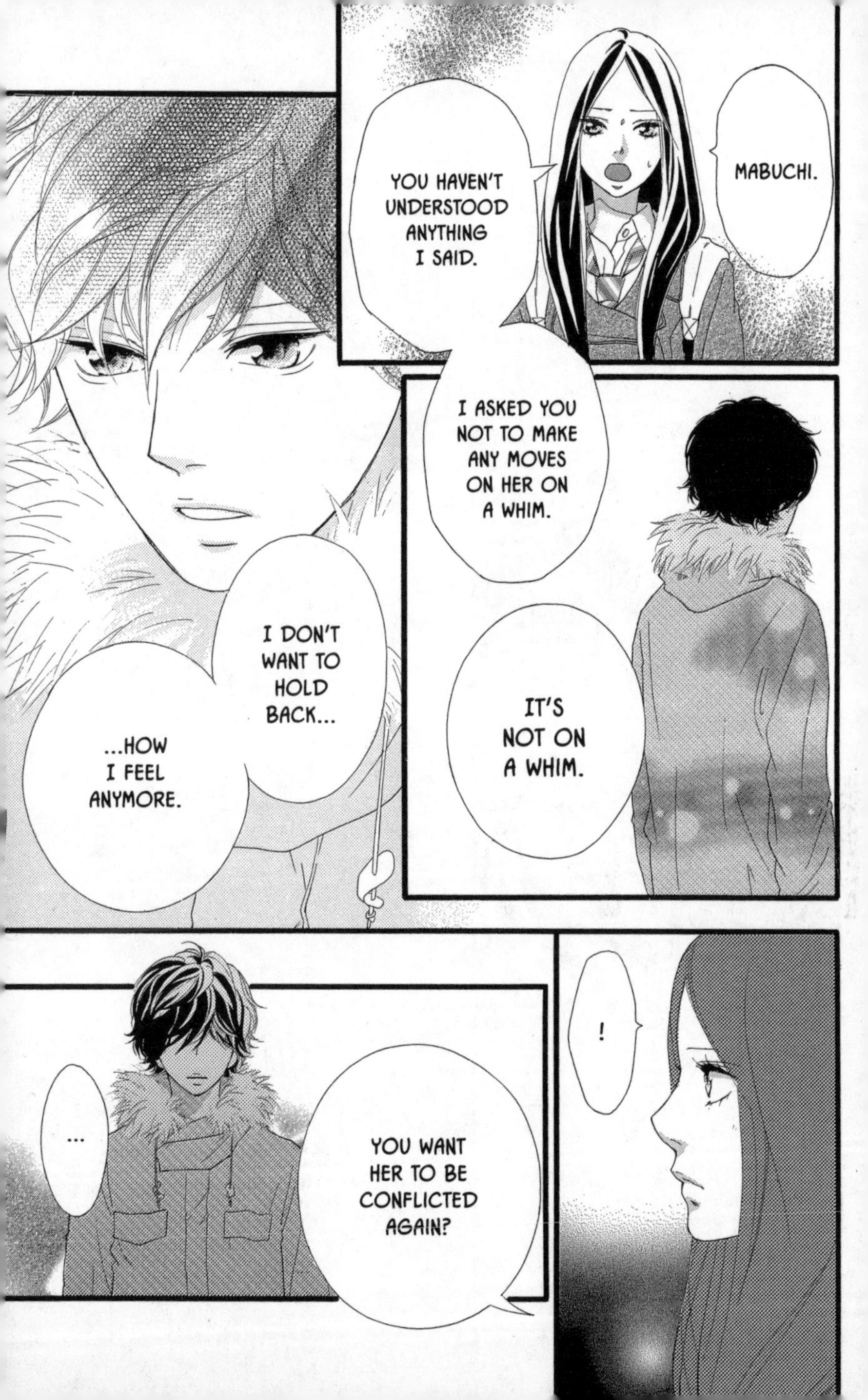
MABUCHI.
YOU HAVEN'T UNDERSTOOD ANYTHING I SAID.
I ASKED YOU NOT TO MAKE ANY MOVES ON HER ON A WHIM.
IT'S NOT ON A WHIM.
I DON'T WANT TO HOLD BACK...
...HOW I FEEL ANYMORE.
!
YOU WANT HER TO BE CONFLICTED AGAIN?
...

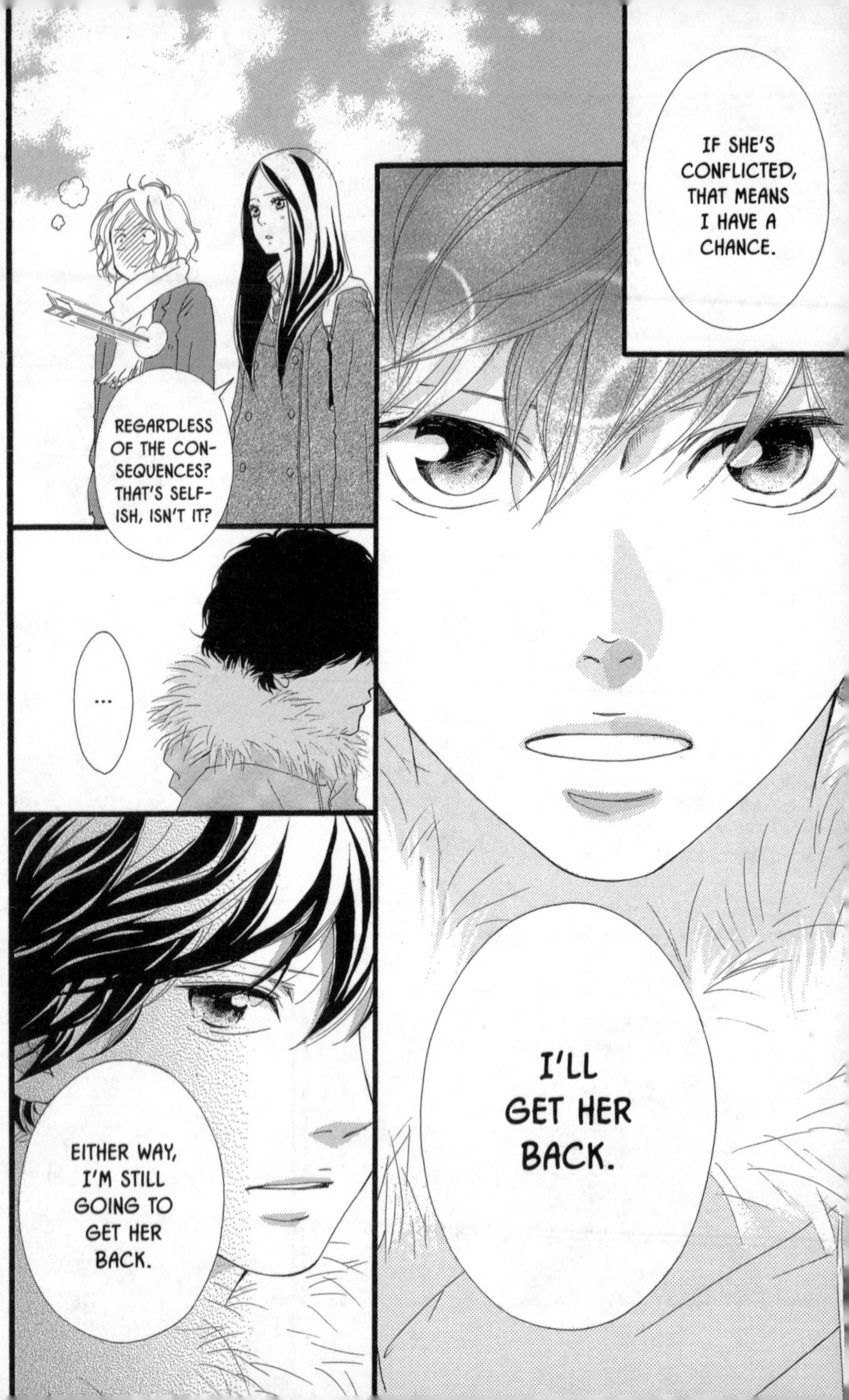
IF SHE'S CONFLICTED, THAT MEANS I HAVE A CHANCE.
REGARDLESS OF THE CON-SEQUENCES? THAT'S SELF-ISH, ISN'T IT?
...
EITHER WAY, I'M STILL GOING TO GET HER BACK.
I'LL GET HER BACK.

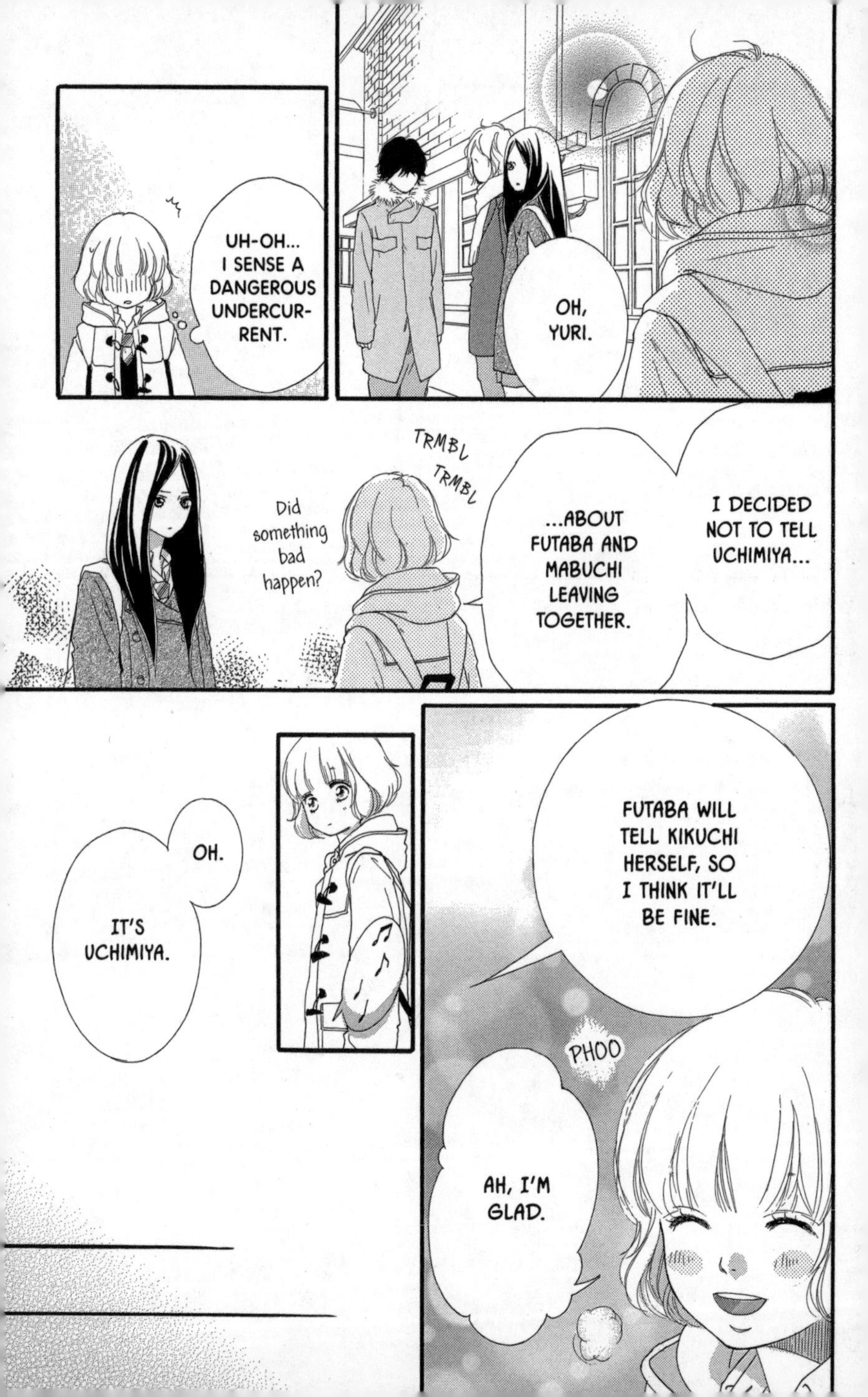
OH, YURI.
UH-OH... I SENSE A DANGEROUS UNDERCUR- RENT.
I DECIDED NOT TO TELL UCHIMIYA...
...ABOUT FUTABA AND MABUCHI LEAVING TOGETHER.
TRMBL TRMBL
Did something bad happen?
FUTABA WILL TELL KIKUCHI HERSELF, SO I THINK IT'LL BE FINE.
PHOO
AH, I'M GLAD.
OH.
IT'S UCHIMIYA.

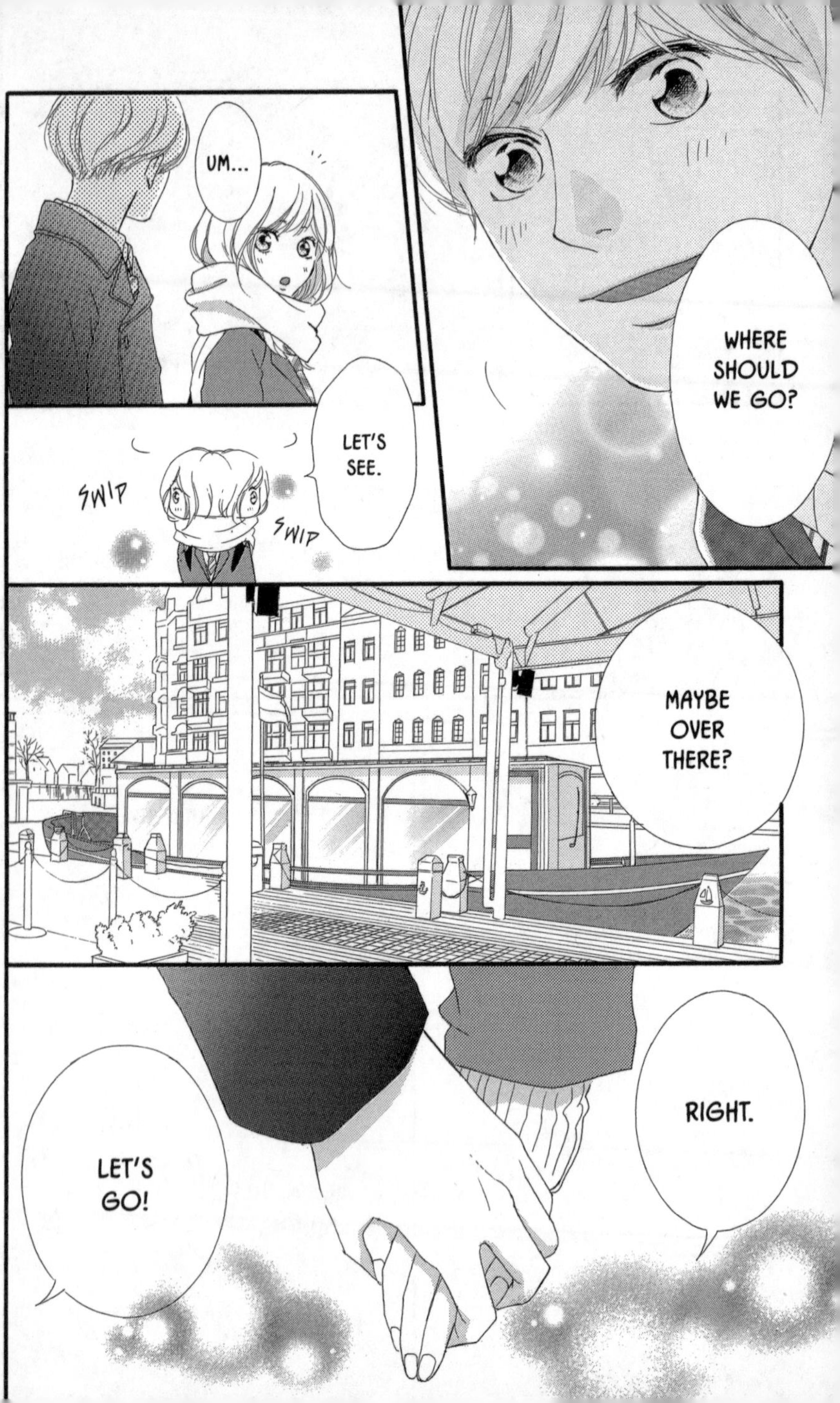
WHERE SHOULD WE GO?
UM...
LET'S SEE.
SWIP
SWIP
MAYBE OVER THERE?
RIGHT.
LET'S GO!

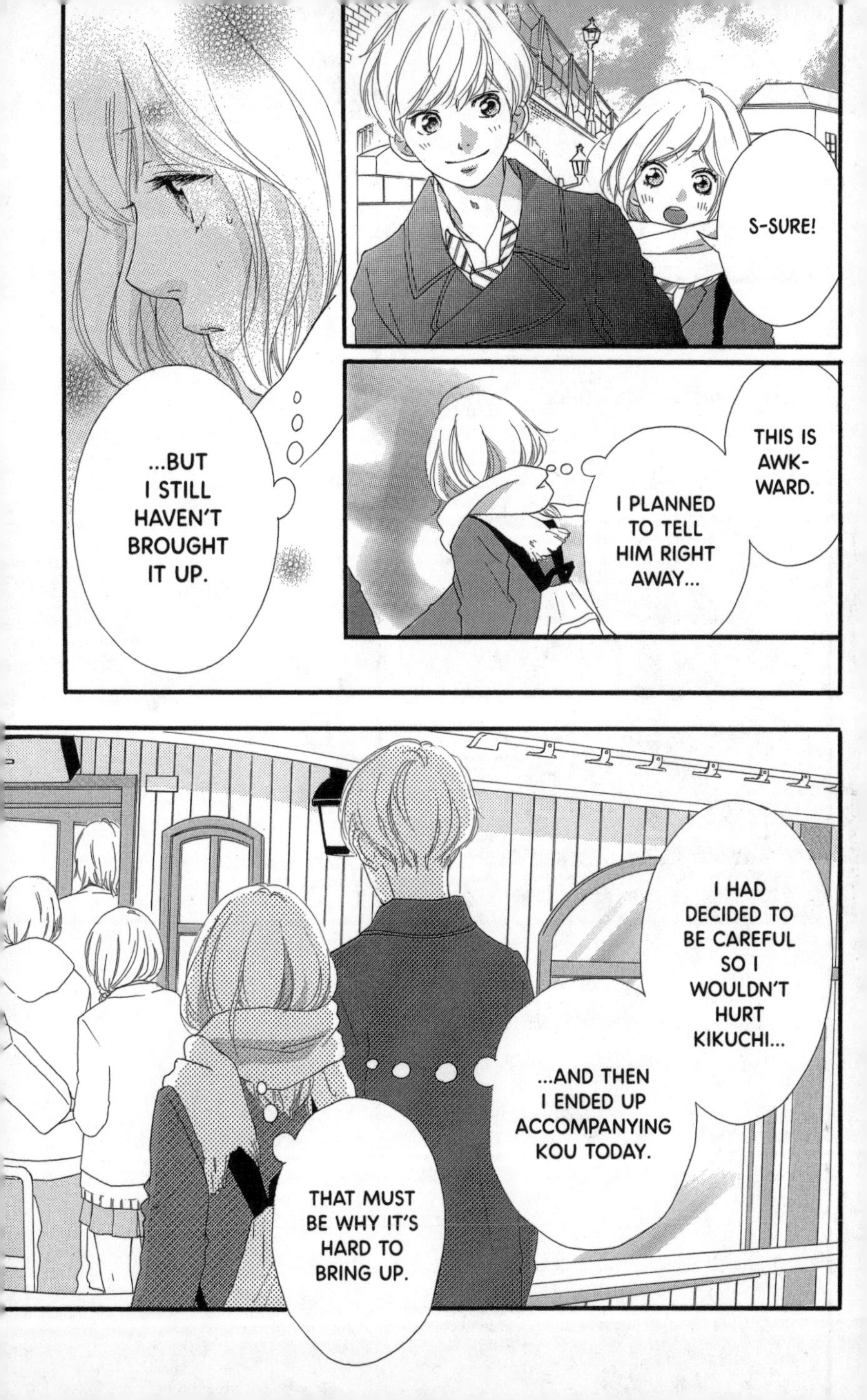
S-SURE!
THIS IS AWK-WARD.
I PLANNED TO TELL HIM RIGHT AWAY...
...BUT I STILL HAVEN'T BROUGHT IT UP.
I HAD DECIDED TO BE CAREFUL SO I WOULDN'T HURT KIKUCHI...
...AND THEN I ENDED UP ACCOMPANYING KOU TODAY.
THAT MUST BE WHY IT'S HARD TO BRING UP.

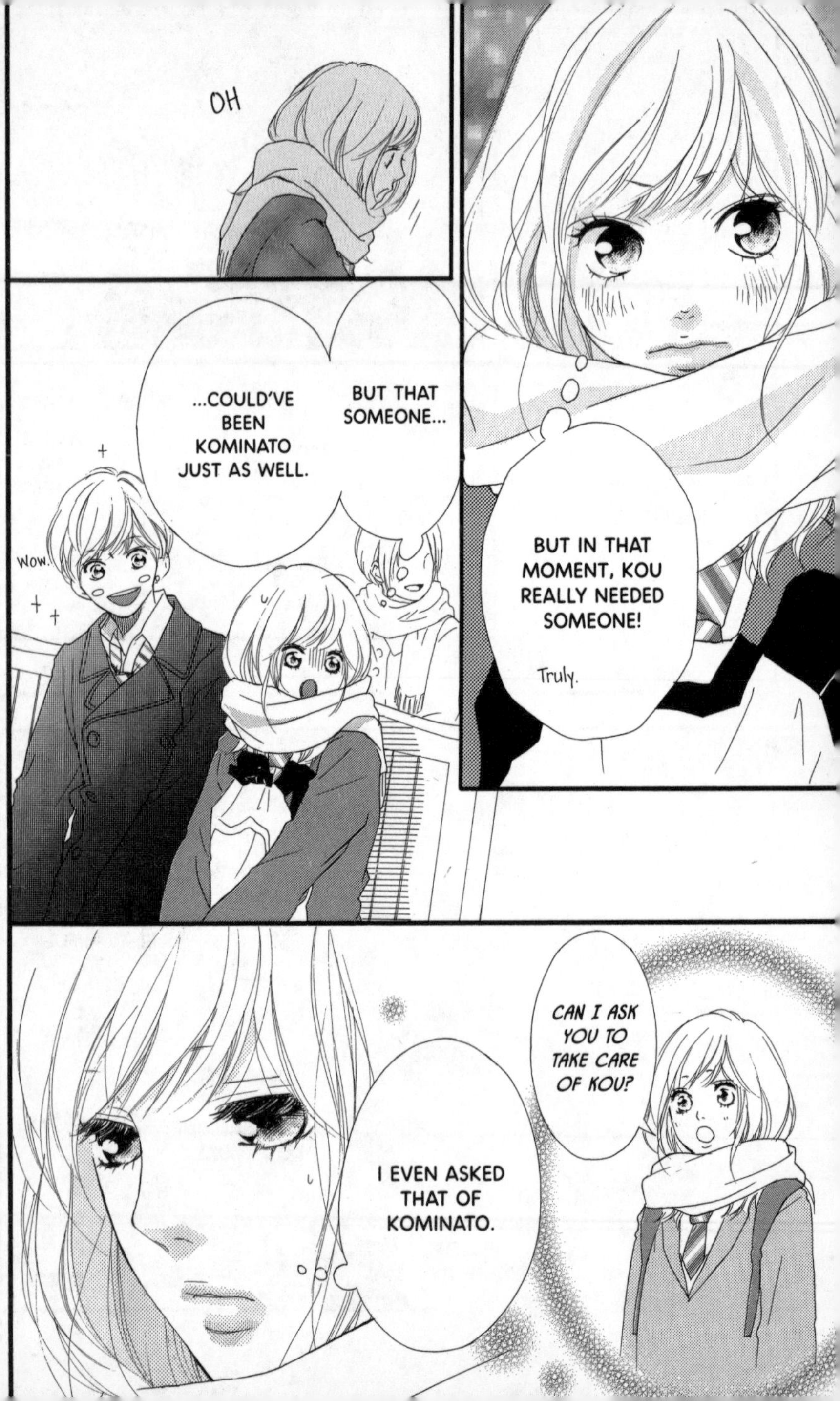
BUT IN THAT MOMENT, KOU REALLY NEEDED SOMEONE!
Truly.
OH
BUT THAT SOMEONE...
...COULD'VE BEEN KOMINATO JUST AS WELL.
Wow.
CAN I ASK YOU TO TAKE CARE OF KOU?
I EVEN ASKED THAT OF KOMINATO.

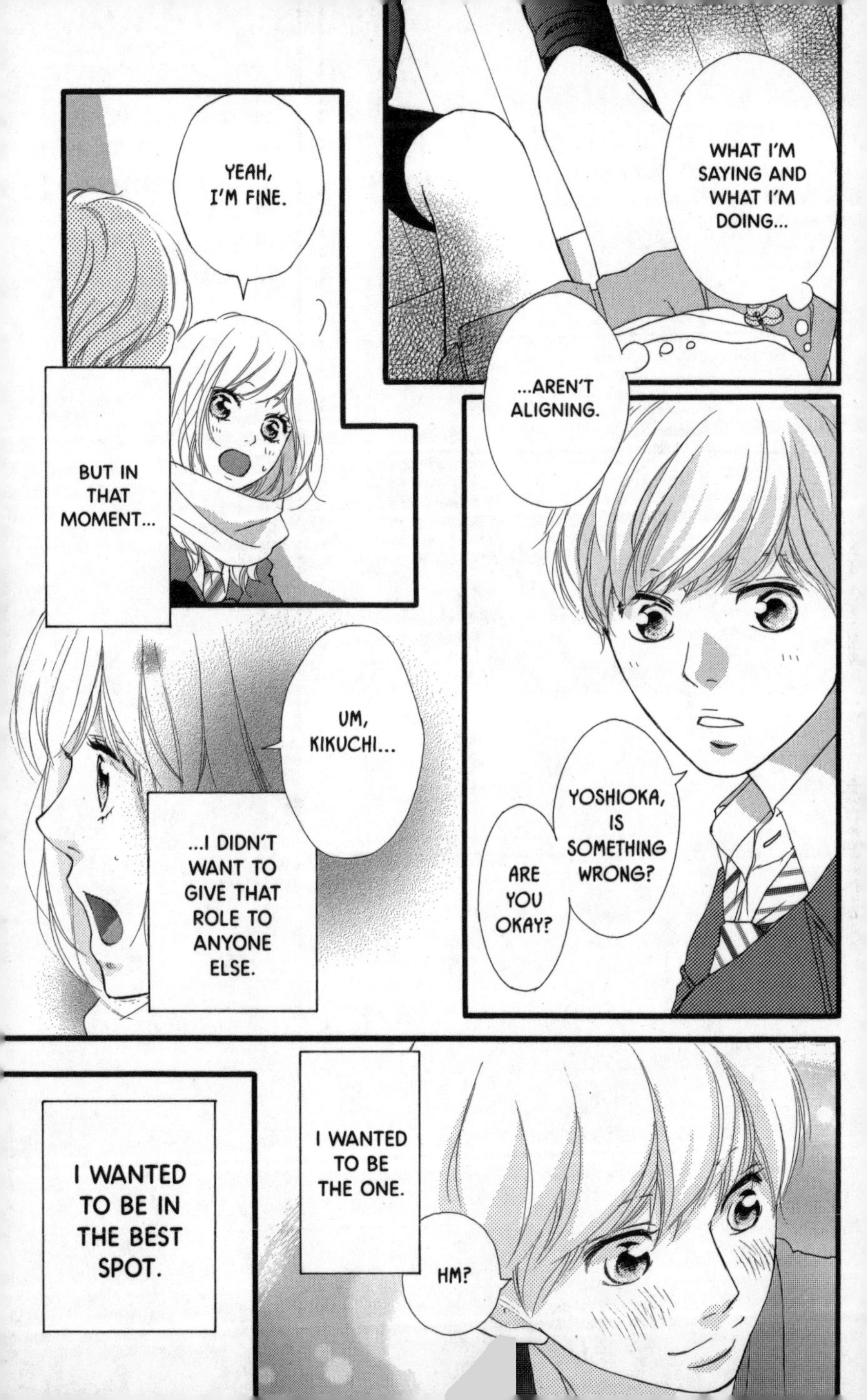
WHAT I'M SAYING AND WHAT I'M DOING...
...AREN'T ALIGNING.
YOSHIOKA, IS SOMETHING WRONG?
ARE YOU OKAY?
YEAH, I'M FINE.
BUT IN THAT MOMENT...
UM, KIKUCHI...
...I DIDN'T WANT TO GIVE THAT ROLE TO ANYONE ELSE.
I WANTED TO BE THE ONE.
HM?
I WANTED TO BE IN THE BEST SPOT.

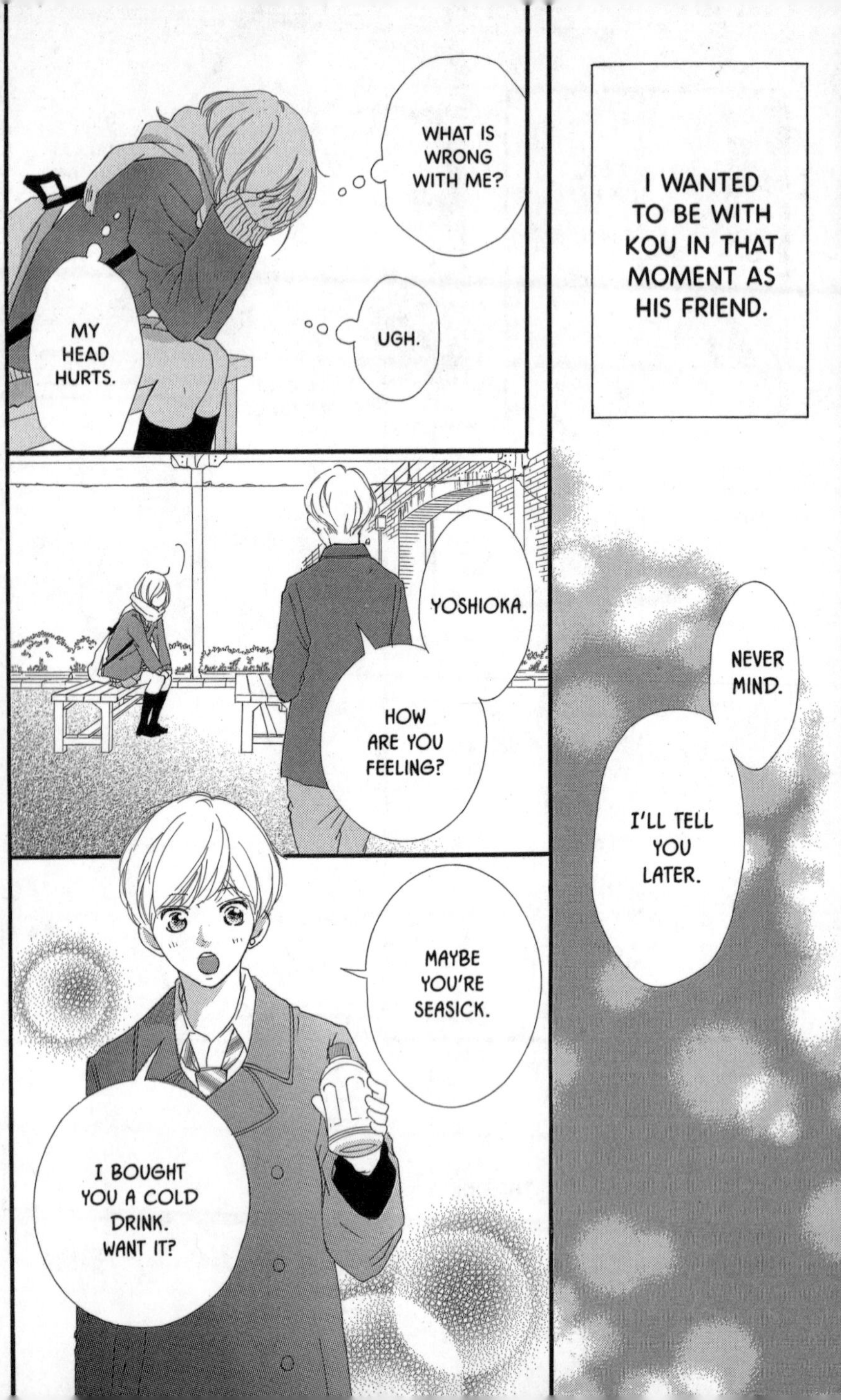
I WANTED TO BE WITH KOU IN THAT MOMENT AS HIS FRIEND.
NEVER MIND.
I'LL TELL YOU LATER.
WHAT IS WRONG WITH ME?
UGH.
MY HEAD HURTS.
YOSHIOKA.
HOW ARE YOU FEELING?
MAYBE YOU'RE SEASICK.
I BOUGHT YOU A COLD DRINK. WANT IT?

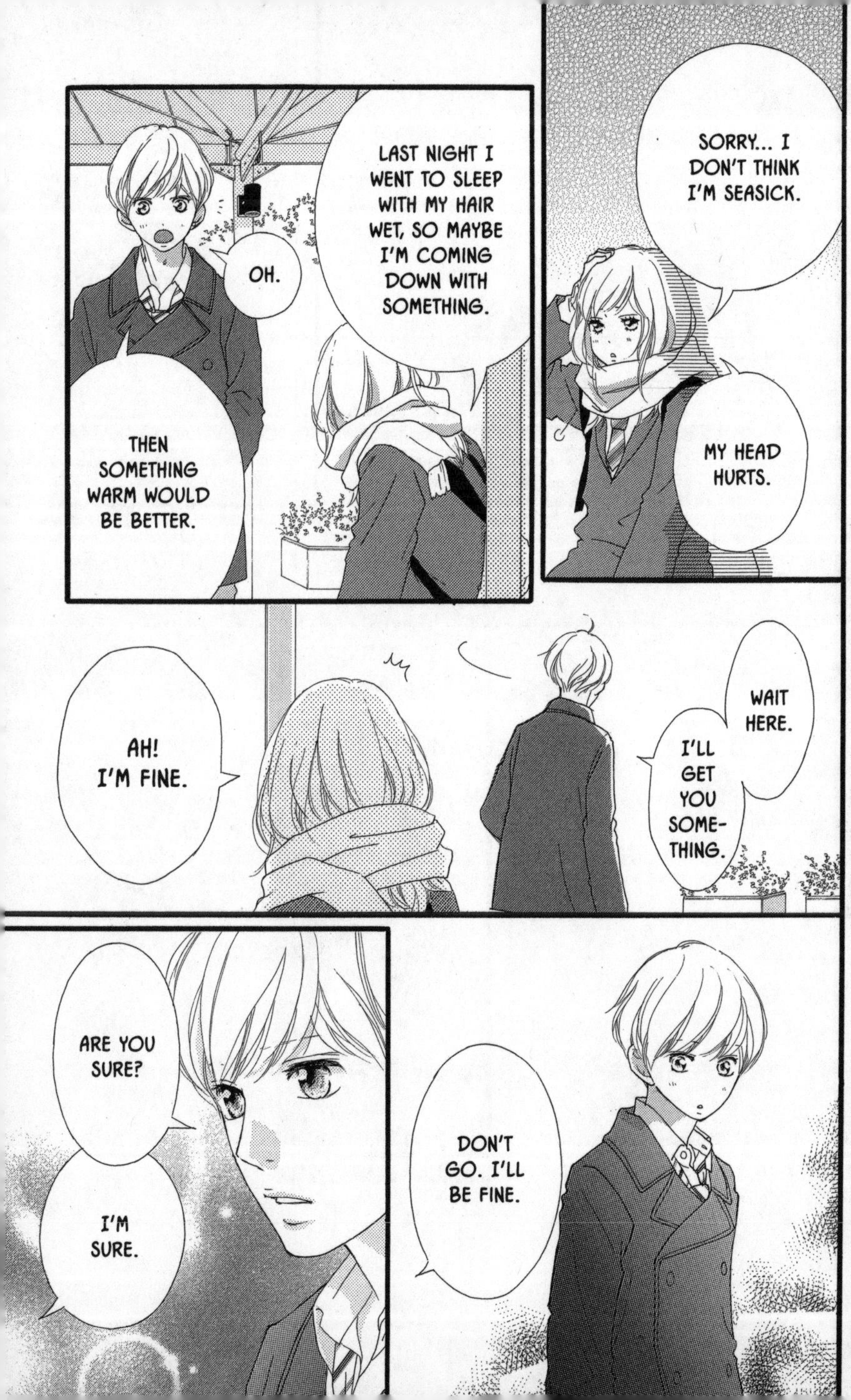
SORRY... I DON'T THINK I'M SEASICK.
MY HEAD HURTS.
LAST NIGHT I WENT TO SLEEP WITH MY HAIR WET, SO MAYBE I'M COMING DOWN WITH SOMETHING.
OH.
THEN SOMETHING WARM WOULD BE BETTER.
WAIT HERE.
I'LL GET YOU SOME-THING.
AH! I'M FINE.
DON'T GO. I'LL BE FINE.
ARE YOU SURE?
I'M SURE.

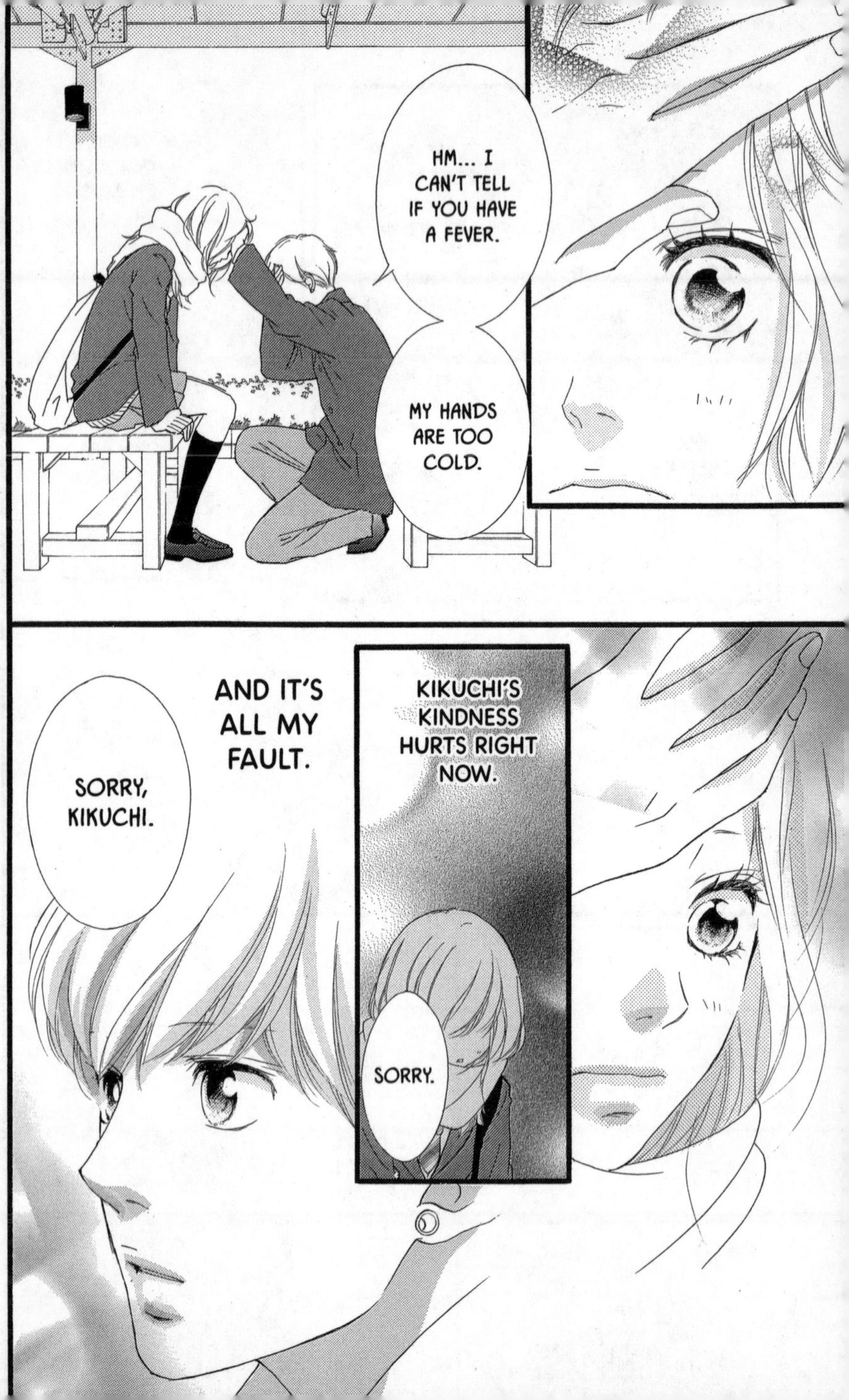
HM... I CAN'T TELL IF YOU HAVE A FEVER.
MY HANDS ARE TOO COLD.
KIKUCHI'S KINDNESS HURTS RIGHT NOW.
SORRY.
AND IT'S ALL MY FAULT.
SORRY, KIKUCHI.

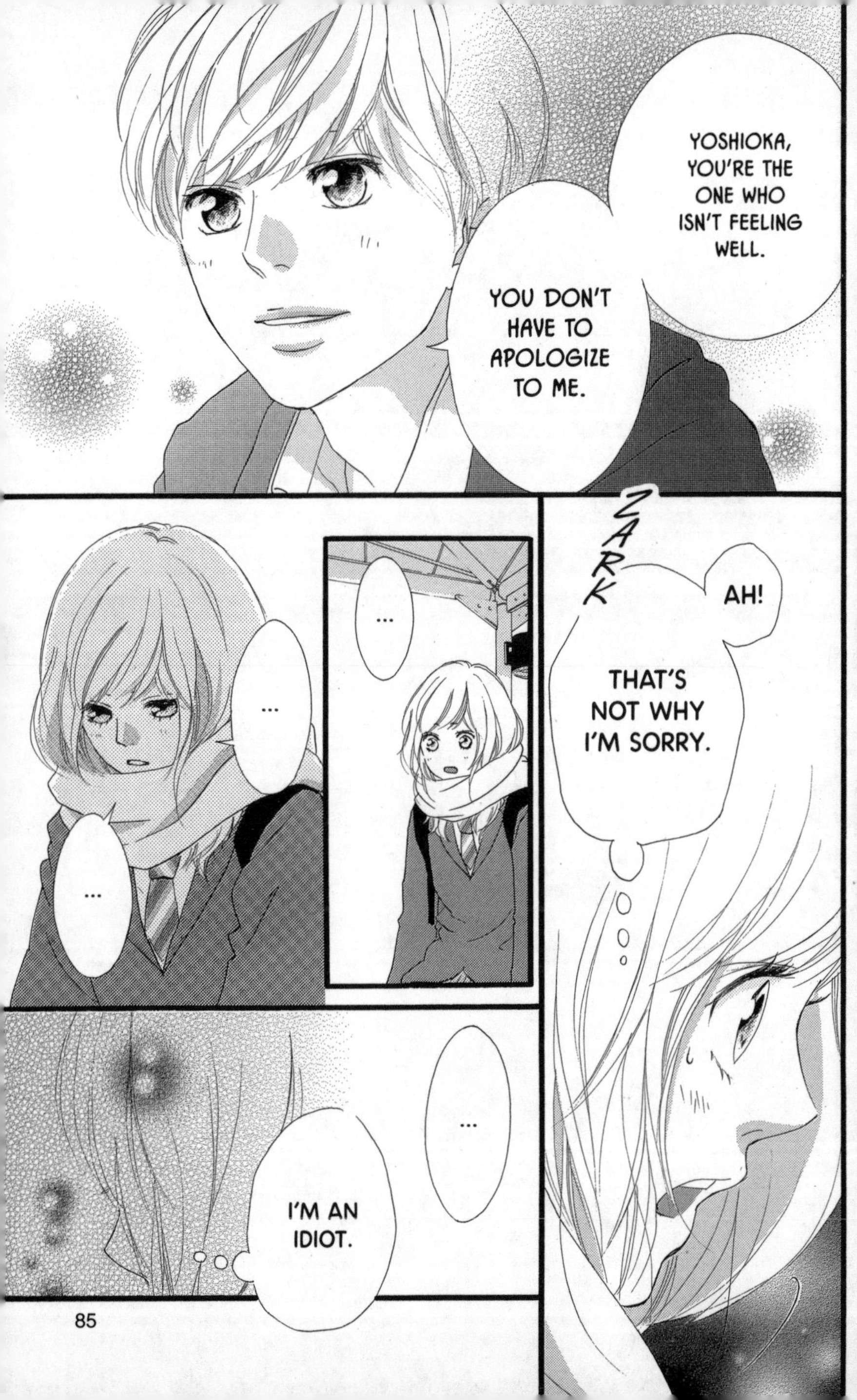
YOSHIOKA, YOU'RE THE ONE WHO ISN'T FEELING WELL.
YOU DON'T HAVE TO APOLOGIZE TO ME.
ZARK
AH!
THAT'S NOT WHY I'M SORRY.
...
...
...
...
I'M AN IDIOT.

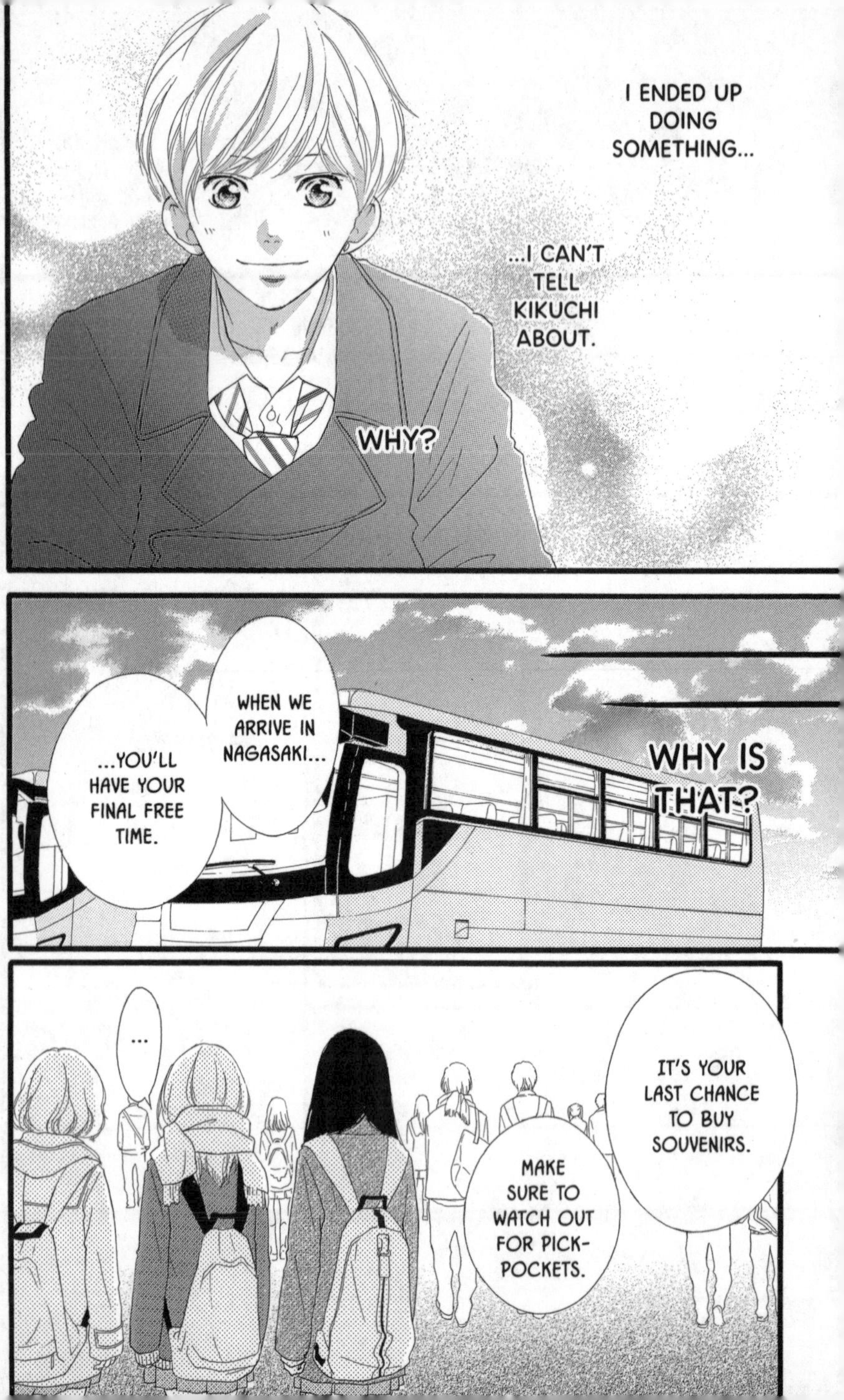
I ENDED UP DOING SOMETHING...
...I CAN'T TELL KIKUCHI ABOUT.
WHY?
WHY IS THAT?
WHEN WE ARRIVE IN NAGASAKI...
...YOU'LL HAVE YOUR FINAL FREE TIME.
IT'S YOUR LAST CHANCE TO BUY SOUVENIRS.
MAKE SURE TO WATCH OUT FOR PICK-POCKETS.
...

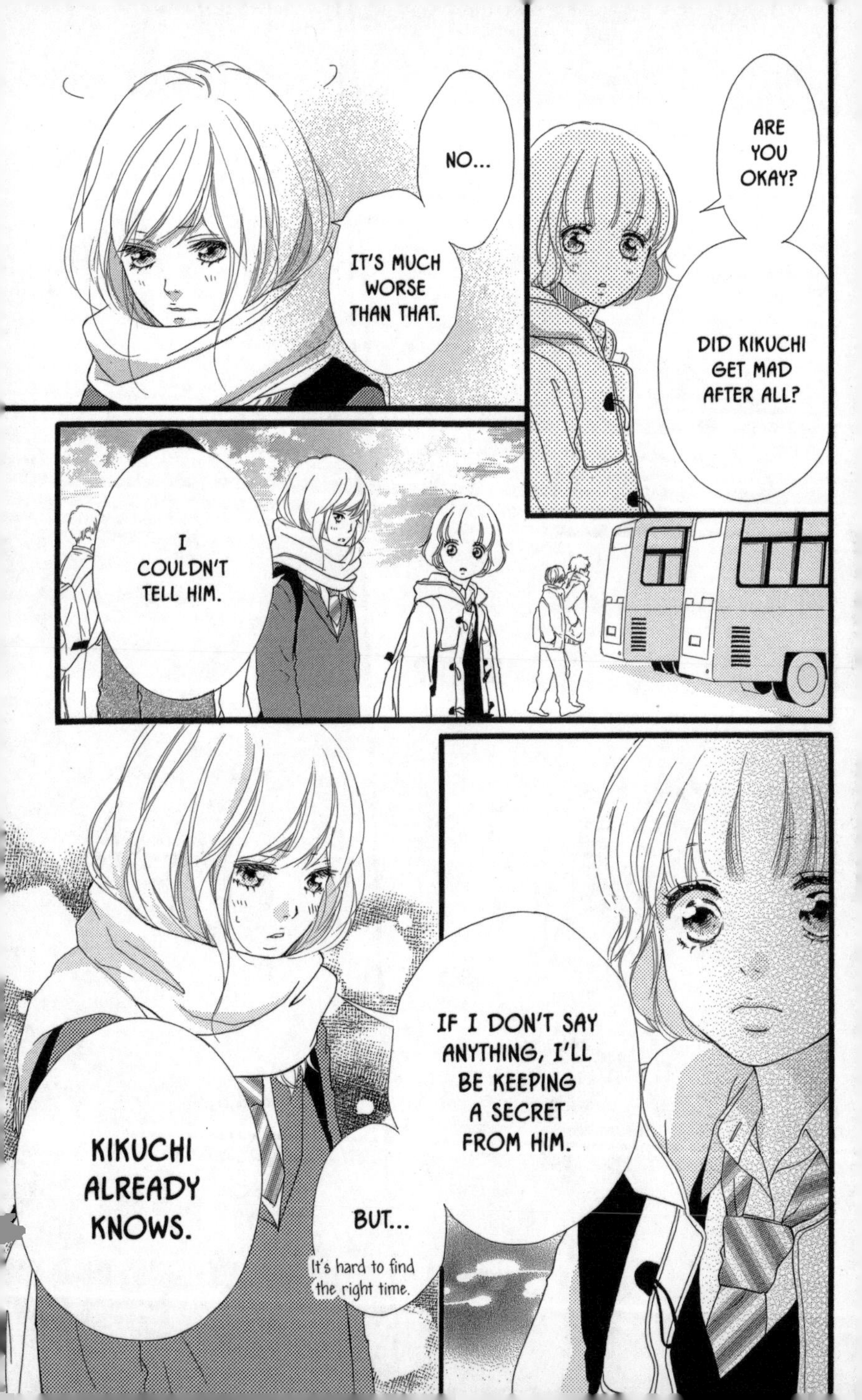
ARE YOU OKAY?
DID KIKUCHI GET MAD AFTER ALL?
NO...
IT'S MUCH WORSE THAN THAT.
I COULDN'T TELL HIM.
IF I DON'T SAY ANYTHING, I'LL BE KEEPING A SECRET FROM HIM.
BUT...
It's hard to find the right time.
KIKUCHI ALREADY KNOWS.

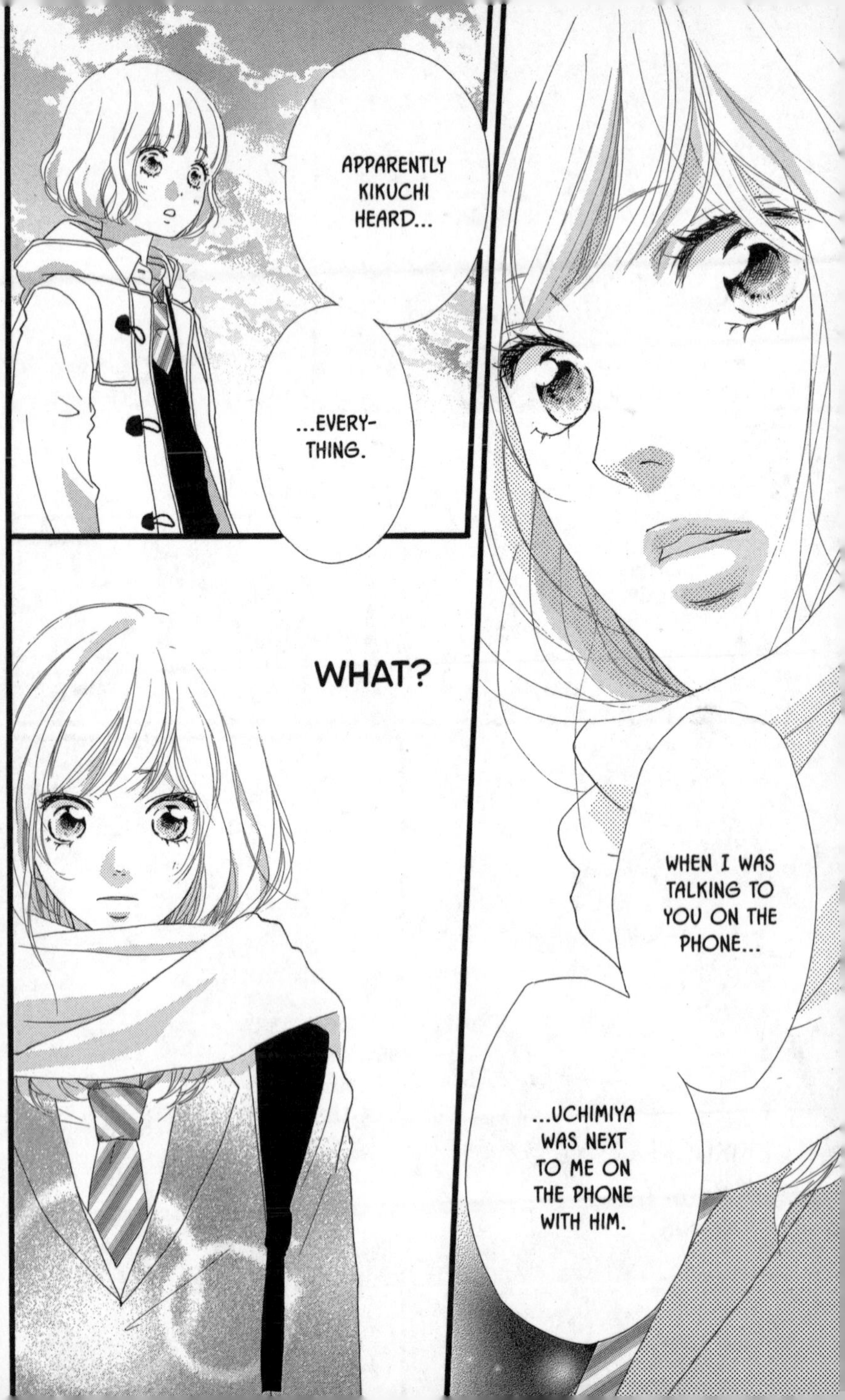
WHEN I WAS TALKING TO YOU ON THE PHONE...
...UCHIMIYA WAS NEXT TO ME ON THE PHONE WITH HIM.
APPARENTLY KIKUCHI HEARD...
...EVERY-THING.
WHAT?

The scent of air after rain...
In the light around us,
I felt your heartbeat.

The anime began in July. (Thank you to everyone who has watched it!) When I was one second into the first episode on TV, I was so overcome with emotion that my tear glands ruptured. I don't think I'll ever forget that moment. On Twitter, when episode 1 began, I received tons of replies, and I was thrilled to be able to share that moment with others. Having worked on the manga, it's incredible seeing everything in color, not to mention my characters moving and talking. If you haven't seen the anime yet, I hope you will. Please watch it!

This is going to turn into an ad, but I'm excited to announce that on September 17, 2014, when the first Blu-ray and DVD are released, the first press will include a special manga. It's called *Awaken,* and it's written from Kou's perspective in junior high! (By the way, I listened to the anime ending song, "Blue," the entire time I worked on the manga.) The anime release will also include a presale ticket form for a special Christmas event. Yuki Kaji, Maaya Uchida, Mikako Komatsu, Ai Kayano, and KENN will all attend—sounds pretty spectacular, wouldn't you say?!

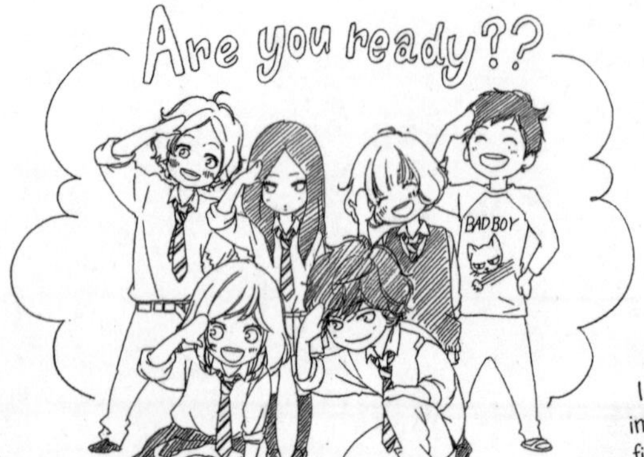
Are you ready??
BAD BOY

I tweeted this image when the first episode of the anime aired.

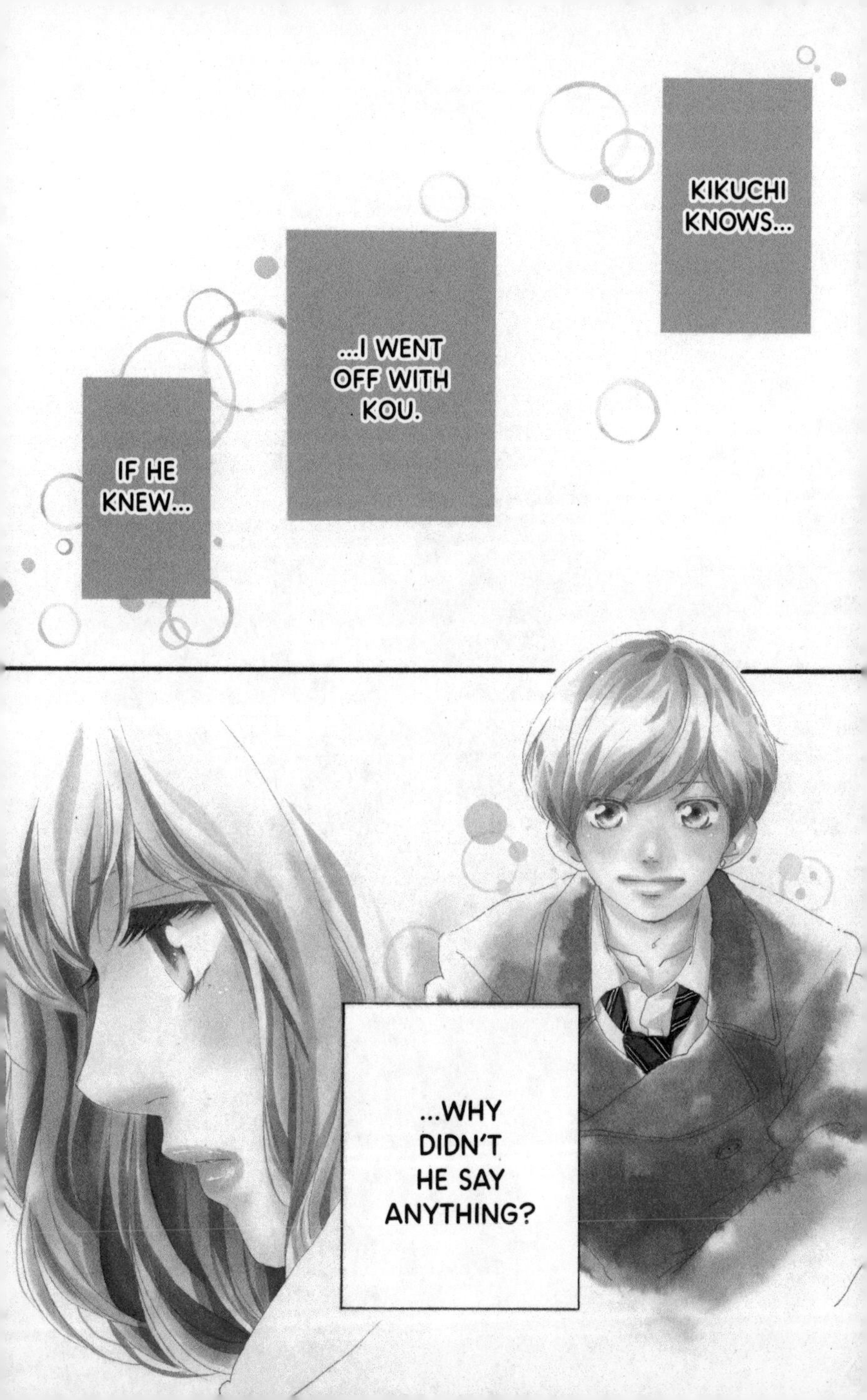
KIKUCHI KNOWS...
...I WENT OFF WITH KOU.
IF HE KNEW...
...WHY DIDN'T HE SAY ANYTHING?

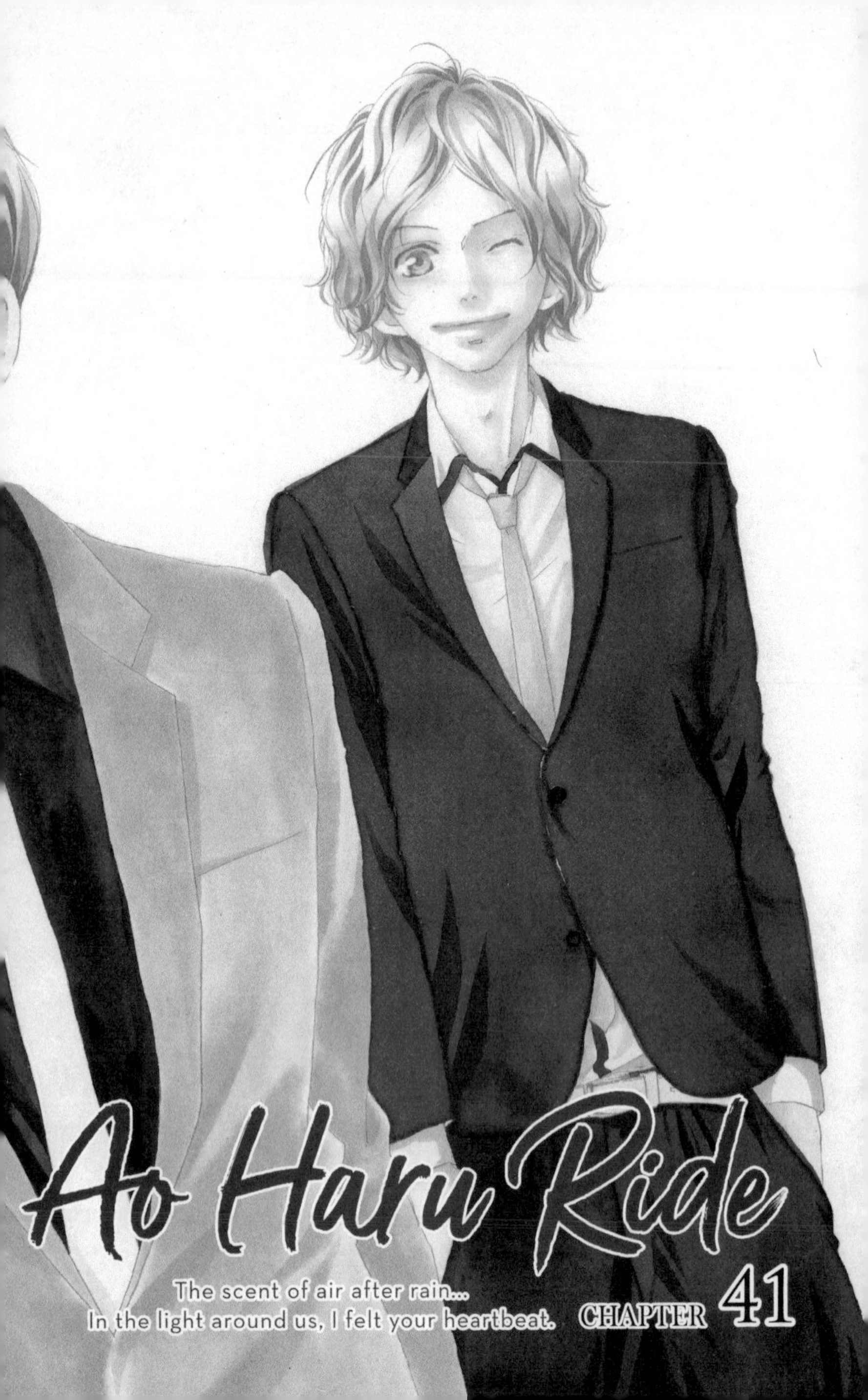
Ao Haru Ride
The scent of air after rain...
In the light around us, I felt your heartbeat.
CHAPTER 41

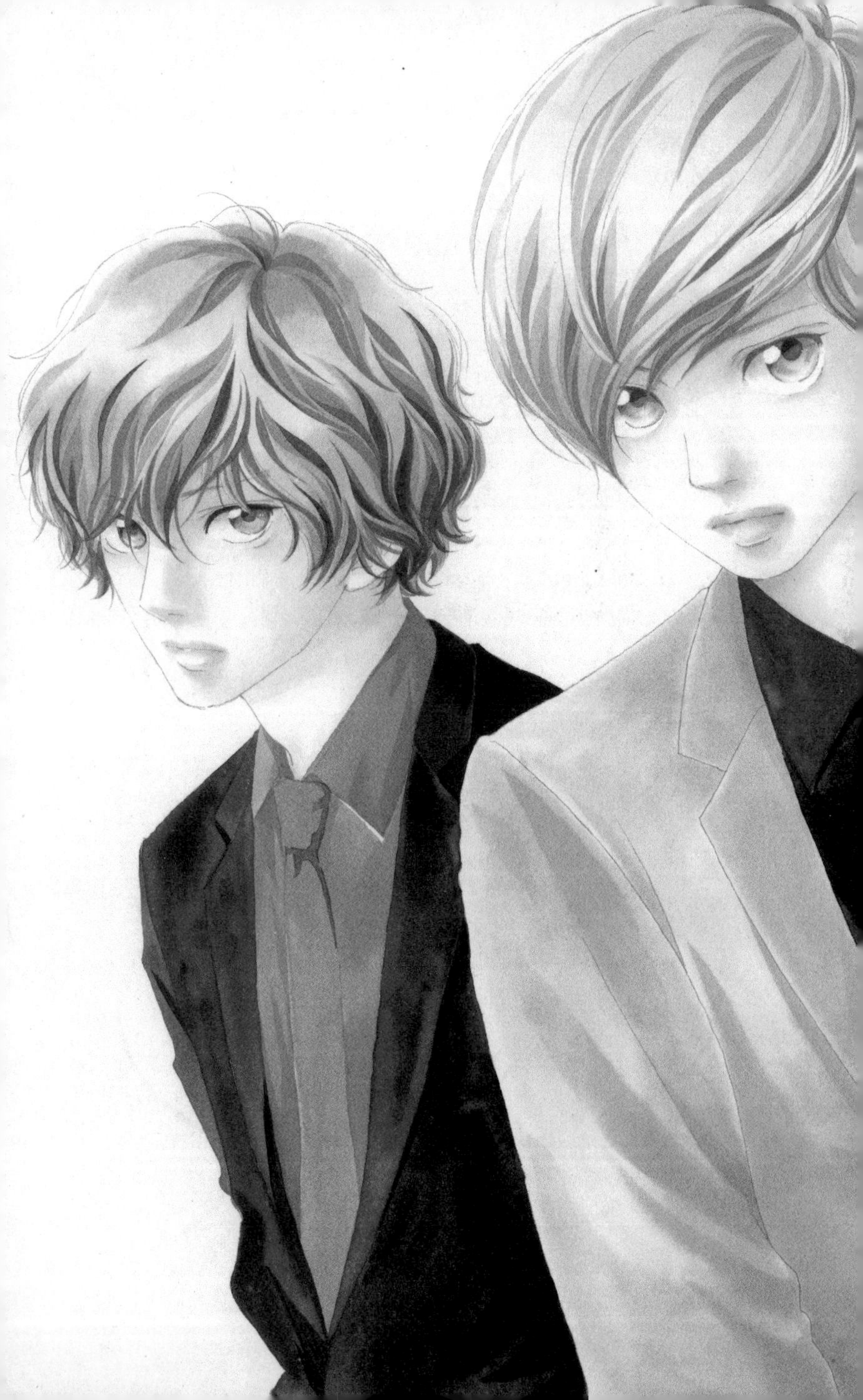

Announcement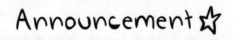

A collection of my short manga stories will be released in *Io Sakisaka's My World Is You: A Collection of Short Love Stories*.

As this is a collection of my past works, some of the art is not very good, but the stories are all ones I love. If this sounds up your alley, I hope you will pick up a copy. ♡

In comparison to my current work, both my art and the way I communicate a story to my readers have changed. At the same time, I can tell that the essence of what I want to convey has not changed much.

There are six stories in all. The new cover art was drawn specifically for this edition. I hope you'll check it out!

Io Sakisaka

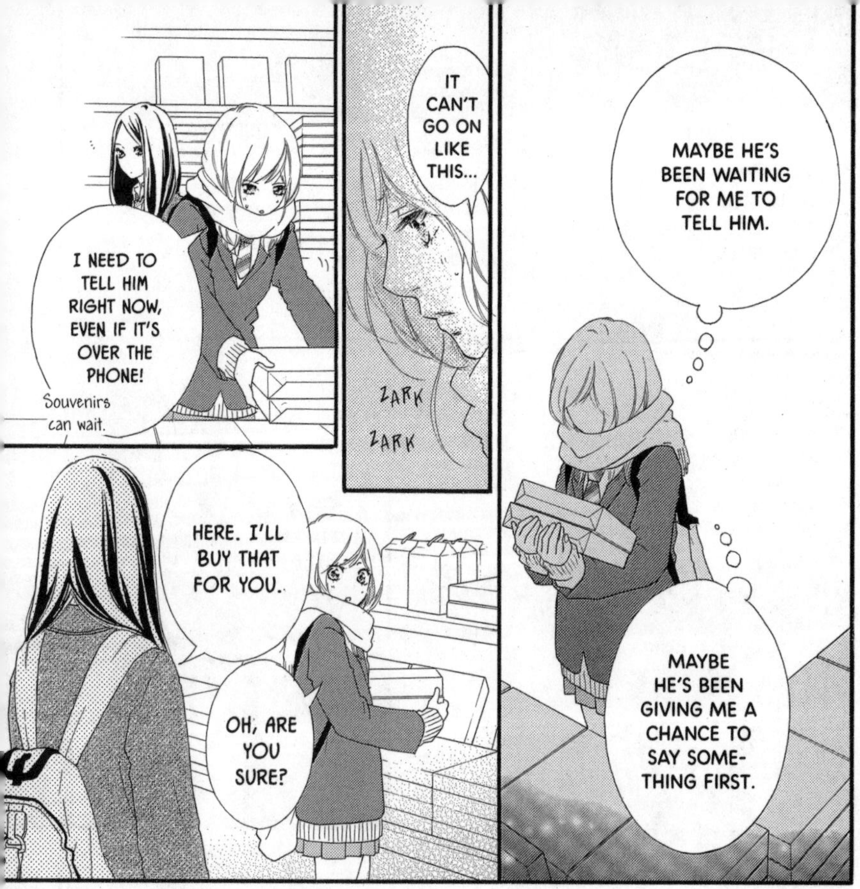
MAYBE HE'S BEEN WAITING FOR ME TO TELL HIM.
MAYBE HE'S BEEN GIVING ME A CHANCE TO SAY SOME-THING FIRST.
IT CAN'T GO ON LIKE THIS...
ZARK
ZARK
I NEED TO TELL HIM RIGHT NOW, EVEN IF IT'S OVER THE PHONE!
Souvenirs can wait.
HERE. I'LL BUY THAT FOR YOU..
OH, ARE YOU SURE?

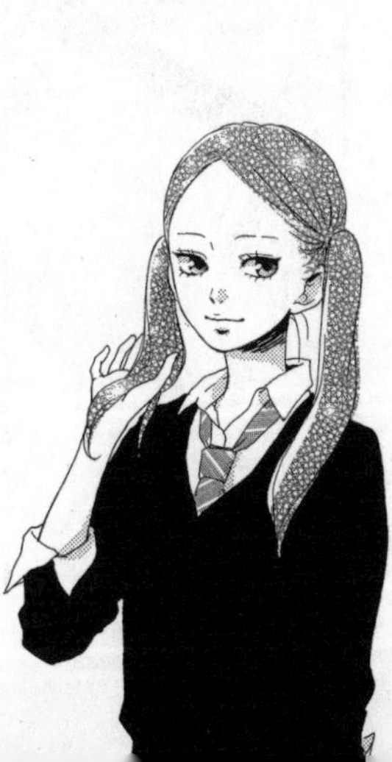

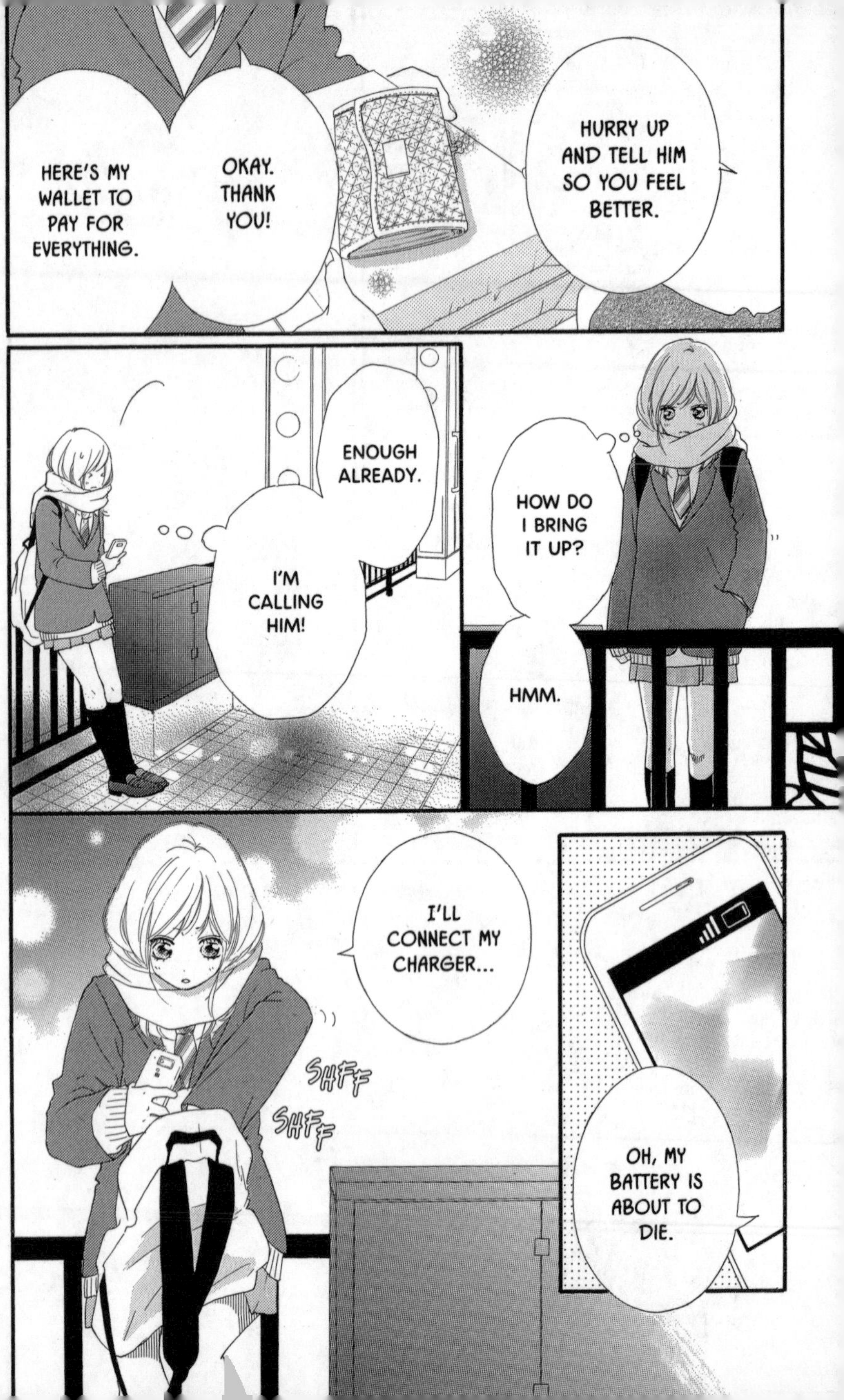
HURRY UP AND TELL HIM SO YOU FEEL BETTER.
OKAY. THANK YOU!
HERE'S MY WALLET TO PAY FOR EVERYTHING.
HOW DO I BRING IT UP?
HMM.
ENOUGH ALREADY.
I'M CALLING HIM!
OH, MY BATTERY IS ABOUT TO DIE.
I'LL CONNECT MY CHARGER...
SHFF
SHFF

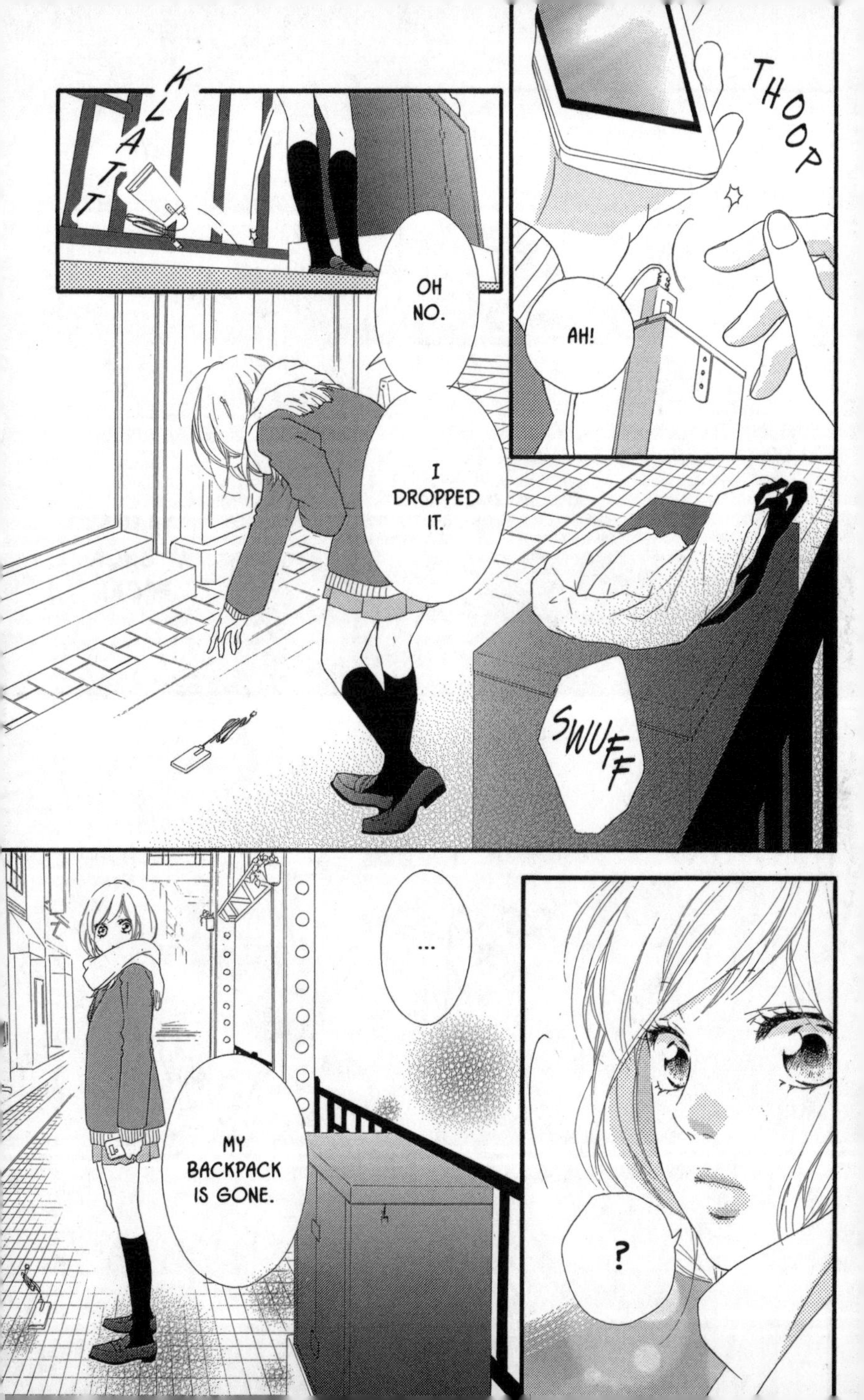
THOOP
AH!
KLATT
SWUFF
OH NO.
I DROPPED IT.
?
...
MY BACKPACK IS GONE.

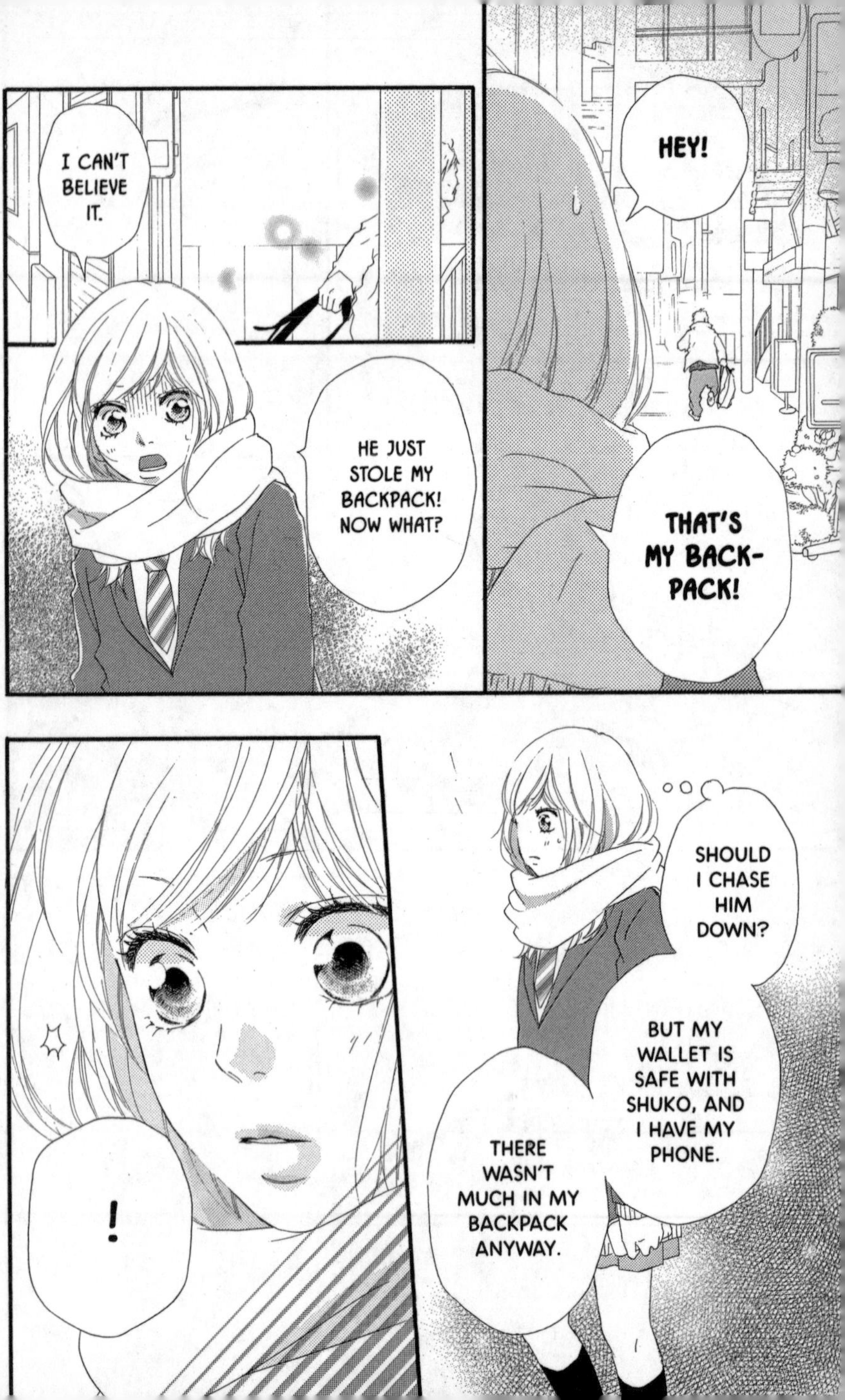
HEY!
THAT'S MY BACK-PACK!
I CAN'T BELIEVE IT.
HE JUST STOLE MY BACKPACK! NOW WHAT?
SHOULD I CHASE HIM DOWN?
BUT MY WALLET IS SAFE WITH SHUKO, AND I HAVE MY PHONE.
THERE WASN'T MUCH IN MY BACKPACK ANYWAY.
!

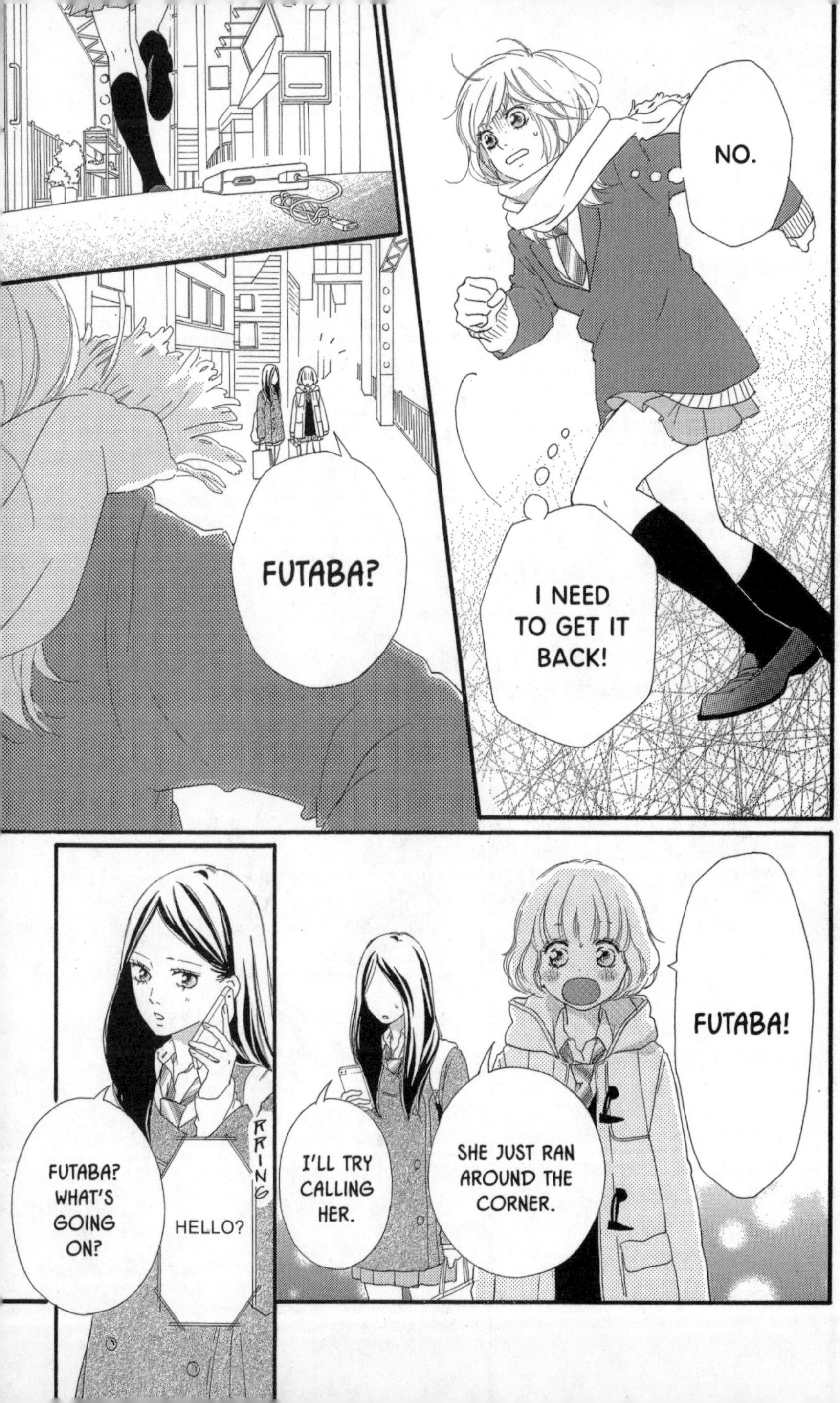
NO.
I NEED TO GET IT BACK!
FUTABA?
FUTABA!
SHE JUST RAN AROUND THE CORNER.
I'LL TRY CALLING HER.
RRING
HELLO?
FUTABA? WHAT'S GOING ON?

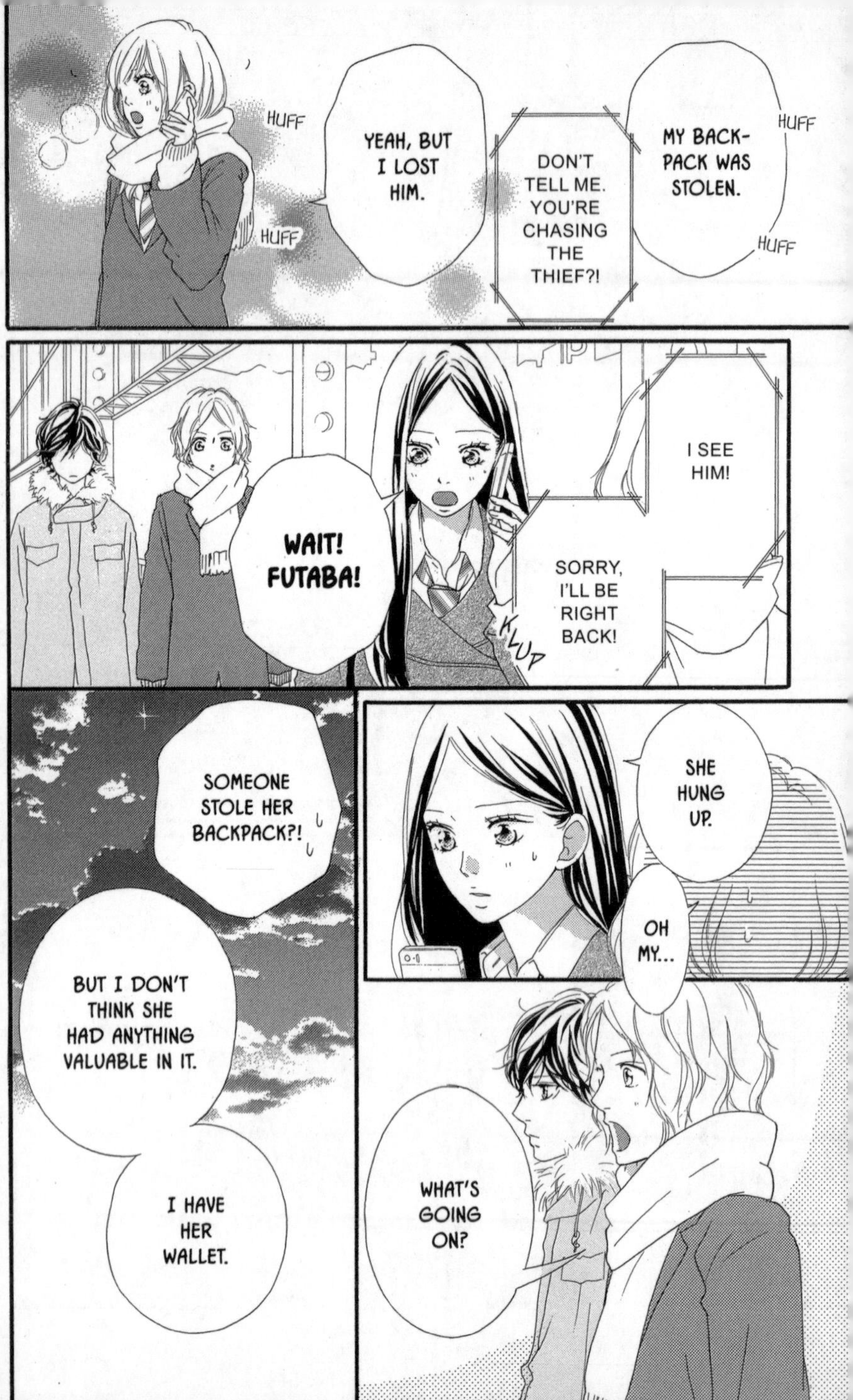
HUFF
MY BACK-PACK WAS STOLEN.
HUFF
DON'T TELL ME. YOU'RE CHASING THE THIEF?!
YEAH, BUT I LOST HIM.
HUFF
HUFF
I SEE HIM!
SORRY, I'LL BE RIGHT BACK!
KLUP
WAIT! FUTABA!
SHE HUNG UP.
OH MY...
WHAT'S GOING ON?
SOMEONE STOLE HER BACKPACK?!
BUT I DON'T THINK SHE HAD ANYTHING VALUABLE IN IT.
I HAVE HER WALLET.

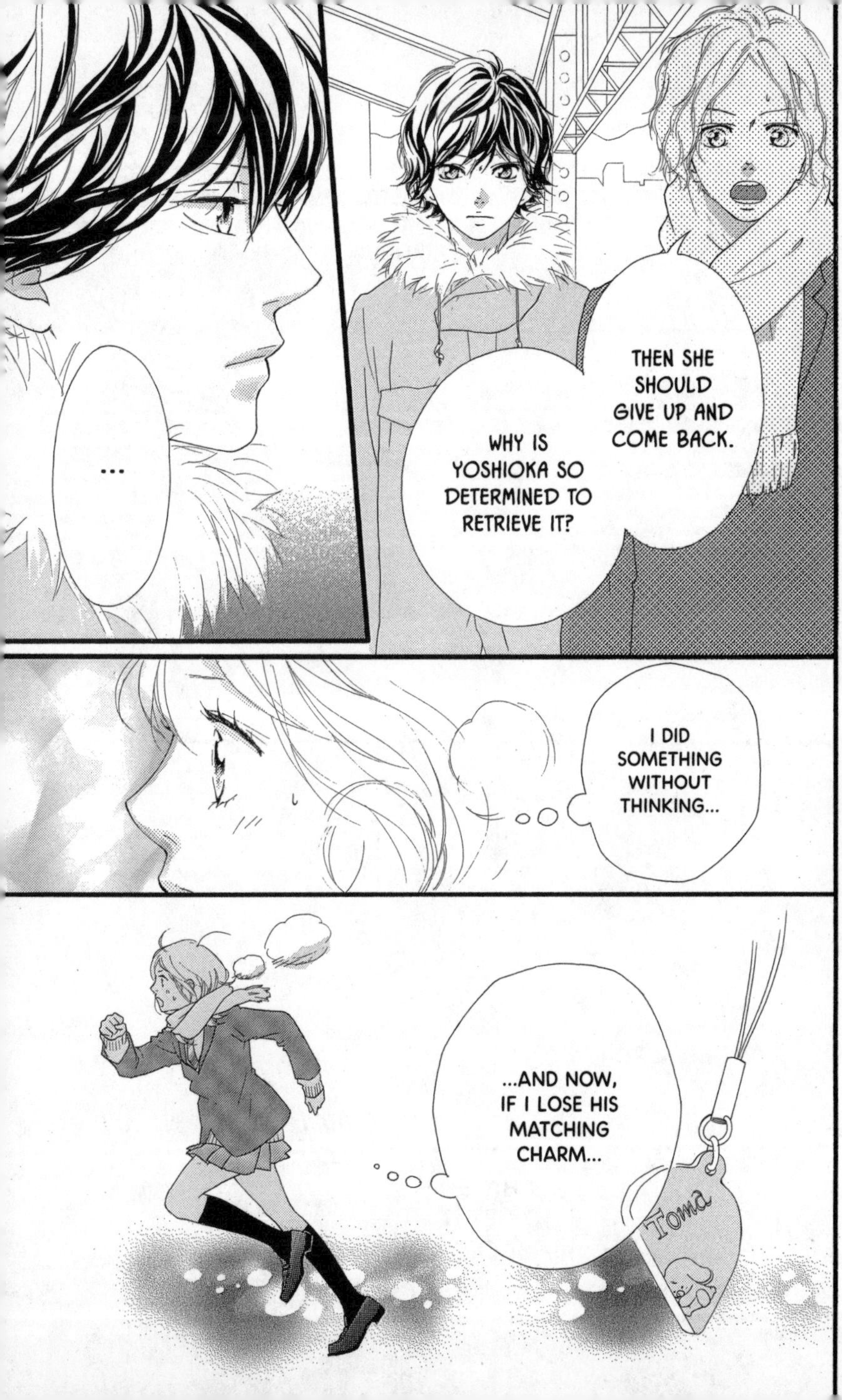
THEN SHE SHOULD GIVE UP AND COME BACK.
WHY IS YOSHIOKA SO DETERMINED TO RETRIEVE IT?
...
I DID SOMETHING WITHOUT THINKING...
...AND NOW, IF I LOSE HIS MATCHING CHARM...
Toma

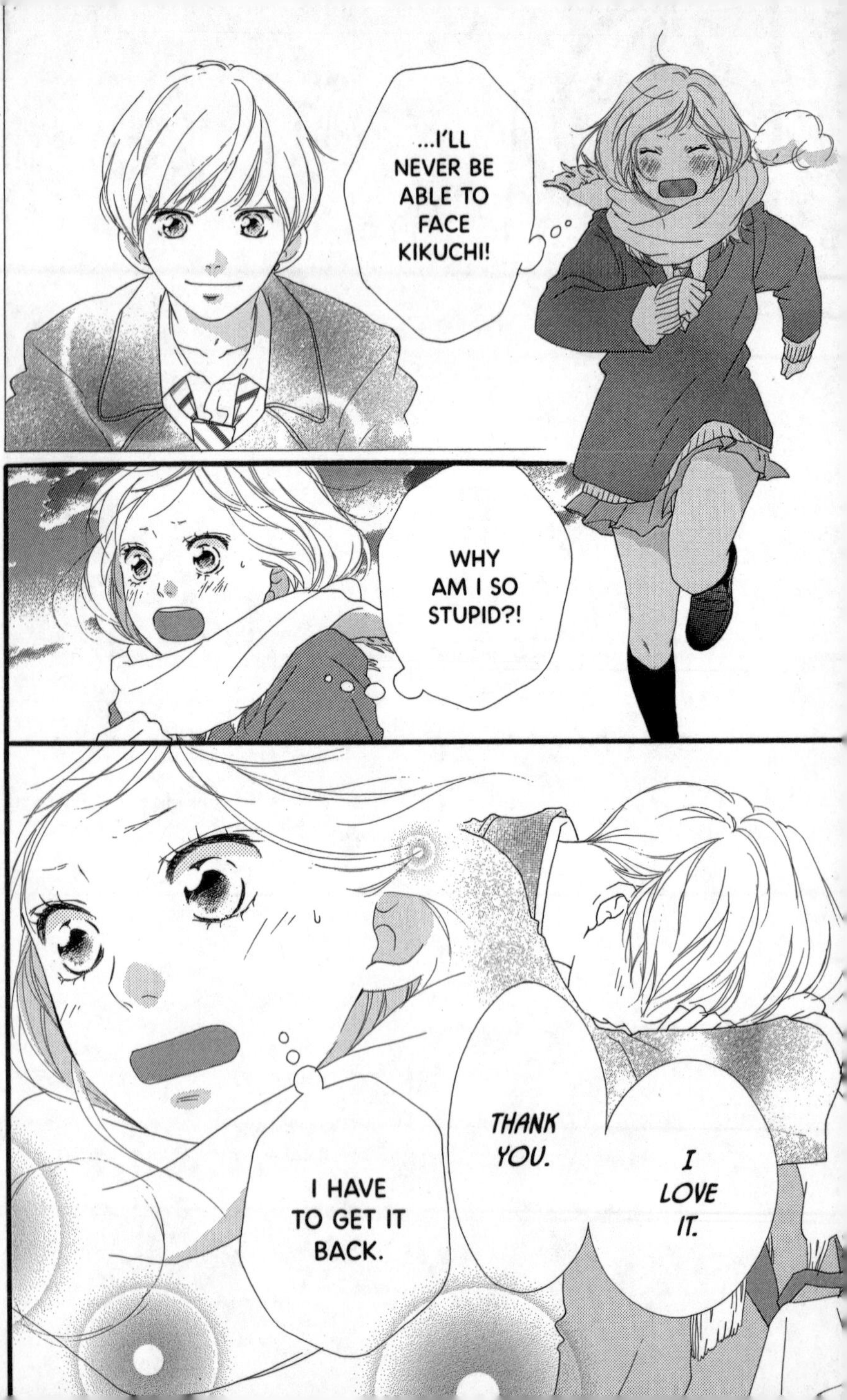
...I'LL NEVER BE ABLE TO FACE KIKUCHI!
WHY AM I SO STUPID?!
I LOVE IT.
THANK YOU.
I HAVE TO GET IT BACK.

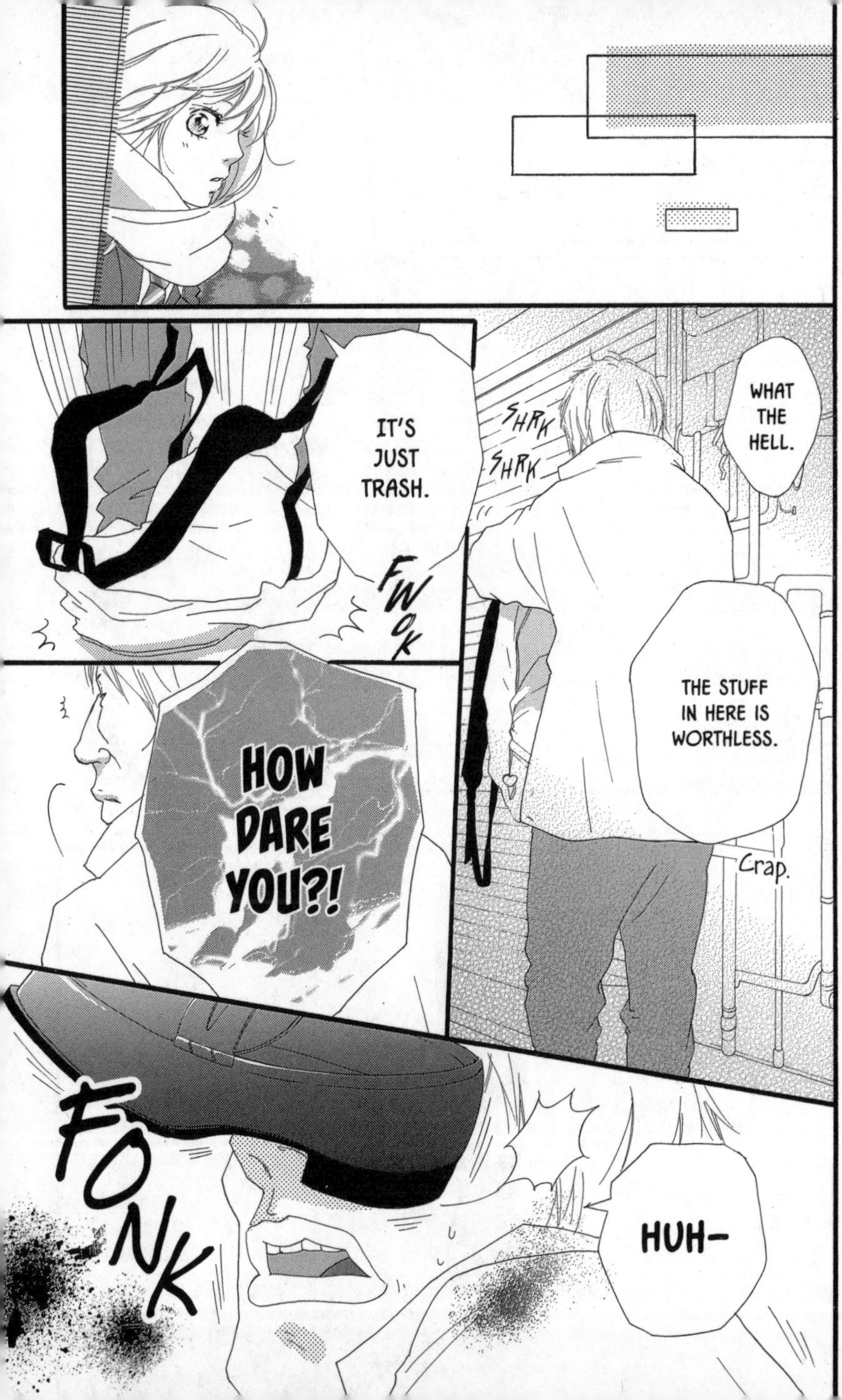
WHAT THE HELL.
SHRK
SHRK
THE STUFF IN HERE IS WORTHLESS.
Crap.
IT'S JUST TRASH.
FWOK
HOW DARE YOU?!
HUH-
FONK

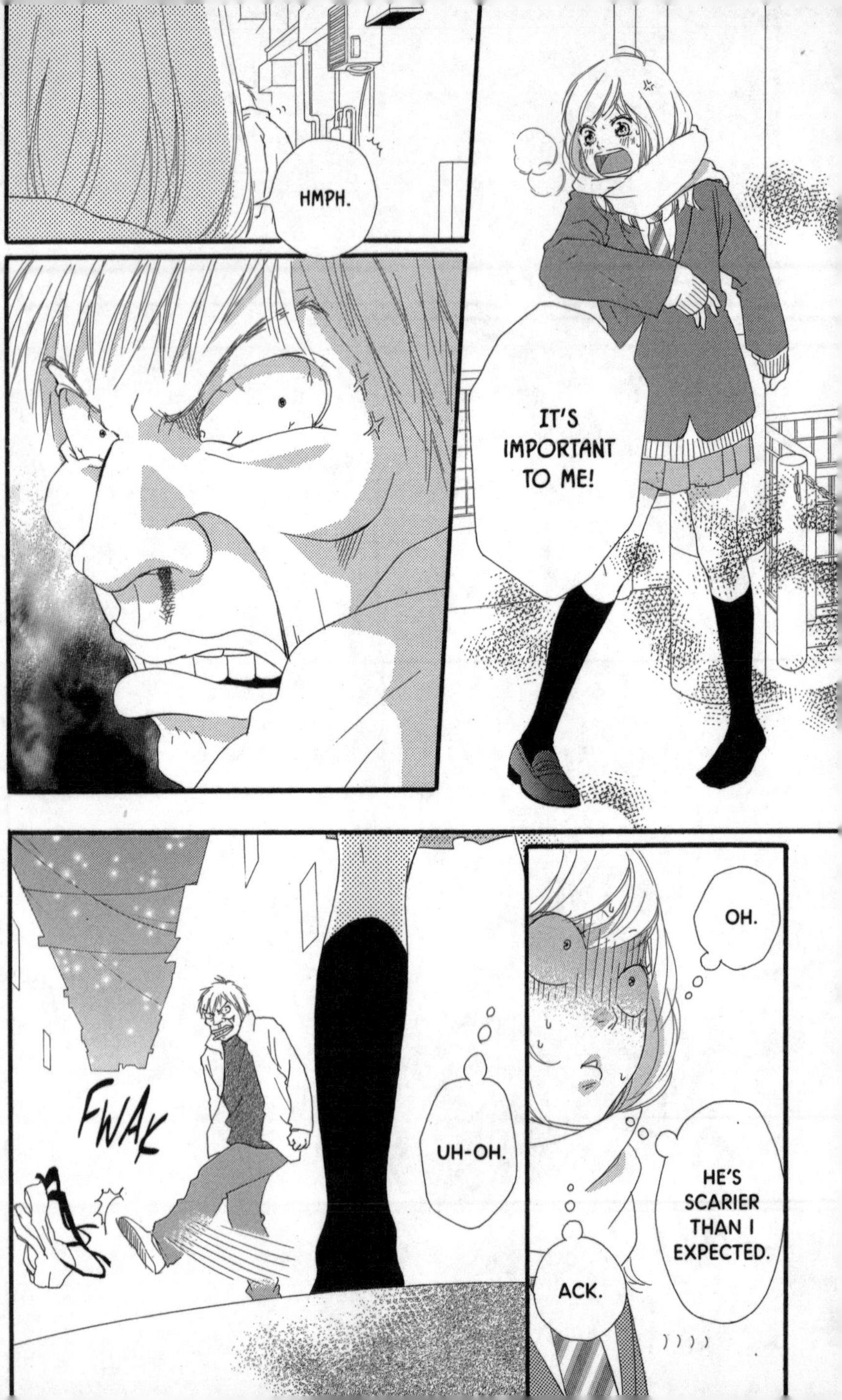
IT'S IMPORTANT TO ME!
HMPH.
OH.
HE'S SCARIER THAN I EXPECTED.
ACK.
UH-OH.
FWAK

By the way, the summer edition of *Betsuma Sister* ran a collaborative feature all about *Ao Haru Ride*. It included comments from the anime cast and musical artists, as well as "tribute illustrations" from other *Betsuma* artists! It's such an amazing feeling to have other mangaka draw your characters. I was soooo grateful to see them! I laughed and cried at all the lovely illustrations, which kept me quite busy. (*laugh*) To top it off, the junior artists who always help me out with my manuscripts also contributed drawings. Those made me cry so much. Those sweet kids! And I got to play around with my own characters in it, which was a lot of fun. Thank you to everyone who participated in this project.

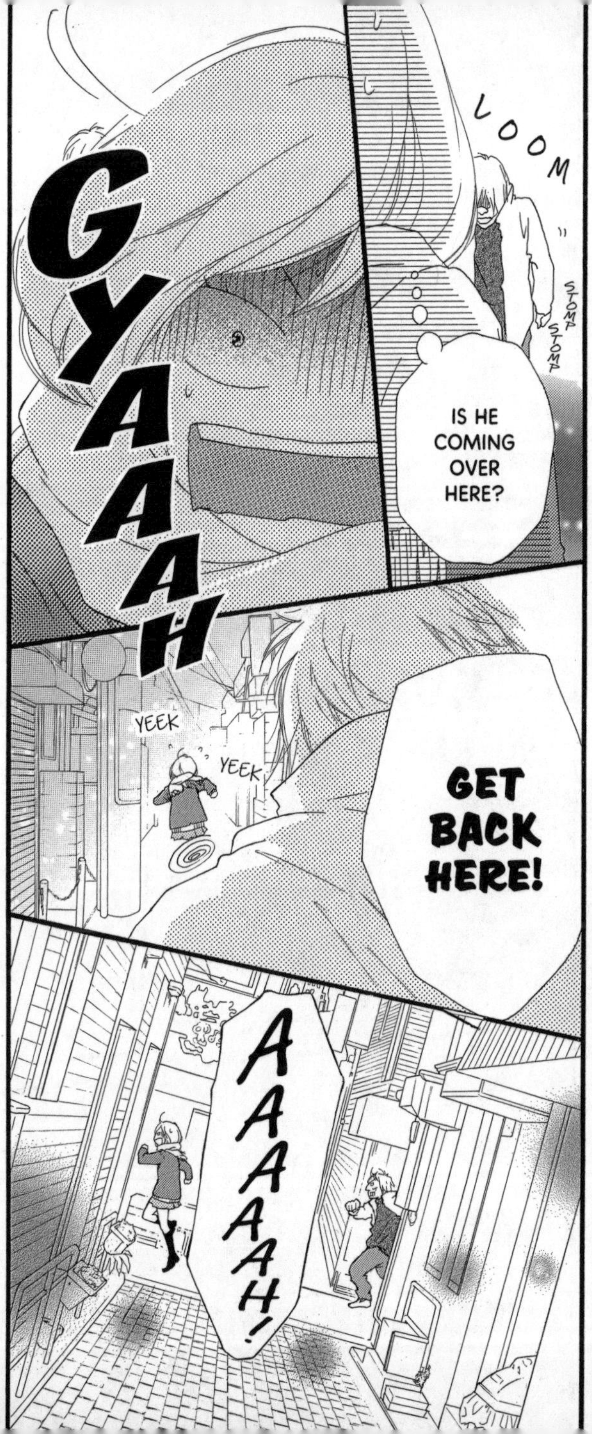

LOOM
STOMP STOMP
IS HE COMING OVER HERE?
GYAAAH
GET BACK HERE!
YEEK
YEEK
AAAAAH!

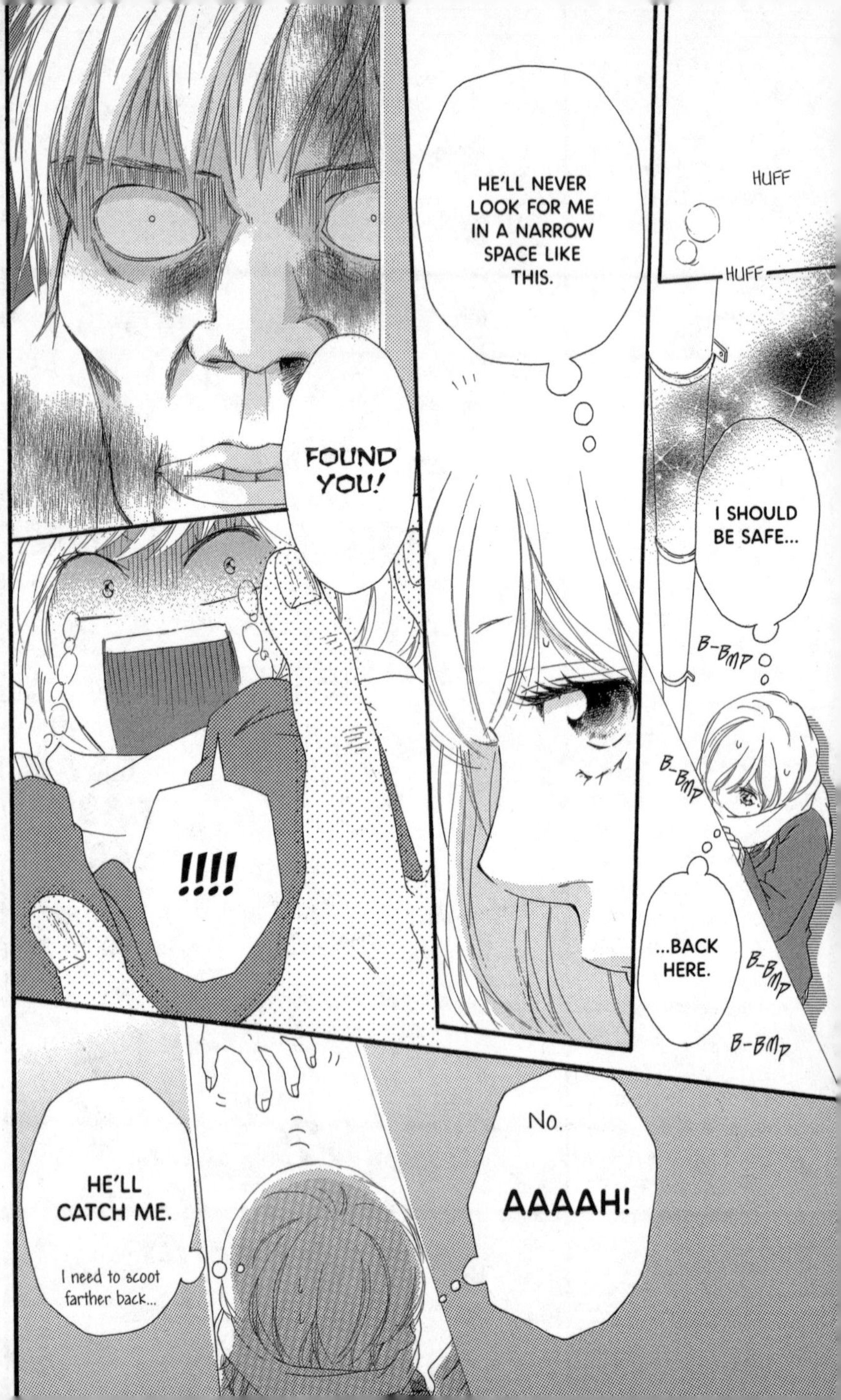
HUFF
HUFF
I SHOULD BE SAFE...
B-BMP
B-BMP
...BACK HERE.
B-BMP
B-BMP
HE'LL NEVER LOOK FOR ME IN A NARROW SPACE LIKE THIS.
FOUND YOU!
!!!!
No.
AAAAH!
HE'LL CATCH ME.
I need to scoot farther back...

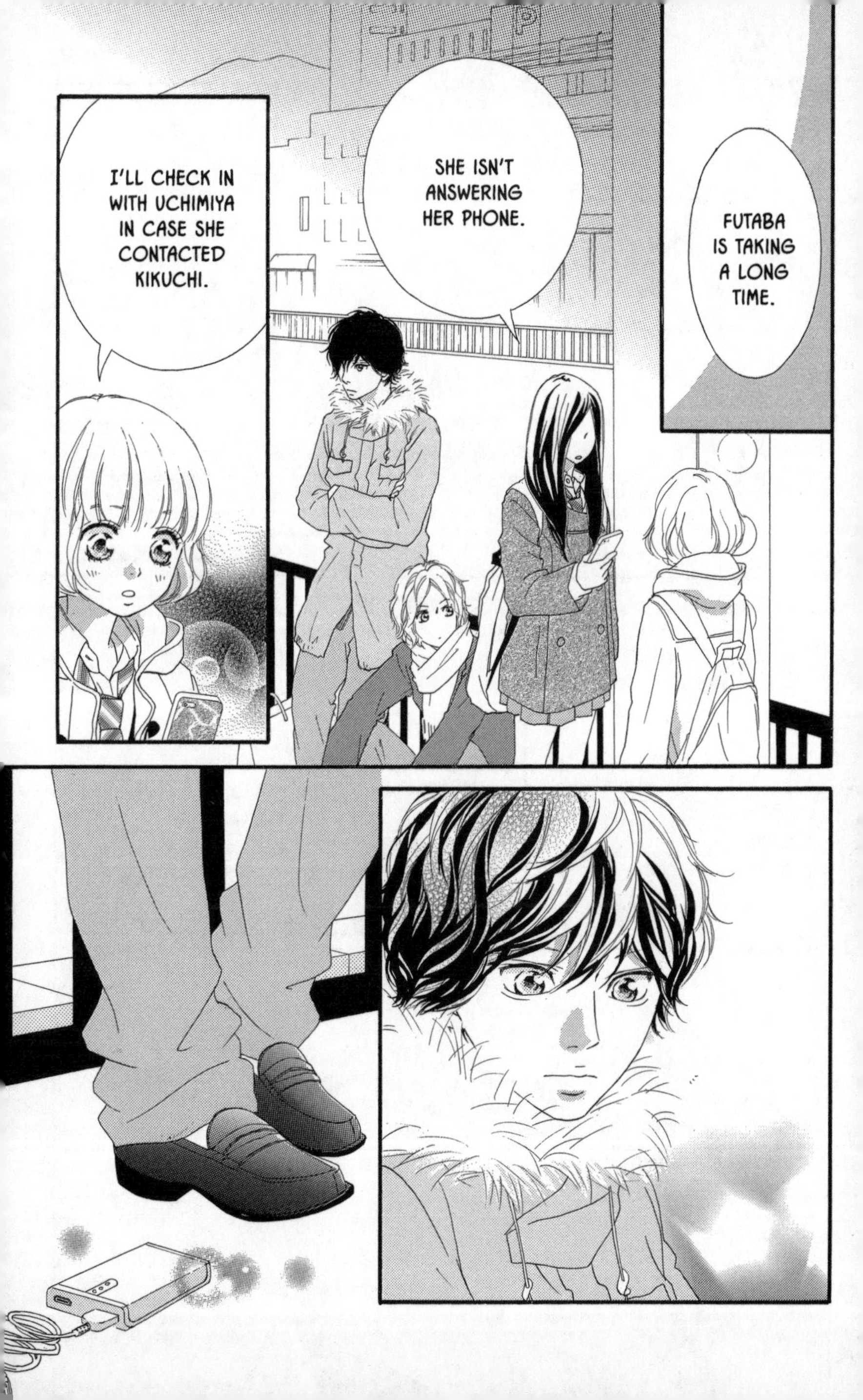
FUTABA IS TAKING A LONG TIME.
SHE ISN'T ANSWERING HER PHONE.
I'LL CHECK IN WITH UCHIMIYA IN CASE SHE CONTACTED KIKUCHI.

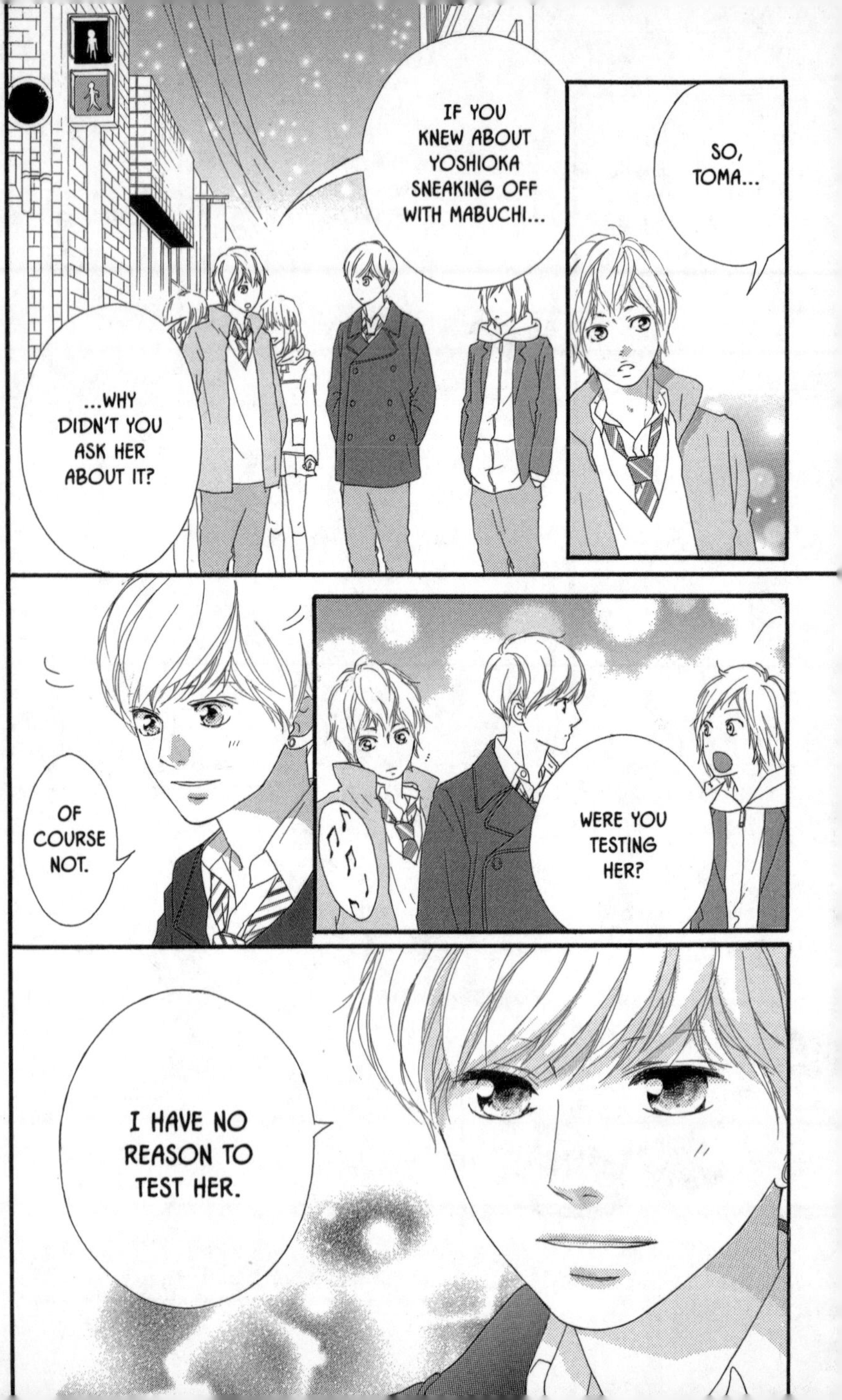
SO, TOMA...
IF YOU KNEW ABOUT YOSHIOKA SNEAKING OFF WITH MABUCHI...
...WHY DIDN'T YOU ASK HER ABOUT IT?
WERE YOU TESTING HER?
OF COURSE NOT.
I HAVE NO REASON TO TEST HER.

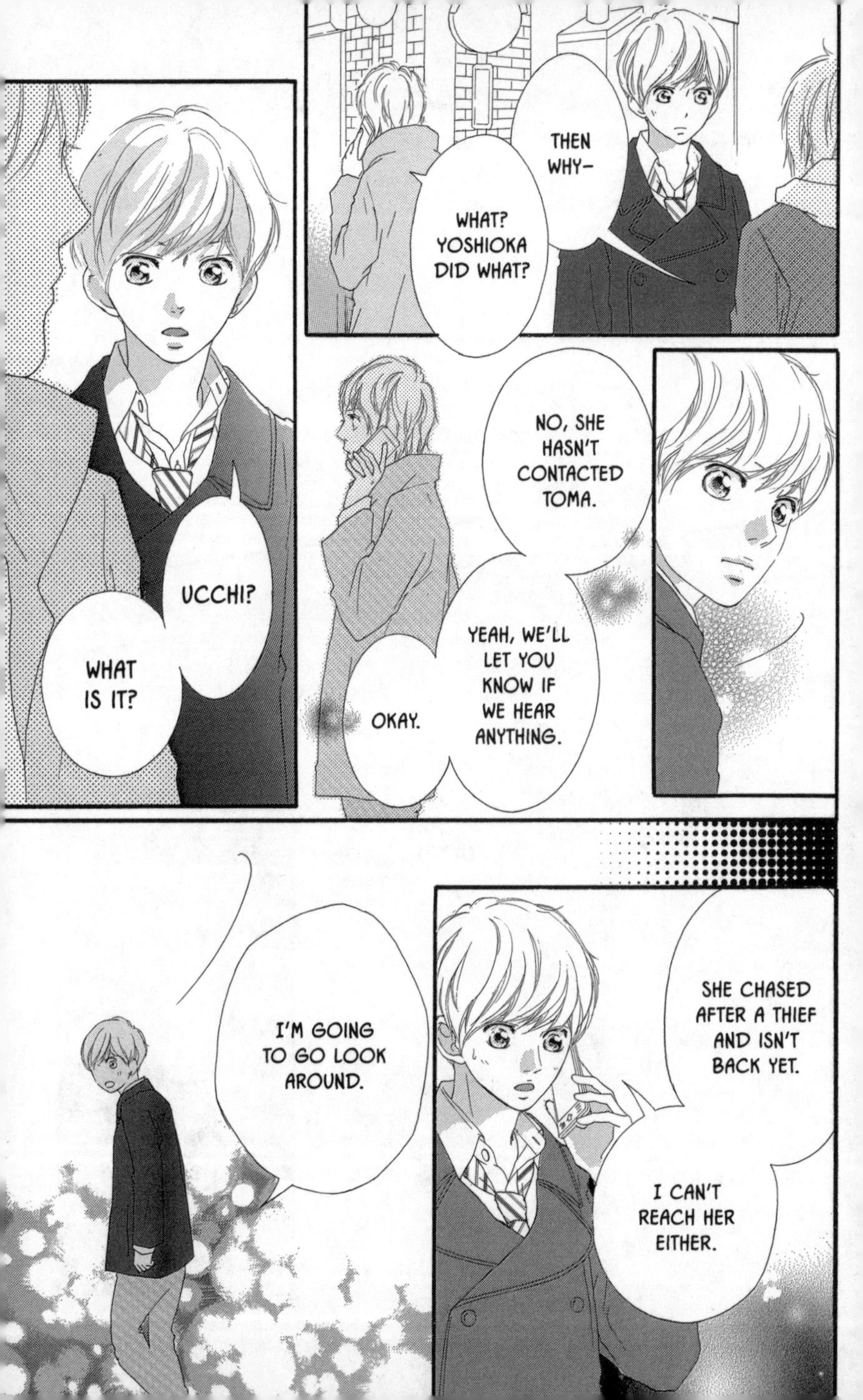
THEN WHY—
WHAT? YOSHIOKA DID WHAT?
NO, SHE HASN'T CONTACTED TOMA.
YEAH, WE'LL LET YOU KNOW IF WE HEAR ANYTHING.
OKAY.
UCCHI?
WHAT IS IT?
SHE CHASED AFTER A THIEF AND ISN'T BACK YET.
I CAN'T REACH HER EITHER.
I'M GOING TO GO LOOK AROUND.

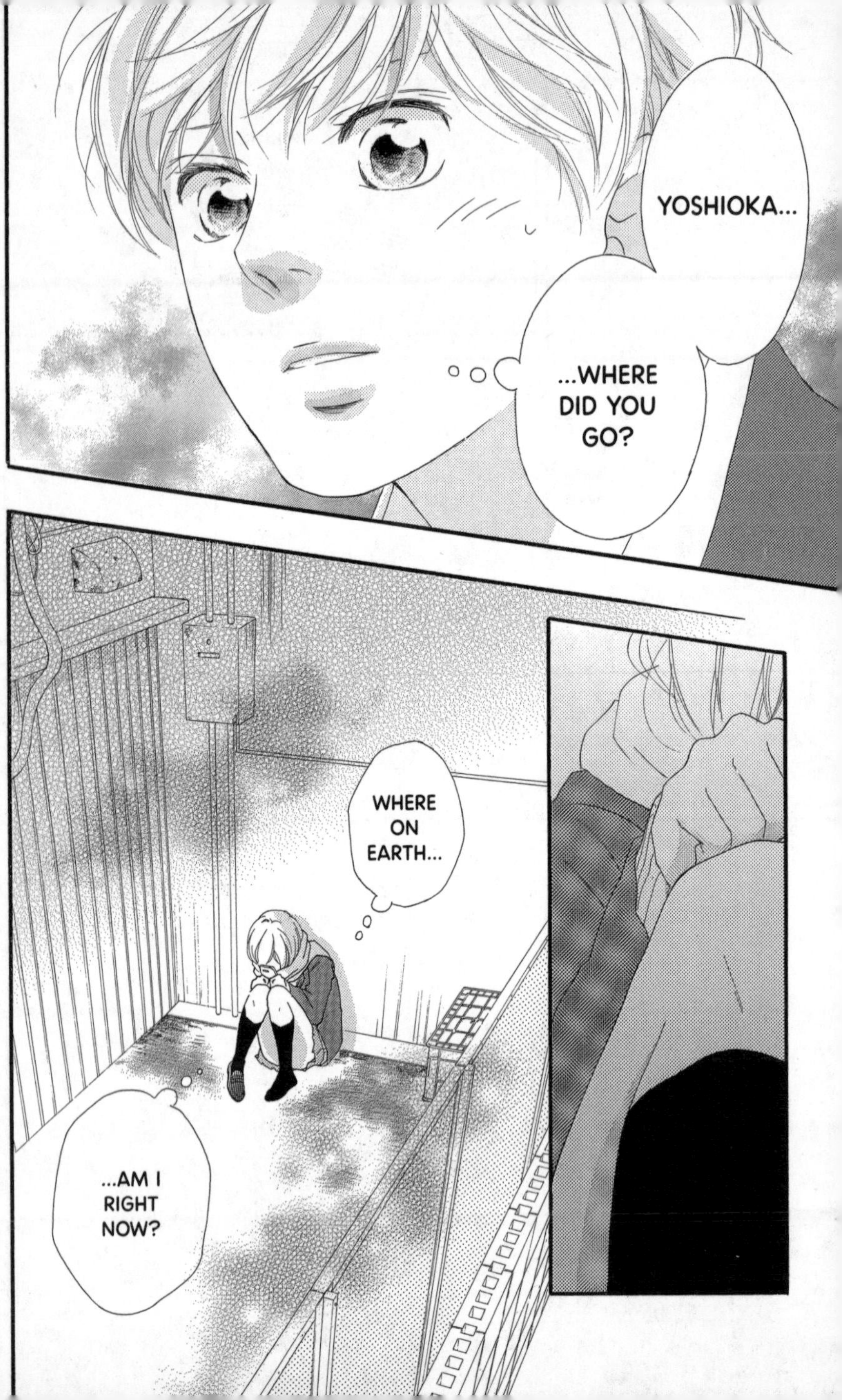
YOSHIOKA...
...WHERE DID YOU GO?
WHERE ON EARTH...
...AM I RIGHT NOW?

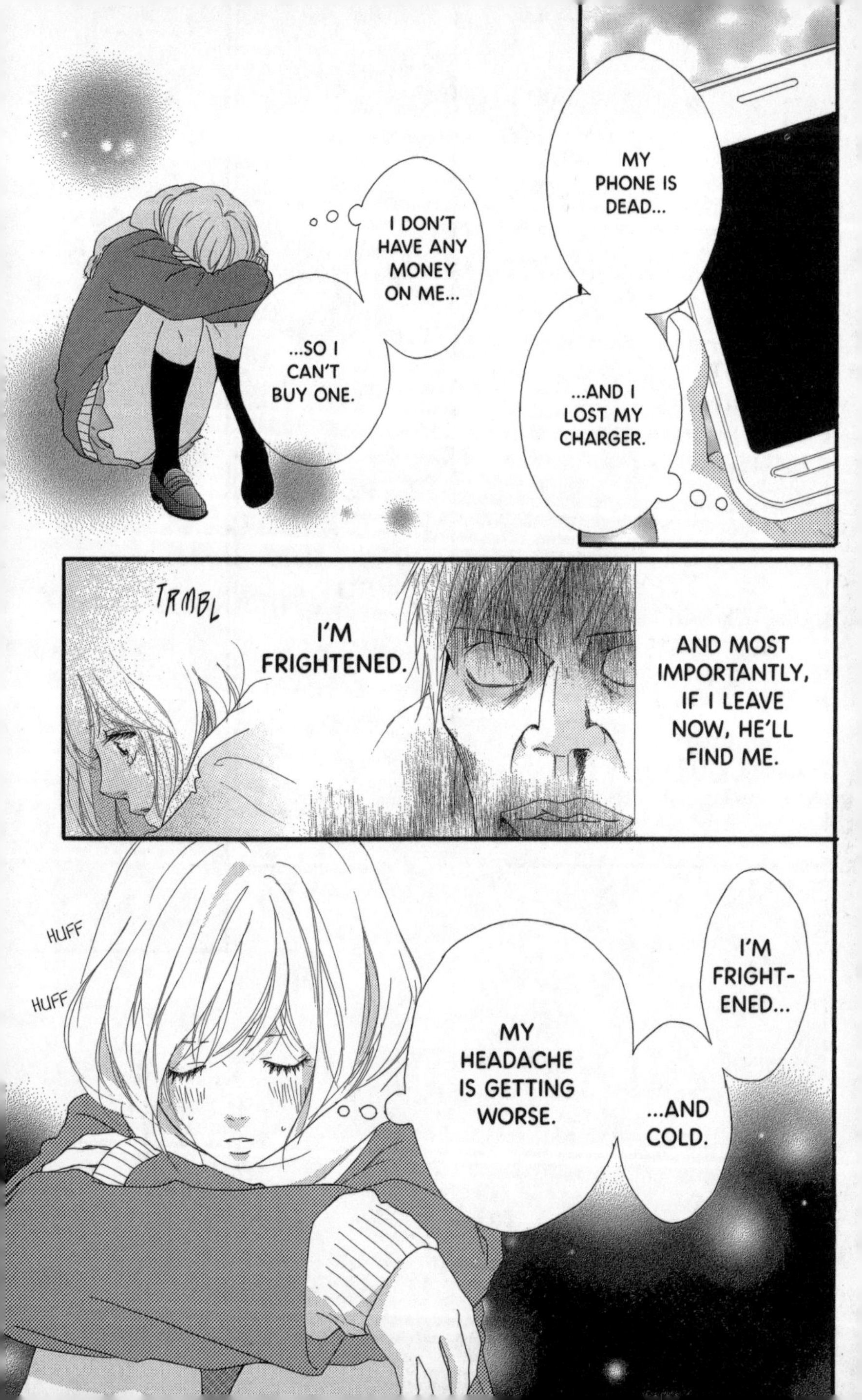
MY PHONE IS DEAD...
...AND I LOST MY CHARGER.
I DON'T HAVE ANY MONEY ON ME...
...SO I CAN'T BUY ONE.
AND MOST IMPORTANTLY, IF I LEAVE NOW, HE'LL FIND ME.
I'M FRIGHTENED.
TRMBL
I'M FRIGHT-ENED...
...AND COLD.
MY HEADACHE IS GETTING WORSE.
HUFF
HUFF

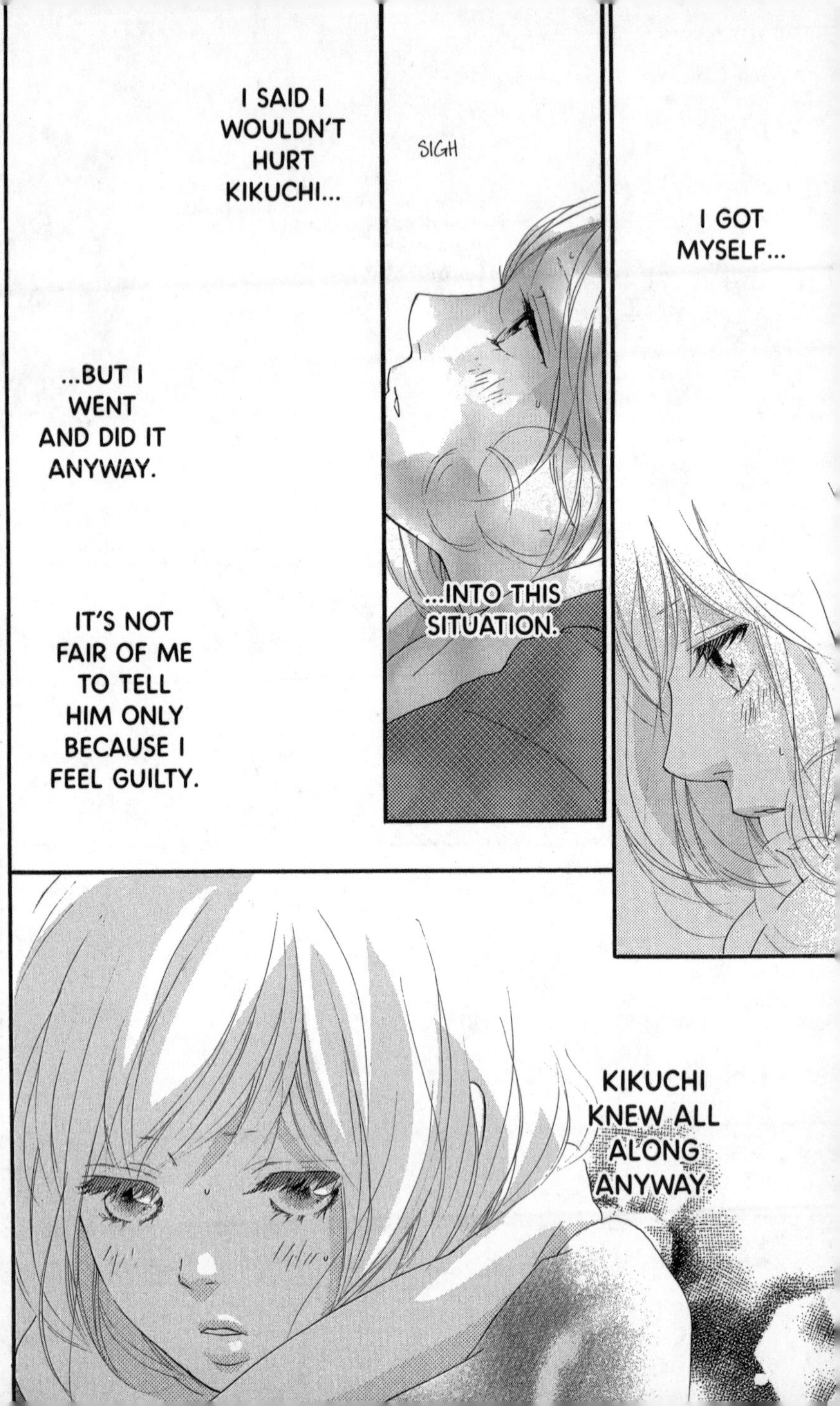
I GOT MYSELF...
SIGH
...INTO THIS SITUATION.
I SAID I WOULDN'T HURT KIKUCHI...
...BUT I WENT AND DID IT ANYWAY.
IT'S NOT FAIR OF ME TO TELL HIM ONLY BECAUSE I FEEL GUILTY.
KIKUCHI KNEW ALL ALONG ANYWAY.

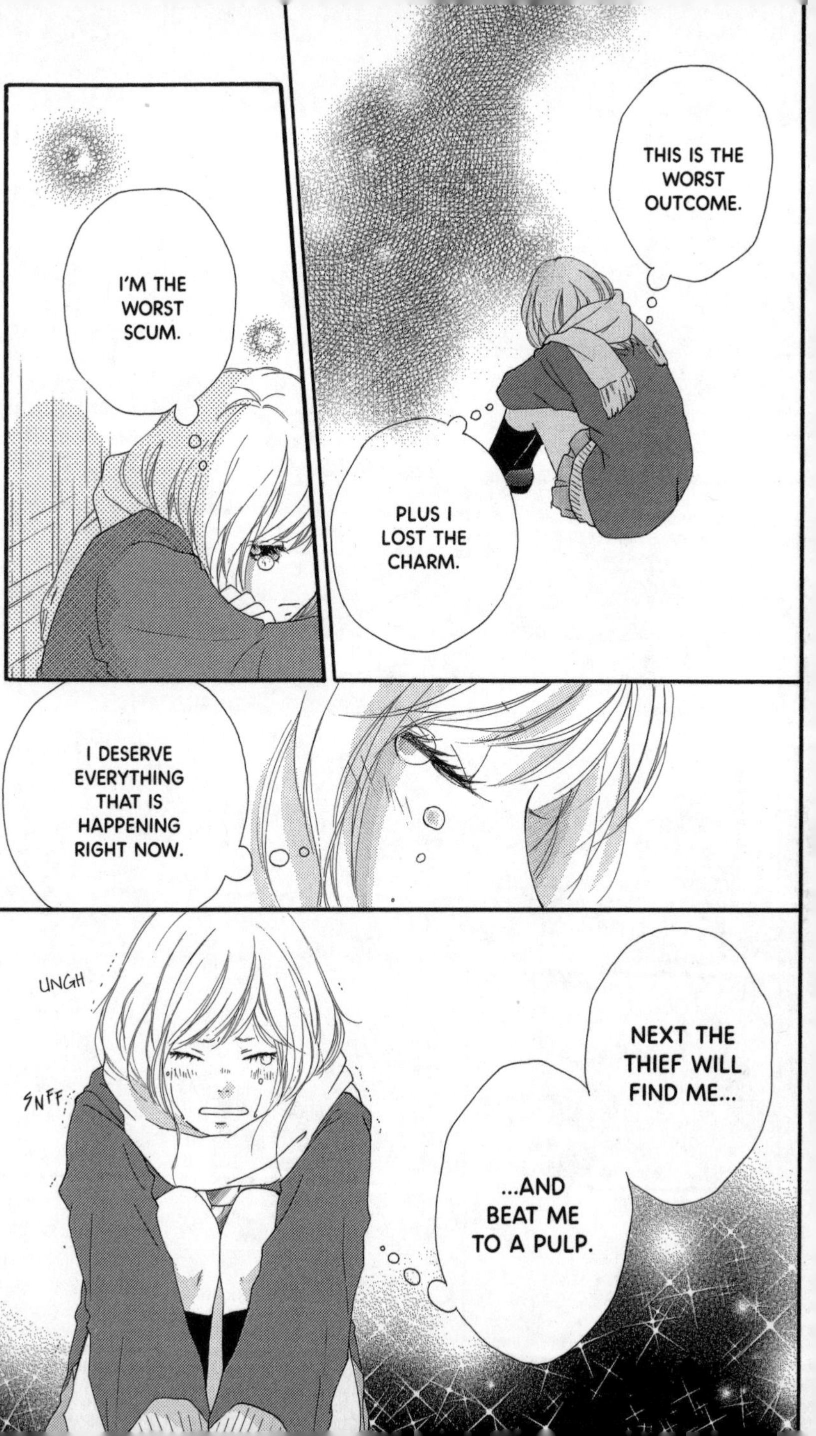
THIS IS THE WORST OUTCOME.
PLUS I LOST THE CHARM.
I'M THE WORST SCUM.
I DESERVE EVERYTHING THAT IS HAPPENING RIGHT NOW.
NEXT THE THIEF WILL FIND ME...
...AND BEAT ME TO A PULP.
UNGH
SNFF

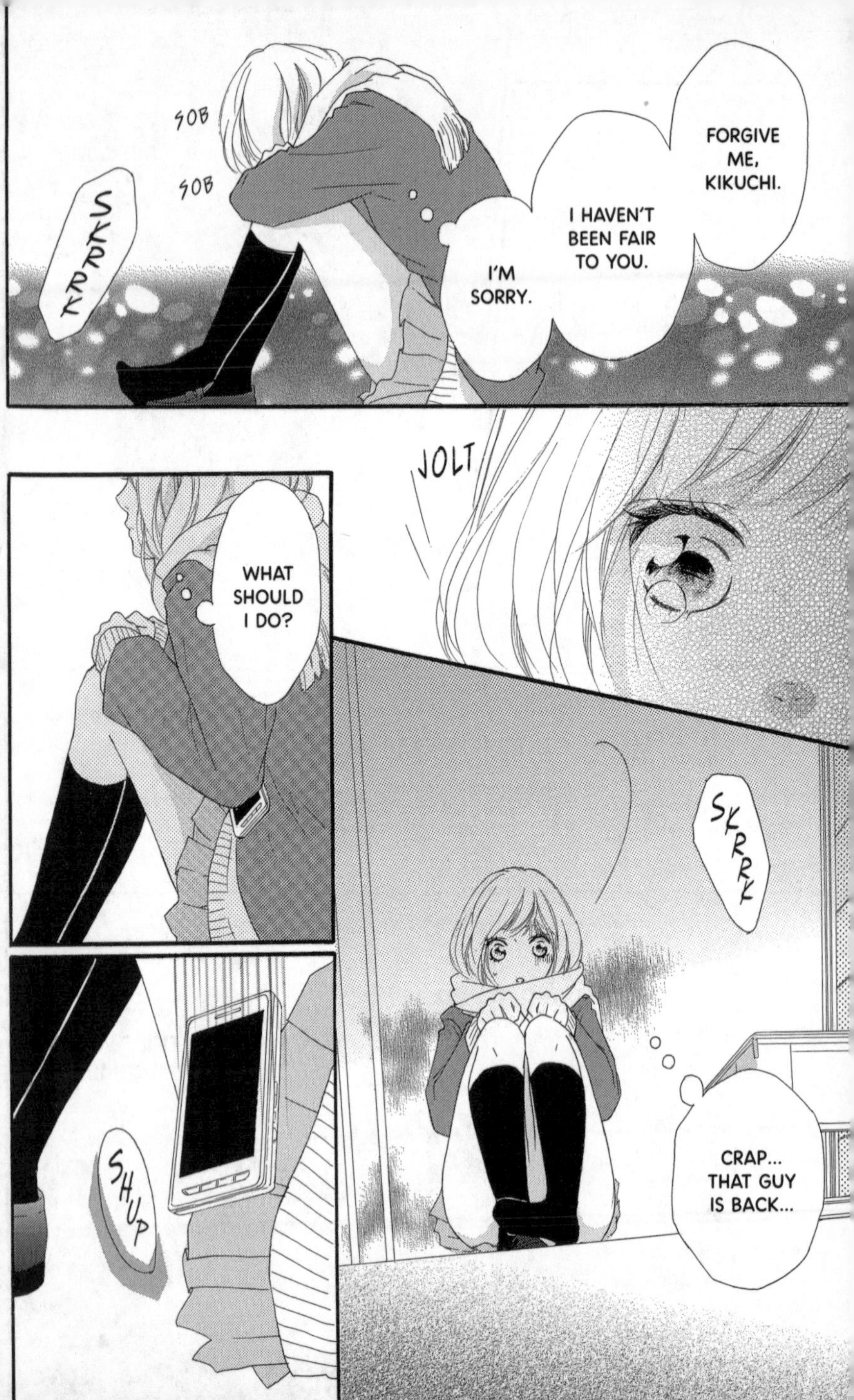
FORGIVE ME, KIKUCHI.
I HAVEN'T BEEN FAIR TO YOU.
I'M SORRY.
SOB
SOB
SKRRK
JOLT
SKRRK
CRAP... THAT GUY IS BACK...
WHAT SHOULD I DO?
SHUP

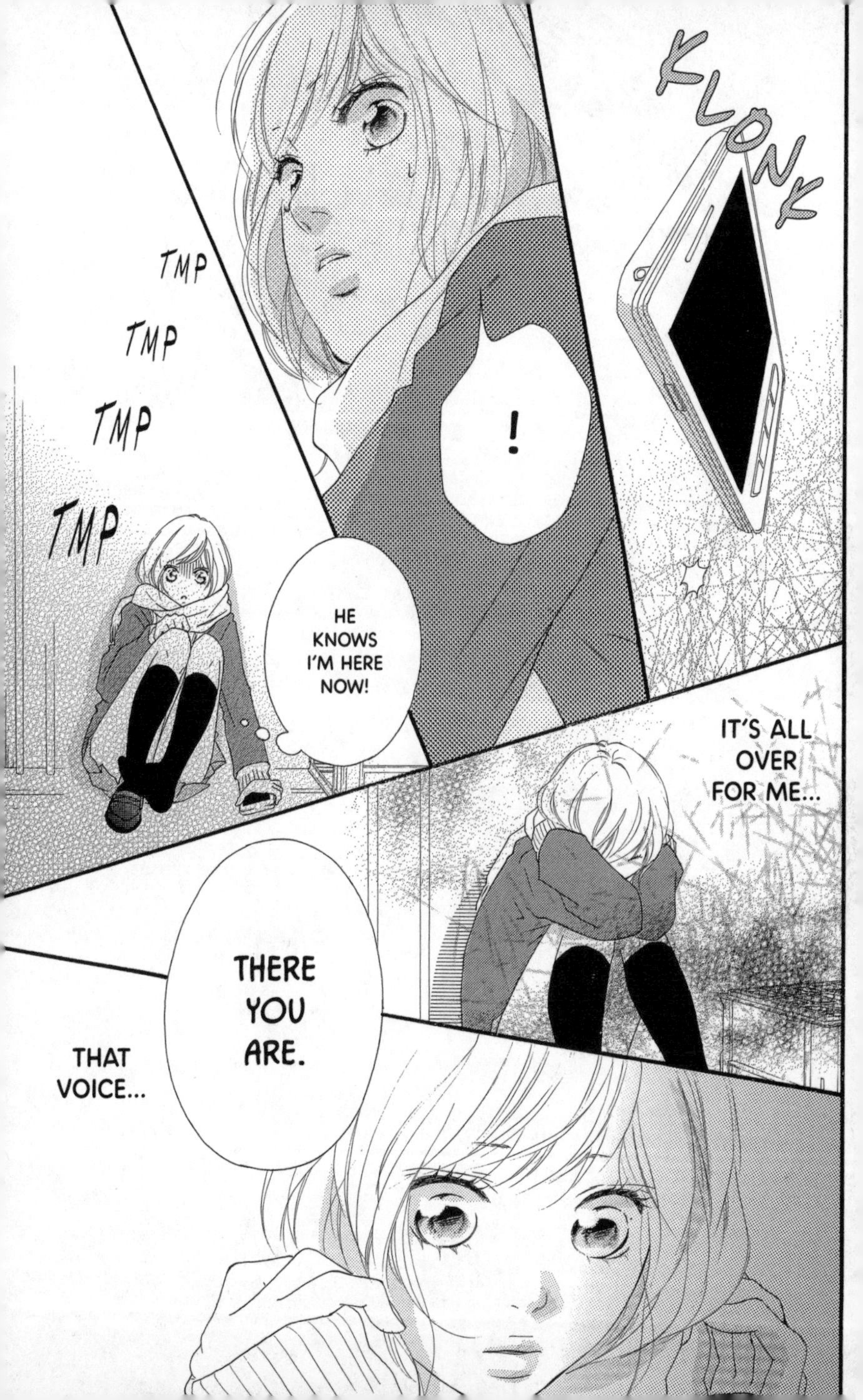
KLONK
!
TMP
TMP
TMP
TMP
HE KNOWS I'M HERE NOW!
IT'S ALL OVER FOR ME...
THERE YOU ARE.
THAT VOICE...

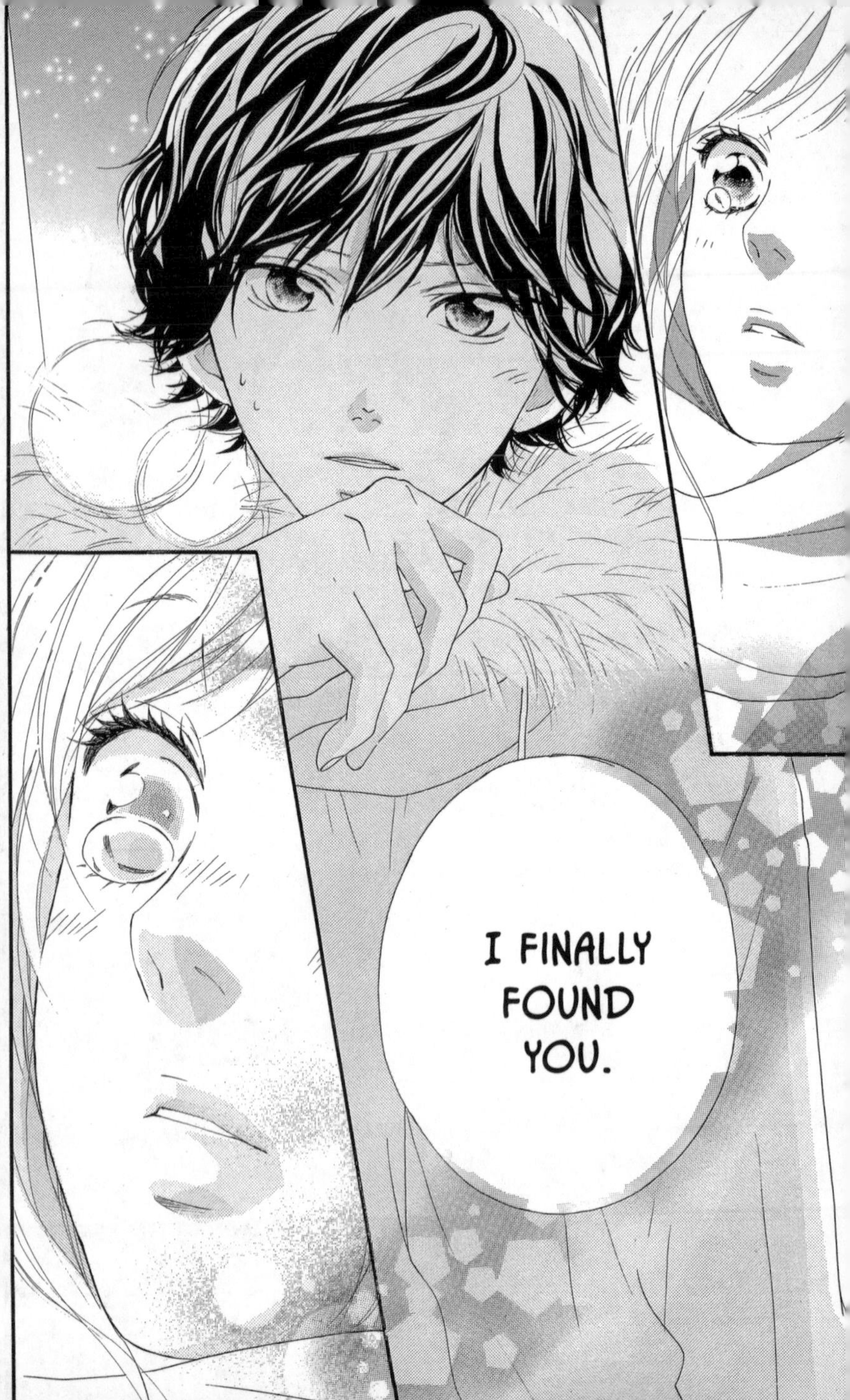
I FINALLY FOUND YOU.

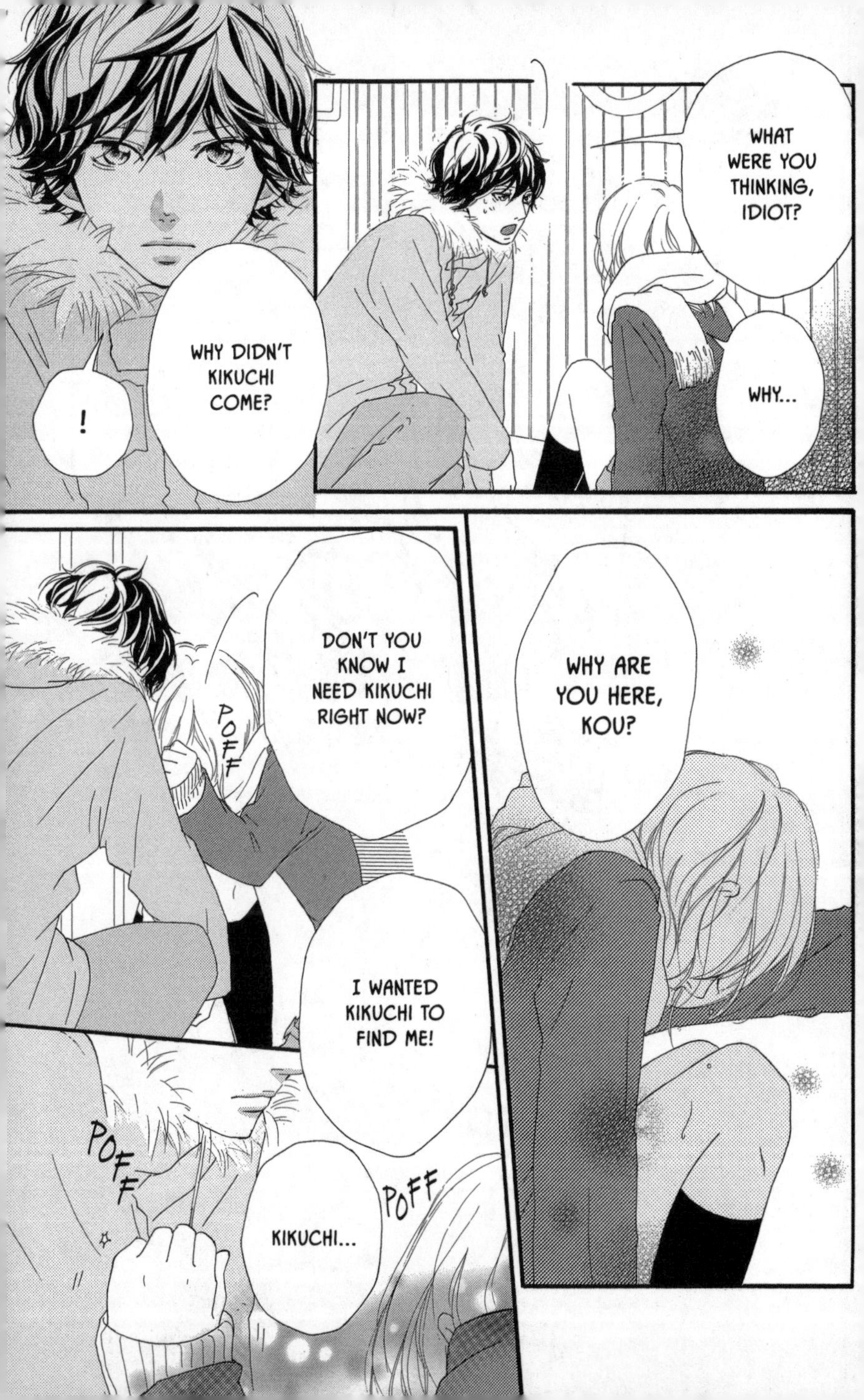
WHAT WERE YOU THINKING, IDIOT?
WHY...
WHY DIDN'T KIKUCHI COME?
!
WHY ARE YOU HERE, KOU?
DON'T YOU KNOW I NEED KIKUCHI RIGHT NOW?
POFF
I WANTED KIKUCHI TO FIND ME!
POFF
KIKUCHI...
POFF

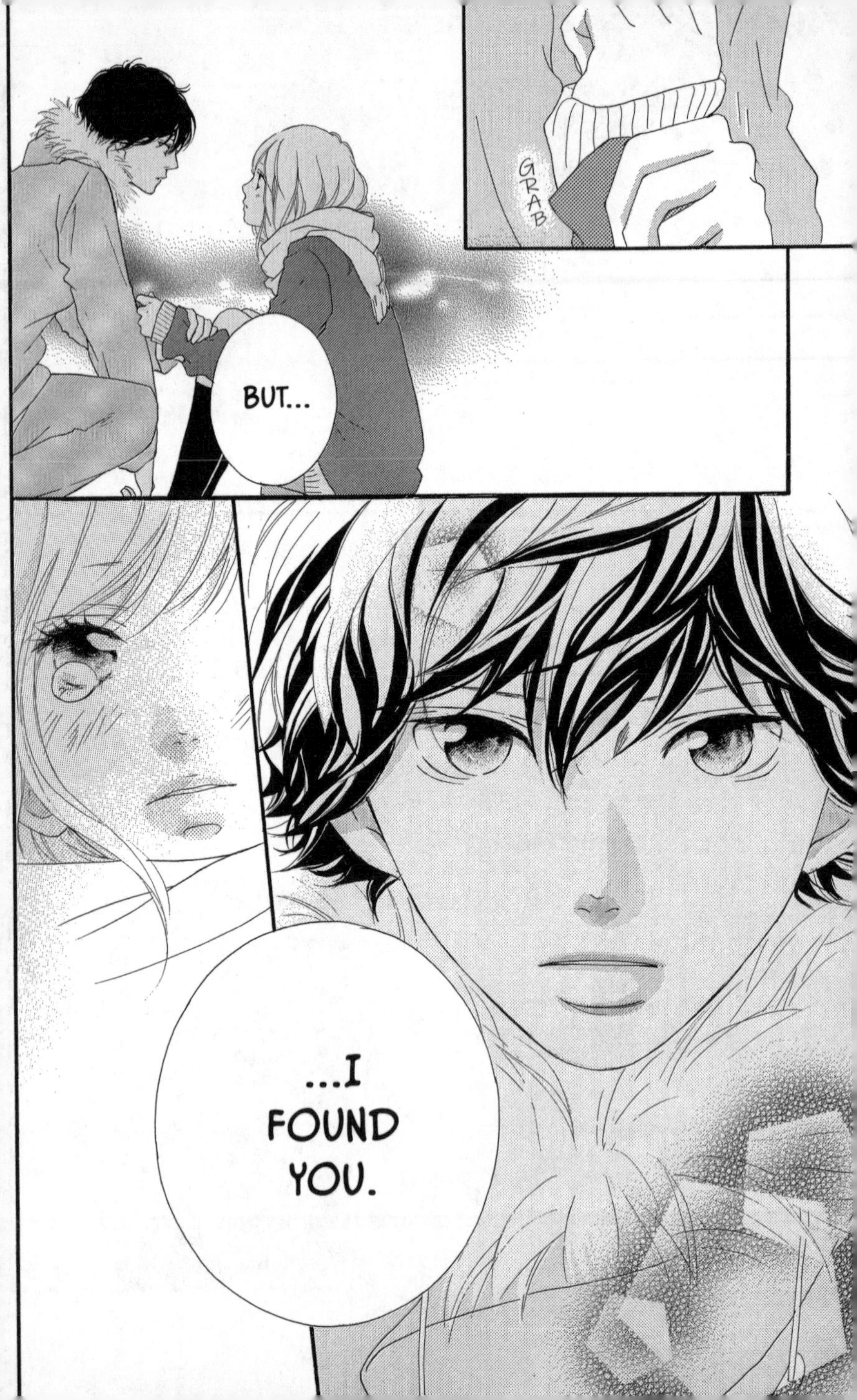
GRAB
BUT...
...I FOUND YOU.

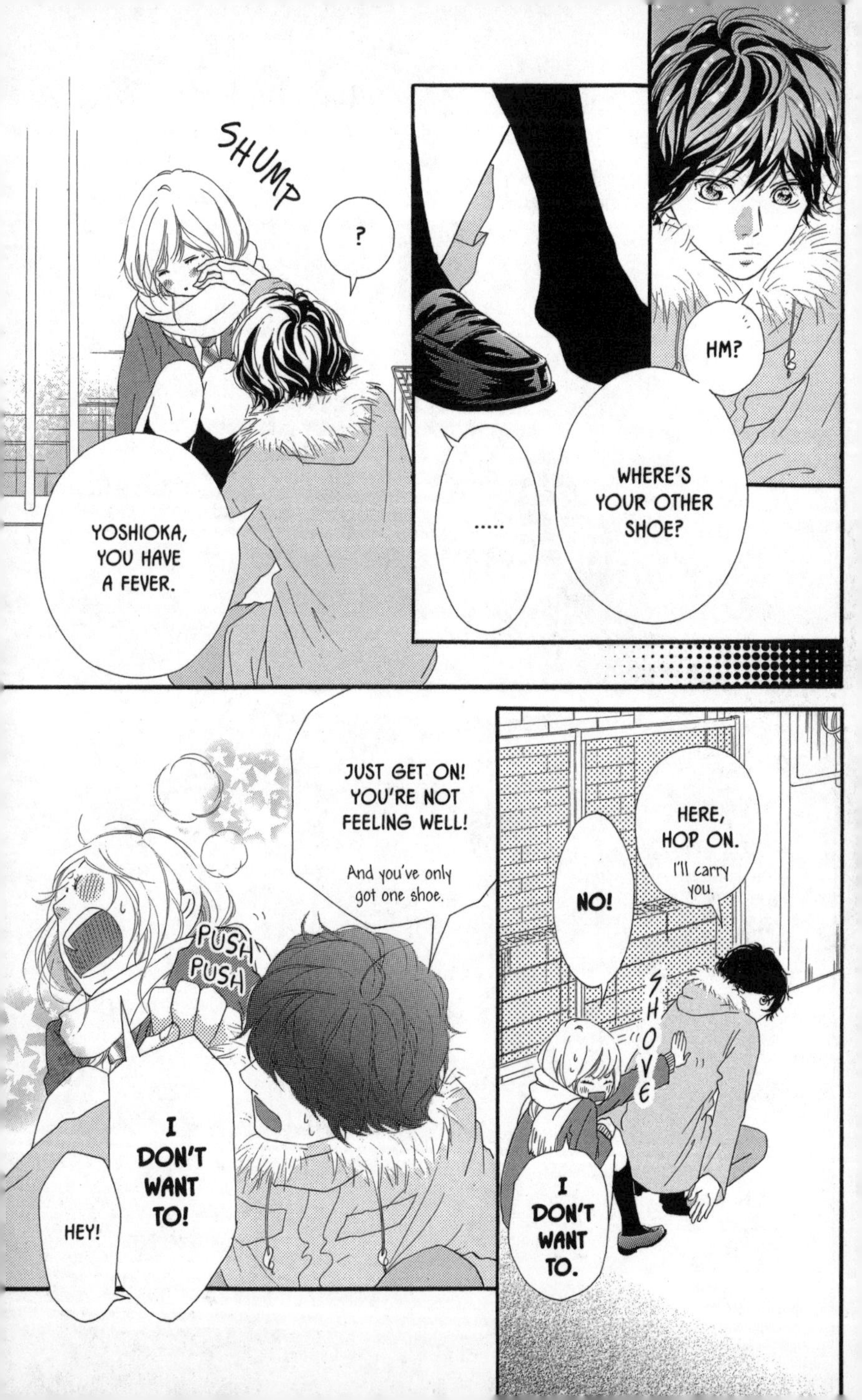
HM?
WHERE'S YOUR OTHER SHOE?
.....
SHUMP
?
YOSHIOKA, YOU HAVE A FEVER.
HERE, HOP ON.
I'll carry you.
NO!
SHOVE
I DON'T WANT TO.
JUST GET ON! YOU'RE NOT FEELING WELL!
And you've only got one shoe.
PUSH PUSH
I DON'T WANT TO!
HEY!

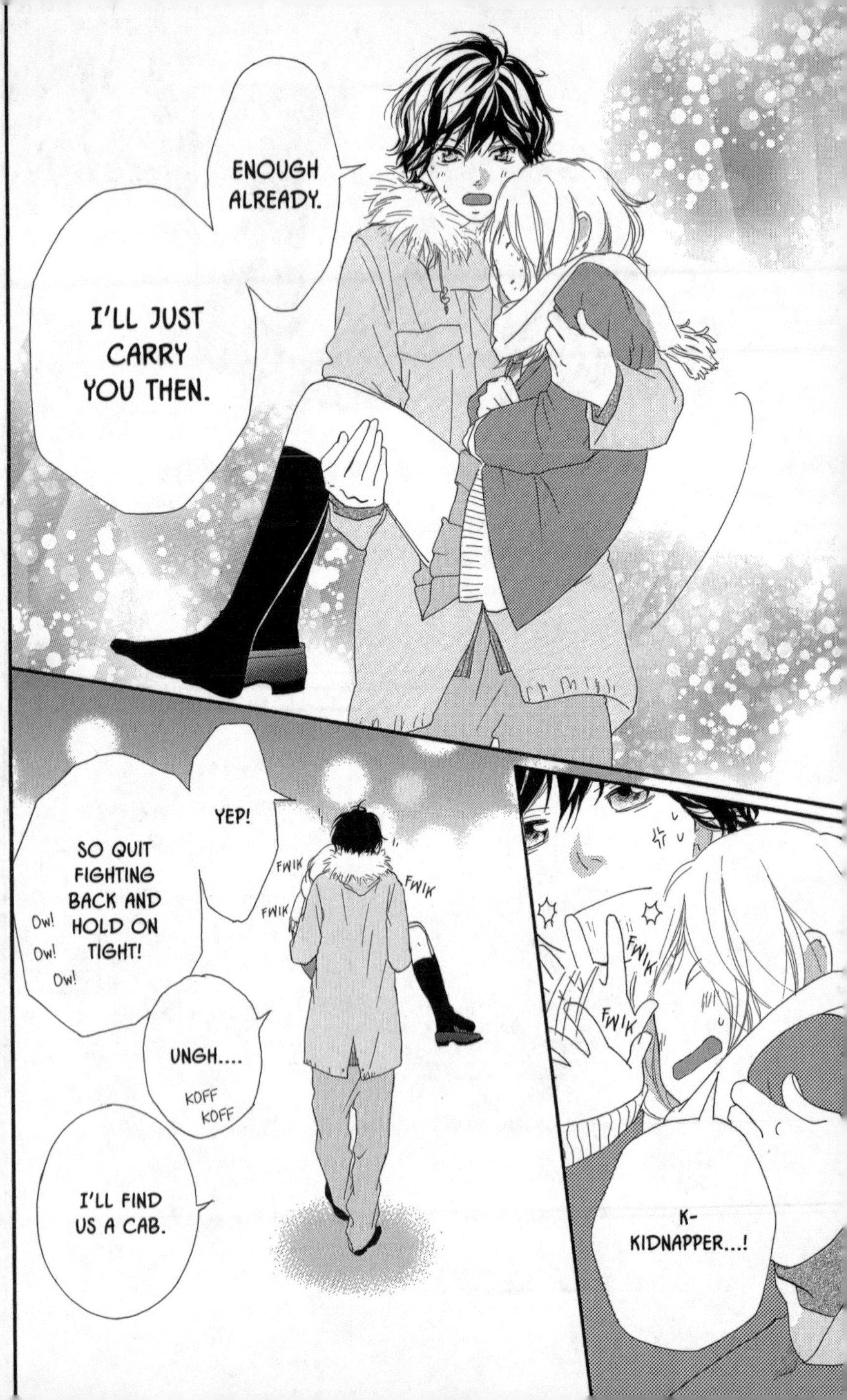
ENOUGH ALREADY.
I'LL JUST CARRY YOU THEN.
FWIK
FWIK
K-KIDNAPPER...!
YEP!
FWIK
FWIK
FWIK
SO QUIT FIGHTING BACK AND HOLD ON TIGHT!
Ow!
Ow!
Ow!
UNGH....
KOFF KOFF
I'LL FIND US A CAB.

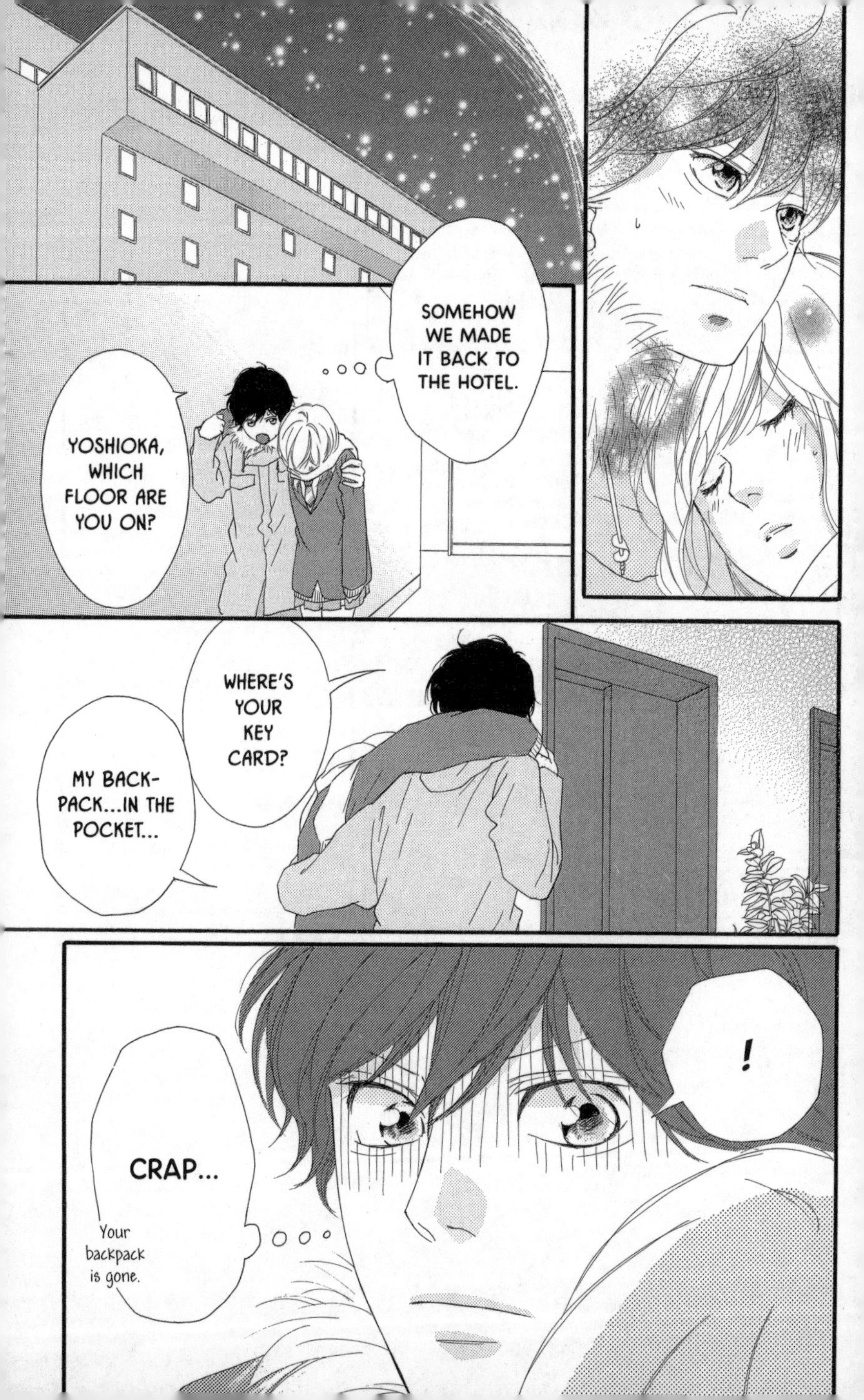
SOMEHOW WE MADE IT BACK TO THE HOTEL.
YOSHIOKA, WHICH FLOOR ARE YOU ON?
WHERE'S YOUR KEY CARD?
MY BACK-PACK...IN THE POCKET...
!
CRAP...
Your backpack is gone.

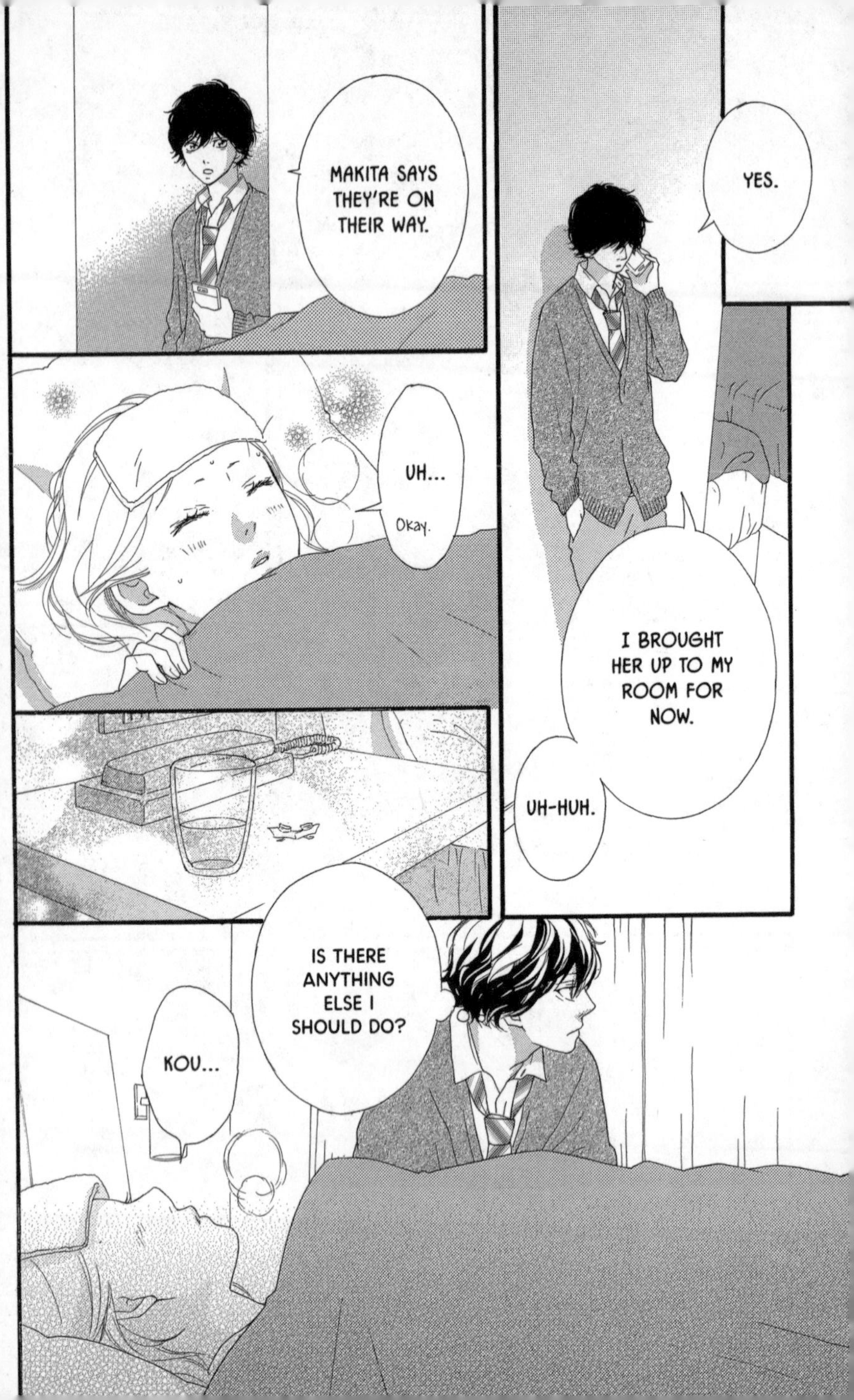
YES.
I BROUGHT HER UP TO MY ROOM FOR NOW.
UH-HUH.
MAKITA SAYS THEY'RE ON THEIR WAY.
UH...
Okay.
IS THERE ANYTHING ELSE I SHOULD DO?
KOU...

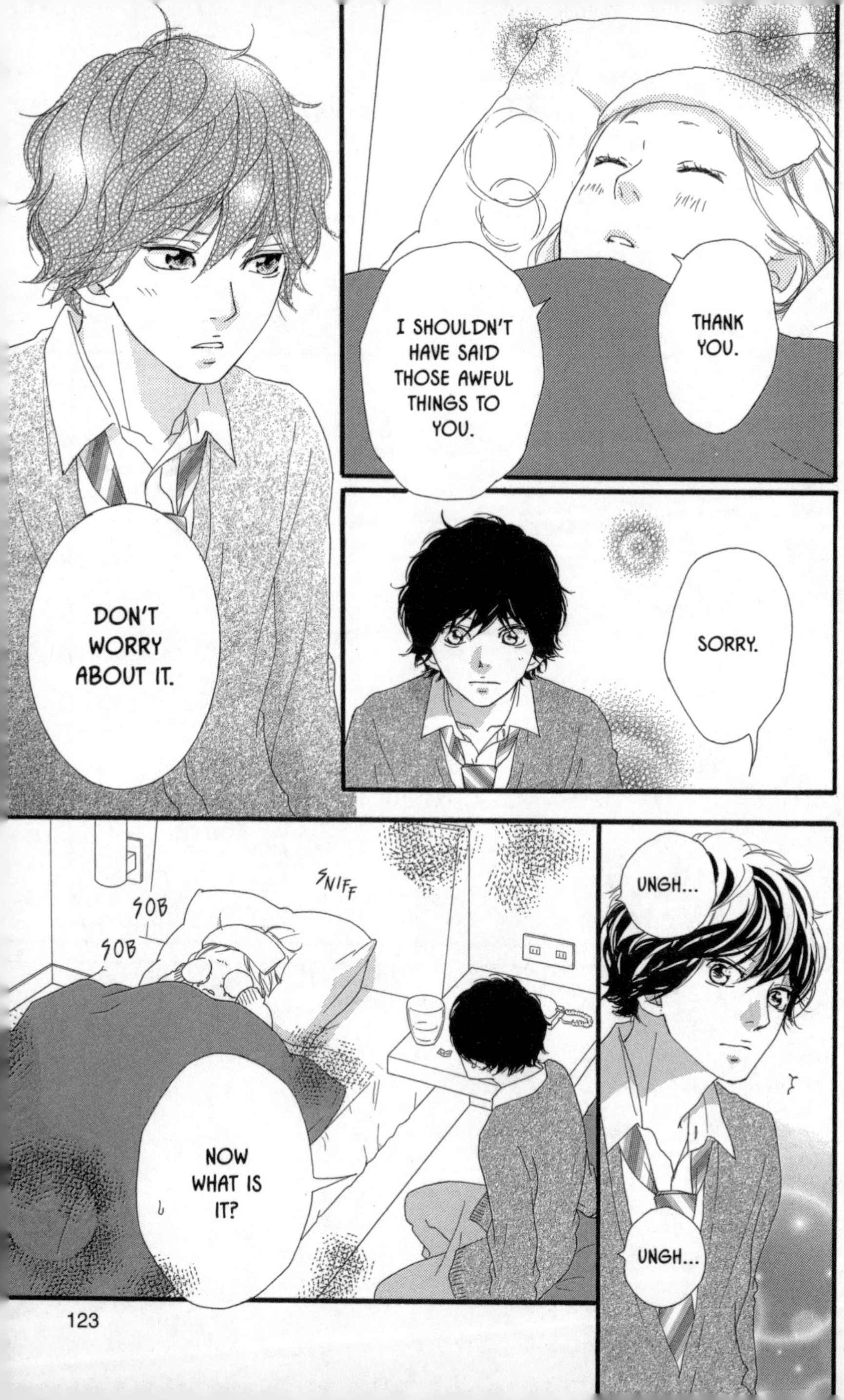
THANK YOU.
I SHOULDN'T HAVE SAID THOSE AWFUL THINGS TO YOU.
SORRY.
DON'T WORRY ABOUT IT.
UNGH...
UNGH...
SNIFF
SOB
SOB
NOW WHAT IS IT?

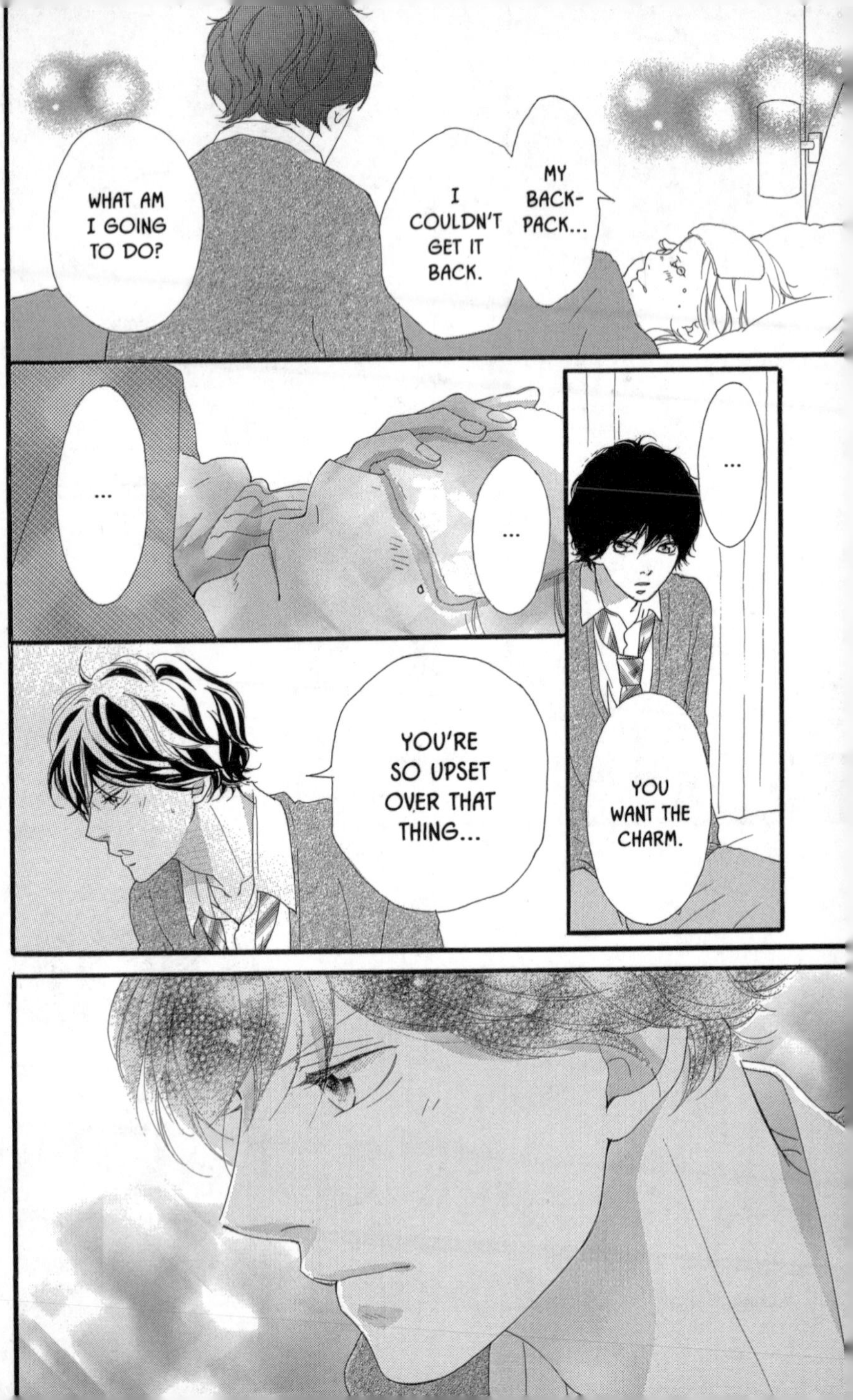
MY BACKPACK...
I COULDN'T GET IT BACK.
WHAT AM I GOING TO DO?
...
YOU WANT THE CHARM.
...
...
YOU'RE SO UPSET OVER THAT THING...

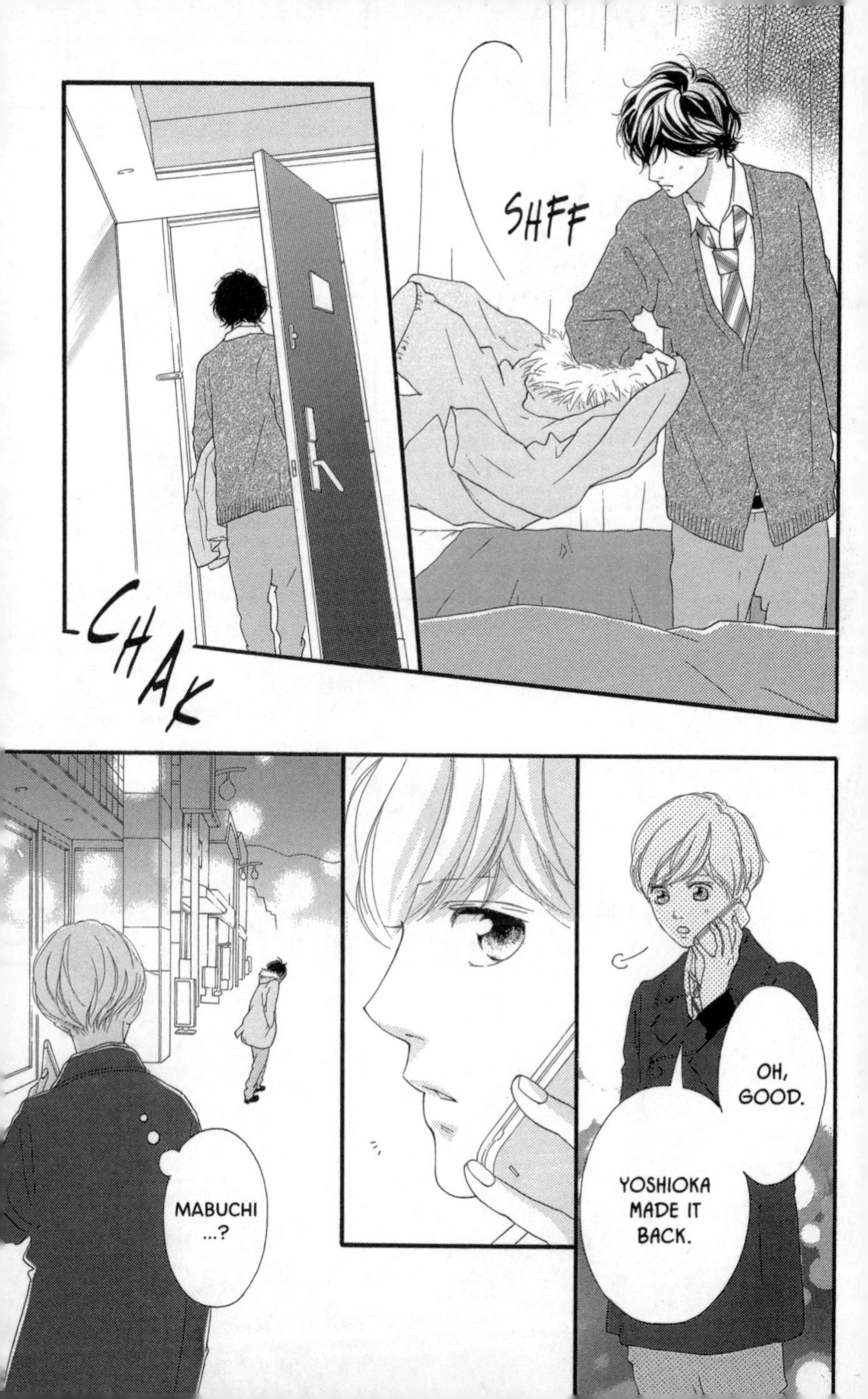
SHFF
CHAK
OH, GOOD.
YOSHIOKA MADE IT BACK.
MABUCHI ...?

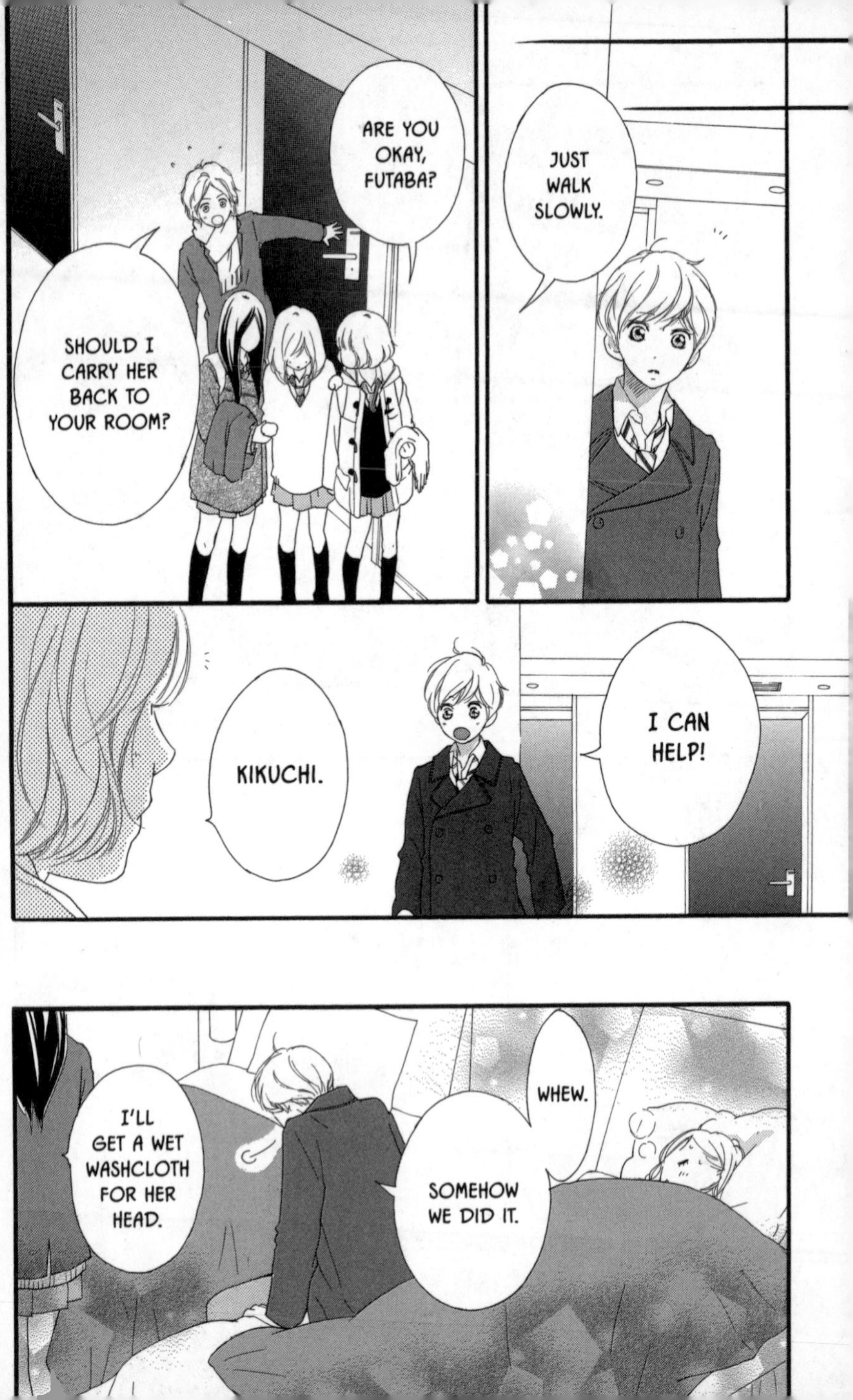
JUST WALK SLOWLY.
ARE YOU OKAY, FUTABA?
SHOULD I CARRY HER BACK TO YOUR ROOM?
I CAN HELP!
KIKUCHI.
WHEW.
SOMEHOW WE DID IT.
I'LL GET A WET WASHCLOTH FOR HER HEAD.

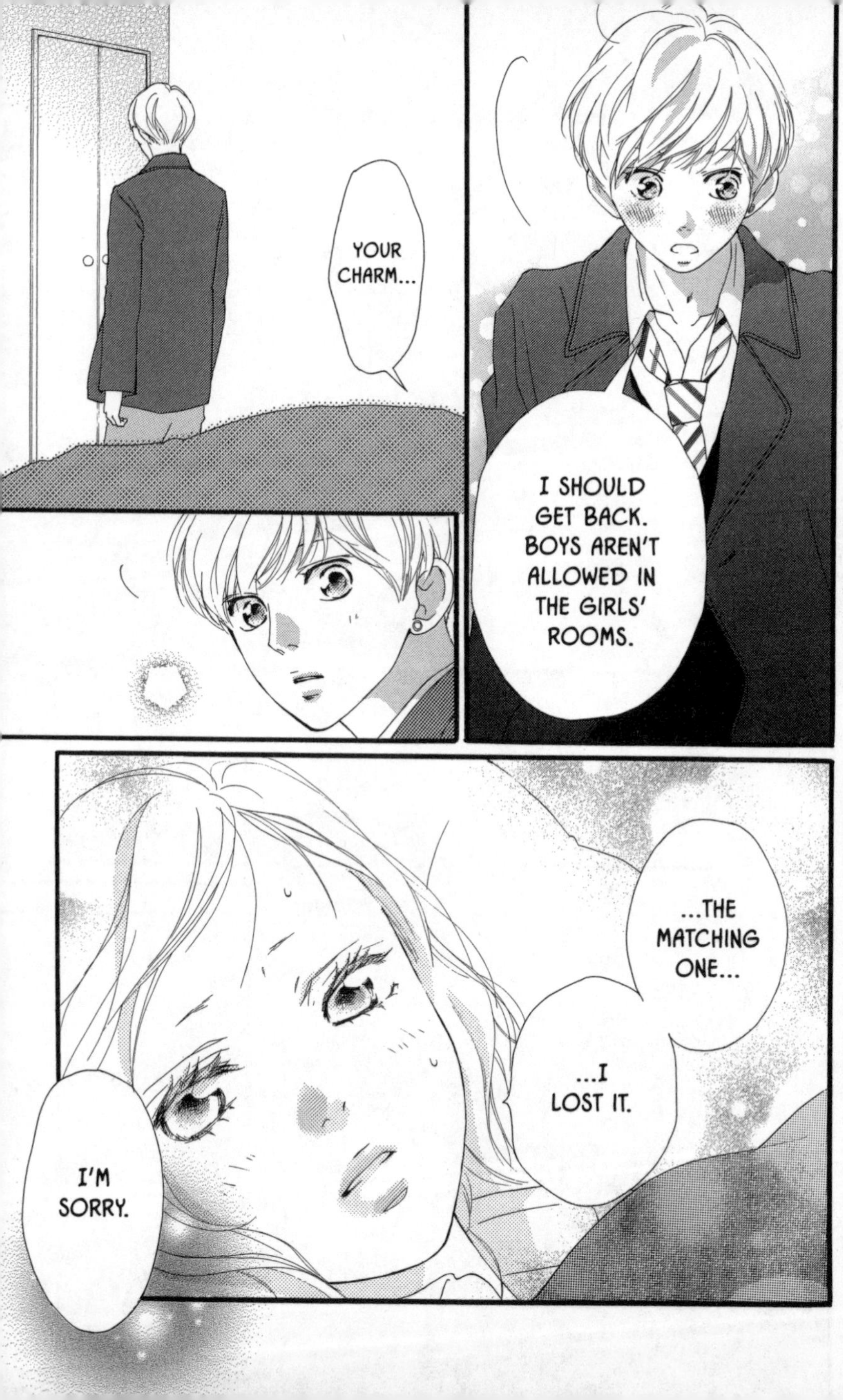
I SHOULD GET BACK. BOYS AREN'T ALLOWED IN THE GIRLS' ROOMS.
YOUR CHARM...
...THE MATCHING ONE...
...I LOST IT.
I'M SORRY.

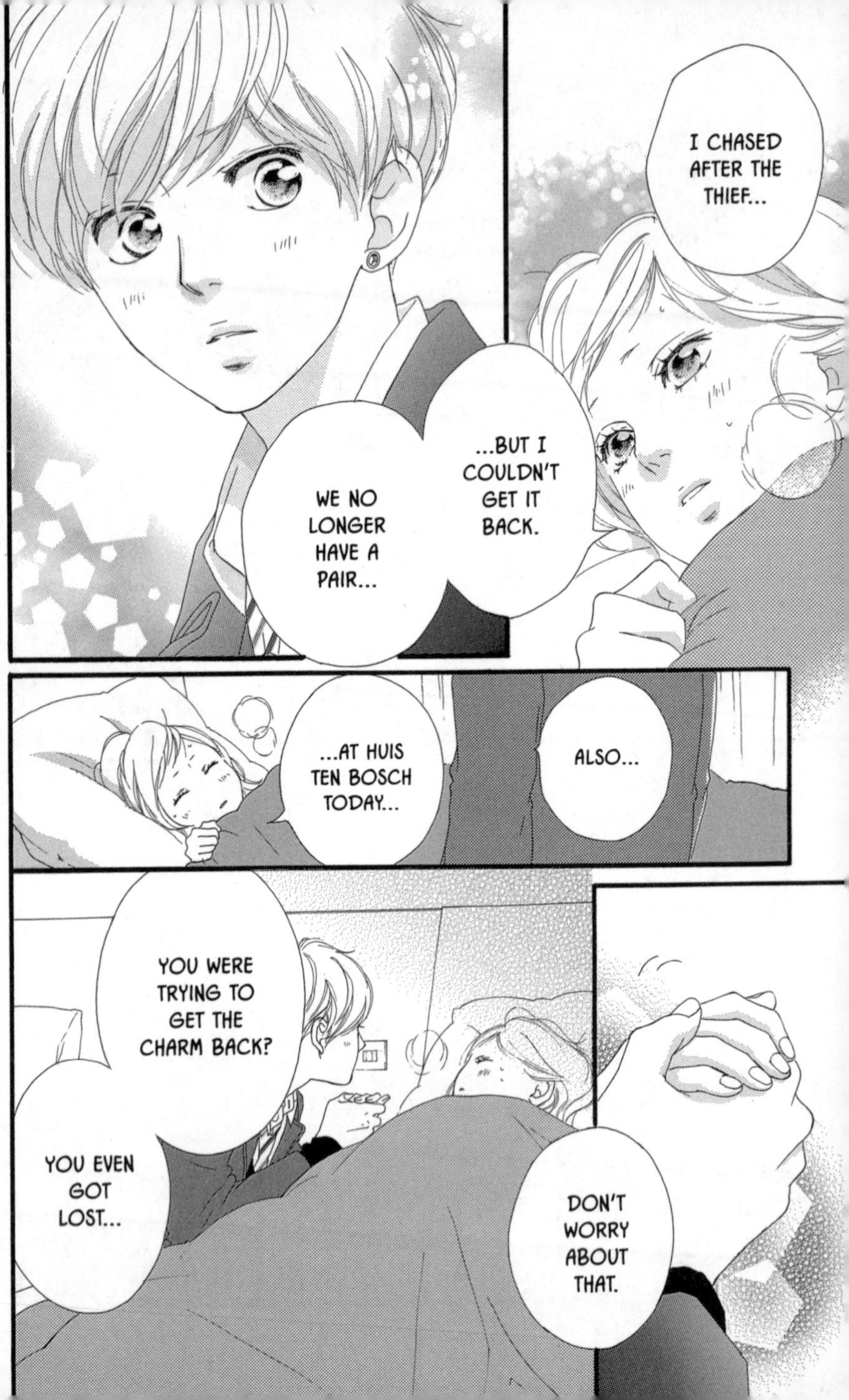
I CHASED AFTER THE THIEF...
...BUT I COULDN'T GET IT BACK.
WE NO LONGER HAVE A PAIR...
ALSO...
...AT HUIS TEN BOSCH TODAY...
YOU WERE TRYING TO GET THE CHARM BACK?
YOU EVEN GOT LOST...
DON'T WORRY ABOUT THAT.

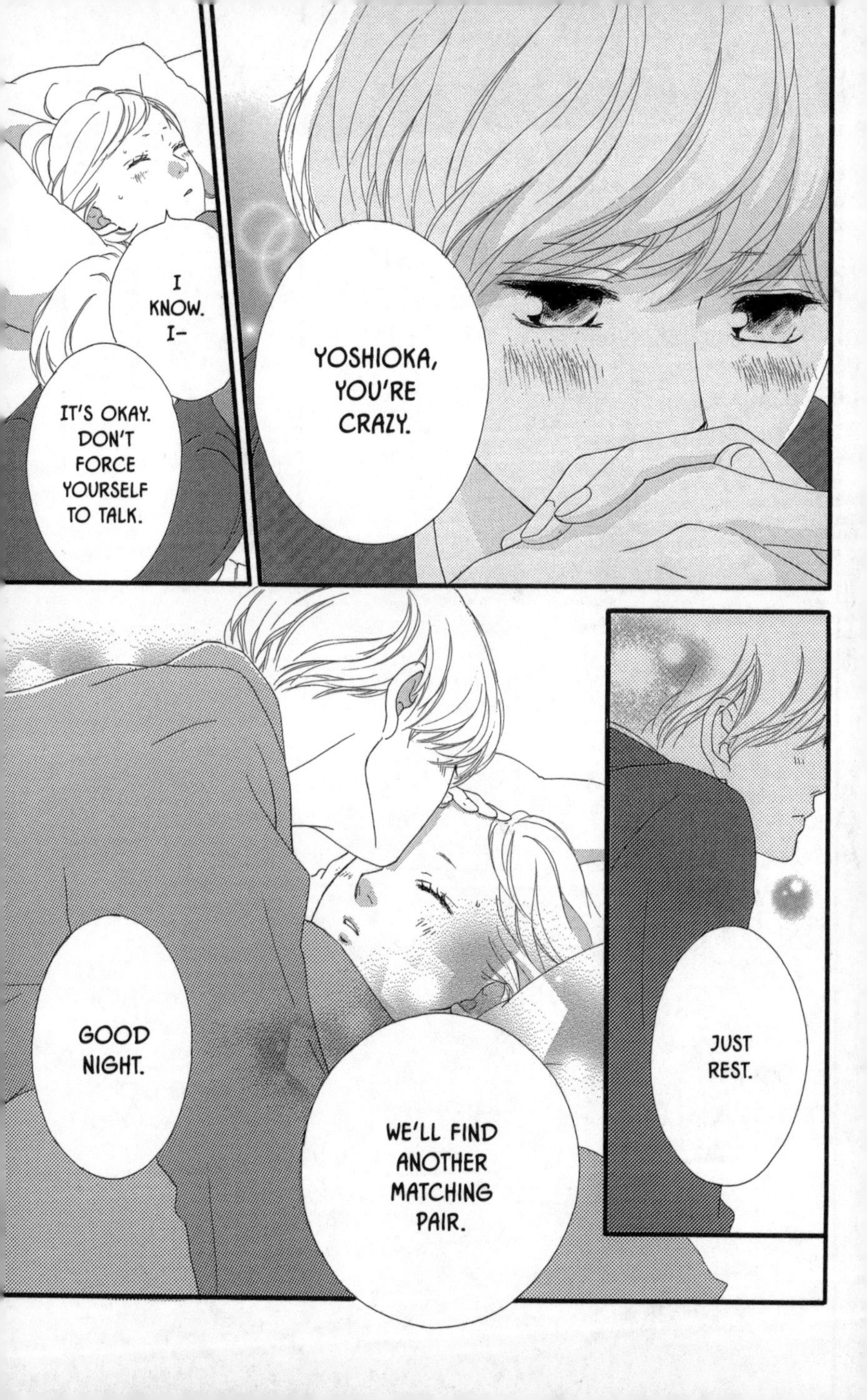
YOSHIOKA, YOU'RE CRAZY.
I KNOW. I–
IT'S OKAY. DON'T FORCE YOURSELF TO TALK.
JUST REST.
WE'LL FIND ANOTHER MATCHING PAIR.
GOOD NIGHT.

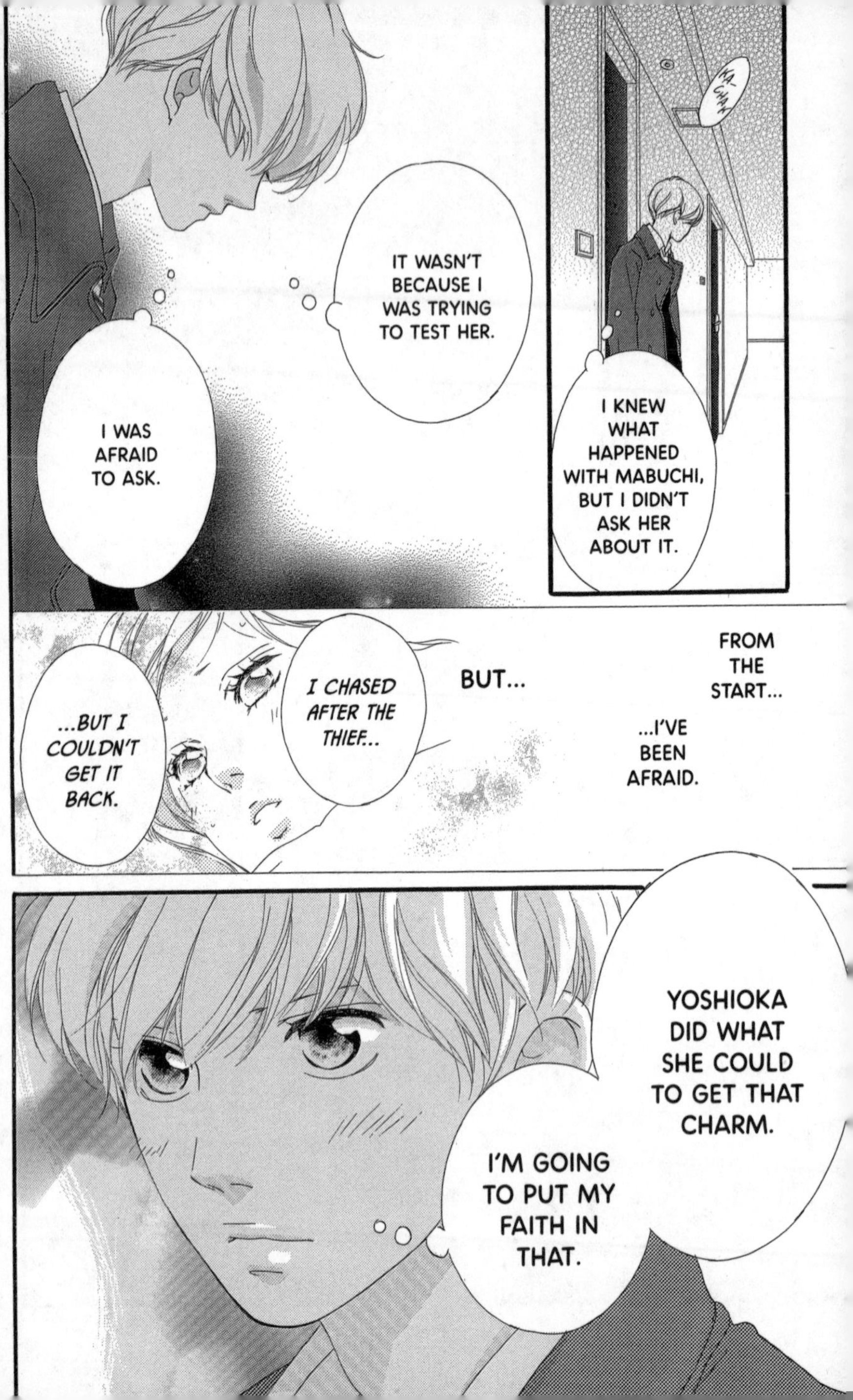
KA-CHAK
I KNEW WHAT HAPPENED WITH MABUCHI, BUT I DIDN'T ASK HER ABOUT IT.
IT WASN'T BECAUSE I WAS TRYING TO TEST HER.
I WAS AFRAID TO ASK.
FROM THE START...
...I'VE BEEN AFRAID.
BUT...
I CHASED AFTER THE THIEF...
...BUT I COULDN'T GET IT BACK.
YOSHIOKA DID WHAT SHE COULD TO GET THAT CHARM.
I'M GOING TO PUT MY FAITH IN THAT.

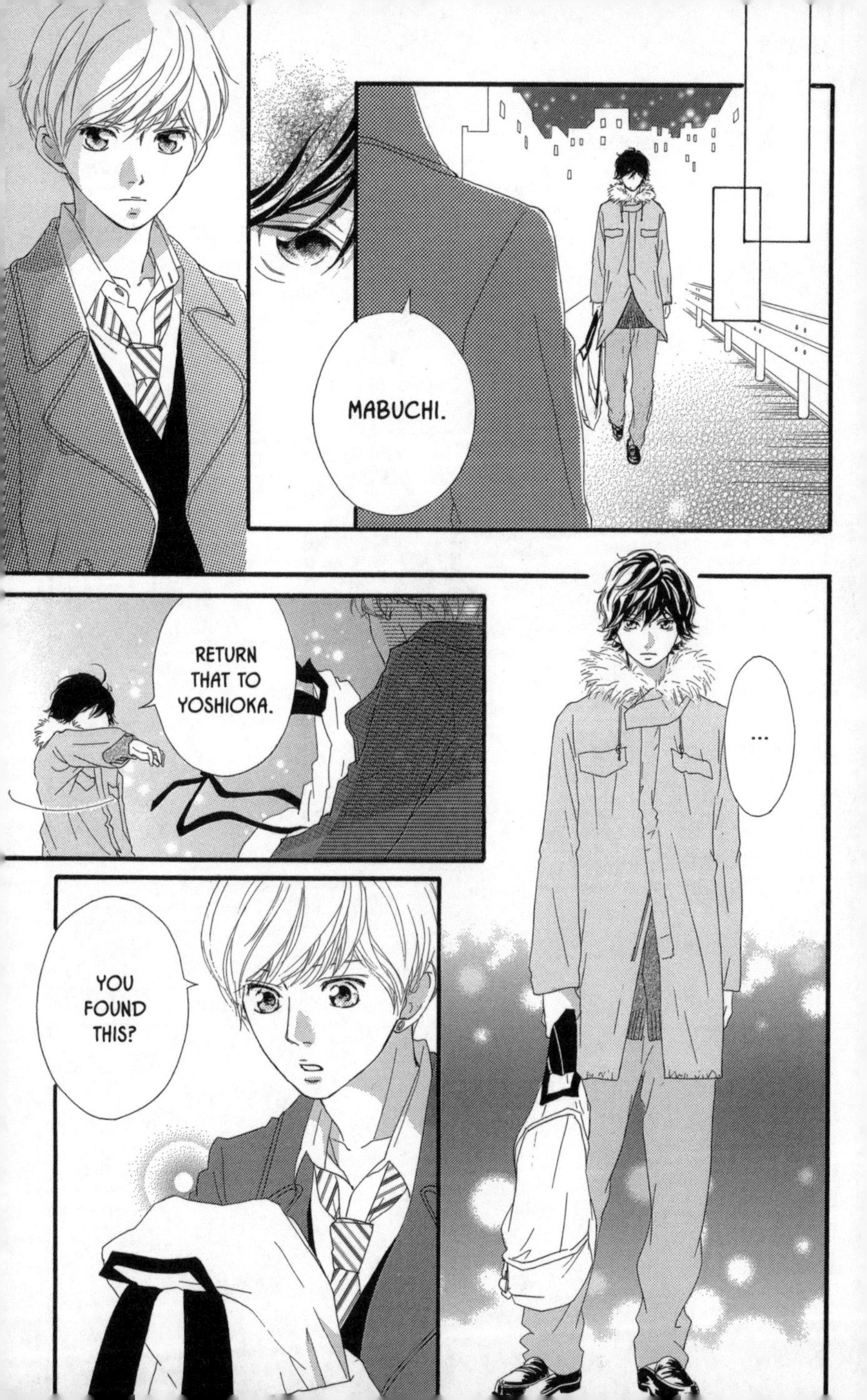
MABUCHI.
...
RETURN THAT TO YOSHIOKA.
YOU FOUND THIS?

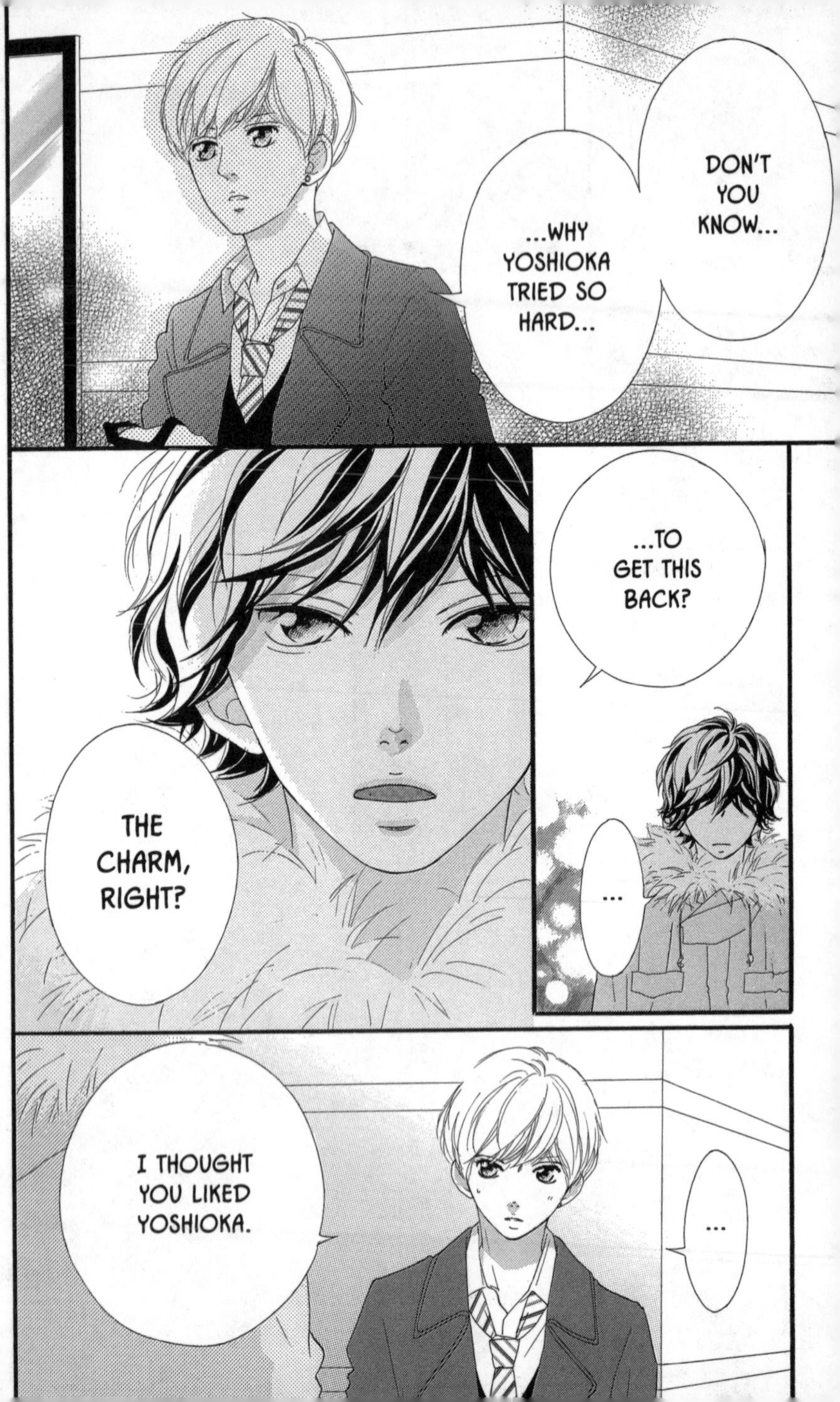
DON'T YOU KNOW...
...WHY YOSHIOKA TRIED SO HARD...
...TO GET THIS BACK?
...
THE CHARM, RIGHT?
...
I THOUGHT YOU LIKED YOSHIOKA.

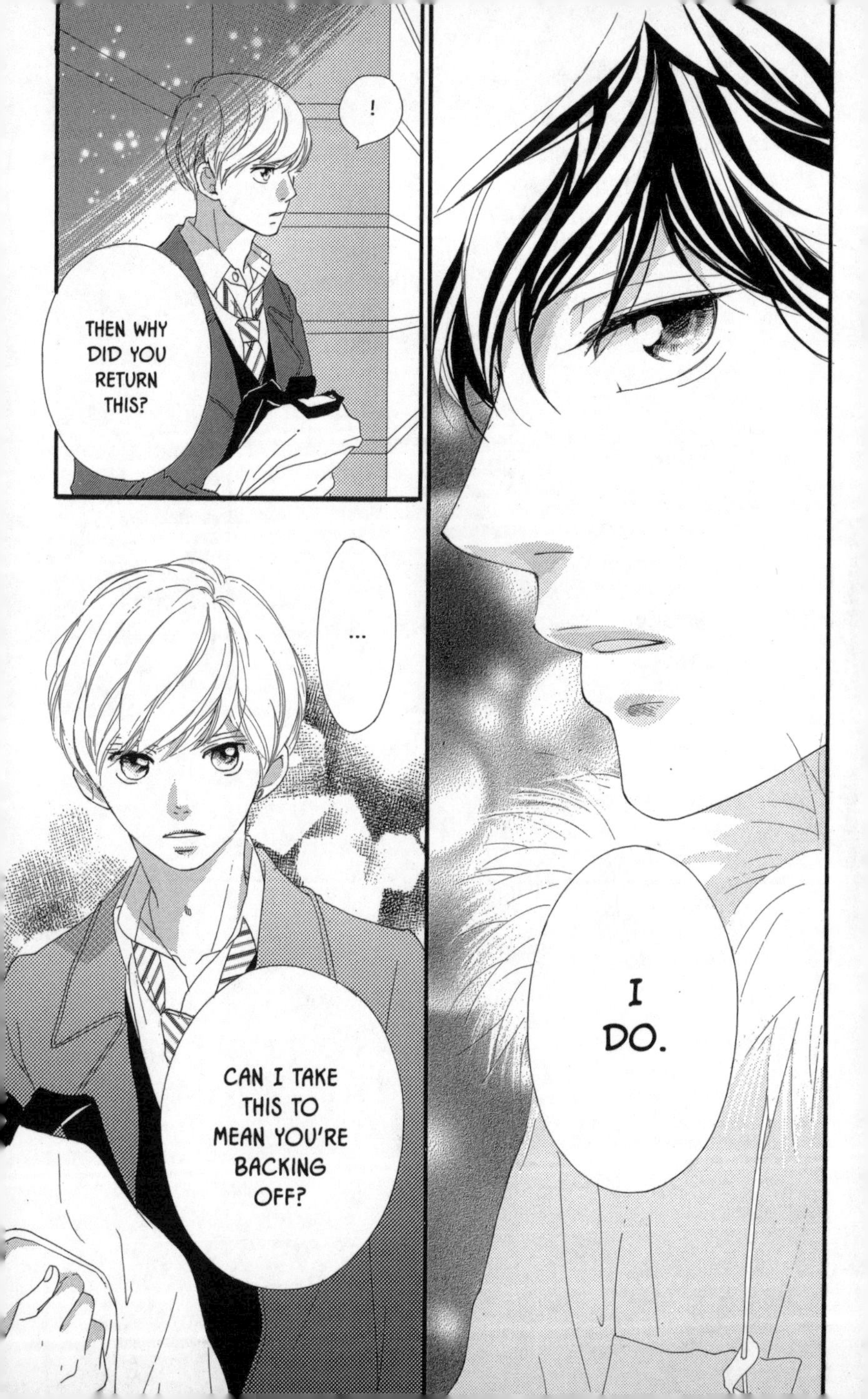
I DO.
!
THEN WHY DID YOU RETURN THIS?
...
CAN I TAKE THIS TO MEAN YOU'RE BACKING OFF?

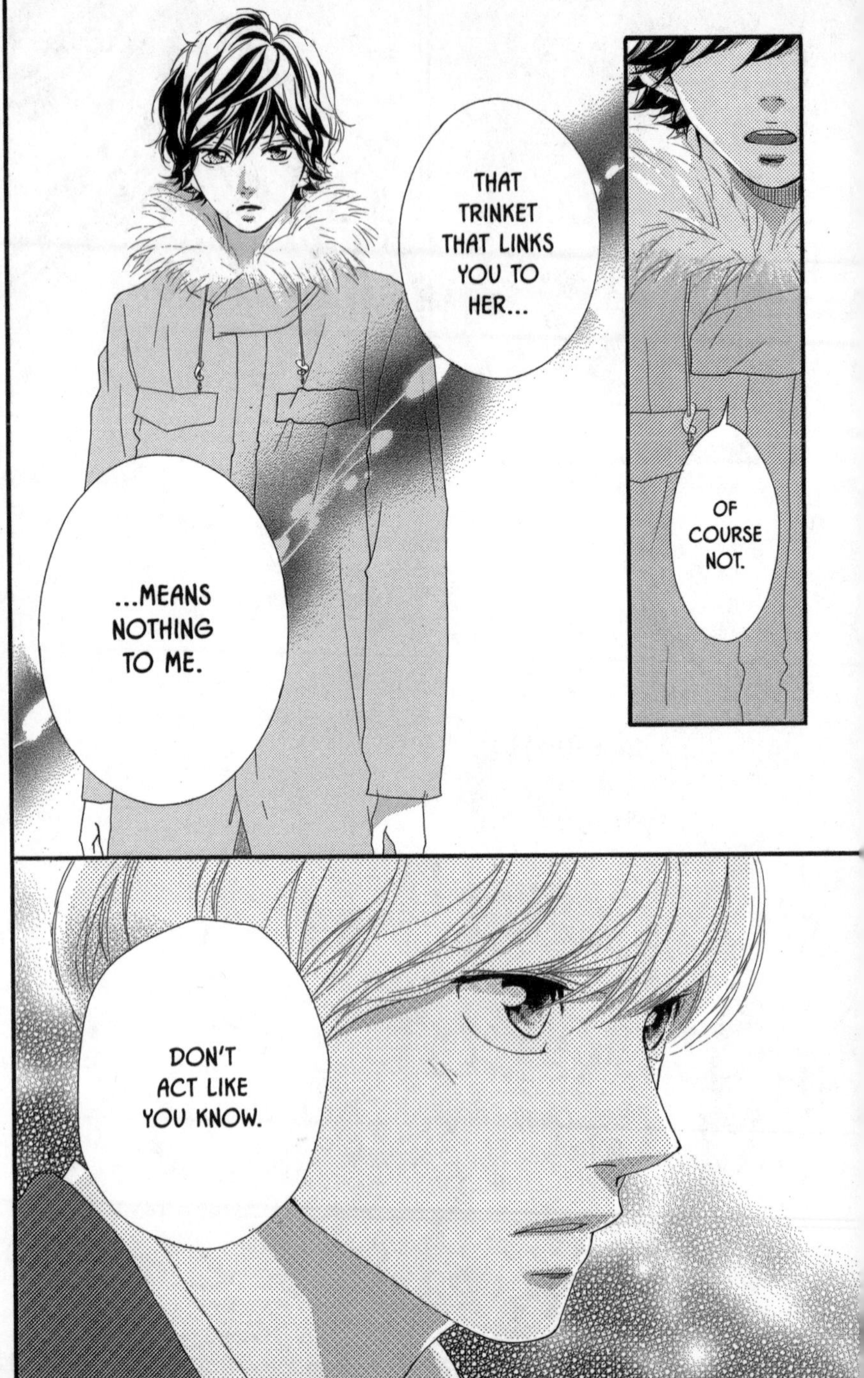

OF COURSE NOT.
THAT TRINKET THAT LINKS YOU TO HER...
...MEANS NOTHING TO ME.
DON'T ACT LIKE YOU KNOW.

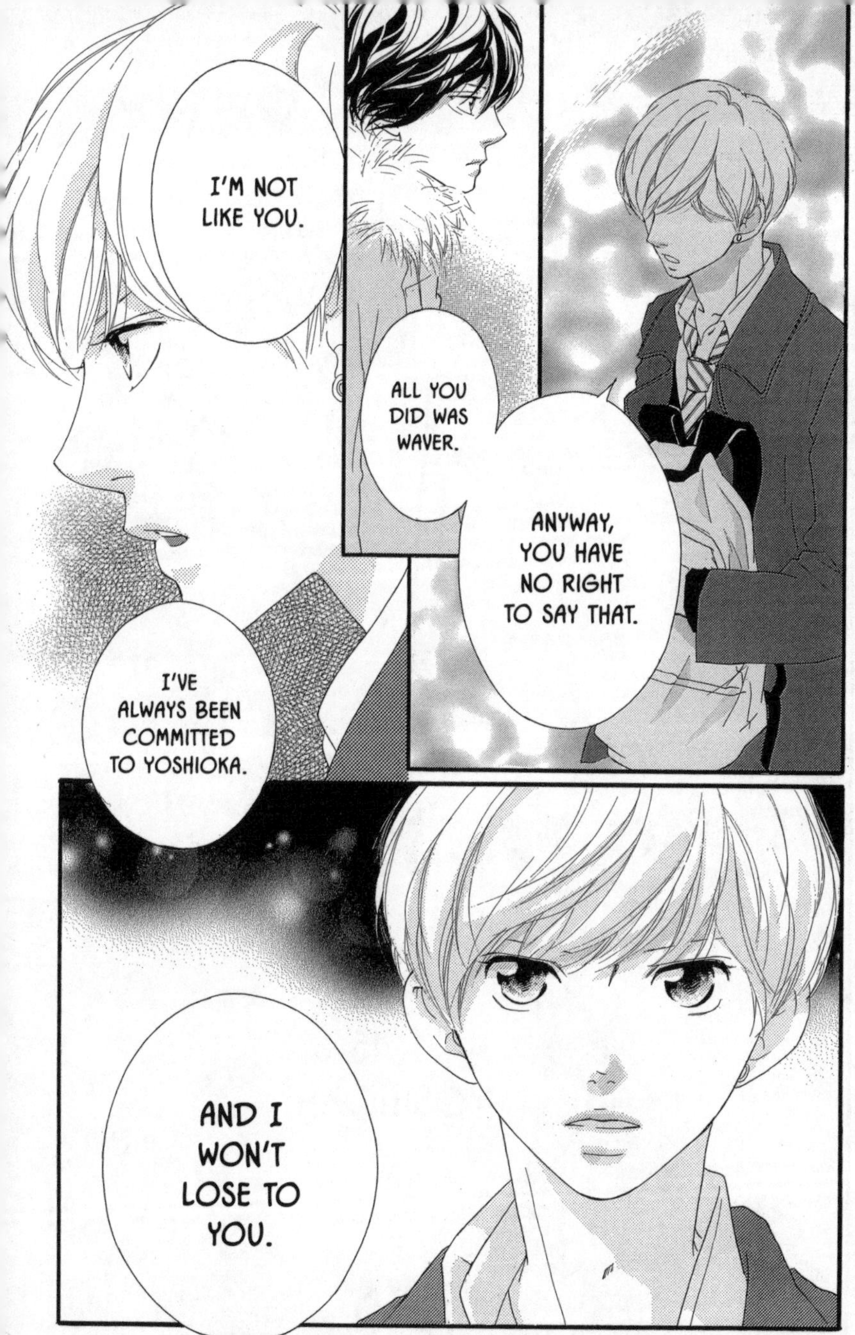
ANYWAY, YOU HAVE NO RIGHT TO SAY THAT.
ALL YOU DID WAS WAVER.
I'M NOT LIKE YOU.
I'VE ALWAYS BEEN COMMITTED TO YOSHIOKA.
AND I WON'T LOSE TO YOU.

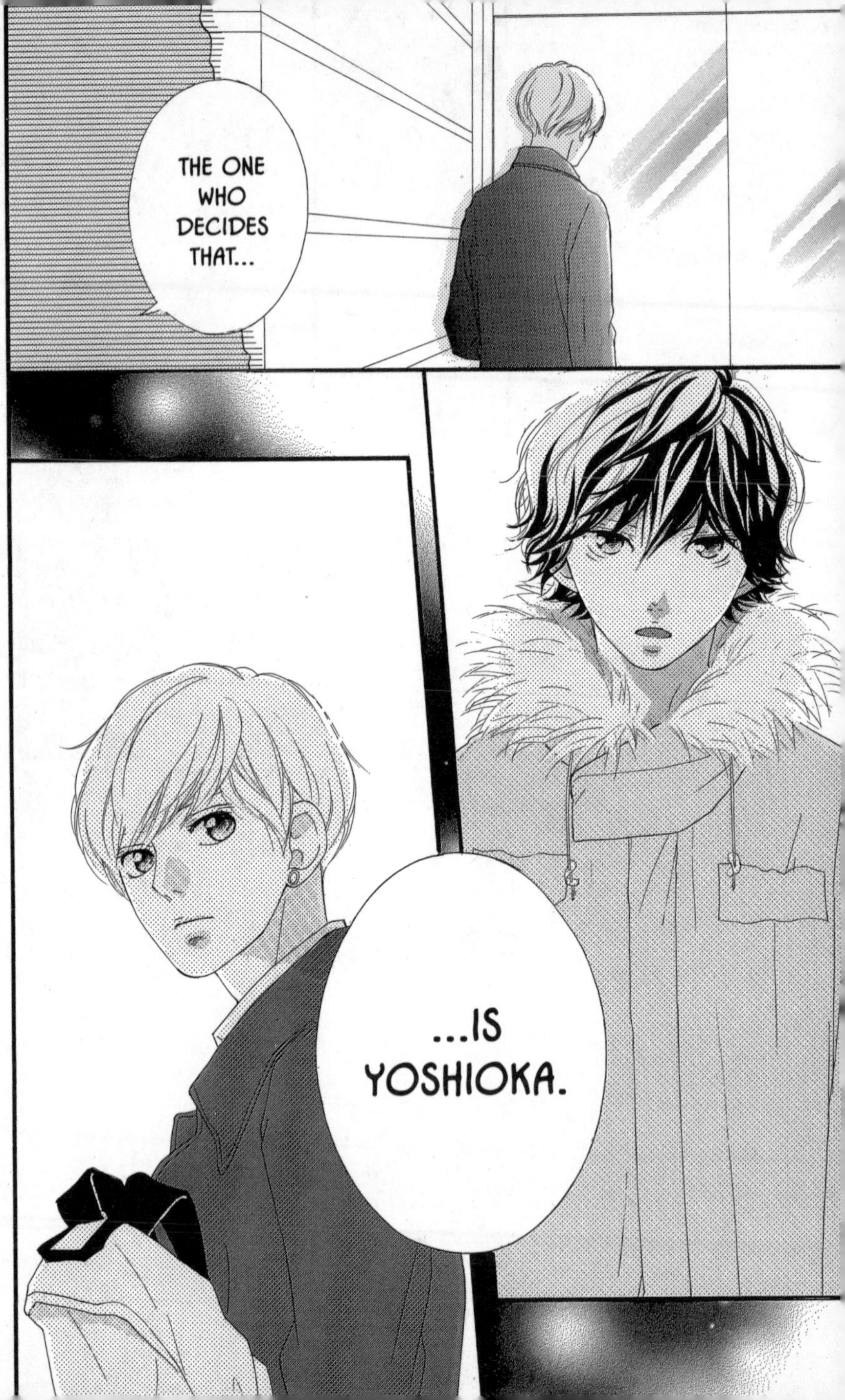
THE ONE WHO DECIDES THAT...
...IS YOSHIOKA.

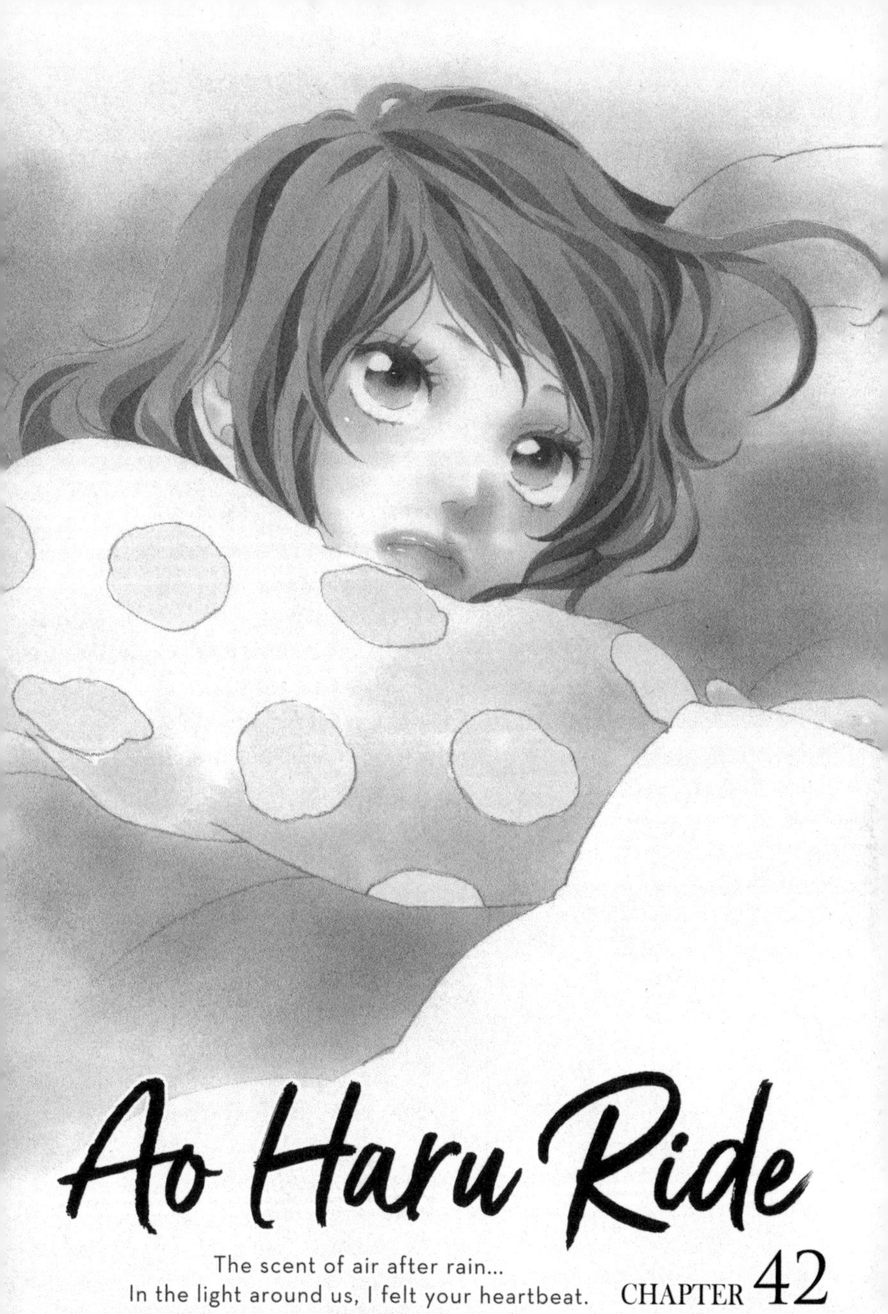

Ao Haru Ride

The scent of air after rain...
In the light around us, I felt your heartbeat.

CHAPTER 42

Announcement ✩

Many of you may already be aware, but *Ao Haru Ride* is going to be made into a live-action movie.

Thank you for this opportunity!

I was invited to visit the film set. It was surprising to see just how many people there were working behind the scenes! Seeing each and every one of them working so passionately moved me. When I am working on the manga with my assistants, there are just a few of us holed up together. That made it all the more exciting to see so many people working together on one project. I thought it was so cool, but it also made me jealous. (Although I'm sure having that many people is a lot to manage.) Then I realized that as the original creator, I am part of their team too, which got me really excited! There's no way to experience all this when I'm working on manuscripts, so I feel very lucky to have been able to see the set. Thank you!!!

The release is scheduled for December 2014. I hope you'll join in too by watching the *Ao Haru Ride* movie!

★ Io Sakisaka ★

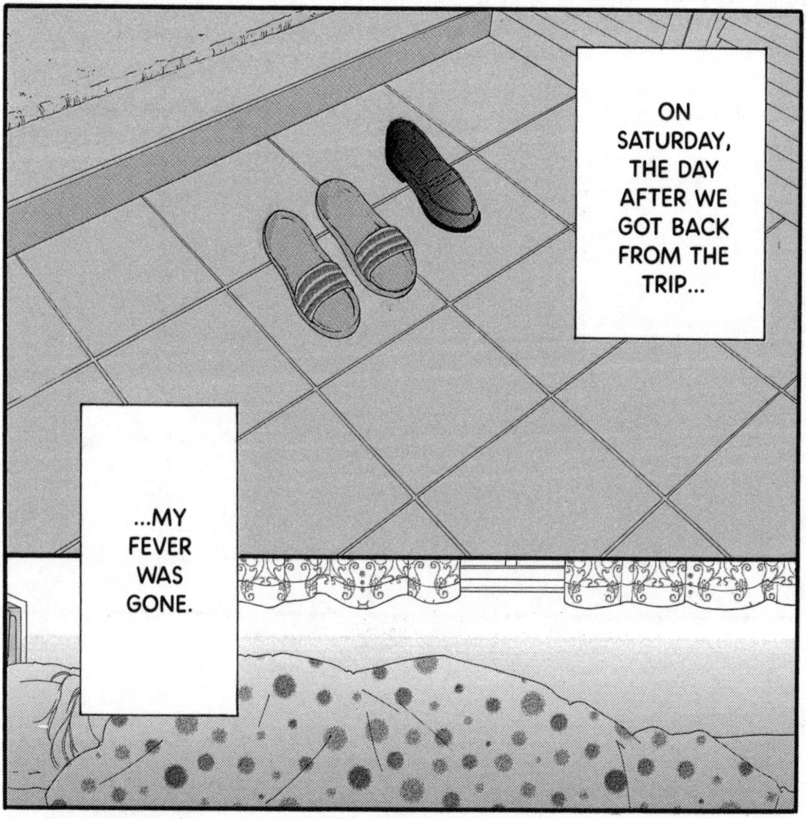
ON SATURDAY, THE DAY AFTER WE GOT BACK FROM THE TRIP...
...MY FEVER WAS GONE.

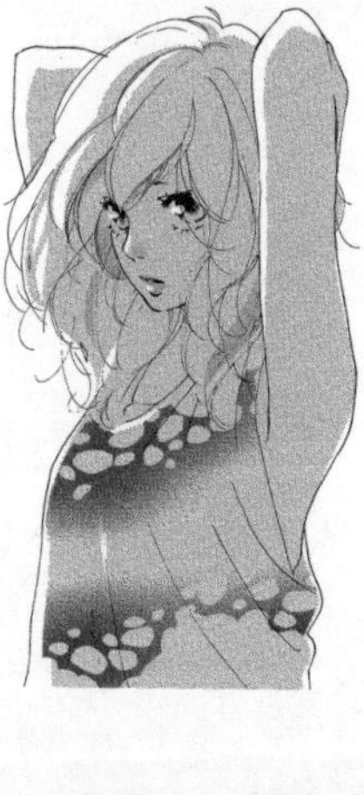

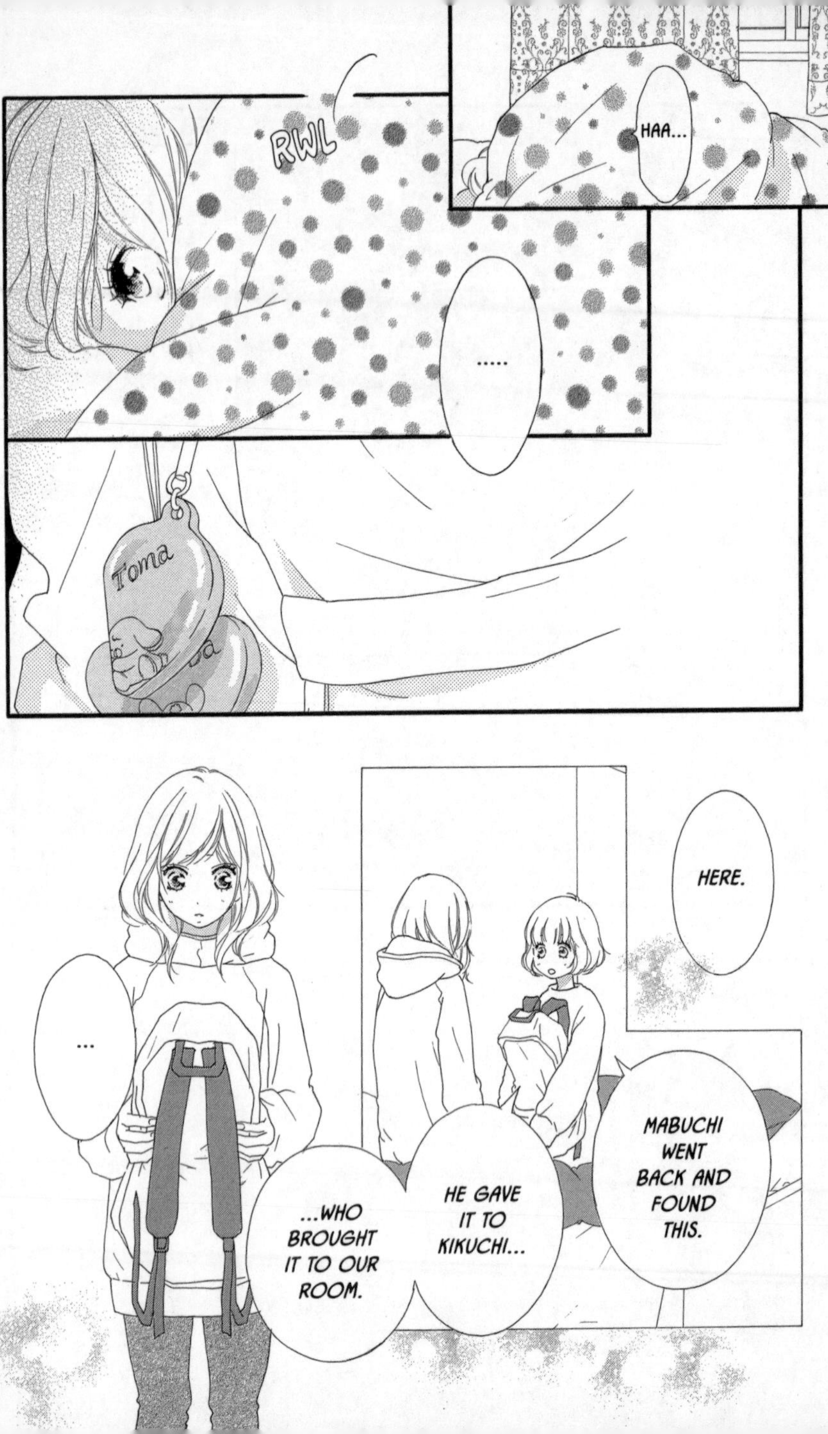
HAA...
RWL
.....
HERE.
MABUCHI WENT BACK AND FOUND THIS.
HE GAVE IT TO KIKUCHI...
...WHO BROUGHT IT TO OUR ROOM.
...

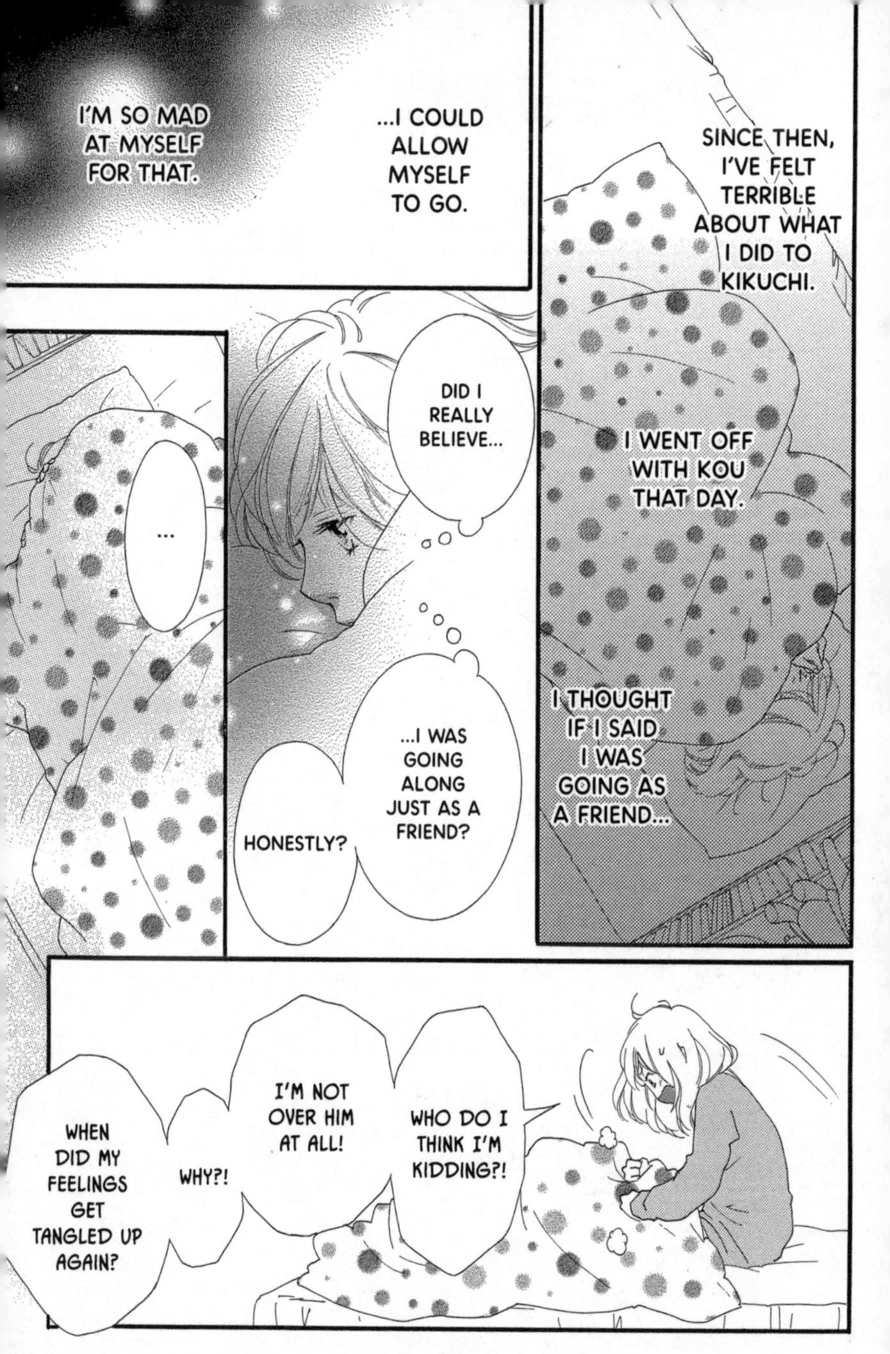
SINCE THEN, I'VE FELT TERRIBLE ABOUT WHAT I DID TO KIKUCHI.
I WENT OFF WITH KOU THAT DAY.
I THOUGHT IF I SAID I WAS GOING AS A FRIEND...
...I COULD ALLOW MYSELF TO GO.
I'M SO MAD AT MYSELF FOR THAT.
DID I REALLY BELIEVE...
...I WAS GOING ALONG JUST AS A FRIEND?
HONESTLY?
...
WHO DO I THINK I'M KIDDING?!
I'M NOT OVER HIM AT ALL!
WHY?!
WHEN DID MY FEELINGS GET TANGLED UP AGAIN?

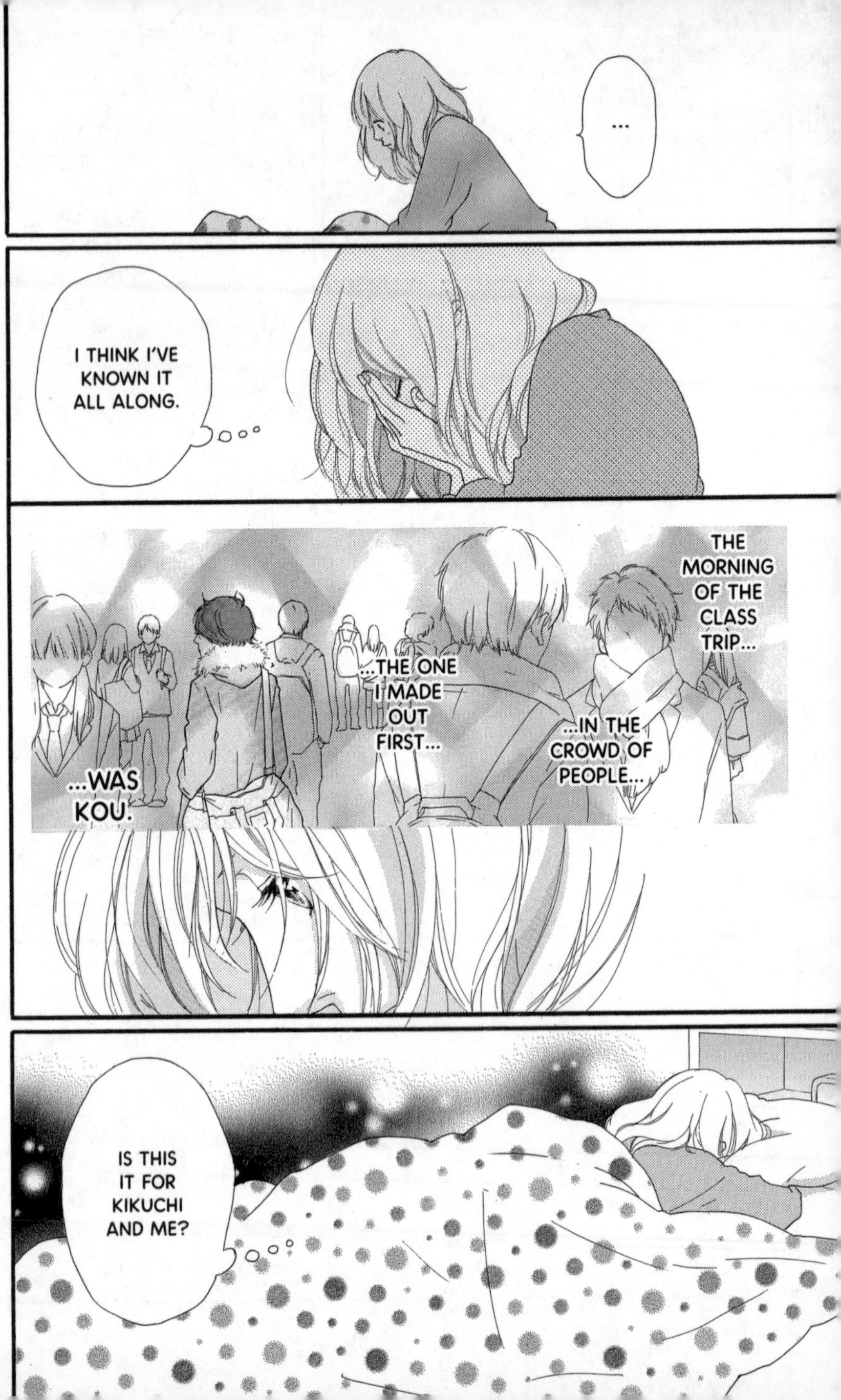
...
I THINK I'VE KNOWN IT ALL ALONG.
THE MORNING OF THE CLASS TRIP...
...IN THE CROWD OF PEOPLE...
...THE ONE I MADE OUT FIRST...
...WAS KOU.
IS THIS IT FOR KIKUCHI AND ME?

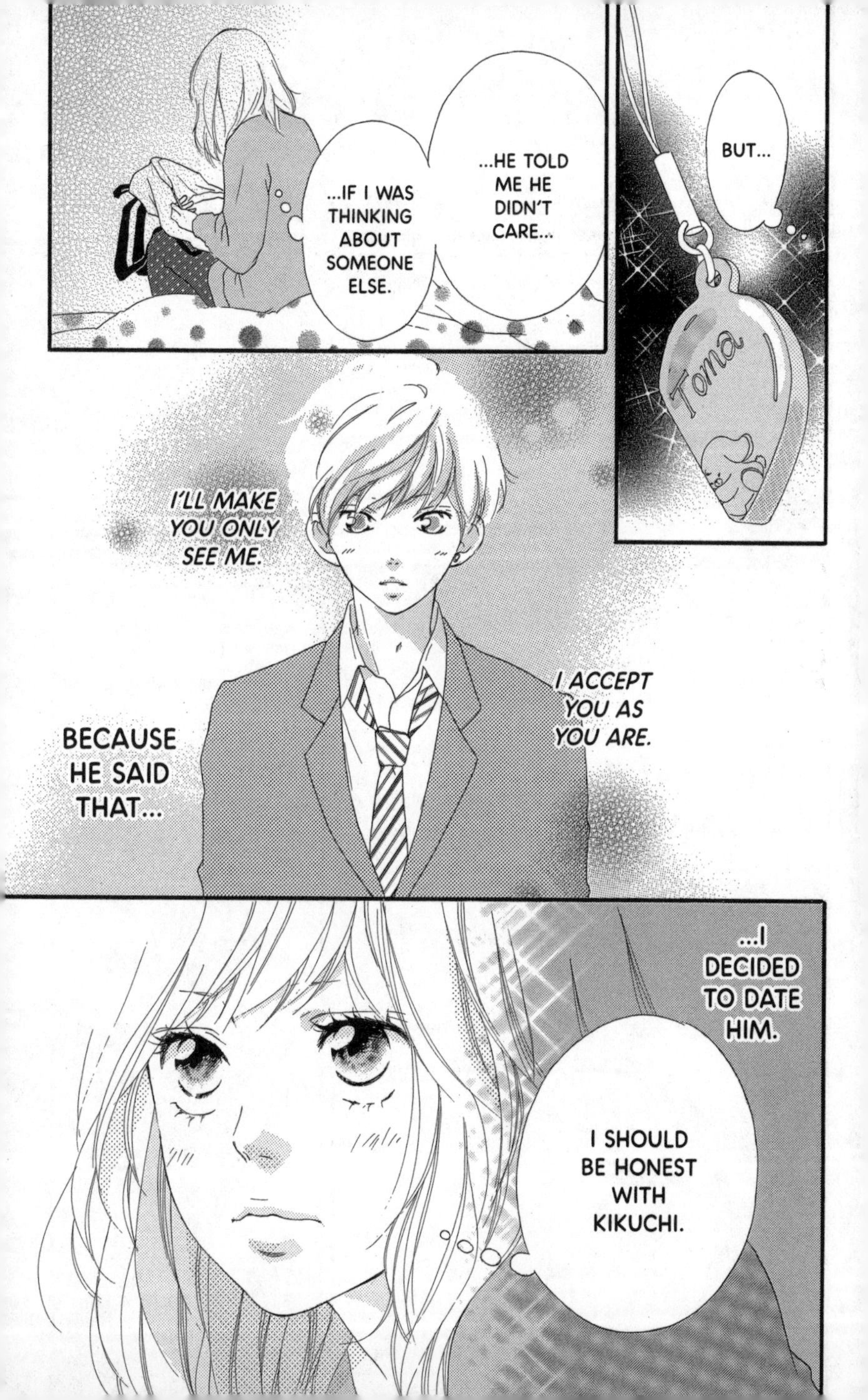
BUT...
...HE TOLD ME HE DIDN'T CARE...
...IF I WAS THINKING ABOUT SOMEONE ELSE.
Toma
I'LL MAKE YOU ONLY SEE ME.
I ACCEPT YOU AS YOU ARE.
BECAUSE HE SAID THAT...
...I DECIDED TO DATE HIM.
I SHOULD BE HONEST WITH KIKUCHI.

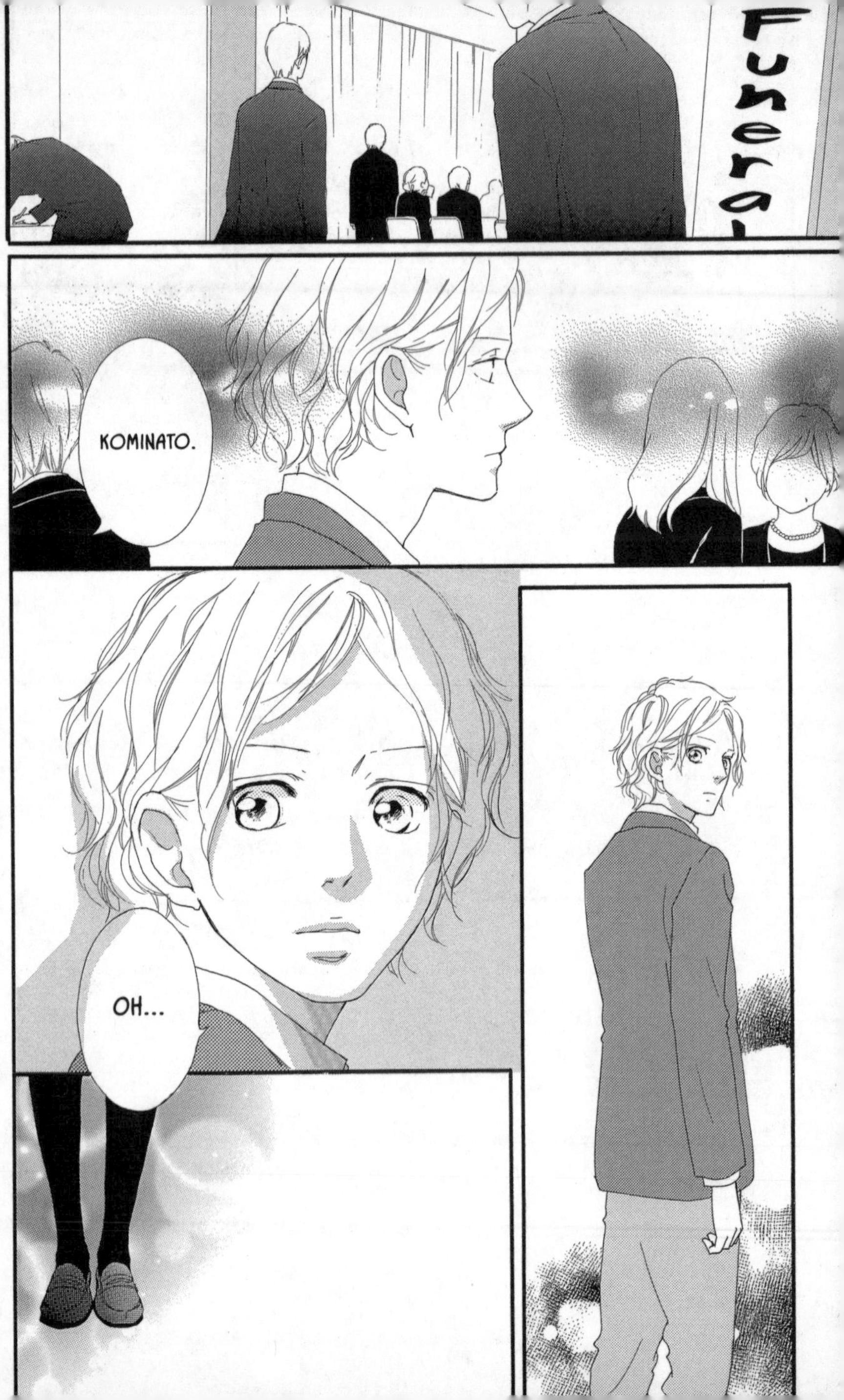
Funeral
KOMINATO.
OH...

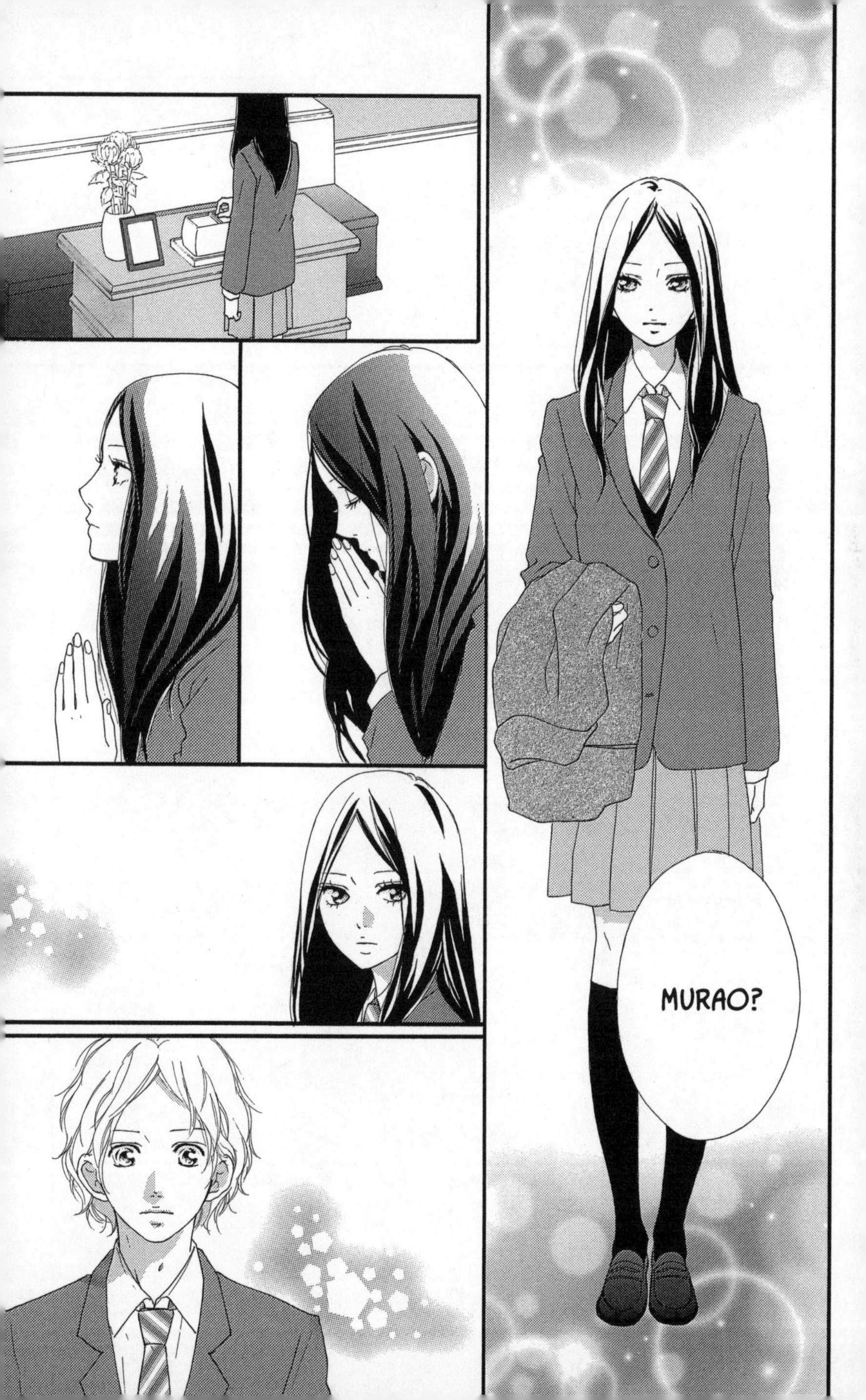
MURAO?

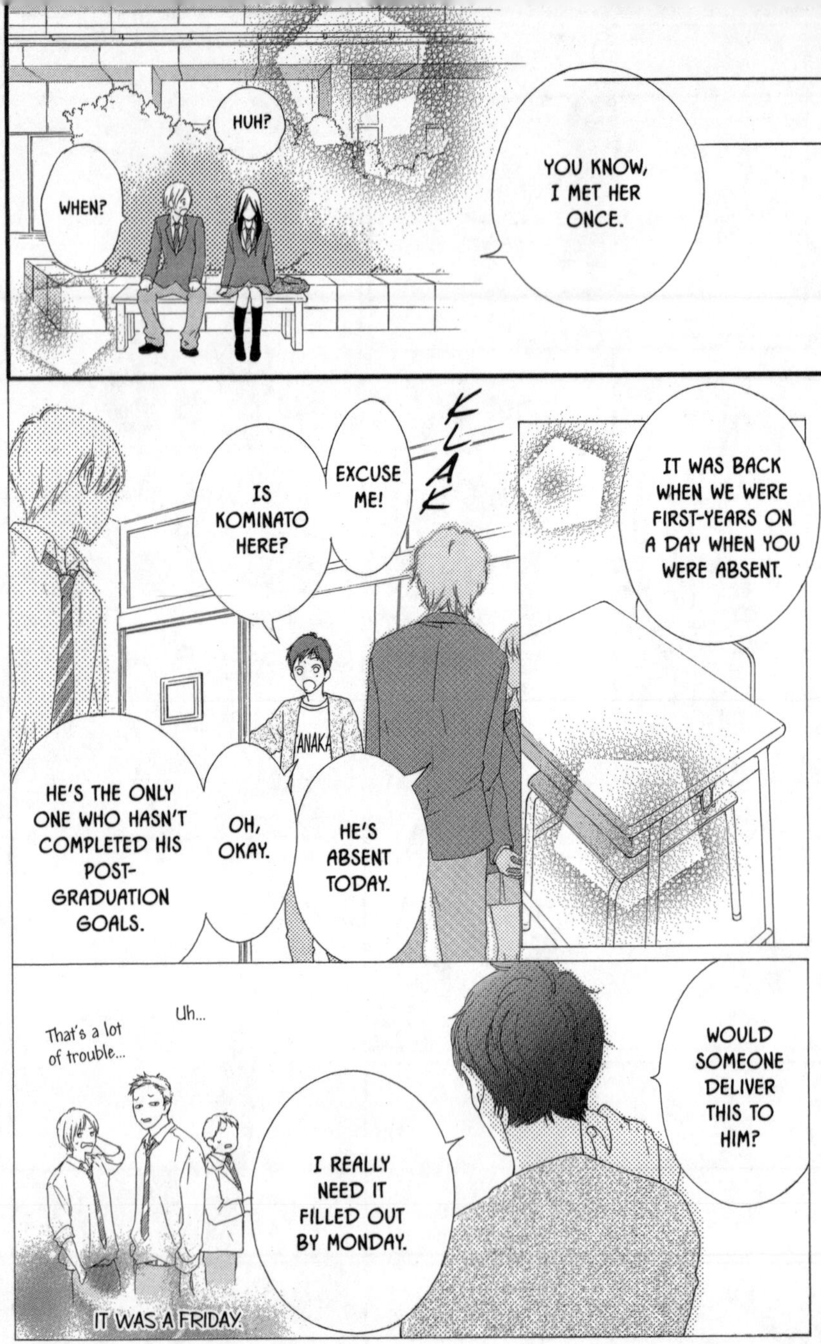
YOU KNOW, I MET HER ONCE.
HUH?
WHEN?
IT WAS BACK WHEN WE WERE FIRST-YEARS ON A DAY WHEN YOU WERE ABSENT.
KLAK
EXCUSE ME!
IS KOMINATO HERE?
TANAKA
HE'S ABSENT TODAY.
OH, OKAY.
HE'S THE ONLY ONE WHO HASN'T COMPLETED HIS POST-GRADUATION GOALS.
WOULD SOMEONE DELIVER THIS TO HIM?
I REALLY NEED IT FILLED OUT BY MONDAY.
Uh...
That's a lot of trouble...
IT WAS A FRIDAY.

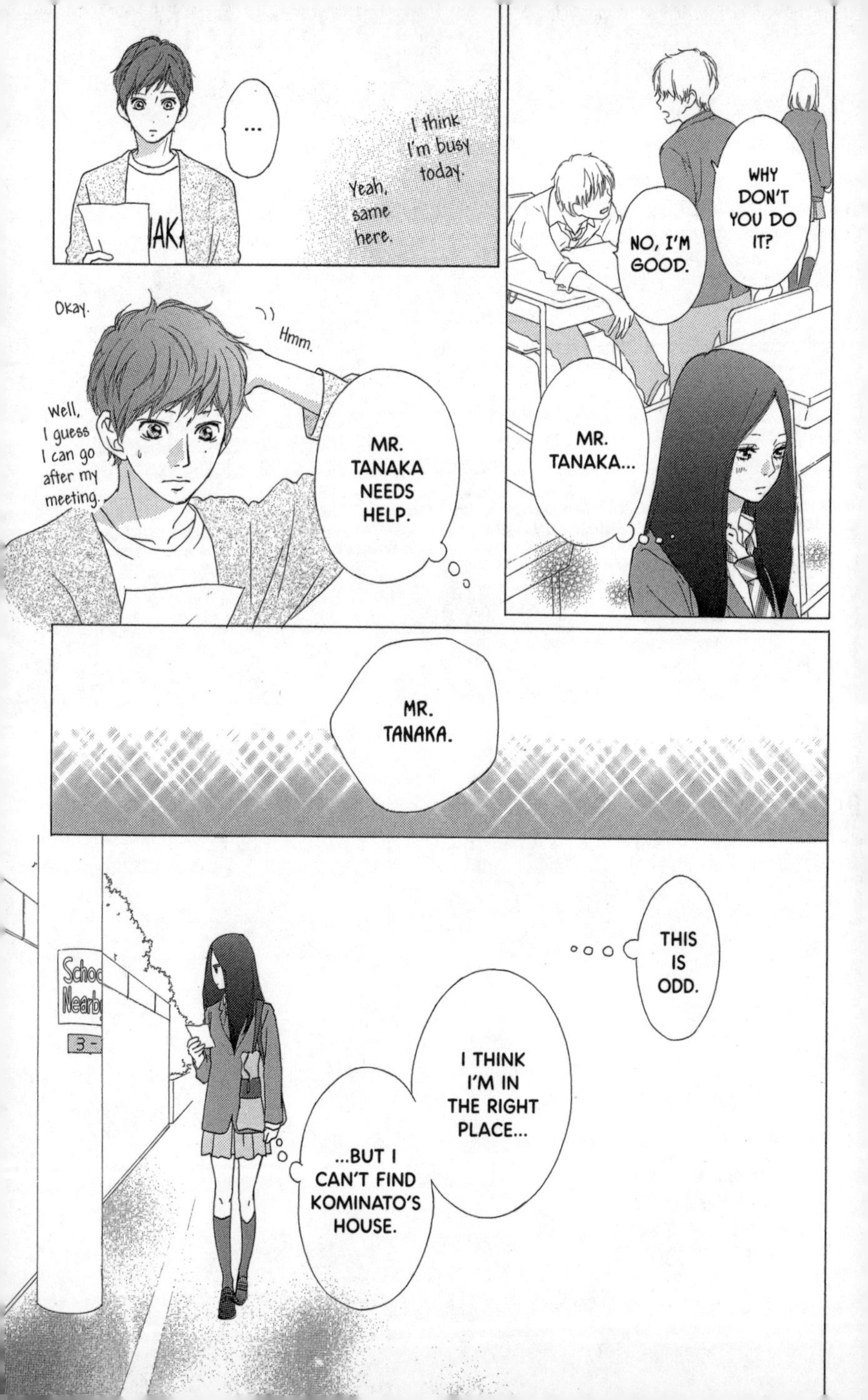
WHY DON'T YOU DO IT?
NO, I'M GOOD.
MR. TANAKA...
...
I think I'm busy today.
Yeah, same here.
Hmm.
MR. TANAKA NEEDS HELP.
Okay.
Well, I guess I can go after my meeting.
MR. TANAKA.
THIS IS ODD.
I THINK I'M IN THE RIGHT PLACE...
...BUT I CAN'T FIND KOMINATO'S HOUSE.

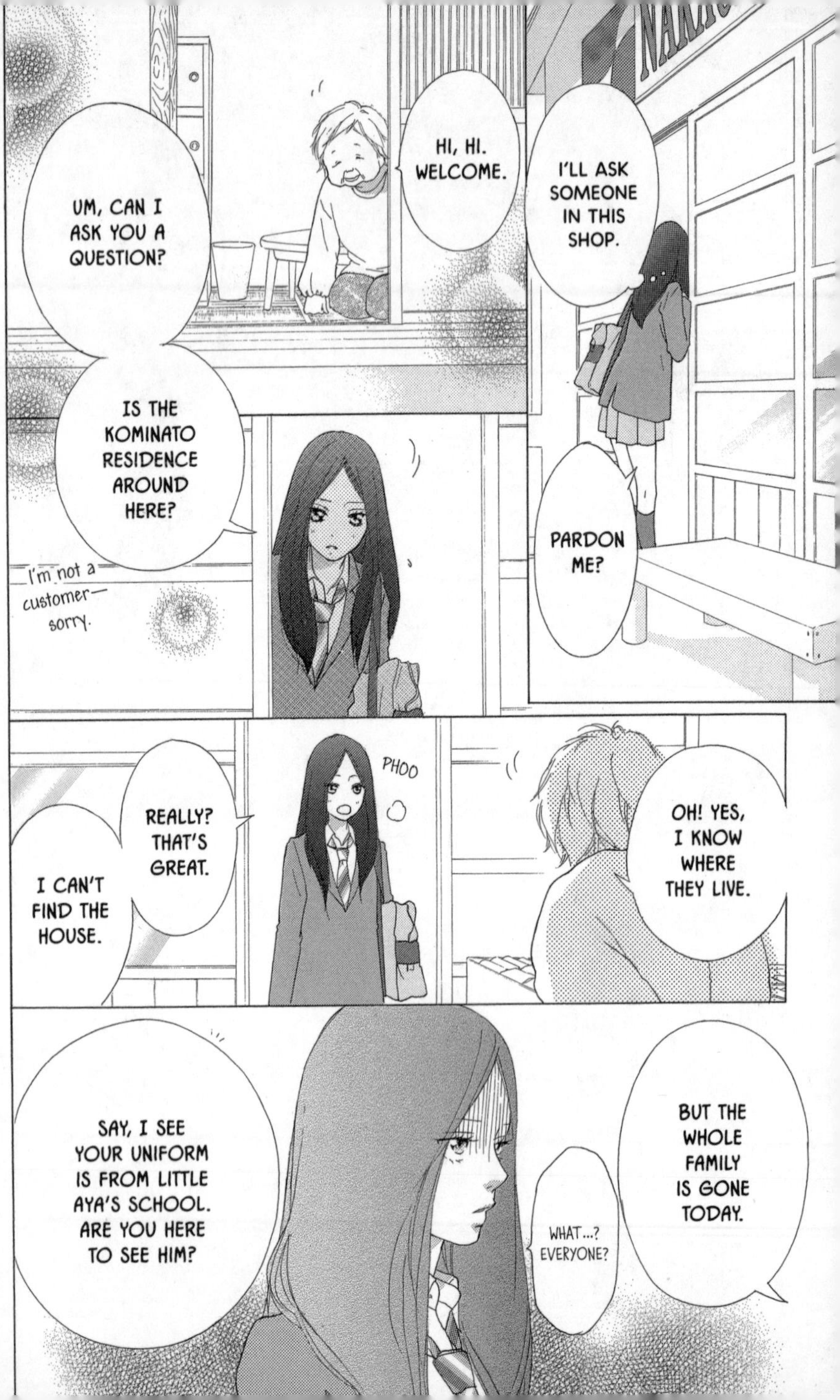
I'LL ASK SOMEONE IN THIS SHOP.
PARDON ME?
HI, HI. WELCOME.
UM, CAN I ASK YOU A QUESTION?
IS THE KOMINATO RESIDENCE AROUND HERE?
I'm not a customer—sorry.
OH! YES, I KNOW WHERE THEY LIVE.
PHOO
REALLY? THAT'S GREAT.
I CAN'T FIND THE HOUSE.
BUT THE WHOLE FAMILY IS GONE TODAY.
WHAT...? EVERYONE?
SAY, I SEE YOUR UNIFORM IS FROM LITTLE AYA'S SCHOOL. ARE YOU HERE TO SEE HIM?

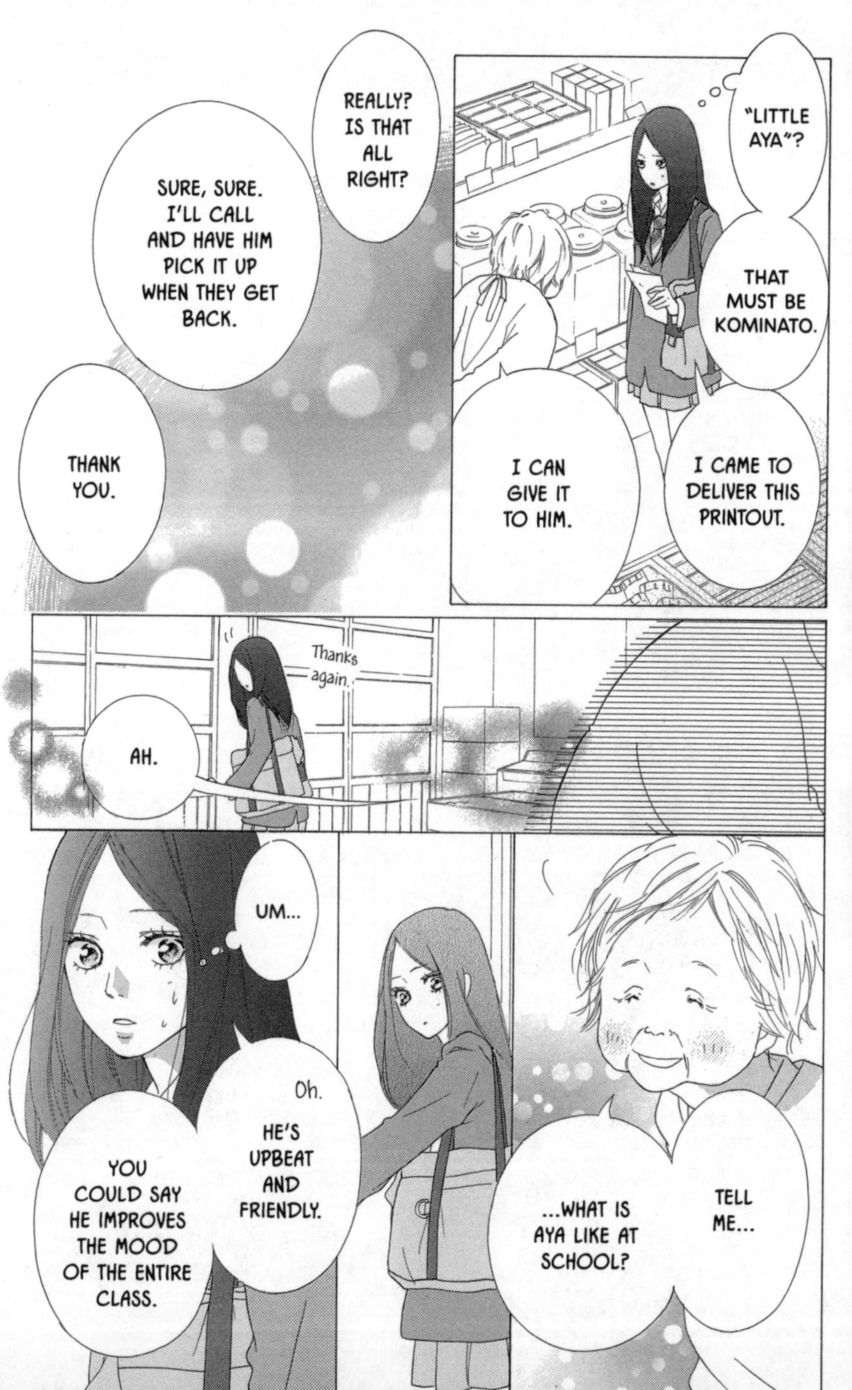
"LITTLE AYA"?
THAT MUST BE KOMINATO.
I CAME TO DELIVER THIS PRINTOUT.
I CAN GIVE IT TO HIM.
REALLY? IS THAT ALL RIGHT?
SURE, SURE. I'LL CALL AND HAVE HIM PICK IT UP WHEN THEY GET BACK.
THANK YOU.
Thanks again.
AH.
TELL ME...
...WHAT IS AYA LIKE AT SCHOOL?
UM...
Oh.
HE'S UPBEAT AND FRIENDLY.
YOU COULD SAY HE IMPROVES THE MOOD OF THE ENTIRE CLASS.

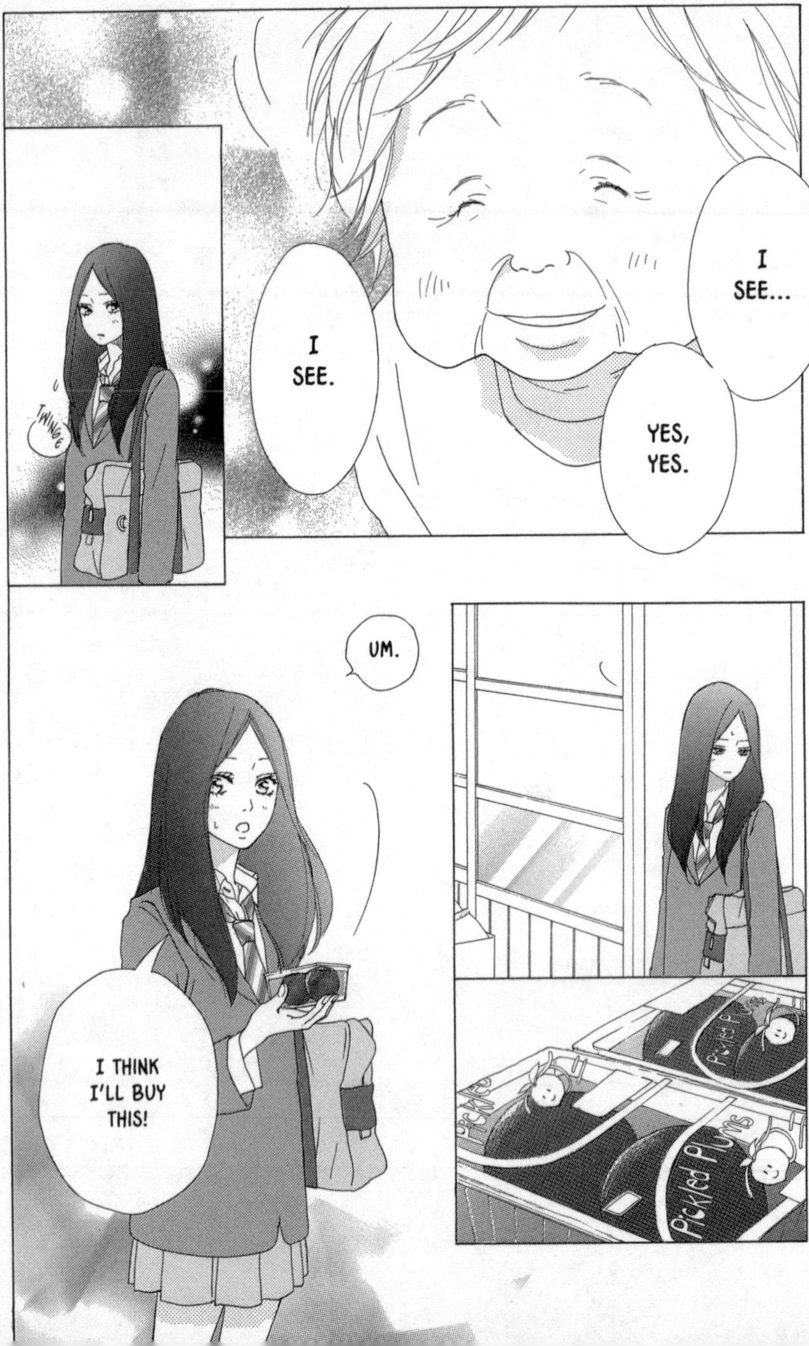
I SEE...
YES, YES.
I SEE.
TWINGE
Pickled Plums
Pickled
Pickled Plums
UM.
I THINK I'LL BUY THIS!

Occasionally I get asked what it was that led me to become a mangaka. I've given this answer before, but the original reason was that I was looking for a way to escape from crowded commuter trains.

I still remember using a dip pen for the first time and thinking it was really difficult. My lines didn't come out straight, and my hand hurt from applying so much pressure... I was not excited about any part of it. Starting from that awful place, I began to gain better control of the pen and to enjoy what I was doing. If you're someone who is interested in becoming a mangaka but you think you can't do it, I encourage you to finish one complete manuscript. It's an absolutely moving experience to flip through the pages of your manuscript and realize, "Wow, this is a manga!" And since you've finished it, why not just send it over to *Betsuma*?! Submissions are welcome.

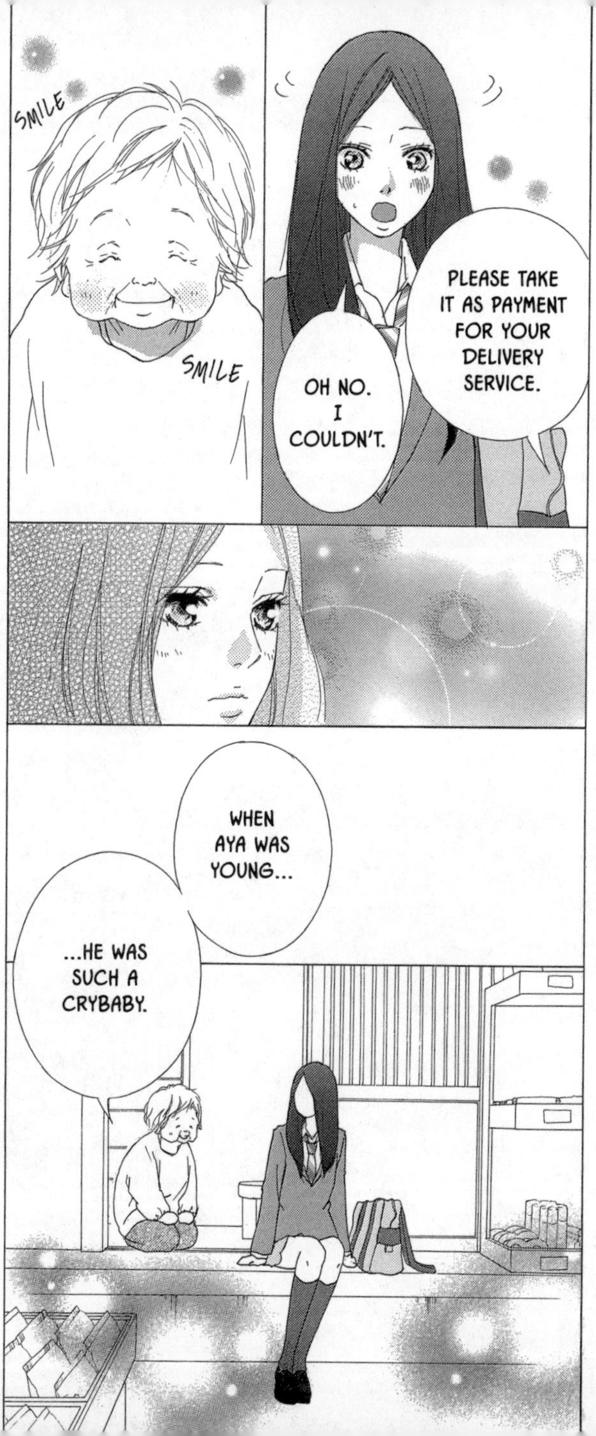
PLEASE TAKE IT AS PAYMENT FOR YOUR DELIVERY SERVICE.
OH NO. I COULDN'T.
SMILE
SMILE
WHEN AYA WAS YOUNG...
...HE WAS SUCH A CRYBABY.

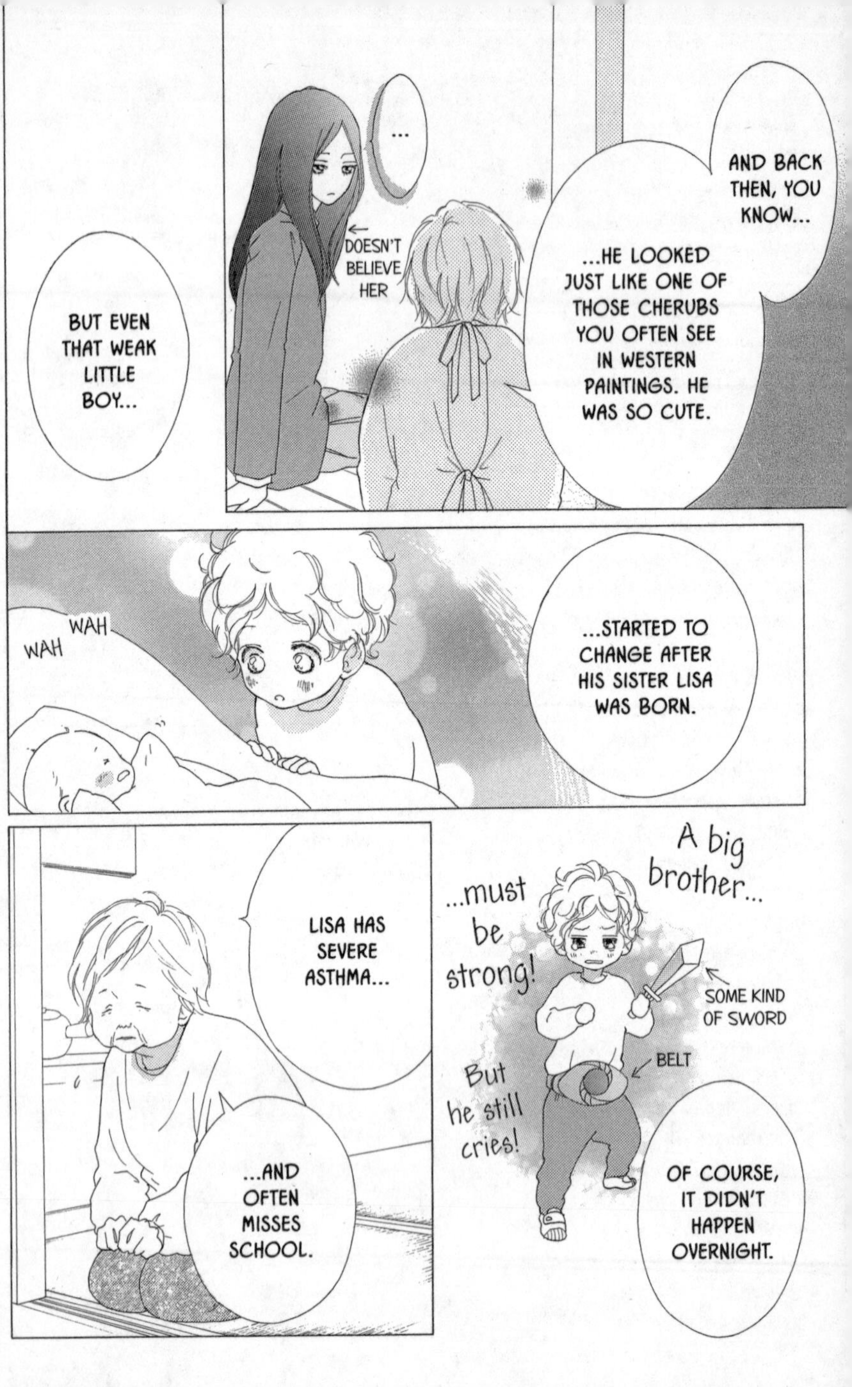
AND BACK THEN, YOU KNOW...
...HE LOOKED JUST LIKE ONE OF THOSE CHERUBS YOU OFTEN SEE IN WESTERN PAINTINGS. HE WAS SO CUTE.
...
DOESN'T BELIEVE HER
BUT EVEN THAT WEAK LITTLE BOY...
...STARTED TO CHANGE AFTER HIS SISTER LISA WAS BORN.
WAH
WAH
A big brother...
...must be strong!
SOME KIND OF SWORD
BELT
But he still cries!
OF COURSE, IT DIDN'T HAPPEN OVERNIGHT.
LISA HAS SEVERE ASTHMA...
...AND OFTEN MISSES SCHOOL.

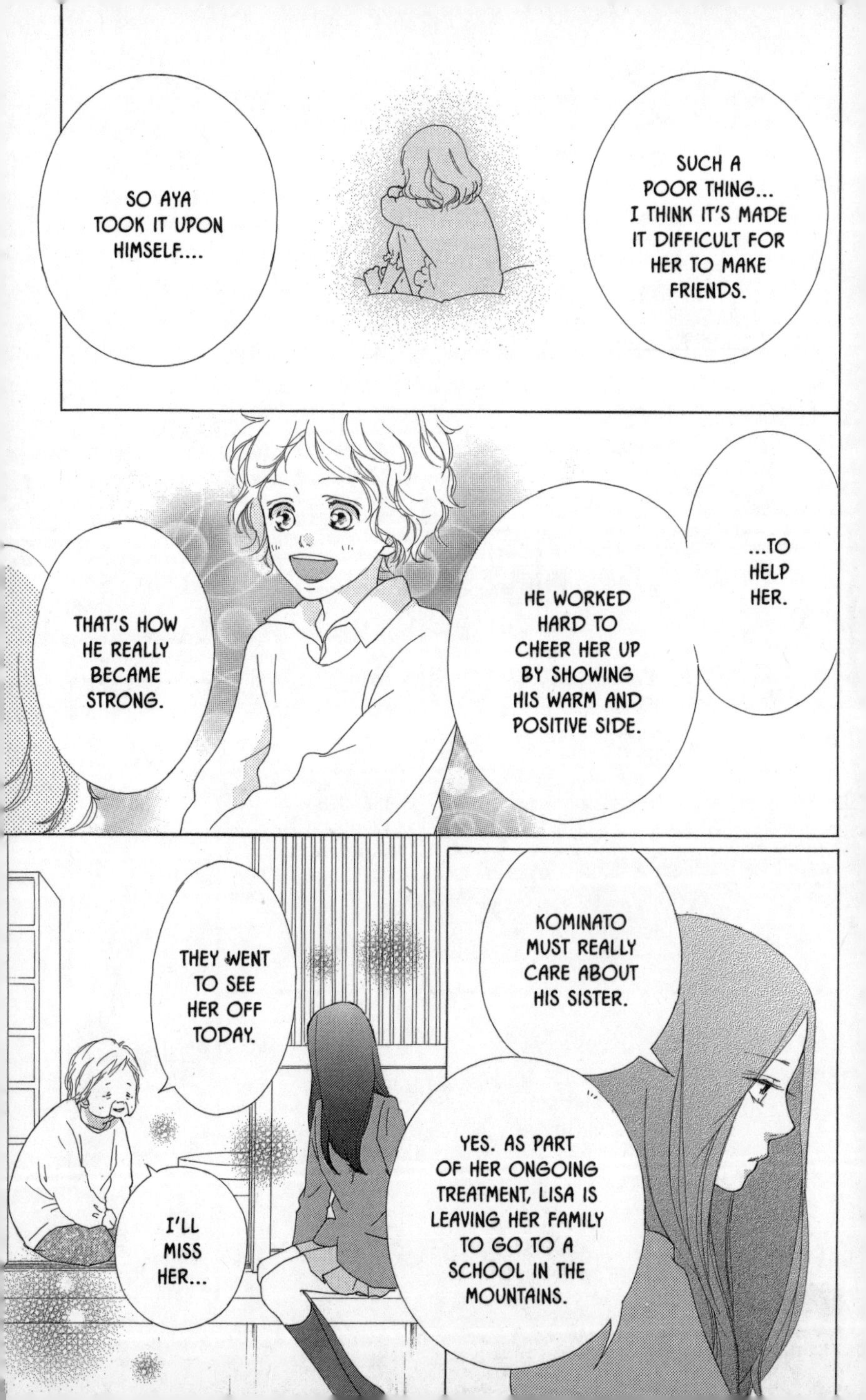
SUCH A POOR THING... I THINK IT'S MADE IT DIFFICULT FOR HER TO MAKE FRIENDS.
SO AYA TOOK IT UPON HIMSELF....
...TO HELP HER.
HE WORKED HARD TO CHEER HER UP BY SHOWING HIS WARM AND POSITIVE SIDE.
THAT'S HOW HE REALLY BECAME STRONG.
KOMINATO MUST REALLY CARE ABOUT HIS SISTER.
YES. AS PART OF HER ONGOING TREATMENT, LISA IS LEAVING HER FAMILY TO GO TO A SCHOOL IN THE MOUNTAINS.
THEY WENT TO SEE HER OFF TODAY.
I'LL MISS HER...

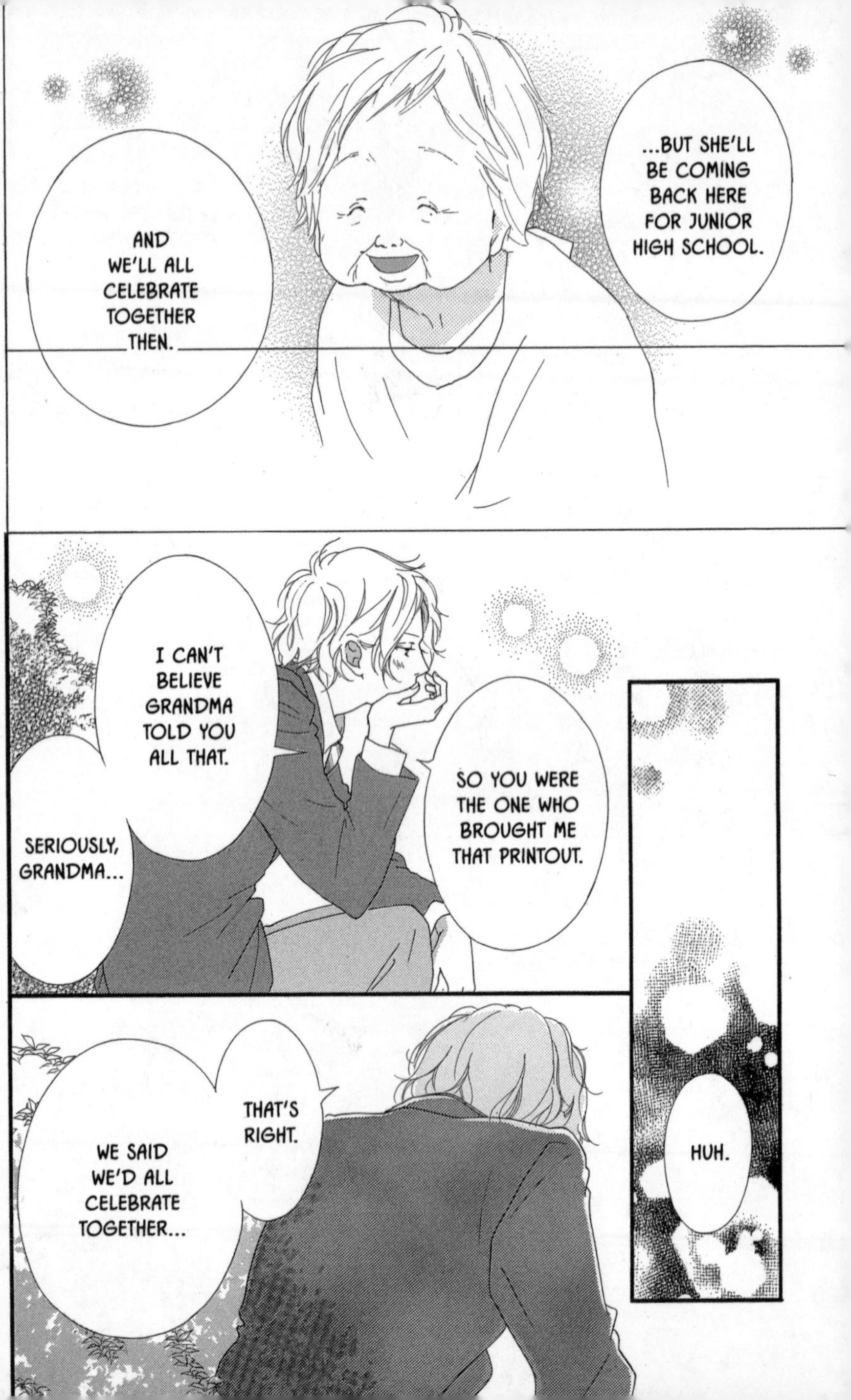
...BUT SHE'LL BE COMING BACK HERE FOR JUNIOR HIGH SCHOOL.
AND WE'LL ALL CELEBRATE TOGETHER THEN.
SO YOU WERE THE ONE WHO BROUGHT ME THAT PRINTOUT.
I CAN'T BELIEVE GRANDMA TOLD YOU ALL THAT.
SERIOUSLY, GRANDMA...
HUH.
THAT'S RIGHT.
WE SAID WE'D ALL CELEBRATE TOGETHER...

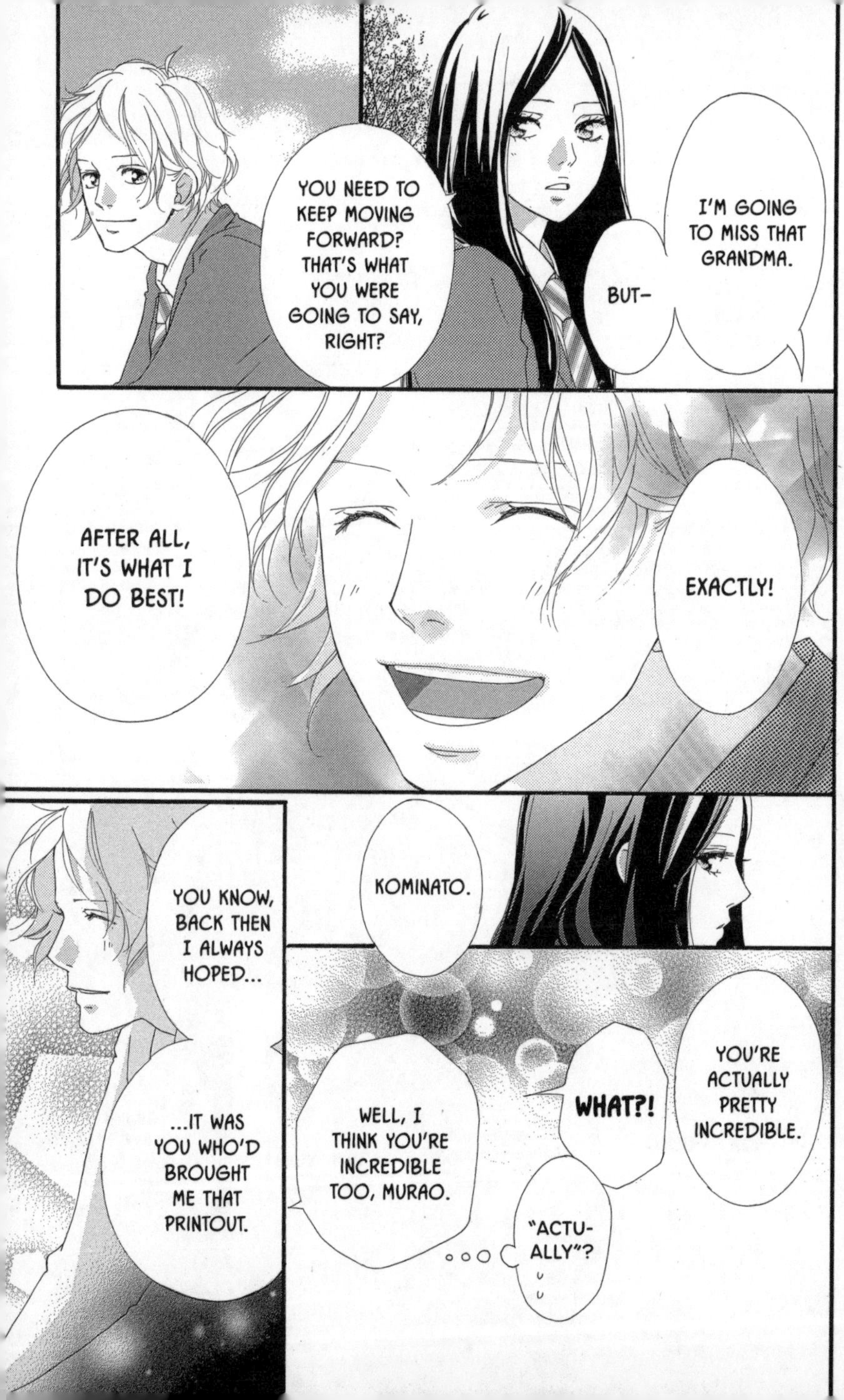
I'M GOING TO MISS THAT GRANDMA.
BUT–
YOU NEED TO KEEP MOVING FORWARD? THAT'S WHAT YOU WERE GOING TO SAY, RIGHT?
EXACTLY!
AFTER ALL, IT'S WHAT I DO BEST!
KOMINATO.
YOU'RE ACTUALLY PRETTY INCREDIBLE.
WHAT?!
"ACTU-ALLY"?
WELL, I THINK YOU'RE INCREDIBLE TOO, MURAO.
YOU KNOW, BACK THEN I ALWAYS HOPED...
...IT WAS YOU WHO'D BROUGHT ME THAT PRINTOUT.

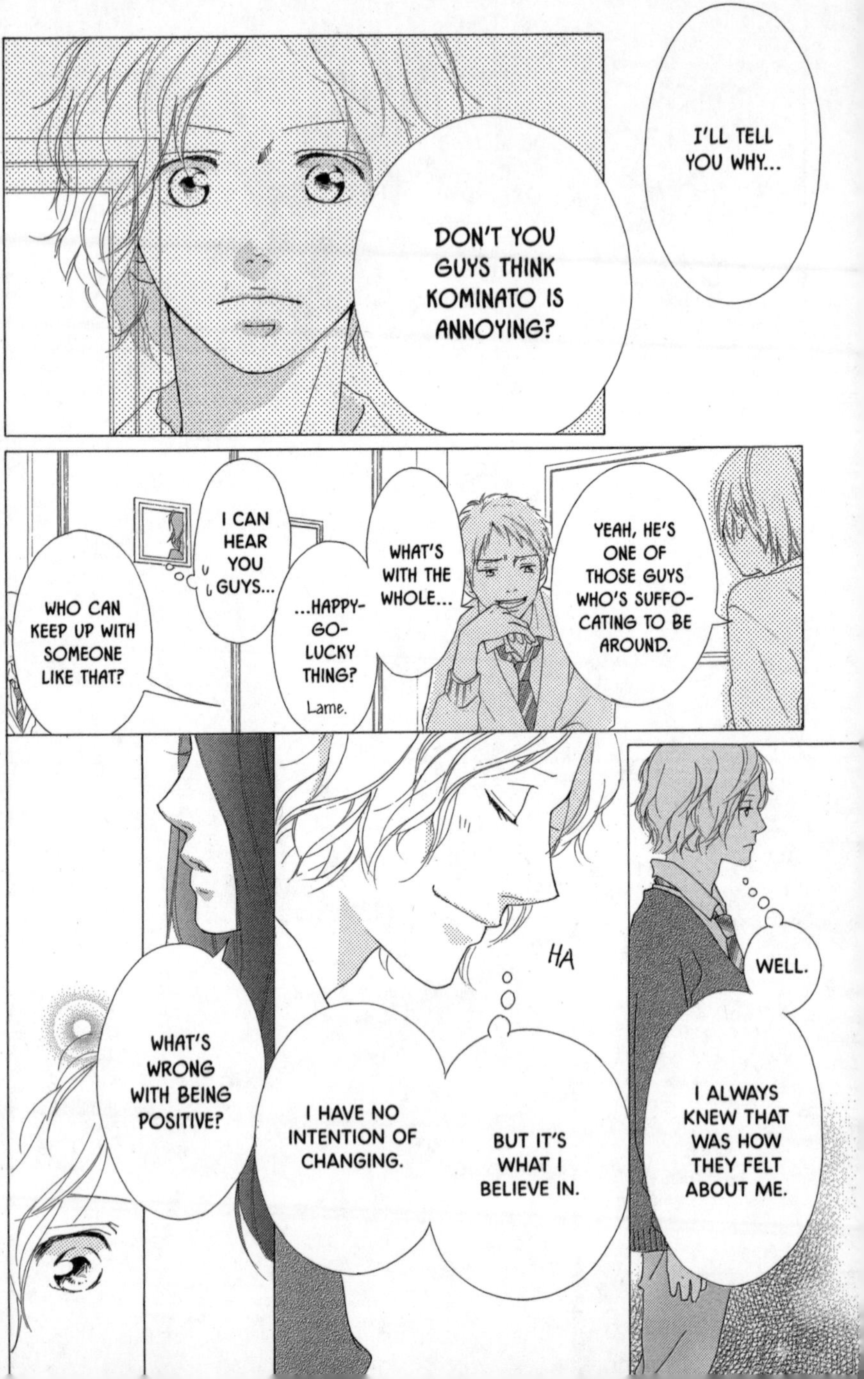
I'LL TELL YOU WHY...
DON'T YOU GUYS THINK KOMINATO IS ANNOYING?
YEAH, HE'S ONE OF THOSE GUYS WHO'S SUFFOCATING TO BE AROUND.
WHAT'S WITH THE WHOLE...
...HAPPY-GO-LUCKY THING?
Lame.
I CAN HEAR YOU GUYS...
WHO CAN KEEP UP WITH SOMEONE LIKE THAT?
WELL.
I ALWAYS KNEW THAT WAS HOW THEY FELT ABOUT ME.
HA
BUT IT'S WHAT I BELIEVE IN.
I HAVE NO INTENTION OF CHANGING.
WHAT'S WRONG WITH BEING POSITIVE?

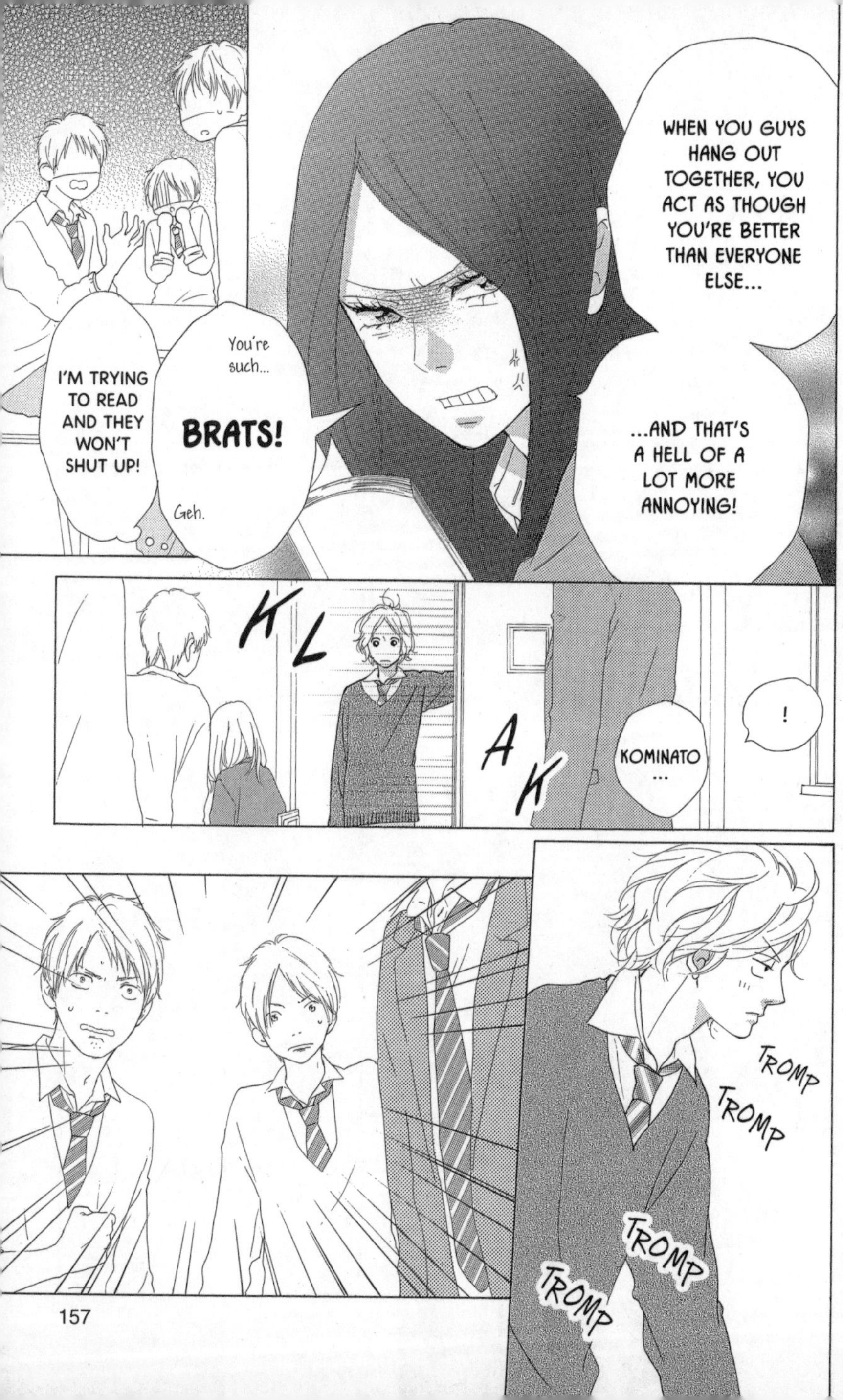
WHEN YOU GUYS HANG OUT TOGETHER, YOU ACT AS THOUGH YOU'RE BETTER THAN EVERYONE ELSE...
...AND THAT'S A HELL OF A LOT MORE ANNOYING!
You're such...
BRATS!
Geh.
I'M TRYING TO READ AND THEY WON'T SHUT UP!
!
KOMINATO ...
KLAK
TROMP
TROMP
TROMP
TROMP

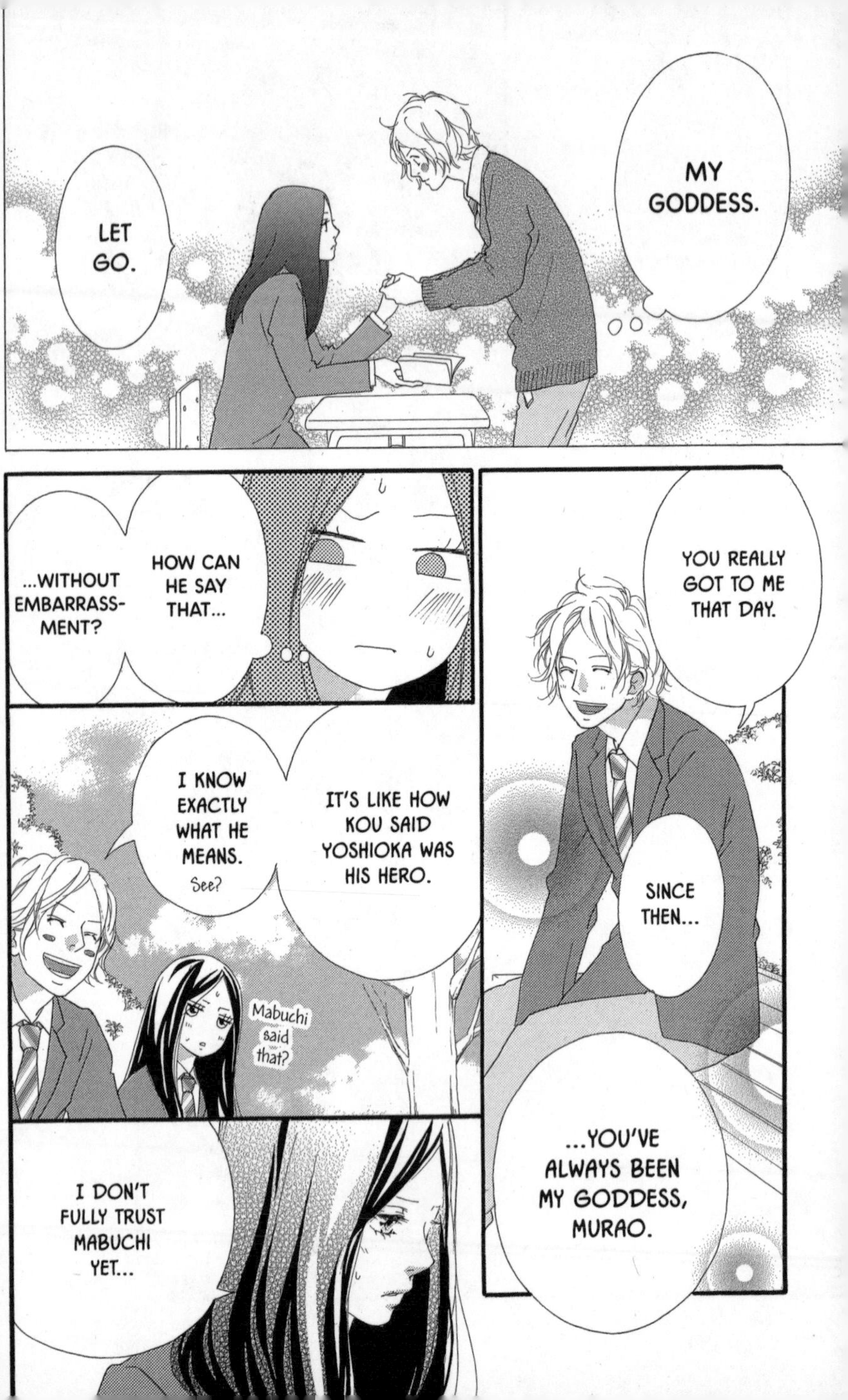
MY GODDESS.
LET GO.
YOU REALLY GOT TO ME THAT DAY.
SINCE THEN...
...YOU'VE ALWAYS BEEN MY GODDESS, MURAO.
HOW CAN HE SAY THAT...
...WITHOUT EMBARRASS-MENT?
IT'S LIKE HOW KOU SAID YOSHIOKA WAS HIS HERO.
I KNOW EXACTLY WHAT HE MEANS.
See?
Mabuchi said that?
I DON'T FULLY TRUST MABUCHI YET...

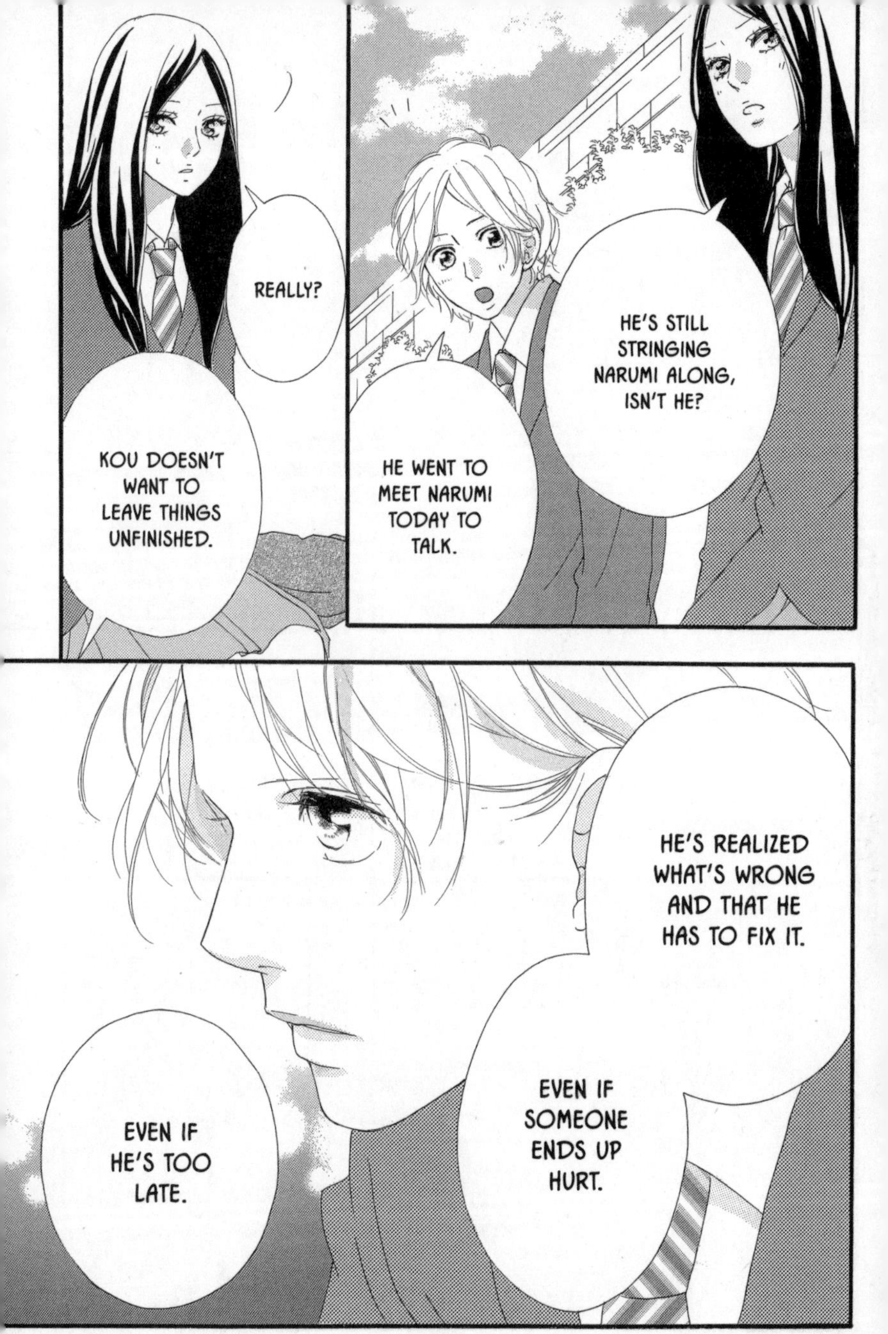
HE'S STILL STRINGING NARUMI ALONG, ISN'T HE?
HE WENT TO MEET NARUMI TODAY TO TALK.
REALLY?
KOU DOESN'T WANT TO LEAVE THINGS UNFINISHED.
HE'S REALIZED WHAT'S WRONG AND THAT HE HAS TO FIX IT.
EVEN IF SOMEONE ENDS UP HURT.
EVEN IF HE'S TOO LATE.

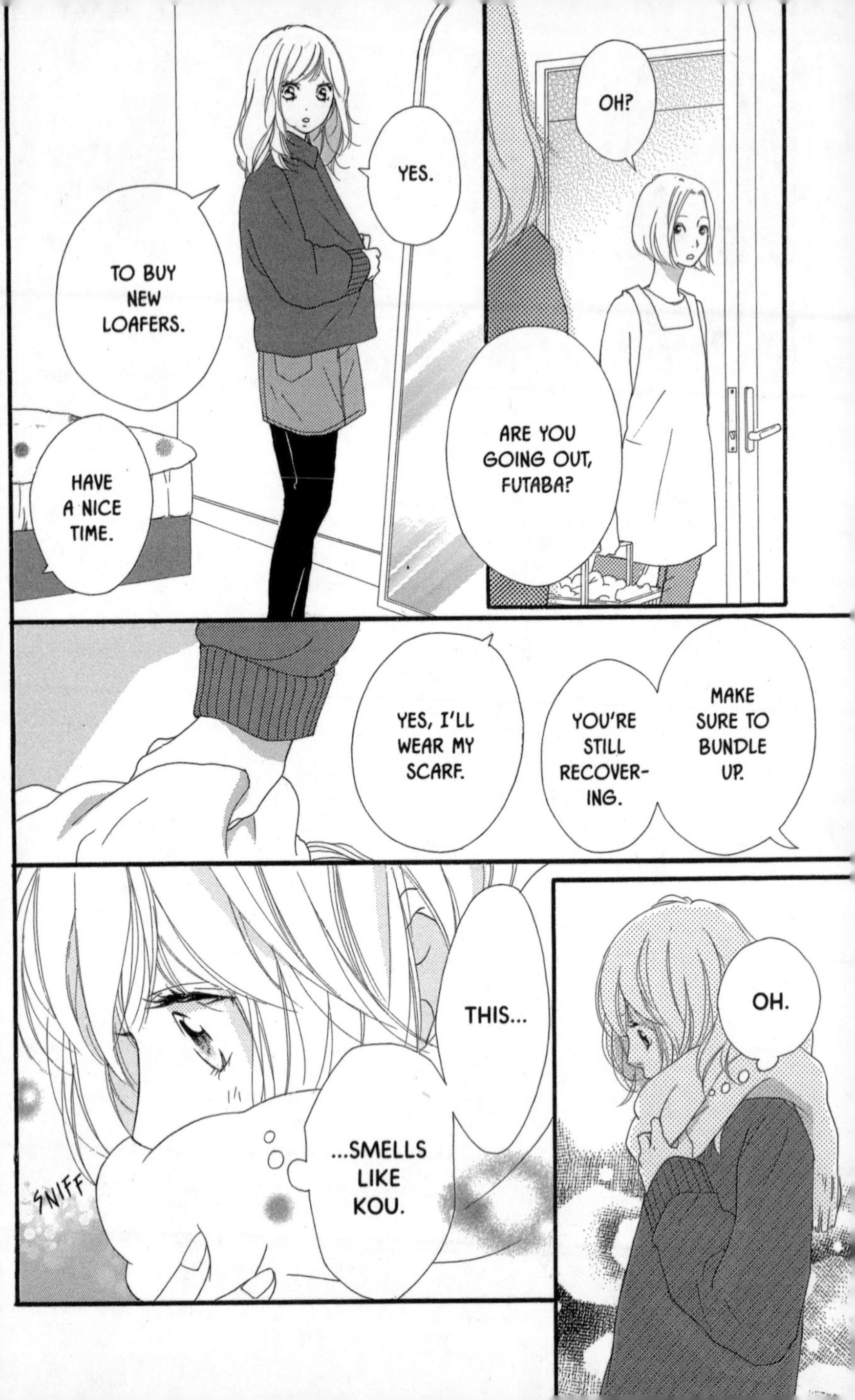
OH?
ARE YOU GOING OUT, FUTABA?
YES.
TO BUY NEW LOAFERS.
HAVE A NICE TIME.
MAKE SURE TO BUNDLE UP.
YOU'RE STILL RECOVER-ING.
YES, I'LL WEAR MY SCARF.
OH.
THIS...
...SMELLS LIKE KOU.
SNIFF

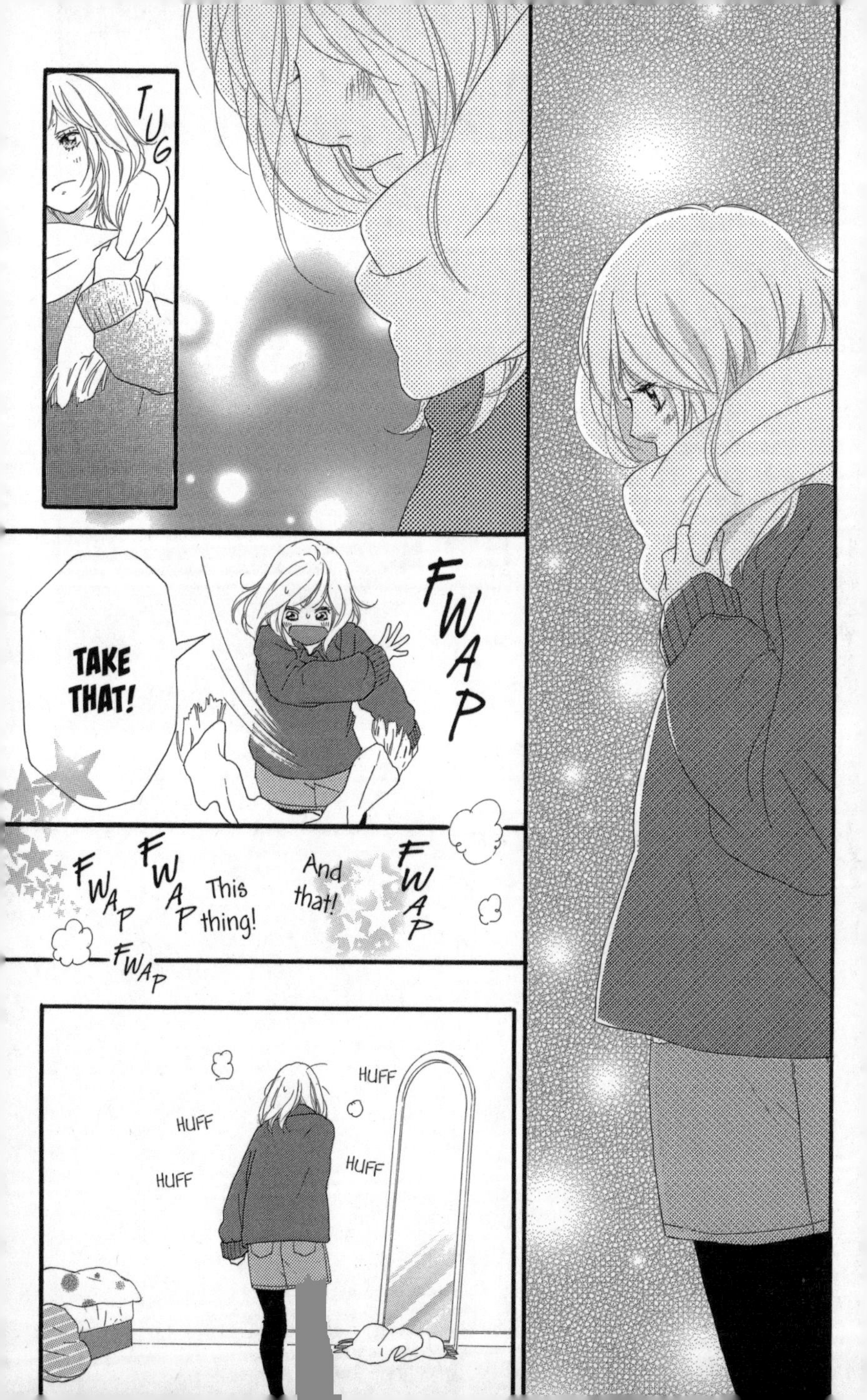
TUG
FWAP
TAKE THAT!
FWAP
And that!
This thing!
FWAP
FWAP
FWAP
HUFF
HUFF
HUFF
HUFF

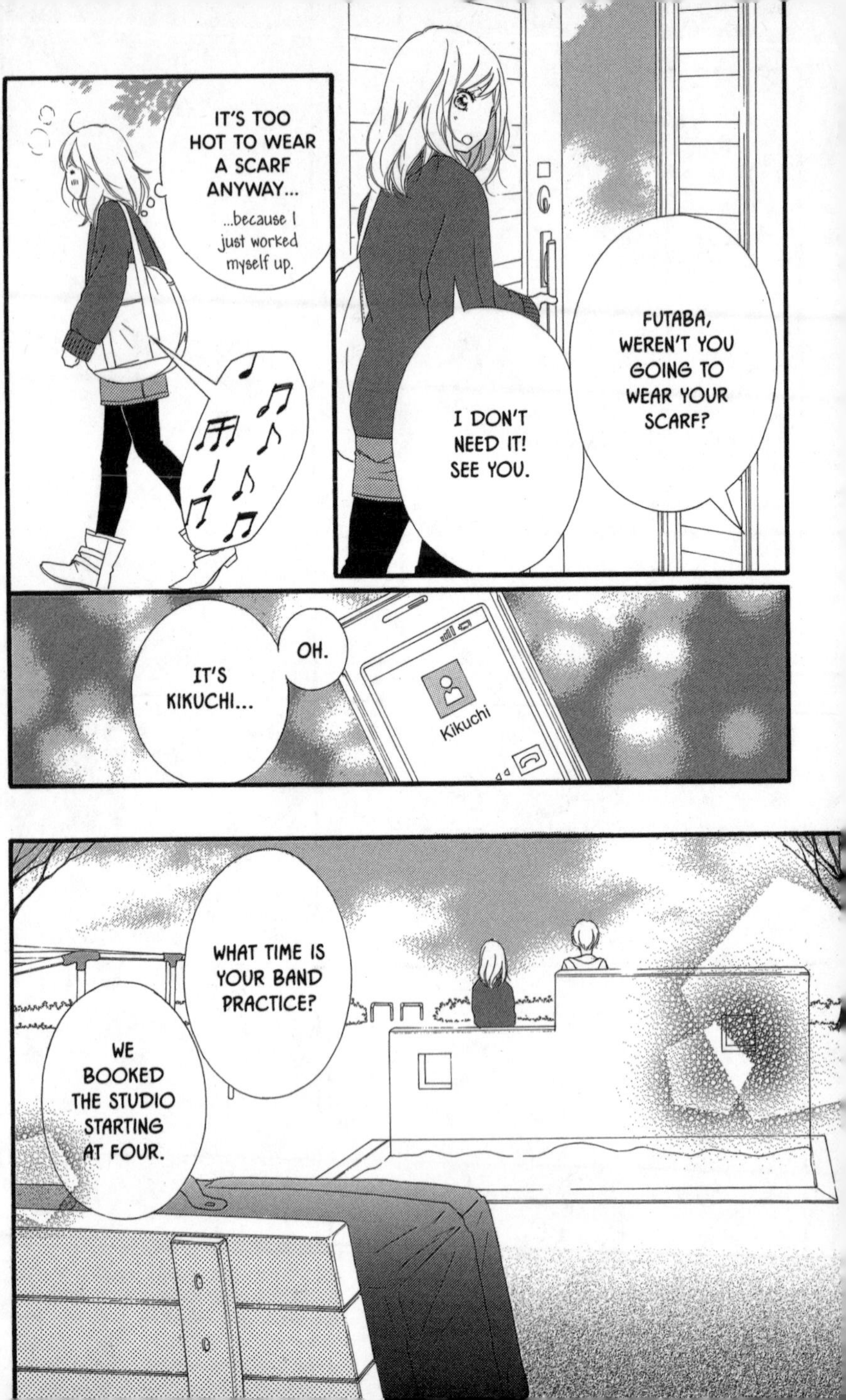
FUTABA, WEREN'T YOU GOING TO WEAR YOUR SCARF?
I DON'T NEED IT! SEE YOU.
IT'S TOO HOT TO WEAR A SCARF ANYWAY...
...because I just worked myself up.
OH.
IT'S KIKUCHI...
Kikuchi
WHAT TIME IS YOUR BAND PRACTICE?
WE BOOKED THE STUDIO STARTING AT FOUR.

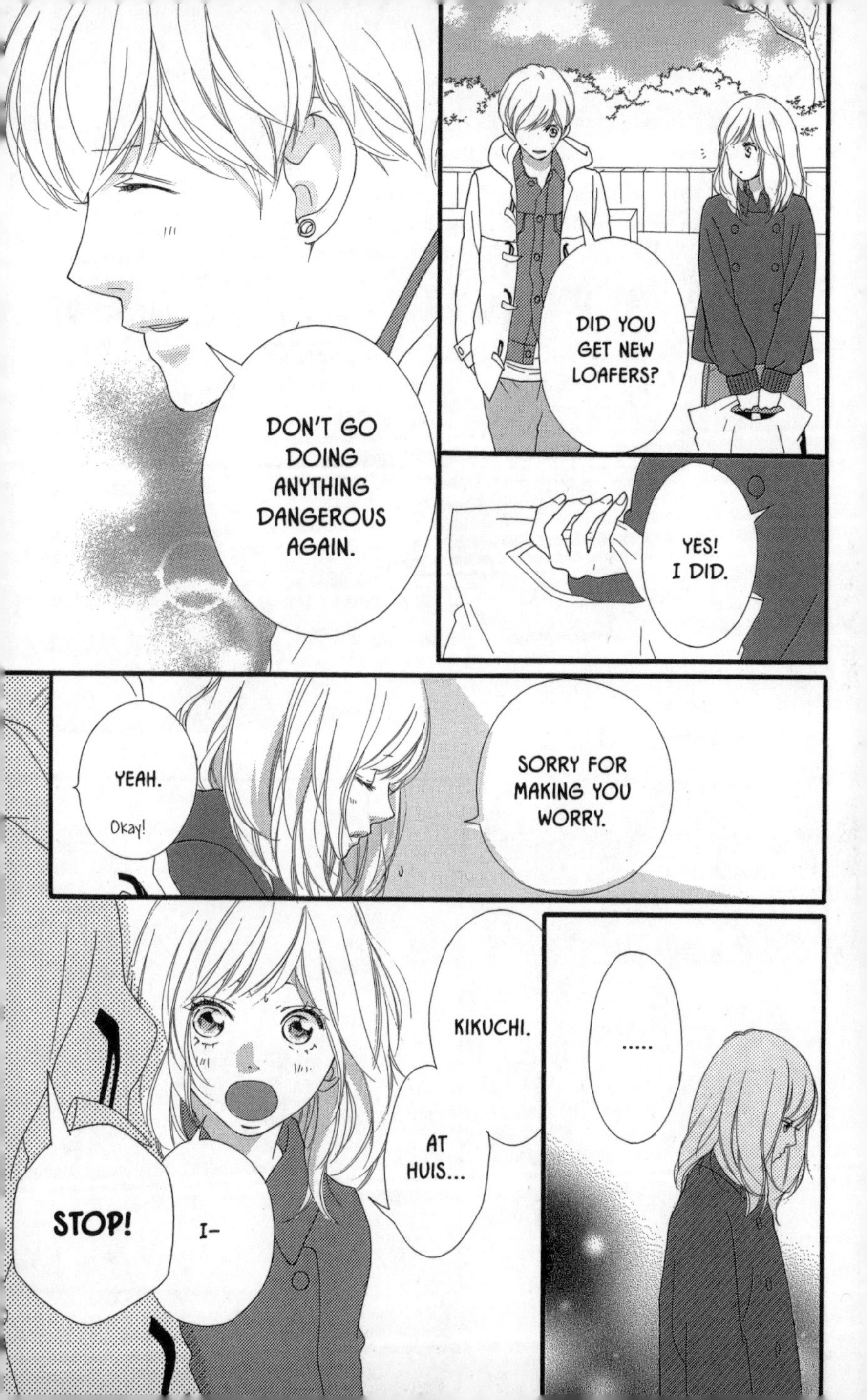
DID YOU GET NEW LOAFERS?
YES! I DID.
DON'T GO DOING ANYTHING DANGEROUS AGAIN.
SORRY FOR MAKING YOU WORRY.
YEAH.
Okay!
.....
KIKUCHI.
AT HUIS...
I–
STOP!

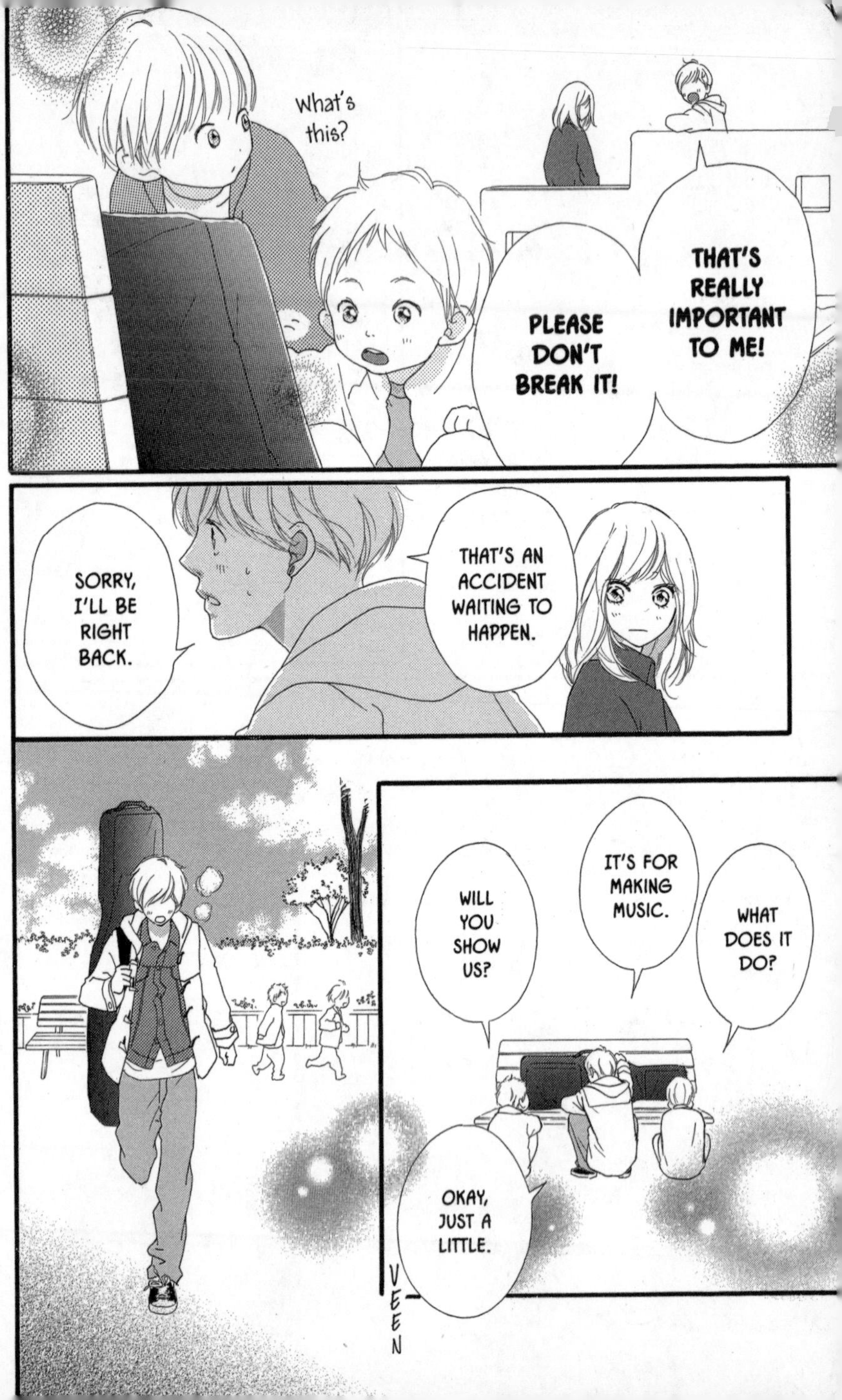
THAT'S REALLY IMPORTANT TO ME!
PLEASE DON'T BREAK IT!
What's this?
THAT'S AN ACCIDENT WAITING TO HAPPEN.
SORRY, I'LL BE RIGHT BACK.
WHAT DOES IT DO?
IT'S FOR MAKING MUSIC.
WILL YOU SHOW US?
OKAY, JUST A LITTLE.
VEEN

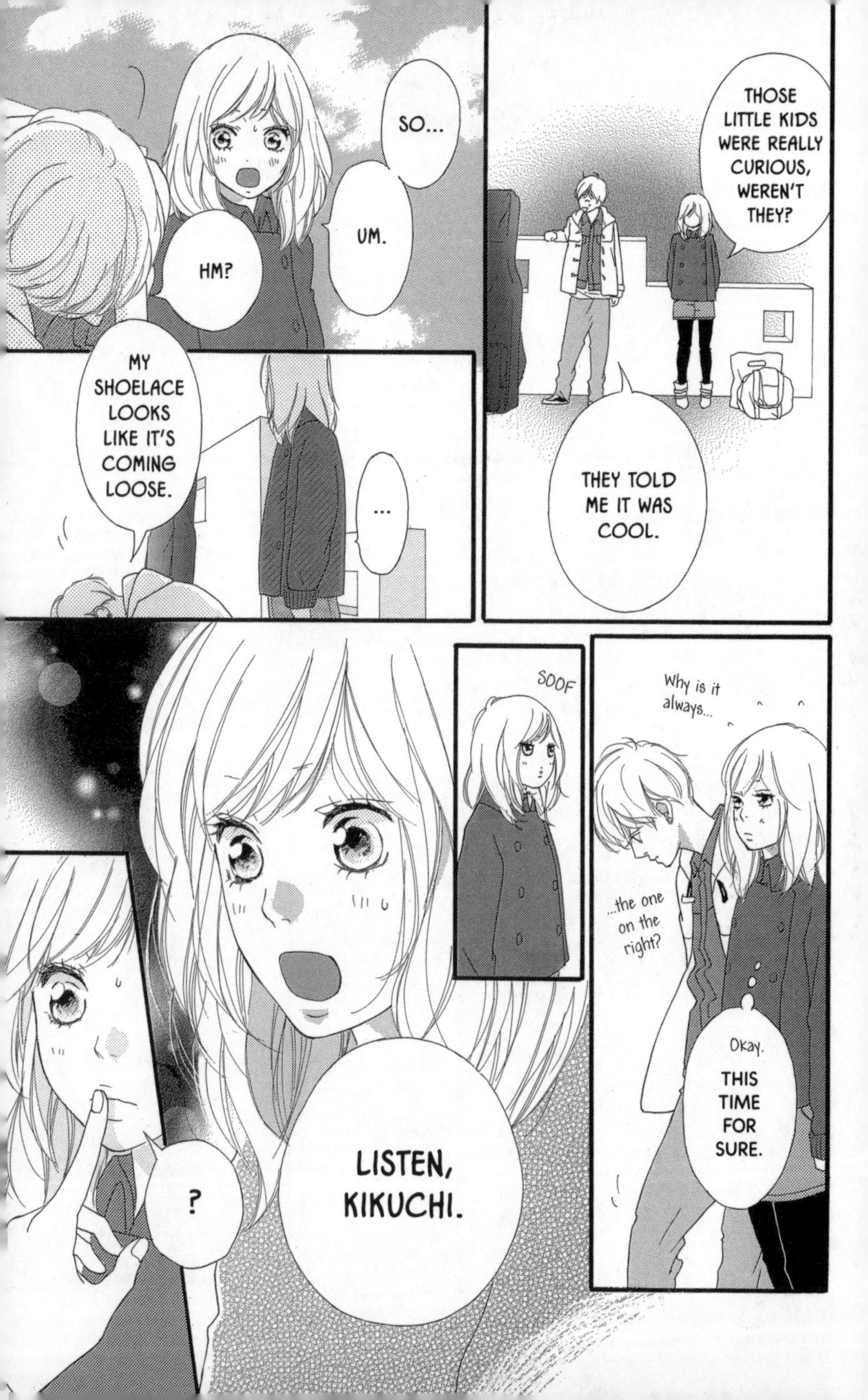
THOSE LITTLE KIDS WERE REALLY CURIOUS, WEREN'T THEY?
THEY TOLD ME IT WAS COOL.
SO...
UM.
HM?
MY SHOELACE LOOKS LIKE IT'S COMING LOOSE.
...
Why is it always...
...the one on the right?
Okay.
THIS TIME FOR SURE.
SOOF
LISTEN, KIKUCHI.
?

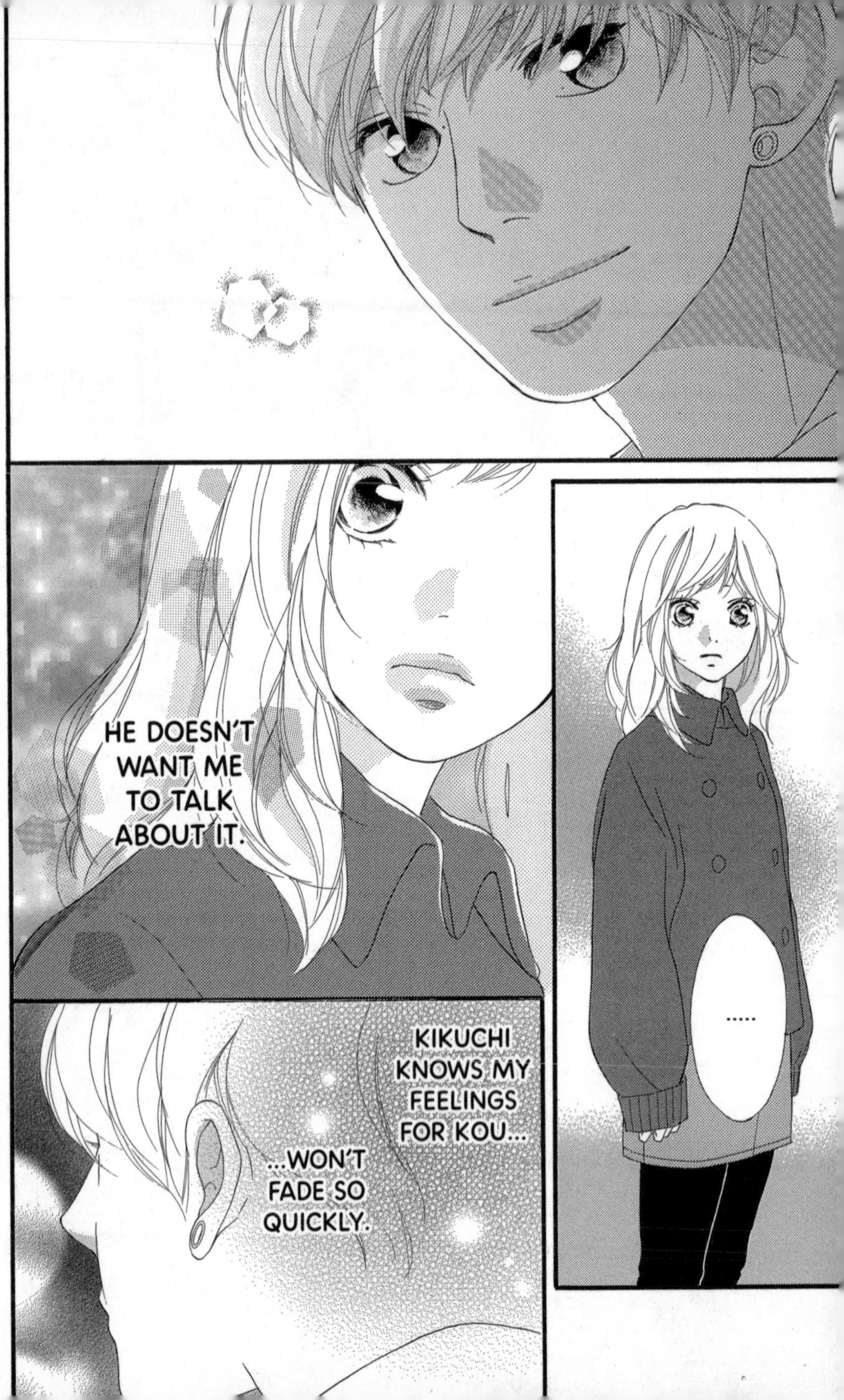
.....
HE DOESN'T WANT ME TO TALK ABOUT IT.
KIKUCHI KNOWS MY FEELINGS FOR KOU...
...WON'T FADE SO QUICKLY.

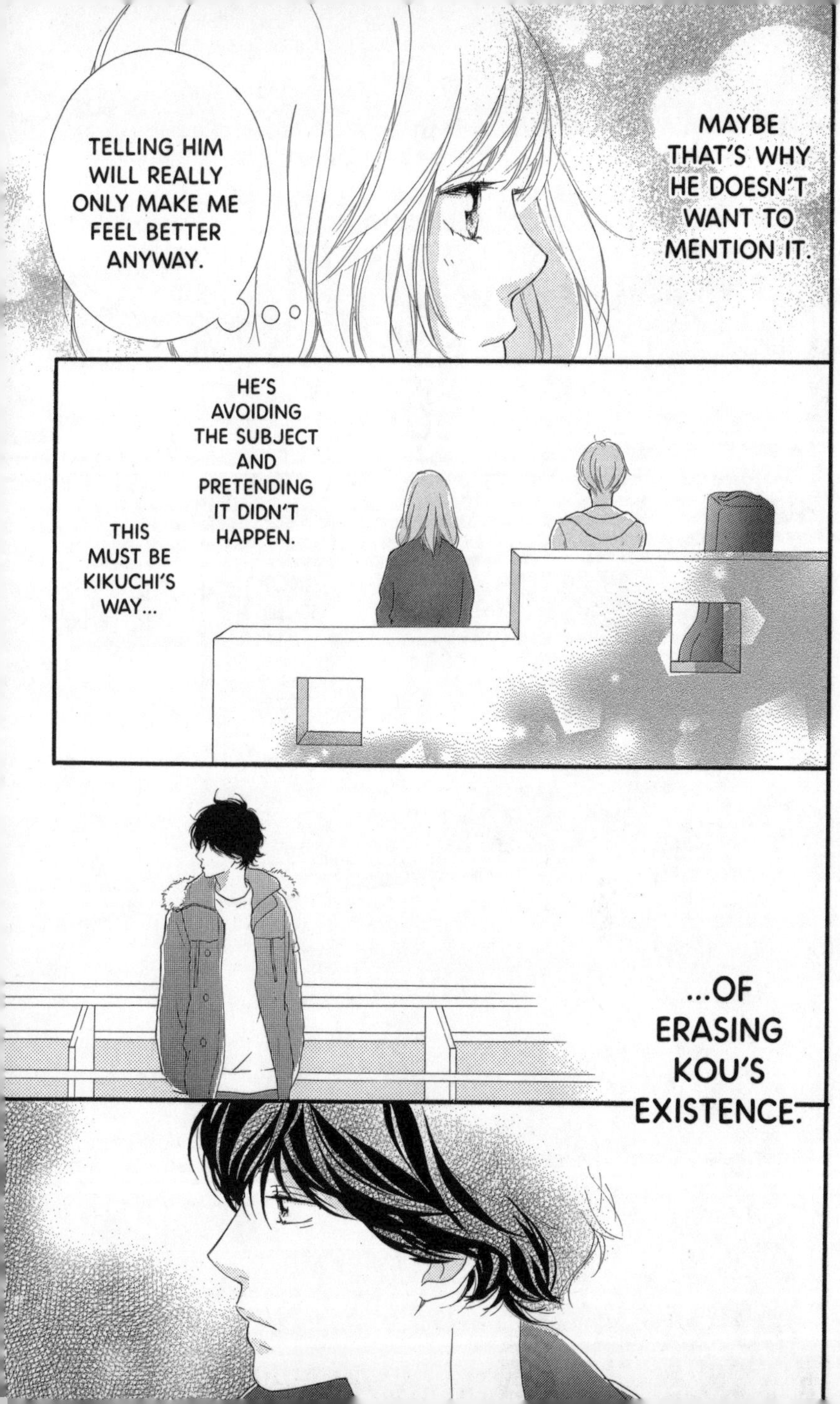
MAYBE THAT'S WHY HE DOESN'T WANT TO MENTION IT.
TELLING HIM WILL REALLY ONLY MAKE ME FEEL BETTER ANYWAY.
HE'S AVOIDING THE SUBJECT AND PRETENDING IT DIDN'T HAPPEN.
THIS MUST BE KIKUCHI'S WAY...
...OF ERASING KOU'S EXISTENCE.

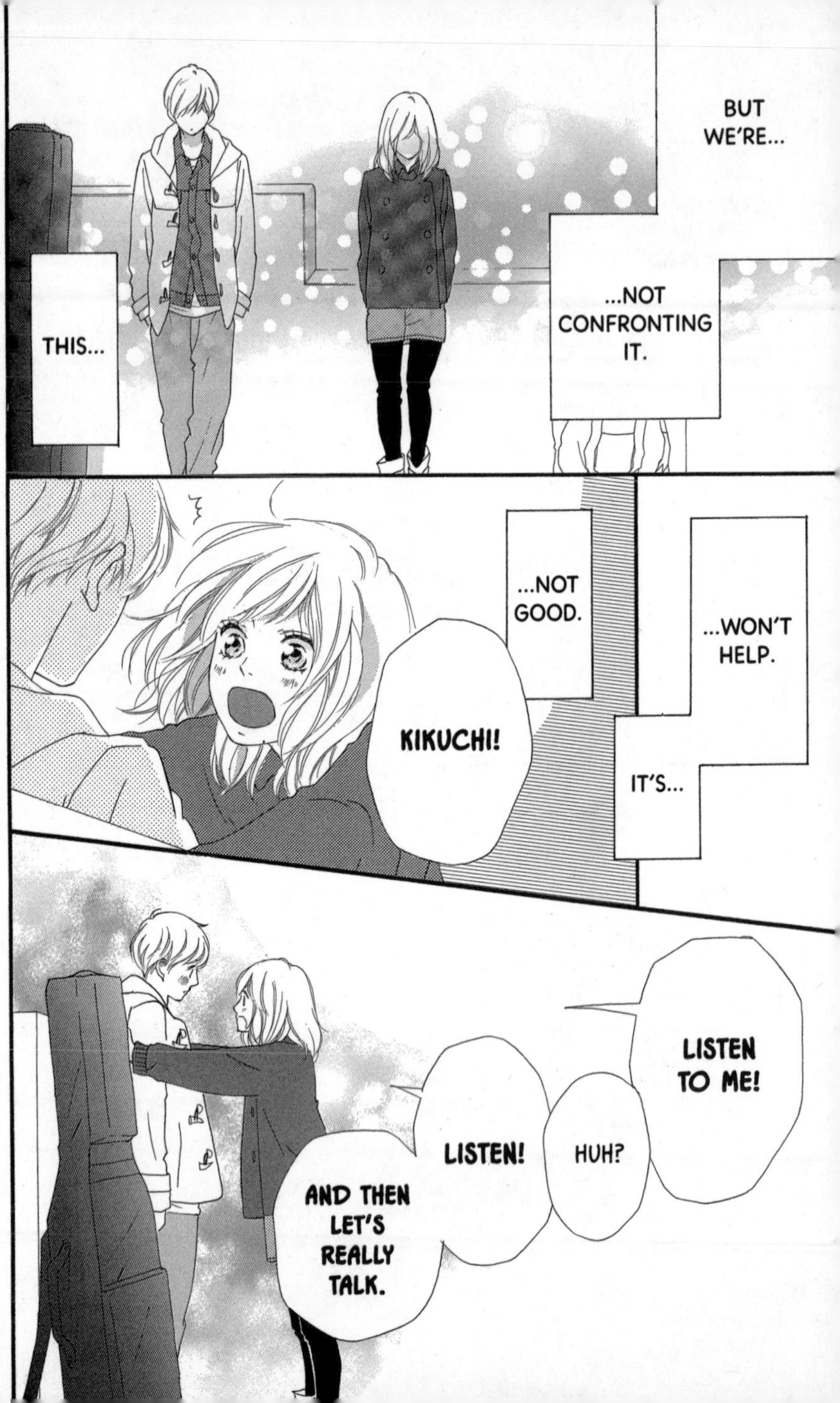

BUT WE'RE...
...NOT CONFRONTING IT.
THIS...
...WON'T HELP.
IT'S...
...NOT GOOD.
KIKUCHI!
LISTEN TO ME!
HUH?
LISTEN!
AND THEN LET'S REALLY TALK.

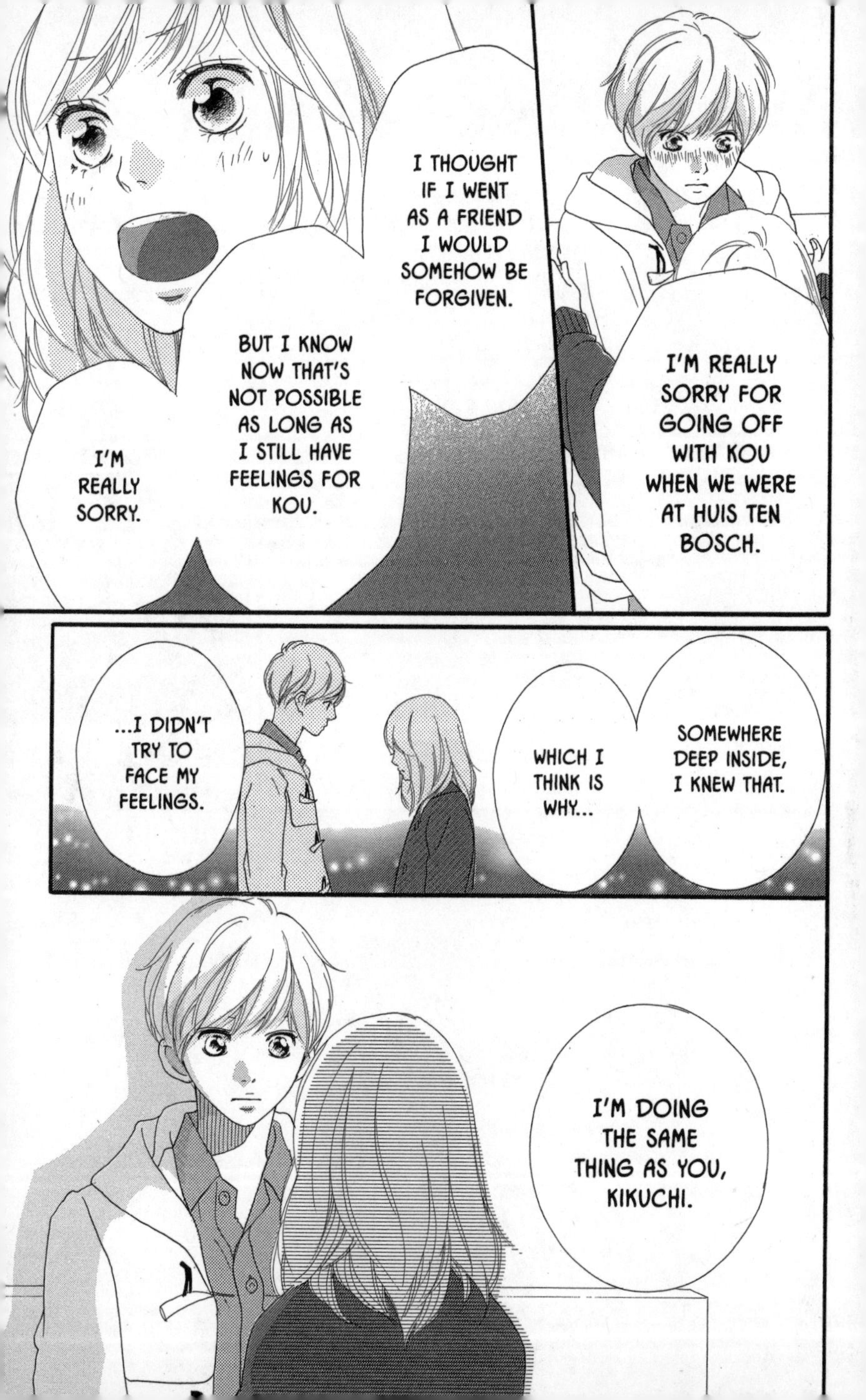
I'M REALLY SORRY FOR GOING OFF WITH KOU WHEN WE WERE AT HUIS TEN BOSCH.
I THOUGHT IF I WENT AS A FRIEND I WOULD SOMEHOW BE FORGIVEN.
BUT I KNOW NOW THAT'S NOT POSSIBLE AS LONG AS I STILL HAVE FEELINGS FOR KOU.
I'M REALLY SORRY.
SOMEWHERE DEEP INSIDE, I KNEW THAT.
WHICH I THINK IS WHY...
...I DIDN'T TRY TO FACE MY FEELINGS.
I'M DOING THE SAME THING AS YOU, KIKUCHI.

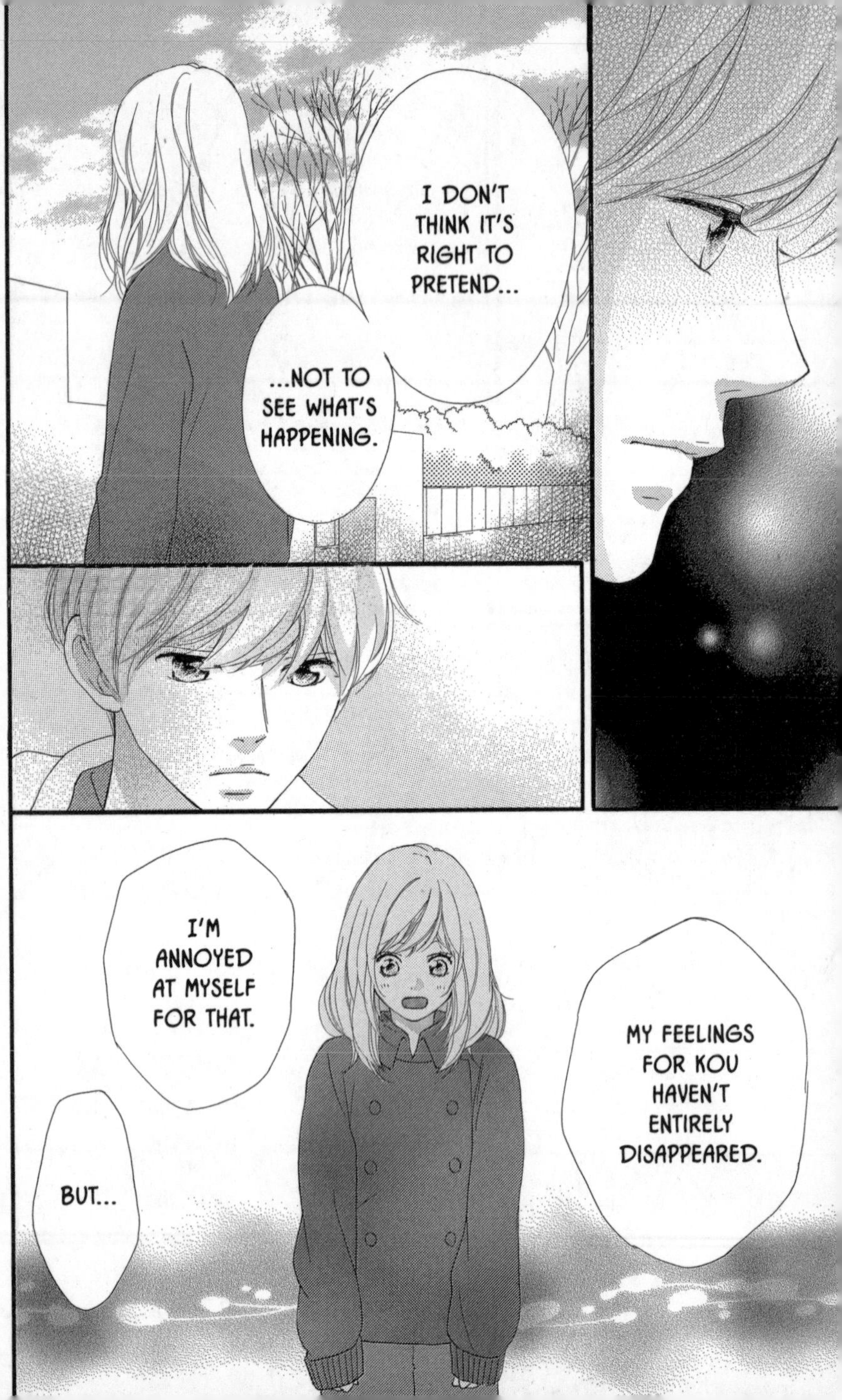

I DON'T THINK IT'S RIGHT TO PRETEND...
...NOT TO SEE WHAT'S HAPPENING.
MY FEELINGS FOR KOU HAVEN'T ENTIRELY DISAPPEARED.
I'M ANNOYED AT MYSELF FOR THAT.
BUT...

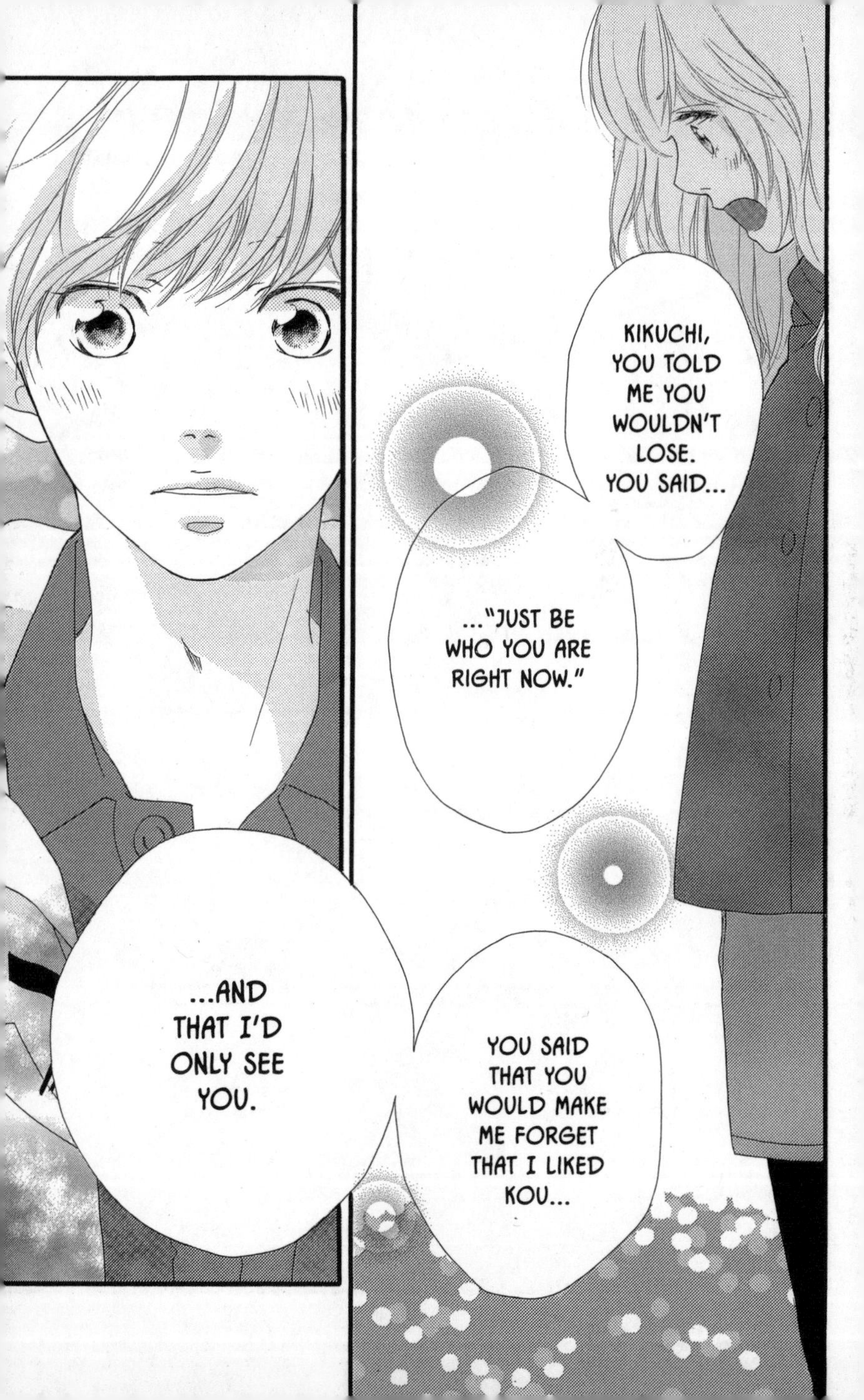
KIKUCHI, YOU TOLD ME YOU WOULDN'T LOSE. YOU SAID...
..."JUST BE WHO YOU ARE RIGHT NOW."
YOU SAID THAT YOU WOULD MAKE ME FORGET THAT I LIKED KOU...
...AND THAT I'D ONLY SEE YOU.

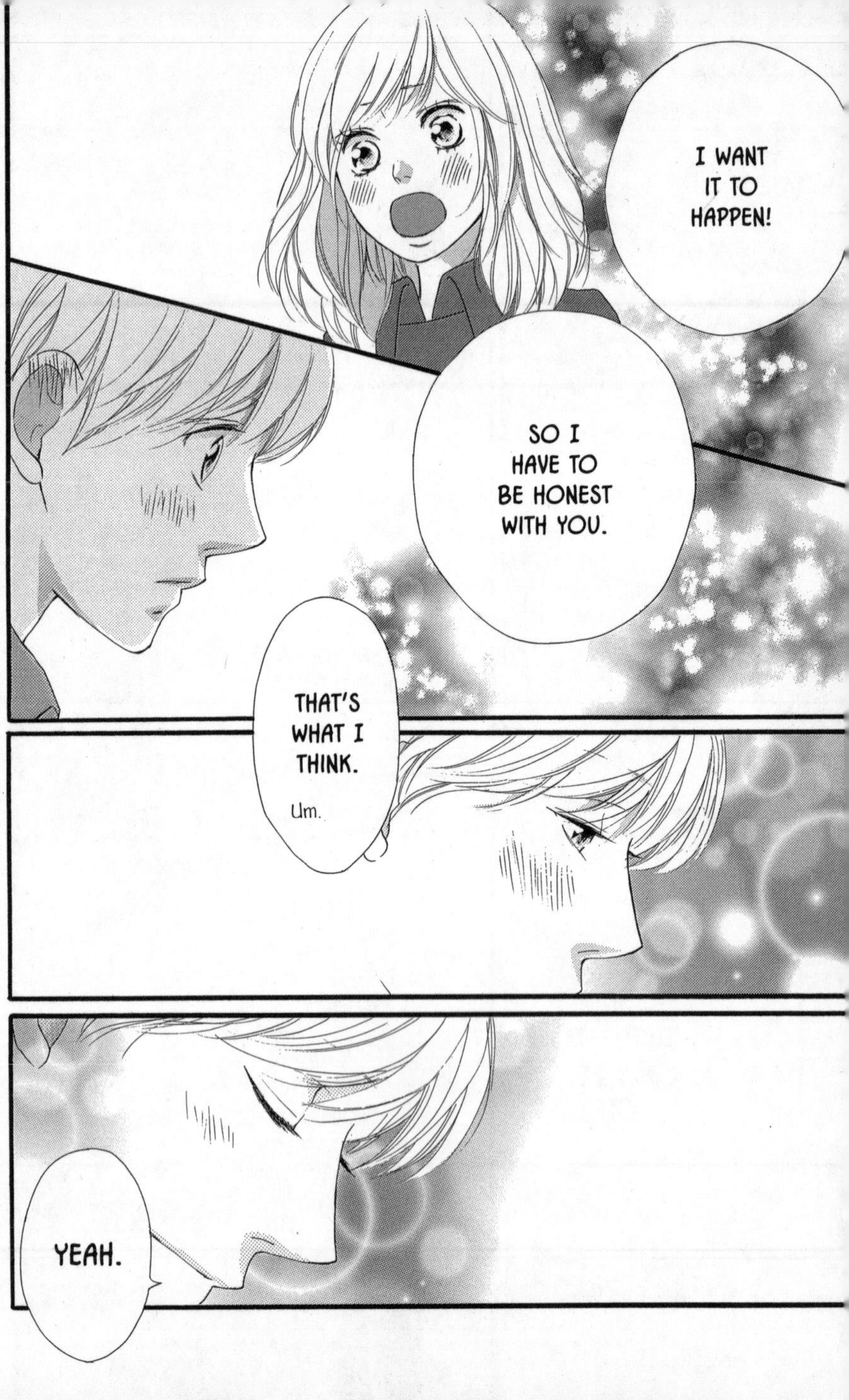
I WANT IT TO HAPPEN!
SO I HAVE TO BE HONEST WITH YOU.
THAT'S WHAT I THINK.
Um.
YEAH.

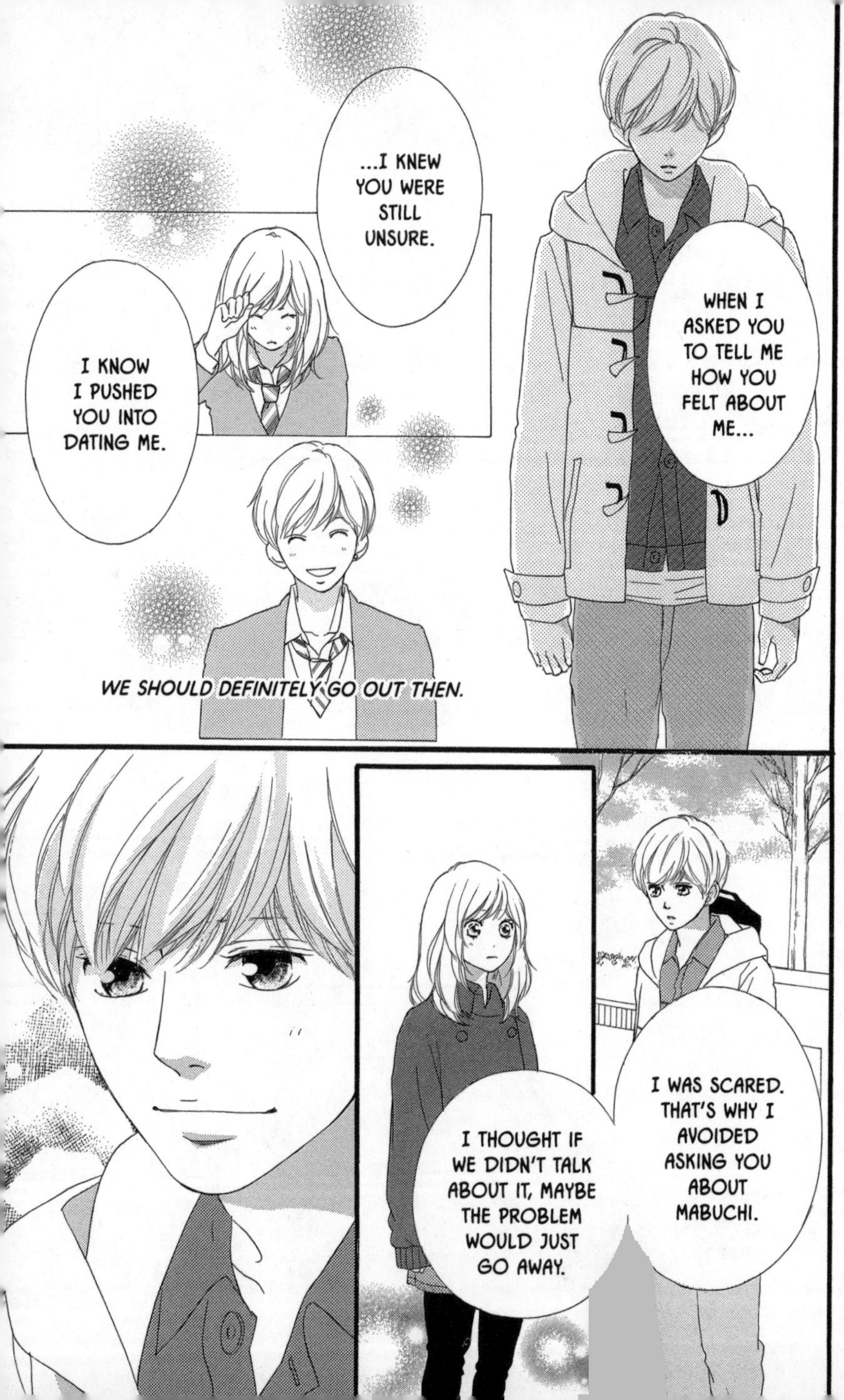
WHEN I ASKED YOU TO TELL ME HOW YOU FELT ABOUT ME...
...I KNEW YOU WERE STILL UNSURE.
I KNOW I PUSHED YOU INTO DATING ME.
WE SHOULD DEFINITELY GO OUT THEN.
I WAS SCARED. THAT'S WHY I AVOIDED ASKING YOU ABOUT MABUCHI.
I THOUGHT IF WE DIDN'T TALK ABOUT IT, MAYBE THE PROBLEM WOULD JUST GO AWAY.

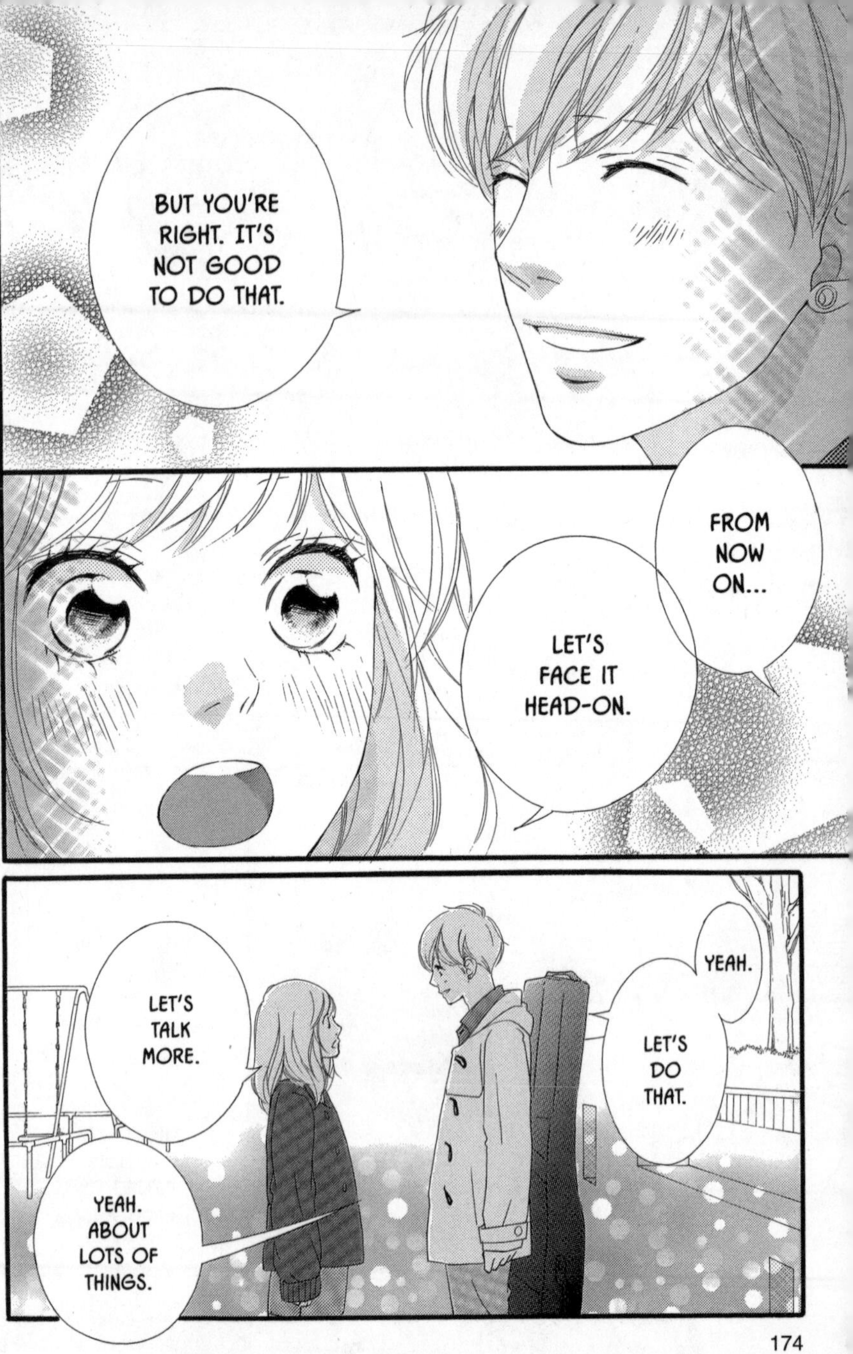
BUT YOU'RE RIGHT. IT'S NOT GOOD TO DO THAT.
FROM NOW ON...
LET'S FACE IT HEAD-ON.
YEAH.
LET'S DO THAT.
LET'S TALK MORE.
YEAH. ABOUT LOTS OF THINGS.

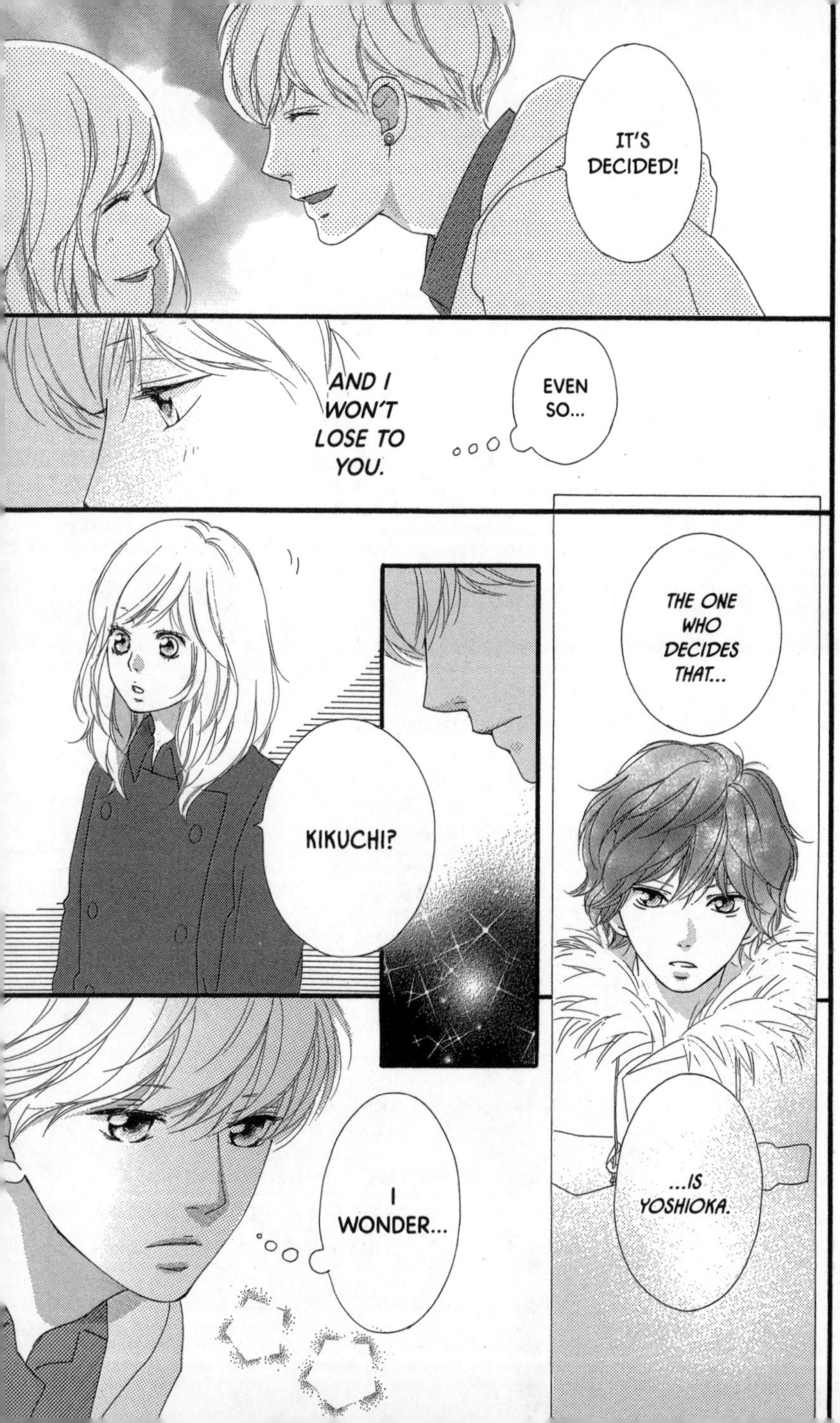
IT'S DECIDED!
EVEN SO...
AND I WON'T LOSE TO YOU.
THE ONE WHO DECIDES THAT...
...IS YOSHIOKA.
KIKUCHI?
I WONDER...

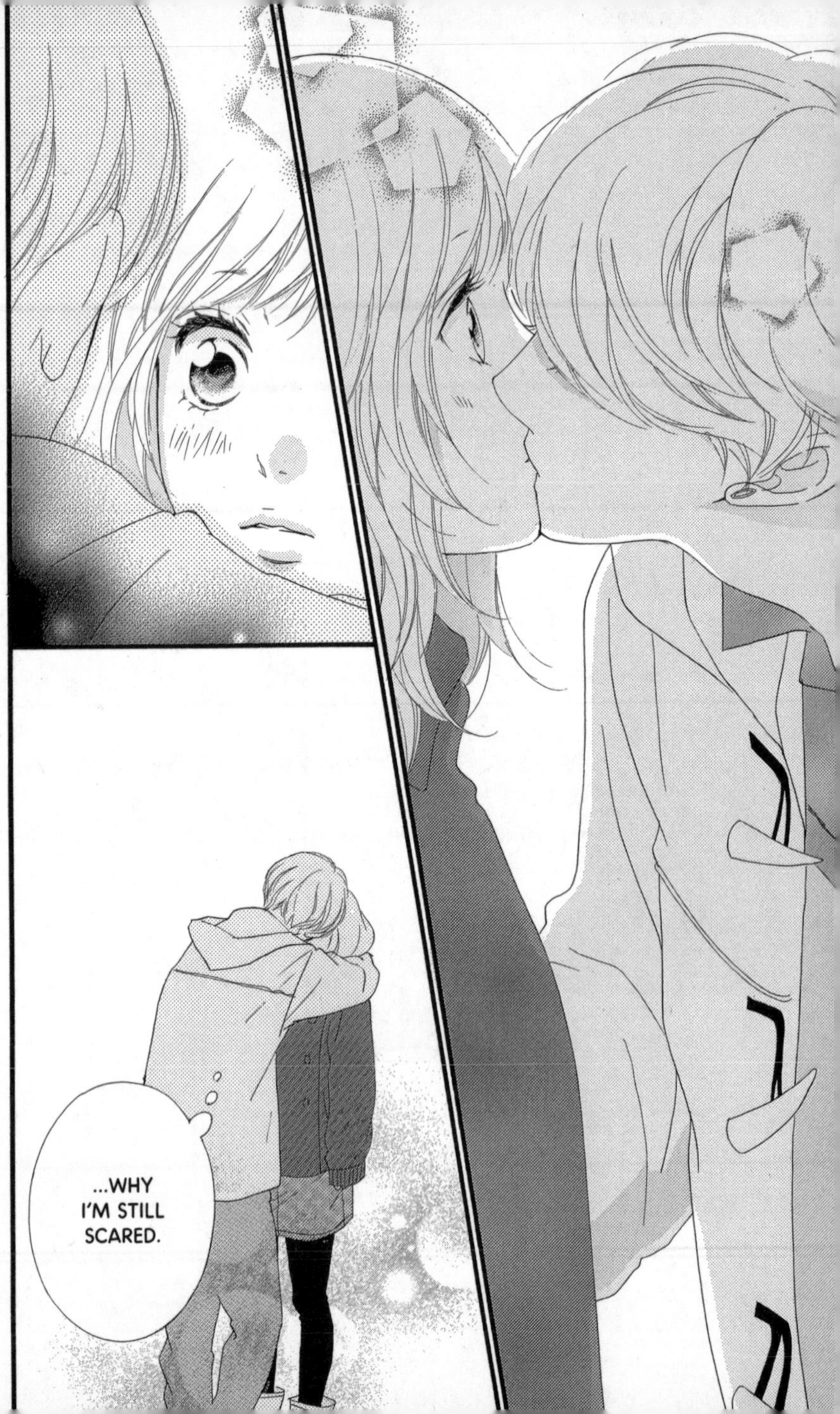
...WHY
I'M STILL
SCARED.

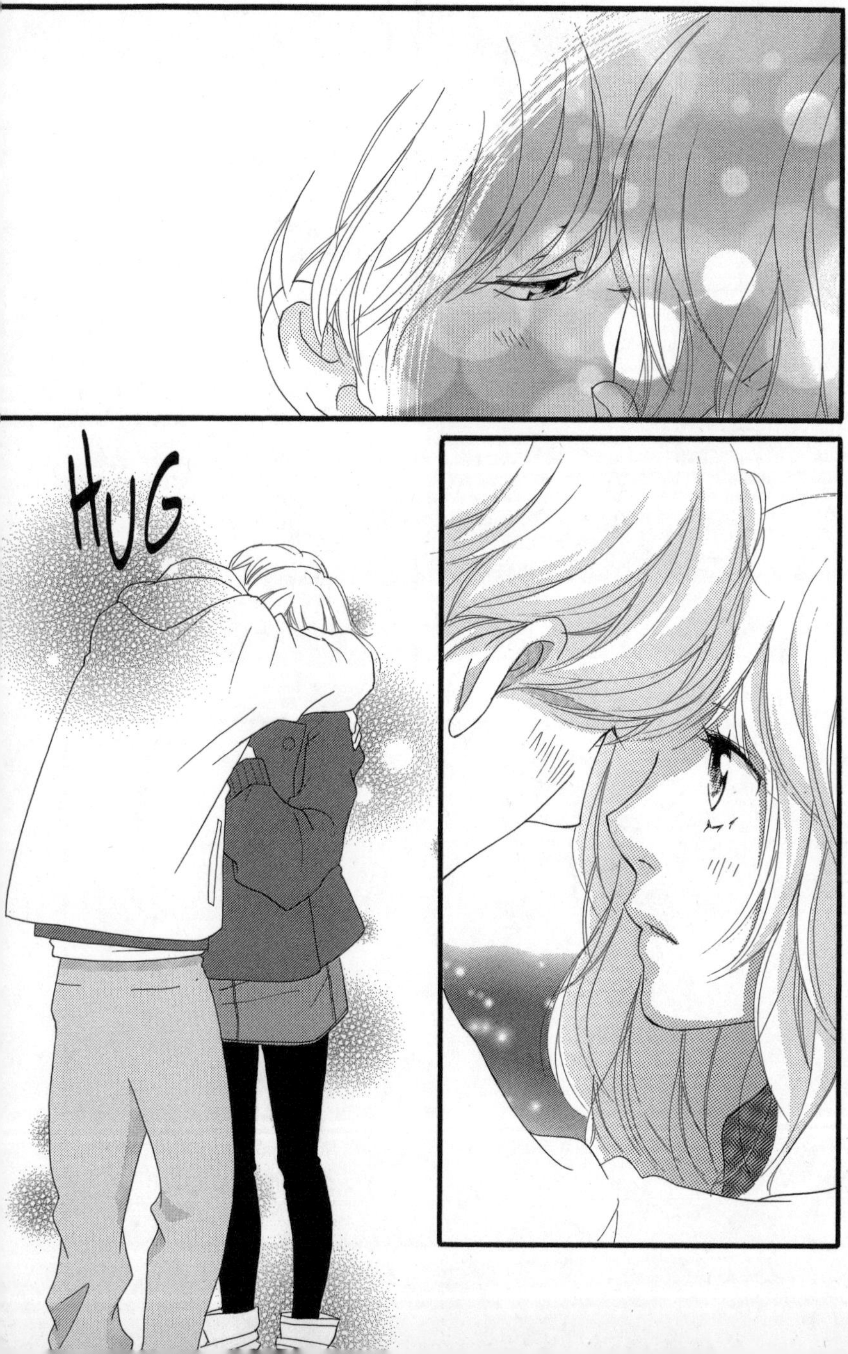
HUG

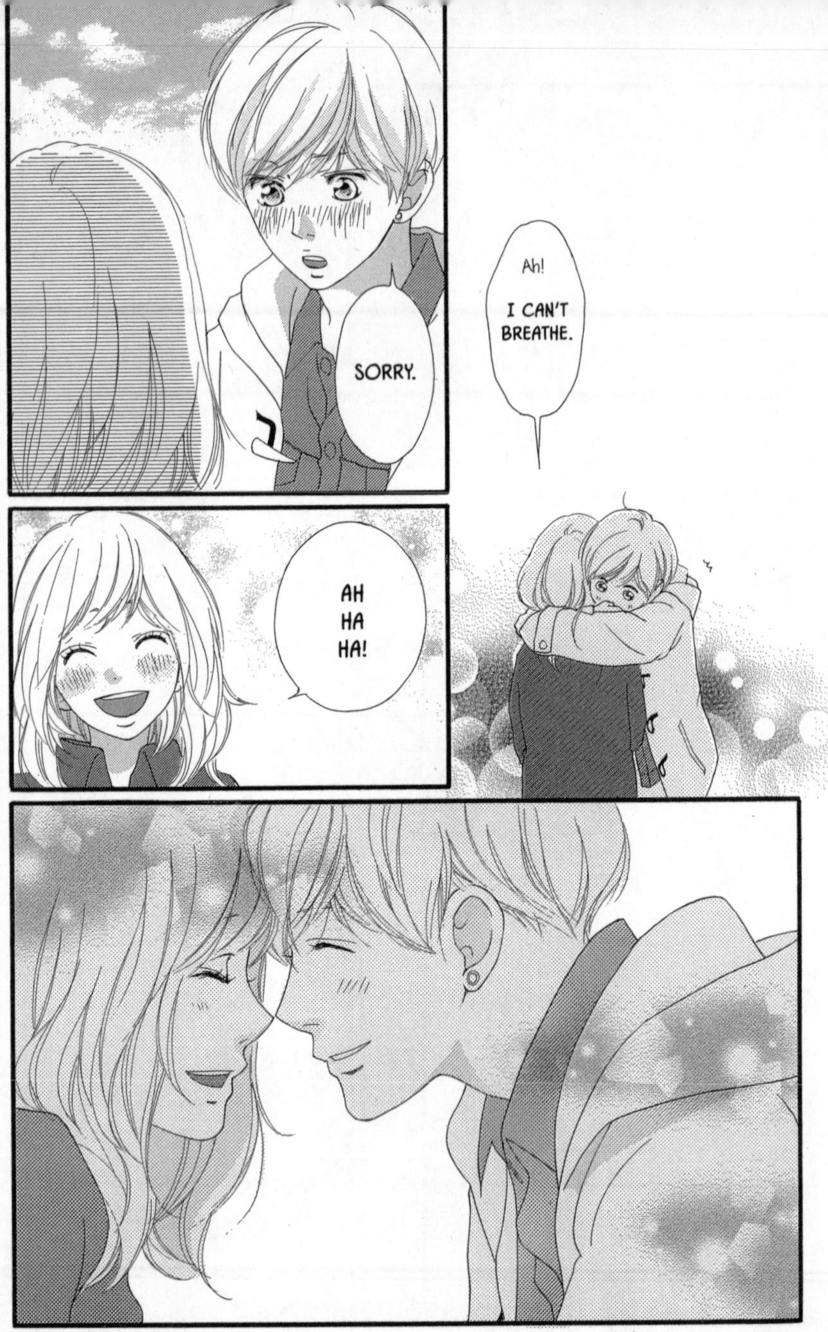
Ah! I CAN'T BREATHE.
SORRY.
AH HA HA!

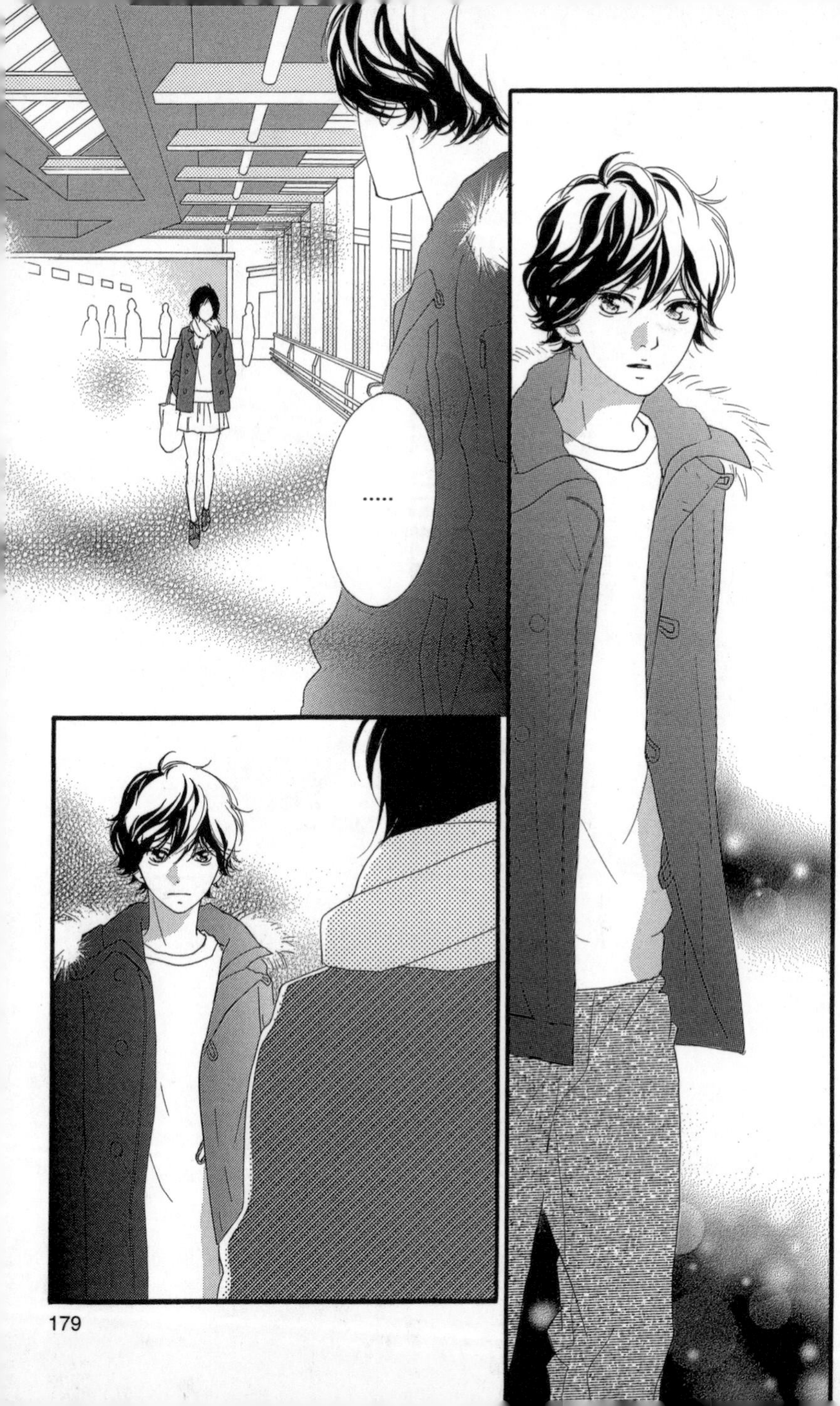
......

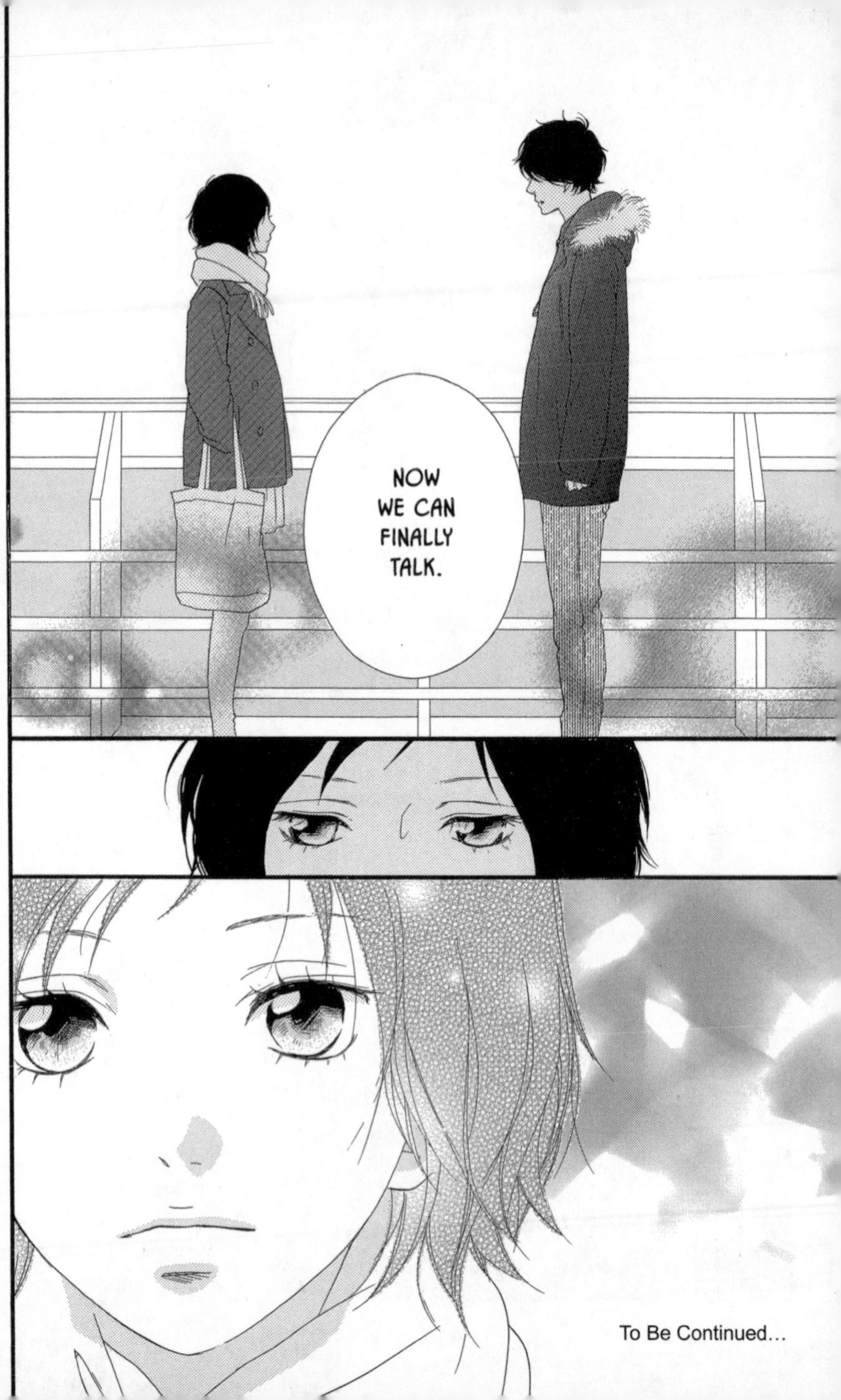
NOW WE CAN FINALLY TALK.
To Be Continued...

Afterword

Thank you for reading through to the end!

The long class trip story has come to an end, and Futaba and the crew are now back to their everyday routines. Because the class trip arc was different from what I usually draw, it was a lot of work, but it was also a lot of fun. I loved drawing little Aya as well as Shun's headstand. Though, while I was enjoying myself, Futaba, Kou and Kikuchi struggled with some heavy stuff. When I consider their feelings, the truth is I start to feel pretty exhausted myself. That said, I rather like drama, so I still enjoyed drawing those scenes. But I also like drawing people having fun. I guess that means I just like drawing everything. That is good!

From here on I hope that, for the most part, I can enjoy my drawing. And with that, see you in the next volume!

Io Sakisaka

Well, after postponing my move for so long, I think I'll have finally done the deed by the time this book is released.

Having said that, if something comes up that keeps me from moving, I'll have to just laugh. In the next volume, I'll let you know whether the move actually happens!

IO SAKISAKA

Born on June 8, Io Sakisaka made her debut as a manga creator with *Sakura, Chiru*. Her works include *Call My Name*, *Gate of Planet* and *Blue*. *Strobe Edge*, her previous work, is also published by VIZ Media's Shojo Beat imprint. *Ao Haru Ride* was adapted into an anime series in 2014. In her spare time, Sakisaka likes to paint things and sleep.

Ao Haru Ride

VOLUME 11
SHOJO BEAT EDITION

STORY AND ART BY **IO SAKISAKA**

TRANSLATION **Emi Louie-Nishikawa**
TOUCH-UP ART + LETTERING **Inori Fukuda Trant**
DESIGN **Shawn Carrico**
EDITOR **Nancy Thistlethwaite**

First published in Japan in 2011 by SHUEISHA Inc., Tokyo.
English translation rights arranged by SHUEISHA Inc.

Printed in the U.S.A.

Published by VIZ Media, LLC
P.O. Box 77010
San Francisco, CA 94107

10 9 8 7 6 5 4 3
First printing, June 2020
Third printing, July 2023

RATED T TEEN ratings.viz.com

PARENTAL ADVISORY
AO HARU RIDE is rated T for Teen and
is recommended for ages 13 and up. This
volume contains the stolen moments of youth.

VIZ MEDIA
viz.com

Shojo Beat
shojobeat.com

STOP!
**YOU MAY BE
READING THE
WRONG WAY.**

In keeping with the original
Japanese comic format, this
book reads from right to left—so
action, sound effects and word
balloons are completely reversed
to preserve the orientation of
the original artwork.